THE FOURTH GOSPEL AND THE JEWS

A Study in R. Akiba, Esther and the Gospel of John

by

JOHN BOWMAN

THE PICKWICK PRESS

PITTSBURGH, PENNSYLVANIA

1975

Library of Congress Cataloging in Publication Data
Bowman, John, 1916-
    The fourth Gospel and the Jews.

    (Pittsburgh theological monograph series ; 8)
    Bibliography: p.
    Includes index.
    1. Bible. N. T. John--Criticism, interpretation,
etc. 2. Akiba ben Joseph, ca. 50-ca. 132. 3. Bible.
O. T. Esther--Criticism, interpretation, etc.
I. Title. II. Series.
BS2615.2.B65   226'.5'06   75-40461
ISBN 0-915138-10-7

CONTENTS

INTRODUCTION vii

TABLE OF TALMUDIC AND RABBINIC ABBREVIATIONS xi

CHAPTER

1. Akiba, Text, Canon and Exegesis 1

2. The Fourth Gospel and Jewish Law. 25

3.   I.   The Immanence of God:
          The *Shekinah* and *Memra* 45

    II.   The *Shemoneh Esreh*--the *Kedushah*
          and the Sanctus. 55

   III.   The Name of God: *YHWH* Savior God,
          the *Memra* and *Kaddish*. 69

4. The Fourth Gospel and the Book of Esther. 99

5. The "Unknown" Feast of John 5:1
   and Esther and Purim 111

6. The Fast of Esther, the Death of Jesus
   and the Death of Haman 133

CHAPTER

7. The Feasts or Banquets in the Fourth Gospel
        and in the Book of Esther. 161

8. The Exegesis of the Fourth Gospel
        and R. Akiba 199

9. Jesus and Lazarus, Esther and Mordecai. 231

10. Which Lazarus?. 245

11. Judas and Haman 275

12. John's Gospel: Christianized *Megillath
        Esther* Superimposed on a Christianized
        Passover Haggadah Pattern. 279

13. The Canonicity of Esther and
        that of the Fourth Gospel. 309

Epilogue 337

NOTES. 341

BIBLIOGRAPHY 375

INDEX TO REFERENCES. 381

INTRODUCTION

One may ask why another book on the Fourth Gospel; and
yet why not? Of the four gospels, the fourth is the most
authoritative and the most challenging, the most demanding.
And its inescapable demand is a response. So New Testament
scholars feel impelled to lecture on the Fourth Gospel and
possibly to write a commentary thereon. Like the writer of
that gospel said (Jn. 21:25) of the deeds of Jesus unrecorded
by him, so too of the potential books on the Fourth Gospel it
could be said: "I suppose that the world itself could not
contain the books that would be written."

The present work *The Fourth Gospel and the Jews* was
written by me and literally lost for some years in my study
until it was found in the process of moving. I happened in
correspondence with Mr. Alfred M. Johnson of Pittsburgh, Pa.,
U.S.A., to mention my original approach set out in it, and at
his suggestion I sent my manuscript to the Pittsburgh Theological Monograph Series for publication. I am indebted to
Mr. Hadidian, the editor of the series, and to Mr. Johnson
for their painstaking editorial work in preparing the manuscript for publication.

The present work is not a commentary on the Fourth Gospel.
As you will note, not only is the work entitled *The Fourth
Gospel and the Jews*, but it has as its subtitle *R. Akiba,
Esther and the Gospel of John*. The present writer accepts
a date for the Fourth Gospel in the last decade of the First
Century A.D. and seeks to introduce the reader to the signifi-
cant happenings in the Judaism of that period. It will be

shown that the Fourth Gospel, a church book, was aware of the new challenges of its age, and the new developments in Judaism, and that it sought to show that its Christ was not only the same, yesterday, today and forever, but was speaking to the new problems of its own day.

The most significant contemporary teacher in Judaism was R. Akiba who played a very significant role in having the Book of Esther incorporated into the Hebrew Bible. Without Akiba's advocacy, Esther might never have been Holy Writ. The connection of the Fourth Gospel and the Book of Esther is a major theme in the present work. The fact that any relationship between Esther and the Fourth Gospel has never been thought of before only highlights the very different ethos in the Fourth Gospel from that in the Book of Esther; the one is universalist and pacifist, the other is nationalist and retaliatory. As the reader will find, the present writer, however, can argue the case of the Fourth Gospel deliberately setting out to present another and better way than the path of nationalistic revenge as the biblical teaching in his day exemplified by the Book of Esther. This latter path was to lead to the Second Jewish Roman War and the death of R. Akiba and his Messiah Bar Cochbah.

There were still Jewish Christians when the Fourth Gospel was written and they could not but be influenced by developments in Judaism. The writer of the Fourth Gospel was aware of the dangers to the Christian Church as well as to the Jewish that another war with the Romans would bring, but he was not for peace at any price.

One must remember that for Christians, even at the end of the first century, the Bible was the Old Testament--of which the Book of Esther was now an integral part. There was a Greek translation of Esther available, some of the vocabulary of which the writer of John's Gospel knew and used. Not only does he seem to evoke literary allusions to the Greek Esther to make implied contrasts between his views and those of the Book of Esther, but he dares in effect to make claims for the canonicity of his own book that recall those argued by R. Akiba and his colleagues for Esther.

It is essential for the reader of this present work to understand the contemporary Jewish background to the Fourth Gospel if the main arguments in the book are to be followed. We make no excuse for having devoted much of the work to helping the reader grasp something of the complexity and variety of the Judaism that the writer of the Fourth Gospel knew and to which he himself owed so much.

It was in the course of researches on "the feast of the Jews" in Jn. 5:1 (afterwards published in *Near Eastern Studies* in honor of William Foxwell Albright, ed. Hans Goedicke, Baltimore and London: The John Hopkins Press, 1971, as "The Unnamed Feast of the Jews in John 5:1") that the present writer became convinced that that feast was Purim. He saw that if it were, then the possibility existed that the Fourth Gospel was, to say the least of it, aware of the newly acquired canonicity of Esther and the teaching of that book. At the end of the article on the unnamed feast in John 5:1 I promised a commentary on the Fourth Gospel which would show the implications of the canonicity of Esther for John's gospel. It has been unduly delayed, but at least the present work does grapple with these problems.

John Bowman

TALMUDIC AND RABBINIC ABBREVIATIONS

A.Z. = 'Aḅodah Zarah

Ab. = 'Aḅoth

Ar., Ara., Arakh. = 'Arakhin

b. = bar, ben

B.K. = Baḅa' Ḳama'

B.M. = Baḅa' M'ẓi'a'

B.B. = Baḅa' Bathrah

Bar. = Baraitha'

Bek., Bekh. = B'khoroth

Ber. = B'rakhoth

Bez. = Beyẓah

Bik. = Bikurim

D.E. = Derekh 'Ereẓ

D.E.R. = Derekh 'Ereẓ Rabah

D.E.Z. = Derekh 'Ereẓ Zuta'

Dem. = D'ma'y

E. = Early authorities
    (Rishonim, till end
    of 15th cent.)

Ed., Edu. = 'Eyduyoth

Eru. = 'Eyruḅin

G. = G'onim

Gem. = G'mara'

Gen. R. = Genesis Rabah
    (Ex. R. etc.)

Git. = Giṭin

Guide = Guide for the Per-
    plexed (Maimonides')

H., Heb. = Hebrew

Hag. = Ḥagigah

Hal. = Ḥalah

Hor. = Horayoth

Hul. = Ḥulin

J. = Jerusalem

Kel. = Keylim

Ker. = K'rithoth

Ket., Keth. = K'thuboth

Kid. = Kidushin

Kil. = Kil'ayim

Kin. = Ḳinim

Koh. R. = Ḳoheleth Rabah

L. = Late authorities
    ('Aḥaronim)

M. = Maimonides (Yad Haha-
    zaḳah)

M.K. = Moeyd Ḳaṭan

M.K. = Ma'aseyh haḲorbanoth
    (Maimonides')

M.S. = Ma'aseyr Sheyni

Maas. = Ma'asroth

Mak. = Makoth

Makh. = Makhshirin

Mekh. = Mekhilta

Meg. = M'gilah

Meg. Taan. = M'gilath
    Ta'anith

Meil. = M''ilah

Men. = M'nahoth

Mid. = Midoth

Mik. = Mikvaoth

Mish. = Mishnah

Mish. Comm.,
  Mish. Comment. =
     Commentary on Mishnah
      (Maimonides')

M.S.Y. = Mekhilta d'R.
     Shim'on b. Yohai

N. = Nahmanides

Naz. = Nazir

Ned. = N'darim

Neg. = N'ga'im

Nid. = Nidah

Oha. = 'Ohaloth

Orl. = 'Orlah

P.Z. = P'sikta' Zutr'tha'

Par. = Parah

Pes. = P'sahim

R. = Rabbi

R.H. = Rosh Hashana

Resp. = Responsa

S.M.L.T. = Sefer haMizvoth
     (Maimonides')
    Lo' Ta'aseh

San., Sanh. = Sanhedrin

Sem. = S'makhoth

Shab. = Shabath

Sh'bi., Shebi. = Sh'bi'ith

Sh'bu., Shebu. = Sh'bu'oth

Shek. = Sh'kalim

Sof. = Sof'rim

Sot. = Sotah

Suk. = Sukah

T. = Tosefta'

T.K. = Torath Kohanim

T.Y. = T'bul Yom

Taan. = Ta'anith

Tam. = Tamid

Tanh. = Tanhuma'

Tem. = T'murah

Ter. = T'rumoth

Toh. = Toharoth

Ukz. = 'Ukzin

Yad. = Yadayim

Yeb. = Y'bamoth

Yo., Yom. = Yoma'

Zab. = Zabim

Zeb. = Z'bahim

CHAPTER 1

Akiba, Text, Canon and Exegesis

It is generally recognized that R. Akiba was associated with
the finalization of the Palestinian Hebrew canon of the Bible and
that he was concerned with the Hebrew text and orthography of the
books accepted within the canon. His interest is said to have
extended also to the Greek version of the Hebrew Bible. R. Akiba
is[1] reputed to have encouraged Aquila to produce a new Greek translation which literally followed the Hebrew Bible text at all costs.
R. Akiba,[2] we are told, was also interested in a revision of the
Targum, the Aramaic translation of the Bible. It is indeed
possible that an early revision of Targum Onkelos, the official
Jewish Targum to the Pentateuch, was made by Aquila[3]/Onkelos at
the behest of R. Akiba. Undoubtedly Targums *qua* Targums had been
in existence long before this. Aquila[4] was certainly *not* the
originator of the Targum Onkelos. It is possible that R. Akiba
saw to it that Aquila revised the Aramaic Targum to the Pentateuch
to bring it into line with his halakah and exegesis. However
Targum Onkelos is in Babylonian and not Palestinian Aramaic. Yet
it is possible that such a literal Targum reflecting the halakah
of R. Akiba was later revised[5] and turned into Babylonian Aramaic.

R. Akiba's interest in Hebrew Bible canon and text and in
the Greek and Aramaic translations of the Pentateuch was based
on a belief in the Torah as being the very word of God. If the
Torah was the very word of God, one must have a text which one
can trust. But there was more to R. Akiba's concern than even
this. The situation which R. Akiba faced, in the decade 80-90 AD,

1

needed an oral law: (a) that was based in its several teachings
on more than the traditional authority of this or that scholar;
(b) that brought all the life of the present under the Torah.
The *Mishnah* form of teaching was well adapted for learning by
rote, but the old *Midrash* form of teaching did show the relationship of the oral law to the biblical text which later was a clear
guarantee of that halakah's biblical authority. There were
Christians who were only too ready to argue with Jews. Then too
there were the Am ha-Arez,[6] i.e. Jews who were not impressed by
the Rabbis' claims of authority. Not everyone that the Mishnah
and Talmud call an Am ha-Arez was an ignoramus, except of course
in the oral law, and even then he might not reject it through a
lack of understanding. There were also the Minim, some of whom
seem clearly enough to have been Jewish Christians, who had a
propensity for arguing with the Rabbis. While it may be true
that the term "Minim" may indeed describe more than one type of
sectarian, the subjects discussed in many a *Ma'aseh* about the
Minim,[7] or encounters with them, seem clearly to point to Jewish
Christians. It became recognized that these Jewish Christians
knew their Bible, which was the common Bible of the Jews. Some
may have argued from the LXX, a Jewish Greek translation, so
this had to be countered by a Jewish Greek translation, that of
Aquila. Some may have argued from the Targum, hence R. Akiba's
interest in standardizing the Targum, or at least in moving
towards an official Targum.

There are two kinds of Targums to the Pentateuch: the
haggadic type typified by the old Palestinian Targum, the Targum
Jerushalmi, with its homiletic developments of the biblical text,
and the halakic type typified by the so-called Targum Onkelos,
principally a straight translation, but concerned with indicating
support for the Halakah. While it is possible that both types
of Targum had originally existed side by side, it is more likely
that the separation of the haggadic from the halakic is *not*

primitive. The haggadic material of the Targum Jerushalmi is midrash. Midrash could be both haggadic and halakic. After the development of the mishnah form in teaching the oral law, the midrash form as a vehicle for teaching Halakah suffered a serious setback from which it never completely recovered. In so far as it did recover, it was thanks to R. Akiba. But R. Akiba first set the Mishnah in order, i.e. not only creating the major divisions, the six *sedarim*, but also the subdivision of each section into tractates. In fact R. Akiba would seem to have been responsible for a first edition of the Mishnah, or at least a Mishnah (the term *Mishnah* here being used in the collective sense, i.e. a collection of individual *mishnayoth* or individual mishnahs). We must bear in mind that obviously his interest in the midrashic method of teaching Halakah was *not* at the expense of the mishnaic method. The mishnaic method lent itself to codification; the midrashic method, where a verse was expounded *in situ*, did not. But the midrashic had the advantage that it demonstrated plainly the dependence of the halakic teaching on the written law.

It was all very well to say: (a) that the Christians of the later Gentile Church did not know the oral law; and (b) that the written law was not enough without the oral law to understand the TORAH. It was for this very reason that God had given the oral along with the written law at Sinai with the injunction to keep the whole law. Such an argument as in (b) seems a counter-charge directed at the Church, when it had clearly said that it and it alone understood how to interpret the written law. One does not believe that such a claim was *consistently* made by Christians before the writer of the Fourth Gospel. On the other hand, one does not think that Judaism as a whole could or would have made such a claim about the oral law being unknown to Christians before R. Akiba's time. One recalls the story of R. Eliezer[8] b. Hyrcanus who wondered why he had been charged by the

(Roman) Governor for being a *Minuth* (here the word *Minuth* certainly means Christianity). R. Akiba encouraged him to recollect what might have led to this, and R. Eliezer recalled how he had heard a hala*k*ic ruling of Jesus with approval from James. It will be remembered that R. Akiba did find R. Eliezer's attitude to the oral law considerably in his way. Nobody doubted that R. Eliezer knew the traditions better than anyone. But while he was in power, there was: (a) no chance of extension of the scope of the oral law; (b) no chance of development and change.

While it is possible that the concept of two laws already did exist, i.e. the oral and the written as both having been given at Sinai, it is most odd that even later (much later) only a very limited number of hala*k*oth are specifically designated as *halakoth le Mosheh mi-Sinai*. We do not know how extensive was the body of oral law on which Beth Hillel and Beth Shammai agreed. We know of 318 differences between them which were supposed to have made the Torah into two Toroth. Though technically the dissension between Beth Hillel and Beth Shammai had been settled by the time of R. Akiba, their respective hala*k*ic rulings still had their champions. Old R. Eliezer was a Shammaite. It is too facile to dub the Shammaites as patrician and priestly, and the Hillelites as plebeian and lay and to interpret the differences in Hala*k*ah merely on social and economic grounds. Yet that approach has at least this much insight, that it actually does take into account the fact that theologians and ecclesiastical lawyers are influenced by their own cultural and economic background.

It could well be that R. Akiba developed his system of exegesis (or rather took over and adapted R. Nahum[9] of Gamzo's system) so as to undermine the position and prestige of R. Eliezer the traditionalist, the living embodiment of the Law.[10] But if

this had been the only goal of R. Akiba, rabbinic Judaism's
debt to R. Akiba would hardly have been so great as it is.
While extending and developing the oral law, R. Akiba actually
succeeded in bringing the oral law and written law together.
The oral law was shown to be rooted in the written law, and
thereafter, for the Jew, the written law could not be understood without the oral law. Akiba's *Middoth* or exegetical
principles provided scriptural support for the halakoth that
he favoured. One can believe that by application of his *Middoth*
he discovered new halakoth. But primarily his *Middoth* were used
for providing support for both old and new halakoth. Akiba was
a systematizer, and he also had a system. Basically the written
law was fundamental for him. It had been given by God to men
through Moses. It was by this instrument that God created the
heaven and earth and all that is. The Law was eternal. It
belonged to man (Israelite man) as well as to God now. God had
spoken and still spoke to Israel in it. The Law was all sufficient both now and forever, if one had the proper means of interpreting it. In a sense God was bound by His own Law. God
even studied the Torah (T. B. Abodah Zara 3b) and could be out-
done by the rabbis (cf. T. B. Baba Mezia 86a). God also kept
His own Law (written and oral). In keeping the Law, and in
studying the Law, God and (Israelite) Man had a bond in common.

Hillel had seen the importance of exegetical rules and
formulated his 7 *Middoth*. Ishmael added to these and restated
Hillel's *Middoth* making 13 in all. But R. Akiba absolutely
literally held the doctrine of verbal inspiration and took this
into account in applying his exegetical principle of inclusion
and limitation.[11] One may not feel that the result of R. Akiba's
application of *ribbui u mīʿūt*[12] is derivable from the text in
question. That is not to the point. R. Akiba convinced himself
and his colleagues. He supplied the means to satisfy the need

to relate the teachings of the traditional oral law of the rabbis to the written law. One no longer needed to depend on the ruling of one rabbi or even on the Beth Din as the final guarantor of his or their interpretation of what constituted the Law on this or that matter. It could now be shown that their interpretation was based on the written Torah. Actually it made little difference for the ordinary individual. What his rabbi said was Torah, and if one was not satisfied there was the Beth Din to appeal to and that was as good as Mt. Sinai itself. However, it was a mighty key that R. Akiba provided to unlock the Torah, so that a never-ending stream of halakoth could be derived from it. It was *not* that tradition was set aside; it was legitimized and supplemented by new halakoth. But the test of all was whether they could be derived on the approved principles of exegesis from the written Torah. The written Torah, thanks to R. Akiba, kept its central place in Judaism without its hampering the development of the oral law.

R. Akiba himself did not give the last word in the development of the Halakah, but his importance is that his work gave a most significant direction and impulse to the development of the oral law. He supplied the principles for justifying this abandoning of absolute reliance on tradition without breaking with the alleged fount of all tradition. In short, he showed how to uncover halakoth which were not revealed even to Moses (cf. T. B. Men. 29b). The Johannine parallel to this is the doctrine of the Paraclete, which justified the Johannine reformulation itself, and made other developments and restatements possible. R. Akiba himself was concerned not only with the halakoth but also with the nature of God and His relation to man. The word *Middah* means both an exegetical principle *and* an attribute of God. And after all if the Torah is the inspired word of God, then by a proper application of exegesis, one should find

not only God's word of command to us, i.e. the expression of
His will, but also God's self-revelation of Himself and His
nature. R. Akiba's reverence for the letter of the Law extended
even to the anthropomorphic passages of the Torah. His God is
both transcendent and immanent, and he would not allegorise away
Torah statements which proclaimed His immanence.

If R. Akiba had an influence on an early revision of what
is now called Onkelos' Targum, we might expect it to reflect R.
Akiba's view of the close relationship of the oral law to the
written law with regard to both Halakah and Haggadah more than
the other Targums. Targum Onkelos like the Targums Jerushalmi
and Pseudo-Jonathan uses the word *Memra* extensively. With few
exceptions it uses the word *Memra* where Targum Jerushalmi does.
Targum Jonathan tends to follow the usage of both the other two
Targums combined as to *Memra*. However, Targum Pseudo-Jonathan
relies more on Onkelos than on Jerushalmi in this, but it also
has the word *Memra* where the others do not. How old the use of
Memra is, one cannot say. It is presumably older than R. Akiba.
It could have been in the Targums before him. If he had anything to do with Targum Onkelos, he may have regulated its use.
It is normally said that the word *Memra* is used to avoid anthropomorphic expressions. If R. Akiba had anything to do with what
is now Targum Onkelos, we would not expect him to avoid anthropomorphic expressions.

The expression *Memra de* [*Yeya*] does not preface the Tetragrammaton in every case. That the word *Memra* is only used
occasionally preceding *Yeya* surely points to the inadequacy of
Moore's[13] explanation that it is a mere translation fill-word
which is itself untranslatable. To the present writer, it would
appear that the expression *Memra* is full of meaning and that it
has been inserted in each Targum according to some specific plan.
In Targum Onkelos we find that it is not used in connection with

any specific Pentateuchal law. Now R. Ishmael, the contemporary
of R. Akiba, held that only where Yahweh specifically gives a
word to Moses to speak (e.g. Ex. 16:32; Lev. 17:2; Num. 30:2,
"this is the *dabar* which Yahweh has commanded") is the Torah
the actual Word of Yahweh. Elsewhere, according to R. Ishmael,
it is Moses' word though the ideas are from Yahweh. This view
of R. Ishmael brought the Torah on to the same level of revelation as the later prophets, where a prophetic oracle is introduced
by "the word (*debar*) of Yahweh to ...". It could be that the
use of *Memra* in the non-legalistic parts of the Torah is deliberately added or (if they are earlier than R. Akiba) retained to
show that throughout the Torah, God is speaking and communicating
with men. It should be noted that Targum Onkelos does *not* say:
"the word of *Yeya* said". It says: "*Yeya* said", both with regard to the so-called words of creation in Gen. 1 and in the
legal portions of the Torah. The interesting thing is that the
Targum in Gen. I substitutes the Tetragrammaton for *Elohim*, as
if insisting that the God of Israel was also the creator God.
Apart from this, it is difficult to see Targum Onkelos (Gen. 1)
as different from the M. T. Hebrew Gen. 1. In short, there is
no development there of creation by the hypostatic Word. In
Targum Onkelos (Dt. 33:27) we are told that: "the world was
made by His Word", and though this is reminiscent of Gen. I,
it may mean no more than the words in Gen. 1:3, 6, 9, 11, 14,
20, 24, 26, 28, 29 "and God said". It is significant, however,
that Targum Onkelos Dt. 33:27 does not say "made by His words",
for M. Pirke Aboth knows of the ten words of creation. It could
be that the statement "the world was made by His Word (*Memra*)"
refers to the use *Yeya* made of the Torah in creation as taught
by the Midrash. In fact there are many cases where *Memra*, as
used in Targum Onkelos, seems to demand the connotation of Torah.
One must remember that while the rabbis were busy showing how

their interpretations of the Torah for their time and its demands on themselves and their fellows were implicit in the Law, they were also claiming that the Torah was in God's lap (if not His bosom) long before creation. In a sense, since every word and every letter of the Torah had existed from before creation, every word of Yahweh in the Torah had already been determined as well as the reactions of the men therein and their deeds. Torah and Word of Yahweh are related, either as R. Ishmael thought that Torah contains the words of Yahweh, or as R. Akiba held that every word of Torah was the Word of Yahweh. One could then presumably say that in R. Akiba's view all the Torah was the Word of Yahweh.

One should remember when reading the Targum that if we have as in Targum Onkelos (Gen. 7:16): "And *Yeya* protected them (i.e. Noah and family, etc.) by His Word" (being the Targumic rendering of "And Yahweh shut him in"), to picture to whom and how this story was read. It was read in the vernacular rendering of God's Word. When one says "read", it was read aloud along with the portion of the Law in the divine service to worshippers who believed the Hebrew Torah was God's Word. If they were told *Yeya* protected the folk in the ark by His Word, they would understand that God protected those in the ark by His Torah just as it also protected them. The Jews were already the people of the Book and Judaism was religion of the Book. In a very real sense God was known principally through the public reading of the Book, the Torah. One notices that in Targum Onkelos, as indeed in the other Targums, the personal pronoun referring to *Yeya* is changed to *Memra*, e.g. Gen. 9:12: "This is the sign of the covenant which I make between Me and you." Onkelos renders the last phrase: "between My Word and you". One may object that if "My Word" means Torah here, it had not been given till Moses' time. But one should recall that in the Targum as in the Book of Jubilees,

the Antedeluvians kept the Festivals of the Law. Nay more in
the Targums, from Seth, the son of Adam, onwards the Patriarchs
had rabbinical schools for studying Torah. Taking into account
the fact that the Targum on the Torah was publicly read, i.e.
proclaimed, in the vernacular along with the Torah in the original
Hebrew, which latter was the very Word of God, it would be
appropriate for the *Meturgeman* to paraphrase the "Me" of the
Hebrew by "My Word" as referring to the Torah in Hebrew. In
any case, the Targum has the needs of the worshippers of its own
day in mind. It was essential to emphasize that the Torah, *Yeya*'s
Word, represents *Yeya* in each and every covenant.

Targum Onkelos Gen. 15:6 states: "And he (Abram) believed
in the Word of *Yeya*, and He reckoned it to him for justification."
Yes, here too one would claim that the Word is Torah. "Word"
here is *Memra* whereas in Targum Onkelos Gen. 15:1 it is "the word
of *Yeya* (*pithgama*) that came to Abram in prophecy". *Pithgama* is
the usual word in Targum Jonathan on the prophets for "the word
of the LORD" to the prophets. The actual phrase in Targum
Jonathan is a *pithgama* of prophecy from before *Yeya*. One recol-
lects R. Ishmael's attempt to bring Torah and Prophecy together
on a level by narrowing the scope of God's word in Torah. R.
Akiba, however, regarded all Torah as the Word of God. We note
pithgama's connection with prophecy is emphasized by Targum
Onkelos 15:1. It is all the more significant that Abram is
assured by the word of prophecy (*ibid.*): "My (*Yeya's*) Word
(*Memra*) shall be your strength", (the 1st personal pronoun of
the M. T. becomes "My Word" in the Targum). There is a contrast
implied. "My Word" (*Memra*) is not the word of prophecy, though
it is corroborated by the word of prophecy. Prophecy was allowed
into the canon of the Hebrew Bible along with the Law because
and only because it was held not to add or to detract anything
from the Law, but to corroborate it. Bearing this in mind, it

seems clear that "My Word (*Memra*) shall be your strength" is clearly "My Torah shall be your strength". But one may note that the Hebrew has "I" (*'anoki*). Here again the personal pronoun referring to *Yeya* is rendered "My Word", and the context in the Targum demands the reference as to the Torah.

We might say that in Targum Onkelos, *Yeya* = My Word = the Torah. To the worshippers to whom the Targum was directed, *Yeya*'s Word or Law was their strength. The Word (*Memra*) of *Yeya* in which Abram believed and which He reckoned to him for justification is also the Torah. One fancies that here we may have an anti-Pauline polemic or at least a corrective to Paul's teaching setting faith over against Law (= Word). *Memra* is Torah in the widest sense. *Memra* being equivalent to Torah and *vice versa* is *Yeya*'s expressed will. In Targum Onkelos, *Memra* is always associated explicitly or implicitly with *Yeya* (= Yahweh) *not* with *Elohim* (God). *Yeya* very often replaces *Elohim* (God) in this Targum.

The *Memra* is Yahweh Himself in communication with men. *Memra* is not used in the Law to introduce individual commands. *Memra* is used in more haggadic (not legalistic) sections of the Law. In the Targum to the Prophets "the word (*debar*) of the LORD" is rendered as the word of prophecy (*pithgama*) from before *Yeya*. The "spirit of the LORD" is the spirit of prophecy. *Memra* does occur in the Targum to the Prophets, but it refers to God Himself, i.e. it is used to translated a personal pronoun referring to God. In Judaism, at least until the 1st century A.D., the Holy Spirit is the Spirit of prophecy. Whereas sometimes *Memra* and Holy Spirit[14] seem synonymous, it would be safer to see their relationship one to the other in and through God. While *Memra* on the one hand is *Yeya* communicating with men, on the other hand, *Memra* is also the communication (i.e. The Torah is the Word). The communication is not the message, but the communicator is the message, and its universal conversive, the message is the communicator. But what of the word of prophecy and the Spirit of prophecy? They are one and the same. The Jews held that the Holy Spirit rested only on prophets who wrote down the words and that every word of holy scripture was inspired by the divine Spirit. The Spirit of holiness was the Spirit of Yahweh who is Holiness or the Holy One. Here the emphasis is not on the Word but on the Spirit that inspires it and is inseparable from it. It would appear that Torah in a special way is *Memra*. It is not just as the haggadic portions of the written Torah, but as we see in the Targums, especially of the Pentateuch, the *Memra* includes later haggadic statements based on the written Hebrew Torah. These later haggadic statements are put into the mouth of *Yeya* as it were. They would be oral first as the Targums were, and then later written down. The Torah is the Word of *Yeya* in which, in the Targum, it is clear that He is still speaking. In fact the Targumic use of *Memra* in the Pentateuchal Targums makes a bridge between the written and the oral law.

This has relevance to the Fourth Gospel. In a way the oral law is the real ante-typical Law, of which the Law and the Prophets and Holy Writings are but types. But the oral law does not call itself the Law. It is the record of the Word and His tabernacling among men. But not only so, it is a manifestation of the *name* of God. The continuity of the revelation is guaranteed by the Paraclete, i.e. the Spirit of truth who should lead the Apostles into all truth. This not only warrants reflection on and extension of the original teaching of Jesus but relates the Spirit to the *Logos/Memra*.

Judaism regarded the Prophets and Writings as *Cabbalah* tradition and as expounding but not adding to or detracting from the Torah. That the Fourth Gospel can quote the Psalms

as Torah is a reflection of the view of the canon of scripture
which R. Akiba championed. The Prophets and the Writings were
closely related to the Torah because they were believed to
expound and confirm the Torah. Even so, the Torah itself was
regarded as not only being on a higher degree of canonicity
but as having existed before creation. It was associated with
the words of creation. One might go further and say that it
held that God created in the very words of the first chapter
of Genesis. Now the Targum, while not abandoning the use of
Memra in the books outside the Pentateuch, may be making a
subtle distinction between the Torah and the Prophets when it
does *not* use the phrase *Memra de Yeya* in introducing a prophetic
utterance, or even introducing it as *dibbur* of *Yeya*, but as a
word (*pithgama*) of prophecy from before *Yeya* or from the Spirit
of prophecy. In the Targum to the Pentateuch when Yahweh states
a command the Targum says, "and *Yeya* said" (*Amar*) - for Hebrew
wa-yomer, *malel* for Hebrew *wa-yedabber*. The Targum obviously
does not want to put a word to a prophet on the level of a
command to Moses. And yet in the books outside the Law the
Targum does use *Memra* extensively with *Yeya within* the prophetic
message, perhaps using *Memra* to show that He who is active in
communication with man in the Torah is also active in the Prophets
and Holy Writings.

    Memra may be associated in the Targum in many cases with
not only Yahweh but the Torah. Sometimes *Memra* occurs instead
of a pronoun[15] referring to *Yeya*. One could then say that *Yeya*
and His Word are one and the same or that the *Memra* is the
expressed will of God. Now, the Torah is the expressed will of
Yahweh. While there are cases in the Targums to the Pentateuch
where His *Memra* seems to refer to what is already mentioned
earlier in the Torah (e.g. cf. Targum Onkelos Gen. 26:5: "Because Abraham obeyed My Word [*Memri* M. T. *Koli*] and kept the

keeping of My Word [*Memri* M. T. *Mishmarti*], My commandments, My
covenants [*Kyamai* M. T. *Hukkothai*] and My laws.") It is in the
Targum to the Psalms and to that on Ps. 119 in particular where
His *Memra* equals His Torah. The Targum to Ps. 119 is actually
following the M. T. Hebrew text faithfully in this. In Ps. 119
there are many synonyms for the Torah. The Targum translated
dabar either by its Aramaic equivalent or by the word *Pithgama*,
whereas the Hebrew *'Imrah* is always translated by the word *Memra*.
It would appear that *Memra* is here a synonym for Torah in its
widest sense, not merely commandments, but as a whole, being
Yahweh's Word to men. So we have *Memra* in the Targums on the
Pentateuch most frequently in close relationship to Yahweh,
e.g. the *Memra de Yeya*. Where in the Hebrew there is no mention
of Word, we have in the Targum on Ps. 119 His *Memra* translating
'Imratho His Word (= His Law). Less frequently we have "by
His *Memra*" in the Targums to the Pentateuch translating "by Him"
of the Hebrew; this latter "by His *Memra*" often could be translated "*in* His *Memra*", i.e. "in His Word", or "in the Torah".
One is reminded of the Samaritan *Memra Marqah* or Marqah's
lengthy discourse on the Torah. Then too there is the Syriac
term *Mimra* for a discourse, e.g. Theodore's Discourses on the
Creed and the Sacraments. But *by* or *in* His *Memra* in the Targums
on the Pentateuch as in the Targum on Ps. 119 can only mean one
discourse - the Law.

Some scholars in the past had been too quick to identify
Memra in the Targums with the Messiah on the basis of Jn. 1:1ff.
Others have been too quick to regard *Memra* as a fill word or a
sort of buffer word to blunt the edge of biblical anthropomorphism
Such explanations are not satisfactory. The Targums have retained
plenty of crude anthropomorphisms. It could be argued that *Memra*
is inserted before *Yeya* = Yahweh. Significantly it does *not*
occur before *Elohim* to show Him communicating with men (Israelites

And it is by His Word that Yahweh communicates with men. One
is reminded of Elijah on Horeb. Yahweh was not *in* the wind
and fire, i.e. He was *not* communicating with him thereby but
in the still small voice. The preposition b^e in Hebrew can
mean either "by" or "in". Although the Targums to Gen. 1
substitute Yahweh for *Elohim*, the phrase "Word of *Yeya*" does
not occur in that chapter. Though the verb "to say" occurs ten
times in that chapter, the noun "word" *Memra* (the Hebrew *ma'amar*)
does not appear. Strikingly the first occurrence of the expression
Memra of Yeya in the Targum is in relation to Man in the Garden.
One would submit that the expression *Memra of Yeya* is used to
emphasize that Yahweh is a God who reveals Himself in Word to
men. His revelation of Himself (as He is) is made to men and
the revelation consists in words. The Targumist could not
separate the revelation from Yahweh. The revelation of Yahweh
was and is Yahweh. The revelation was by word (or words) and the
Word was Yahweh. Yahweh could not be separated from His Word.
Word and name are the same. In fact a new name of God (cf. Ex.
3:6) constituted a new revelation of God, i.e. of His nature.
The name of God has been called theology in a nutshell. Appellatives are attributes. Compare how Yahweh (Ex. 34:6, 7) in re-
vealing Himself to Moses on Sinai proclaimed His name, Yahweh
then described Himself. First He states He is El. This can
mean that He Yahweh is an *El* (i.e. a God), but it is more likely
that He is identifying Himself with El: the God whose attributes
are set out in the appellatives in Ex. 34:6b and 7, e.g. merciful
and gracious, slow to anger, and plenteous in mercy and truth,
etc. When the Jews had the Law, i.e. Yahweh's revelation of Himself, they had as it were God Himself. Mention has been made
above (cf. p. 5) that *Middoth* in Hebrew means both hermeneutical
rules and divine attributes. One remembers how R. Eliezer b.
Hyrcanus, the old traditionalist at the end of the 1st century

A.D., was overruled by R. Akiba and his colleagues in his
opinion regarding the possibility of a purification of the
'Aknai Tannur (oven).[16]   R. Eliezer called on the course of
nature to be reversed to prove his point was right. He called
for a heavenly voice to witness to the correctness of his
opinion. The course of nature was reversed; the heavenly voice
testified; but R. Akiba was not impressed. R. Joshua b.
Hananiah said that the Law was not in heaven, but is with men.
It was given at Sinai and now it was up to men to interpret it.
Akiba with his special hermeneutics could extract hosts of laws
from tittles and ornamental crowns on letters of the alphabet.
Yahweh had to study His own Law to keep up with these clever
sons of men who, as remarked above, could beat Him. Was Yahweh
separate from His Word? Did He exist apart from the Torah?

Akiba and his colleagues were interested primarily in
halakic matters. Torah comprises both halakic (legalistic)
as well as haggadic (homiletic) materials. But in the normative Judaism which Akiba was creating, the emphasis was to be
on Halakah. It was the Halakah that was the way of life. The
Pentateuch contains both halakah and haggadah. The so-called
historical portions are haggadic midrash. This is especially
clear in the historical addresses of Moses in Deuteronomy.
However the laws, and one means not only the Ten Commandments
but the whole 613 positive and negative commands of the Law,
form the basis of all the development of the so-called oral
law now enshrined in Mishnah and Talmud. The Law had to be
kept relevant to the different ages. In the Pentateuch itself
there are different codes and the modification of some of the
laws is evident. Even supposing that the written law, which
the people in the time of Ezra (in the first few decades of
the fourth century B.C.) swore to observe, was not subsequently
modified, there must have been different ways in which its

individual laws were interpreted in different places and
succeeding periods. According to early rabbinic tradition,
until the pupils of Beth Hillel and Beth Shammai in the first
century became numerous, there had been few differences on the
interpretation of the written law. Actually there are only 318
recorded differences between the two schools. This is, however,
a huge increase throughout the first century as before that
there had been only *one* difference between Hillel and Shammai.
Much is to be said for the identification of the Sadducees of
Josephus and the New Testament with the Shammaites, and the
Pharisees of Josephus and the New Testament with the Hillelites.

It has always been a puzzle just how the Temple could be
run at all if the Sadducees had their own rules as to how it
should be run and the Pharisees had different views. But the
situation was more complicated if the Pharisees were divided into
two groups themselves. In any case, apart from Paul, who called
himself a Pharisee? And who called himself a Sadducee? Each
term is a nick-name given by opponents to the other. The identification Sadducee = priest, over against Pharisee = layman,
reflects the bias of those who hold it. Even if we do not go
all the way with Louis Ginzberg we can say at least that there
was very much in common between the Shammaites and the Sadducees.

The fact that Pharisees and Sadducees had existed since
the middle of the second century B.C. shows that different
attitudes to the written Torah were possible. The Sadducees
are supposed to have held only the written law as authoritative.
Whereas the Pharisees gave much weight to the traditions of the
Fathers, just as to the written law (cf. Jos. Ant. XIII 297, 298).
This does not mean that the Sadducees gave no weight to the
traditions of the Patriarchs or had none. It would be most
surprising if they did not emphasize these traditions since the
priests were a very learned hereditary aristocracy. Incidentally,

there are only some nineteen recorded differences between the
Pharisees and the Sadducees, and these are all on religio-legal
matters. The Sadducees had their interpretation of the written
law and the Pharisees theirs. It was basically a difference in
exegesis. The Qumran sectarians also had their exegesis and,
as we can see from the Zadokite document, they regarded those
who did not subscribe to their interpretation of the Torah as
not having the Law, nor keeping the Statutory Feasts. The
calendar divided the Jewish community into sects, e.g. Samaritans,
Qumranites, Pharisees and Sadducees, differing on the date of
Pentecost. But the calendar itself was largely based on biblical
exegesis.[17] It is unthinkable that the Sadducees did not have
their own traditions of how the biblical ordinances of religion
based on the Law were to be fulfilled. They obviously had their
traditions as to how the Temple and its services and sacrifices
were to be carried out, though one could not find them set out
in the Torah. So they were not lacking a kind of oral law.
Actually before R. Akiba we have very little rabbinic oral law
of the first century.

The staunch traditionalist, R. Eliezer b. Hyrcanus, represents the tradition of his teacher, Rabban Johanan b. Zakkai. But
although many halakoth of R. Eliezer are preserved covering most
aspects of the oral law as represented in the Mishnah, one could
not say that he felt that there was a halakah for every conceivable situation and thing. R. Eliezer's Halakah, however,
updated and extended the Law to cover much of life. As we saw
above (pp. 15, 16), R. Akiba was the cause of R. Eliezer's excommunication on the question of purifying an oven. This incident is significant as it brought to a head the tension between
the older type of Pharisaic rabbinism typified by the traditionalist *par excellence*, R. Eliezer b. Hyrcanus, and R. Akiba who
stressed his exegesis as more important than tradition. R. Eliezer

was the greatest exponent of traditional oral law at the end of the first century A.D. But he refused to extend the scope of the oral law. Akiba could and did extend the oral law to cover all contingencies by his own method of exegesis, while at the same time claiming that it was not new but a rediscovery of an alleged oral law in its totality as given to Moses on Sinai along with the written law. The written law was not enough by itself. The oral law was *the* Law to be obeyed, and it was aimed at bringing all life under the aegis of that Law.

If Eliezer b. Hyrcanus were asked a halakic point on which he had no tradition, he had to say that he had nothing to say. Whereas R. Akiba by his hermeneutics could give a halakic ruling and at the same time relate his ruling to some dictum in the Law. The haggadah in T. B. Men. 29b shows how Moses was at one and the same time impressed with R. Akiba's halakic skill in the vision granted him at Sinai, but was puzzled at how his findings were derived from his Torah. And yet R. Akiba was of the literalist[18] and *not* the allegorical school. This may seem surprising. His contemporary R. Ishmael, who said: *"Talmud lomar belishon Adam"*, i.e. "the Bible speaks in the language of men", was an allegorist; and yet R. Ishmael seems to take the plain sense of the Torah. Akiba was indeed a literalist in that he stressed the importance of every[19] word, letter, tittle and ornamental crown on a letter. He and his school must have given much impetus to the standardizing of the Hebrew text and orth-ography of the Bible, especially of the Torah. It was essential for him and his school to have a Bible text in which there was no variant reading or doubt about the reading letter by letter, because every letter was important in the discovery of new halakoth. R. Akiba's hermeneutical principle of *Ribbui-u-Mi'ut* went far beyond the 13 *Middoth* or hermeneutical rules of R. Ishmael. R. Ishmael's results might seem to give what we call

the literal sense, while R. Akiba's were farfetched. And yet
R. Akiba's results were indeed literal in that on his premises
they gave importance to every letter. In fairness, some of
R. Akiba's halakoth may have been old rulings or practices,
which were formerly enunciated by some sage, but without
biblical support. R. Akiba by his skillful (if somewhat forced)
exegesis contrived to give such an interpretation the support of
the written Torah. This was not all, part of his aim was to
bring all life under Torah, and it was all the easier when such
vestiges of national life as had been granted the Jews before
70 A.D. were now lost. One of the earlier impulses given to the
development of the oral law was the desire to prevent the in-
fringement of the written commands of the Torah, by putting a
fence about the Law. But by R. Akiba's time the fence had
become the Law itself and hedged in some aspects of life, but
theoretically its totality. When R. Akiba and his school came
to anthropomorphic expressions relating to the Deity, they
tended to treat them literally. But here again the term
"literal" requires some qualifications. R. Akiba (T. B. Hag.
14a) in explaining the two thrones that were set in Daniel
7:9 says that one was for the Ancient of Days and the other
for the son of David, the messiah. His concern was to take
account of the fact that there were *two* thrones instead of only
one. When R. Joshua b. Hananiah objected, R. Akiba allowed that
the second throne was a footstool for the Almighty. R. Joshua
was an allegorist, but it is difficult to see where R. Akiba,
as a literalist, got any reference to the son of David, the
messiah, in Dan. 7:9.

Haggadah was not as important as Halakah for R. Akiba and
his colleagues, yet even then haggadah had more weight than say
in the time of Shemuel ha-Nagid, who regarded haggadic views as

an individual's private opinions expressed on the spur of the
moment. R. Akiba and his colleagues did dabble in Merkabah
Mysticism, and Aher's (Elisha b. Abuya) statement[20] about seeing
the Metatron beside the Almighty, i.e. that there were two
deities, led to Aher's exclusion. There is the interesting story
in M. Gen. R. 1 of two boys (one of whom was Akiba) and how they
explained to the sages the mysteries of the creation and God's
providence from the letters of the alphabet.[21] This story may
have led to the ascription to him of the later Midrash: *The
Alphabet of R. Akiba*. As we have them, the different versions
of *The Alphabet of R. Akiba* cannot go back to R. Akiba, but
there are sufficient points of contact with the story in M. Gen.
R. 1 to show a continuing belief that R. Akiba's concern with
letters was literal in what may seem to us to be a truly startling
way. Briefly the Midrash points to creation by the Law, but
before the Torah had existed the alphabet was with the Holy One.
Each of the letters of the alphabet requested the Holy One to
create with him. Then the Holy One quotes from the Hebrew Bible
(all of which is regarded as Torah in this Midrash) a verse where
the petitioning letter will be used in an unworthy sense, thus
disqualifying it from being used to introduce creation. *Beth*
is chosen for creation and *Aleph* is given the reward of introducing the Torah at Sinai with *'Anoki* (Ex. 20:1). From a more
esoteric aspect, the Midrash presents how much each letter counted
for R. Akiba.

Belief in the coming of the Messiah belonged to the realm
of Haggadah rather than Halakah, yet R. Akiba did acknowledge
Bar Cochbah as such.[22] I would submit that for R. Akiba and
those who followed him, there was a real connection between the
halakah and haggadah. It has always puzzled the present writer
why R. Akiba and his colleagues and successors went on codifying
and developing all the niceties of sacrificial law and temple

practice and all the laws of Levitical purity[23] till more than
two-thirds of the Mishnah was given over to laws that cannot
be kept nor could be kept because when they were formulated
there was no longer a temple. But we forget the rationale of
the whole process. R. Akiba and many of his colleagues were
"messianists". The messiah's reign was to be a reign of Law
and his state a Torah state. For the implementation of the
Torah, the temple was necessary. Till then study was as good
as doing. This gave much of the impetus to R. Akiba's drive
to discover more and more halakoth from even the tittles and
crowns of the individual letters in the words of the Law. It
was the revelation of the blueprint for the constitution of
the Messianic Age. R. Akiba was not dependent on tradition
but on the Torah itself, which existed with the Holy One before
creation and was His agent in creation. So the haggadic story
of the events which led to the excommunication of R. Eliezer is
very important as highlighting these two different approaches
to religion. R. Eliezer calling for a reversal of the law of
gravity for a heavenly voice to witness to his being correct
is rather like the Johannine Jesus calling his miraculous works
and God Himself as witnesses. R. Akiba was not impressed. The
Law is not in Heaven, but it has been with men since Sinai and
it has been in their power to determine, interpret, and define
it, had they known how to do so before R. Akiba came. While it
would be going too far to say that Yahweh was absolutely identical with the Torah for him, there was more than a casual connection between the two. For R. Akiba the Torah surely expressed
the revealed will of God and declared the nature of God. God
could not be untrue to Himself which would be impossible. It
was essential in dealing with the written Torah to exercise
maximum care in interpreting the Torah so as to extract from it
each and all its commandments for the way (the halakah) of life.

The 613 commandments were the revealed will of God not just for
man but in a sense required by God. God needed man to sanctify
Him. Did not R. Akiba say that all is foreseen,[24] but freedom
of choice is given? There is also the saying: everything but
the fear of Heaven is in the power of Heaven.[25] And heaven[26]
is God by metonymy. R. Akiba, who died a martyr with the
Shema' on his lips and declaring the uniqueness of the Lord
(Yahweh), knew that man cannot love the Lord his God with all
his mind, might, and strength unless he keeps all the commands
of the Torah. Man could not be holy so as to sanctify the LORD
unless he kept the whole Law. It was a holy duty to find out
new ways of sanctifying the LORD his God. The temple had gone;
the sacrifices had ceased; the *Shekinah* had departed; but the
Jews had still the Law. In a sense, the Law was more central
than ever for R. Akiba and his colleagues. The Law was not in
heaven: it was with man (Jewish man). The Law had existed with
the LORD before creation, and it would be supreme when the
messiah came. With the Law and in the Law, the Jews, as God's
witnesses, could find God's will and could help Him to be true
to Himself. God needed them to sanctify Him and bind His resolve. The haggadic portions of the Law, as anthropomorphic as
they might be in describing Yahweh's dealings with men, were all
the more precious and could not justifiably be allegorised away.
The Lord had been near to their Fathers, and it was a *miẓwah*
to perform a remembrance of His wondrous acts at the great
feasts and to magnify them, even if it meant multiplying the
plagues of the Egyptians and His wonders at the Sea (cf. the
Passover Haggadah). In a real sense, R. Akiba in his haggadic
statements magnified Yahweh's power, wisdom and might, just as
in his halakic statements he extended His will for those under
the covenant of Sinai. If the Torah declares Yahweh's will, it
also reveals His nature. And because of this, R. Akiba, in so

far as he could, was careful in interpreting the stories of
Yahweh's dealing with his people. Their actuality is heightened,
even if the anthropomorphism was overdone. Every preacher and
every exegete, to a greater or lesser extent, projects not only
his view of his God but much of himself. If the Law is not in
heaven, if it is with men to define and explore to the fullest
and, if it is God's revealed will and revelation of Himself, may
not men be determining God's will and not merely describing
His nature, but determining it for the faithful? Of course this
applies to any great and influential theological work and to the
reinterpretation of God and His demands on men. God is ontologi-
cally the same yesterday, today, and tomorrow. But men's views
of Him change, and different emphases are put on different aspects
of His nature. This applies even when men have the same written
testimony of His revelation of Himself. The revelation is made
to reveal the God they seek. One is not saying that R. Akiba
denied the transcendence of His God, but he certainly found the
God he sought, and glorified Him in His Torah. R. Akiba's
Middoth (i.e. hermeneutical principles) provided him with the
Middoth (i.e. attributes of God). We cannot say that he was consciously creating by his *Middoth* (i.e. hermeneutical principles)
God's Law and His attributes. He used the *Given*, the written
Torah and what tools he had at hand, i.e. his hermeneutical
principles, and he was confident of the result, for the Law
was not in heaven.

CHAPTER 2

The Fourth Gospel and Jewish Law

Galilean Christianity had hoped to liberate men from the Law, the Temple and all its functionaries, priests, Sadducees and Pharisees, and the like. The Temple had been destroyed by the Romans in 70 A.D., but the Torah was more powerful than ever, and its influence over the lives of Jews was even more all-embracing. Jesus the Messiah had *not* come back in glory as Mark had predicted in the chapter (Mk. 13) which began with his curse on the Temple; and the Roman yoke was heavier. The priesthood *qua* priesthood had lost their power, but such priests as were left had cast their lot with the rabbis who now had full charge of a new Sanhedrin. Not that the latter had even the trappings of secular power; it was more an academy than a court and their writ was not supported by the Roman authority. And yet because it was the self-appointed custodian of the Torah and the Torah was more central to Judaism than ever, the Beth Din had a real moral power over the remnants of Palestinian Jewry. It is important to be aware of the actuality of the crisis that the Roman War caused for *both* Judaism *and* Christianity. The Jews had lost their Temple; and the Zion City of Yahweh their God, who had abode in the Holy of Holies, had been abandoned by Him or so the Christians told them. There were Jews who felt the same.

The Christians had seen the fulfillment of Jesus' prediction on the fate of the Temple. At last its sacrifices were no more and the system of atonement and purification centering on the

Temple was unrealiable. But the Son of Man had not returned in
glory on the clouds. Until 70 A.D. the Christians could stress
the return of their messiah and hope that when he came the second
time it would be in glory (and not in humility as the first time).
And then the Jews would recognize him. It is not that the
Christians necessarily saw the full implications of His non-
return immediately. At least the Temple had gone. The fact
that part of the prediction was fulfilled and the pride of the
high-priesthood overthrown, might seem to be an earnest
of the full accomplishment of Mk. 13. Matthew's and Luke's
gospel did cling to the hope of their Davidic messiah's imminent
return. But already in Matthew and especially in Luke there are
significant changes from the old Petrine gospel of Mark. However Paul's preaching, even before Mark's gospel, had stressed
less the life and work of Jesus of Nazareth and even his messiahship and had emphasized more the unbroken continuity of His redemptive activity with that of the pre-incarnate Son of God. The
gospel form of the preaching alone in Luke's gospel (ca. 80 A.D.)
specifically in its annunciation and birth narratives made it
clear that Jesus was both the eternal Son of God and son of
David. Particularly striking is (Lk. 2:9) the appearance of the
angel of the Lord and the heavenly glory (or *Shekinah*) of the
Lord to the shepherds, with the declaration (v. 11): "Today in
the city of David a Saviour has been born to you. He is Christ
the Lord." The application of the title "Lord" to the Christ is
significant since "Lord" is a title which the Old Testament
reserves for Yahweh. Matthew does not go so far (cf. Mt. 1:18-
23). While telling that Mary was with child through the Holy
Spirit (v. 18) of which Joseph, a son of David, was informed
by the angel of the Lord in a dream (v. 20), Matthew's comment
is that this took place to fulfill Isa. 7:14: "The virgin will
conceive and give birth to a son and they will call him
Emmanuel", a name which means "God-is-with-us".

Theodore of Mopsuestia in his preface to his *Commentary
on the Gospel of John the Apostle*[27] tells why the Fourth Gospel
came to be written. He states that the Christians of Asia came
to John and asked him his opinion of the three Synoptic Gospels.
John commended them but pointed out their lack of doctrine,
adding that while they dwelt on the incarnation ministry, they
were silent on his divinity. Therefore John wrote on the doctrine of his divinity. Ishodad of Merv at the beginning of his
Commentary on the Gospel of John[28] repeats Theodore's story.
However, one should not necessarily accept Theodore's tale as
history, any more than his statement that John, writing for
these Asians who had the gospels of Matthew, Mark and Luke,
signifies events already known to them from these other gospels
by his fairly frequent use of *meta tauta*. Bacon[29] did point out
the difficulties that John in Ephesus would face in coming to a
church accustomed to Pauline preaching. The argument is that
such a church would find it difficult to accept the gospels of
Mark, Matthew, or even of Luke and their emphasis on tales of
his ministry. If this were the case in Ephesus, one would have
expected the same difficulty in other Pauline churches too. One
is not entirely convinced by Bacon's argument. The Christians
of Rome had the preaching of both Peter and Paul. Afterwards
they could hold the gospel of Mark as well as the Epistle to the
Romans in high esteem. One could allow for a swing away from
the Pauline doctrine because of the attractiveness of the
narrative form of the gospels and their apparent emphasis on
the Christ of history. Neither messianism nor nationalism was
dead among the Jews after the fall of the Temple. In fact
messianism had always been the quintessence of the old Jewish
nationalism. The early Christian Church was still largely
Jewish and could not but be influenced by the national aspirations
of the Jews. Some Christians would want to stress that Jesus was

messiah all the more and dwell on his second coming in majesty
to set up God's kingdom on earth. Whereas the Jewish religion
suffered intermittent persecution by the state in the last
quarter of the 1st century A.D., Christianity,[30] never having
been a *religio licita* was the more suspect.

It is usually held that docetism with its tendency to
explain away the real humanity of Jesus is what the Fourth
Gospel sets out to contend with. Theodore did not seem to have
thought that this was the case. John's archenemy at Ephesus
is alleged to have been Cerinthus.[31] But was Cerinthus entirely
docetic? It would depend on one's definition of docetism.
Irenaeus said that John wrote his gospel to root out the
erroneous doctrine which had been spread by Cerinthus and some
time before by the Nicolaitans. Cerinthus was a Jew by birth
and was educated in Alexandria where he taught. The main points
in his system borrowed from gnosticism are the concepts of a
pleroma,[32] aeons and demiurge. But these are adapted to fit his
system. The God of the Old Testament, the demiurge, is sub-
ordinate to the true God whom he had formerly resembled in
nature. When the demiurge's nature deteriorated, the true God
was determined to subvert his power by means of one of the aeons
whose name was Christ. This aeon/Christ entered into a certain
very righteous Jew called Jesus, the son of Joseph and Mary, by
descending upon him in the form of a dove when he was baptized
by John in the Jordan. After his union with Christ, this Jesus
vigorously assailed the demiurge, the God[33] of the Jews. It
was at the instigation of the demiurge that Jesus was seized
by the rulers of the Jewish nation and crucified. But when
Jesus was apprehended, the aeon Christ flew away to heaven so
that only the man Jesus was put to death. Cerinthus required
his followers to worship the supreme God, the Father of Christ,
along with the Christ himself. But the demiurge[34] who, besides

creating the world, had given the Law to the Jews was *not* to be
worshipped. Though some parts of the Mosaic Law were retained,
emphasis was placed on the precepts of Christ as a guide to
life. Cerinthus taught the resurrection of the body with the
delights of the millenium under Christ reunited to Jesus the
man and reigning in Palestine. Thereafter there would follow
a happy and never-ending life in the celestial world. Presumably the writer of the Fourth Gospel had to face such[35]
teaching and show (1) that the God of the Old Testament is *the*
God and not just the God of the Jews and (2) that Jesus is the
Christ the Son of God, who suffered and died for men and rose
again. It is odd however that Theodore of Mopsuestia,[36]
Nestorius, and the Nestorians--all of whom were much influenced
by the Fourth Gospel--see the man assumed, i.e. Jesus as the
Temple of the Word/God. Theodore in his catechetical lectures
and his commentary on John actually distinguishes places in
that gospel where it is the Word/God who speaks from where it
is the man Jesus who is talking. Theodore and the Nestorians
claim that the Word/God stood apart from the man assumed, i.e.
Jesus, when the latter was on the cross, though ready to help
if he required it. Theodore[37] bases this withdrawal on Paul
(Phil. 2:8 read as *"Apart from God* he [Jesus] tasted death").
However the Monophysite reads "Because He, God, by His grace
tasted death for every man".

One has the impression that Cerinthus' teaching, apart
from the gnostic phraseology, sprang from a Judaeo-Christian
background. Even the pre-existence of the messiah was possibly
due to a type of Judaism represented by I Enoch. We err if we
think that the messiah must be human. Cerinthus' millenarianism
is as much Judaeo-Christian as the New Testament Apocalypse which
has been given the name of John. Early Christianity was faced
with the dilemma of what its attitude to the Law was to be. To

the Law of Moses, Christianity could *not be* neutral. Either
the gospel superceded the Law and released one from most of
the 613 laws and all the injunctions and prohibitions of the
rabbinic oral law, *or* the gospel fulfilled the Law in such a
way that its 613 laws were transcended and the rabbinic oral
law was negated. Such would seem to be the approach inculcated
by the gospels of Mark and Matthew respectively. Luke, with
his emphasis on Jesus' proclamation of the Jubilee year of
release, seems to imply that the gospel releases one from the
jurisdiction of the Torah. In the face of Jewish apologetic
on behalf of the Law and polemic against Christian Jewish gospel
preaching, while some Jewish Christians may have held fast to
the Law, the tendency would be to declare the gospel to be the
new Law. In the period after the destruction of the Temple and
the increasing emphasis on the centrality of the written and
oral Torah by the rabbis, the Christians may have felt that it
was impossible to come to terms with the Law of Moses. In
short, one could maintain that in the period when the Torah
under R. Akiba and his colleagues was actually being made[38] to
cover all of life (as had been claimed for it before) the
attitude of the Christians to the Torah also changed. Cerinthus'
teaching may be symptomatic of this and indeed later Marcion
may have been irritated by similar continuing and increasing
claims of the Jews for their Law. One has to see Cerinthus and
later Marcion as reacting against the Judaism of their own
times. According to the Christian view, Judaism was superceded
when Christ came. Later Judaism lost its Temple, but the Jews
not only clung to the Law, but Jewish teachers made more and
more claims for it and extended its influence. In fact by the
oral law they remade the Law and revitalized it, claiming, of
course, that this was and always had been the Torah. Since
divine approval and sanction were given for the oral law, God

was implicated and involved. One should surely take this
situation into account. It must have been felt so painfully
by some Christians who, while they had been willing to use
the Law and the rest of the Old Testament as pointing to Christ,
were now, nevertheless, willing to jettison it and with it the
God Who gave it. At the same time they were willing to adopt
gnostic terminology and some of its concepts to make their
approach appear more "with it"!

The writer of the Fourth Gospel, we are told by Irenaeus,[39]
was opposed to Cerinthus. It is our contention that he was not
only opposed to Cerinthus' gnosticism[40] in general but in particular to his attitude towards the God of the Old Testament and the
Law. One might add that he was especially opposed to Cerinthus'
doctrine of Christ, but this was contingent on his opposition
to the latter's doctrine of God. The writer of the Fourth Gospel
was also opposed to Judaism--not only the Judaism which had
opposed the rejected Jesus Christ but also that Judaism which,
by its new claims for the Law and its authority, continued to
reject the claims made for Jesus Christ by the apostles and
their successors. It could be that the writer of the Fourth
Gospel felt he had to go beyond Luke in bridging the gulf between the Synoptic Gospels and Pauline theology. That his gospel
was written in Ephesus does not preclude his actual concern with
Jews and Judaism. The Jewish Diaspora was strong, and there
was constant coming and going between Jerusalem and the Diaspora.
It would appear that the writer of the Fourth Gospel was more
fundamentally concerned with a dialogue with Judaism than with
the gnostics and Cerinthus. In any case, he may have met some
gnostics in Judaism. The writer of the Fourth Gospel had to
provide propaganda to use in answering "the Jews" so often
mentioned in that gospel. His gospel shows the Jews making
enquiries (e.g. Jn. 1) regarding John the Baptist and the latter's

testimony to Jesus Christ (cf. also the visit of Nicodemus the
ruler of the Jews in Jn. 3). There is also the cross-questioning
of the man born blind (Jn. 9) who was healed on the Sabbath (v.
14) and the threat to excommunicate him (v. 12). Much of the
Fourth Gospel deals with rejection and this need not mirror only
the rejection of Jesus but also that of his followers even in
the gospel writer's own time.

The writer of the Fourth Gospel knew much about Judaism and
not just about the religion of the old Testament. It is indeed
clear that he knew of Jewish personages known to the Talmud and
Midrash. His Jesus, he shows, has influential friends. Nicodemus
may be the same as Nakdimon[41] who seems to have been both a priest
and Pharisee who was wealthy and public-spirited. The rub is
that Nakdimon, who was known to the rabbis, was according to them
one of the leaders of the so-called Peace Party during the Roman
War. Martha,[42] who was also known by the rabbis, belonged to the
important high priestly family of Boethius and was herself the
wife of one of the last high priests Jesus b. Gamla.[43] One could
press the argument that the Talmud's *forte* is not history and
perhaps Nakdimon really is a contemporary of Jesus. But this is
unjustifiable when we see that the rabbinic stories about Nakdimon and Martha, if they are to have any point at all, demand
our acceptance of the fact that they are about people who were
well-known during the siege of Jerusalem by the Romans.

There is no real doubt that the writer of the Fourth Gospel
knew about the Temple services. This is clear enough on internal
evidence without having to refer to Irenaeus' statement cited by
Torrey[44] about John the Elder wearing the *Petalon*. Even if John
the Elder were not the writer of the Fourth Gospel, it is still
a very interesting statement because the *Petalon* in the LXX[45]
is the translation of the *Ẓiẓ*, i.e. the high priestly plate worn
on the forehead of the incumbent of that office with the legend
"holy to Yahweh". John the Elder must at least have been close

to one of the high priestly families of the first century A.D.
The interest in the feasts shown by the Fourth Gospel, and not
merely in the feasts themselves but in relation to the divine
acts of power and deliverance which they proclaim, shows the
liturgical context in which its writer set the gospel and through
which he reveals it. Liturgy does not belong to the temple
feasts alone but was an essential daily element in the temple
worship. One thinks in particular of the prayer service which
was an integral part of the daily morning Tamid sacrifice and
which became the nub of the daily Synagogue office. This Tamid
prayer service took place in the Temple and Synagogue on the Sabbath as well as on the week-day. To this day in private morning
devotions the observant Jew will say the benedictions before and
after the *Shema'* as they were said in the first century. For
first century Jewish theology study of these prayers is essential.
Granted they have had additions added after the destruction of
the Temple, but the basic themes are most likely the same. These
prayers flank the *Shema'* as they did in the temple prayer service.
The *Shema'* is central. It is possible that the accompanying
prayers were intended to tell one of The LORD (*YHWH*) our God who
is one LORD (*YHWH*) so as to make a better witness to Him. The
first benediction before the *Shema'* blesses the LORD (*YHWH*) our
God, King of the *'Olam* universe or world as *Yozer 'Or* former[46]
of light and creator of darkness, the maker of peace and creator
of all things who, in mercy, gives light to the whole earth and
those who dwell therein; and in His goodness every day constantly
renews the work of creation. The second benediction begins either
as in the Askenazis: "With great love", or in the Sephardis:
"With everlasting love" (*Ahabath 'Olam*). This benediction ends
"Blessed art Thou, O LORD, who hast chosen Thy people Israel in
love". The benediction dwells on God's love to His people manifested chiefly in His having given them His Torah. Their prayer

is "Enlighten our eyes in Thy Law and make our hearts one that
we may love and fear Thy name, and not be ashamed". In this
benediction we note the emphasis on the love of the Lord (*YHWH*).
His love to those that pray this prayer is to enlighten their
eyes in His Law. Law is central; through the Law they can love
and fear God. The LORD (*YHWH*) is declared to be the God who
works salvation for those who trust in His holy name. These two
benedictions and the Fourth Gospel share a common vocabulary.
This is not surprising as both were heirs of the same scriptures
and liturgical traditions, but there are also significant differences.

The Sephardi ritual's opening formula *'Ahabath 'Olam* is
surely very significant for the student of John's gospel. *'Olam*
can mean "eternity" or "world". While *'Ahabath 'Olam* can be
translated "with everlasting love" (lit. "love of/for eternity"),
it could be translated "love of the world". Not that the benediction envisages it thus. The phrase in the benediction occurs in
Jer. 31:3 (A.V.): "Yea, I have loved you with *an everlasting love*.
therefore with loving kindness have I drawn you". But while *'Olam*
in mishnaic Hebrew can mean world: in Aramaic and Syriac *'Alam*
likewise can mean world or eternity. I therefore suggest that
Jn. 3:16: "For God so loved the world, that He gave His only
begotten Son, that whosoever believes in Him should not perish,
but have everlasting life" is a commentary not only on the opening
words of this benediction but also on its whole underlying theology
which later is particularistic and has the Torah as the means of
grace. Jn. 3:16 is universalistic and has the Son as the means
of grace provided by the Father. In both John as much as in this
benediction preceding the *Shema'*, the one God is central. Thus
Christians as well as Jews can say "make our hearts one (quite a
Johannine note) that we may love and fear Thy name, and not be
ashamed. For in Thy holy name we trust; we rejoice and exult in

Thy salvation. For Thou art the God who worketh salvation and brought us nigh to Thy great name in truth." *'Emeth* (truth) has also the overtone of faith. We should note that the emphasis on "Thy great name" is quite understandable and most appropriate as this benediction precedes the *Shema'* which is the declaration of the name of God. We should also note that the emphasis on the unity of God's name is matched by the requirement of making "our hearts one", this latter being produced by having their eyes enlightened in/by the Law. Christians would, following Johannine teaching, say that they attained unity of heart by their love of Jesus. The Christian too can proclaim the unity of God in love (cf. Jn. 10:30 "The Father and I are one." And Jn. 15:9 "As the Father has loved me, so have I loved you."). The Christian could also say, "Blessed art Thou, O Lord, who hast chosen Thy people Israel in love", for the Church believed it was the true Israel.

It is of interest to us to ask what were the feasts that the writer of the Fourth Gospel includes. There are three passovers in the Fourth Gospel--the first and last of which Jesus attended at Jerusalem. There was also the Feast of Tabernacles which Jesus attended. The water-pouring is naturally a part of the Feast of Tabernacles in the Fourth Gospel. This had been a Pharisaic innovation and probably was not included as a part of the ritual of this feast before Maccabean times. Alexander Jannaeus had been strongly opposed to it. There is no doubt that it was an important part of the Feast of Tabernacles in the first century A.D. As far as Passover and Tabernacles are concerned, the Fourth Gospel might have been written while the Temple was still standing. As to the unnamed feast of Jn. 5:1 and the Feast of the Dedication, one is not so sure. What was the unnamed feast? Purim, Passover, Pentecost, New Year (Rosh ha-Shanah), The Day of Atonement and Tabernacles have all had their claims supported. If Jn. 5 and Jn. 6 be thought to be out of order, the unnamed feast can be the Passover mentioned in Jn. 6:4

as being "at hand". However the Manna, to which reference is
made, did not start till after the Passover. In any case, there
is no MS. evidence for altering the order of Jn. 5 and Jn. 6.
If the reading "*the* feast" found in one important MS. is stressed,
then the unknown feast could be Tabernacles or rather the
Sabbath therein. It is not likely to be Rosh ha-Shanah which
is not a pilgrimage feast nor the Day of Atonement which was a
fast not a feast. However there is a temporal indication at the
end of Jn. 6 with reference to the number of months to harvest.
If we take this time indication seriously and remember that the
harvest meant is a grain harvest, then the Feast of Tabernacles
of the seventh month is ruled out. While Pentecost has been
suggested because of a reference to Moses (Jn. 5:45-47) and his
writings (i.e. the Law), it is the note of deliverance that is
most important. If the years the paralytic had waited in the
porticoes refer indirectly to the years in the desert, this still
does not rule out Passover. Under Joshua the Israelite tribes
had crossed the Jordan and sacrificed the Passover at Gilgal.
But the Jews later were to remember another deliverance celebrated
at the Feast of Purim (in Adar, one month before the celebration
of Passover). If we take the Johannine textual order as it
stands, the unnamed feast coming as it does so close after the
statement that there were four months to harvest could be more
easily identified with Purim in Adar, than Passover in Nisan.
There are not three months between Passover and Pentecost, but
there are three months between Purim and Pentecost. One difficulty with Purim that is often mentioned is that it would be too
cold for a man to be out of doors. This takes no account of the
claim that he had been lying there for 38 years. More difficult
is the question as to whether Purim was celebrated in temple
times. There is, of course, the tractate Megillah in the Mishnah.
This tractate is concerned primarily with reading the *Megillath*

Esther and represents the usage of the 2nd century A.D. There is evidence that in the discussions on the Palestinian Hebrew Bible canon in the last quarter of the first century doubts were expressed about the fitness of Esther. R. Akiba who was active in the defense of the inclusion of the Song of Songs in the canon was also active on behalf of Esther. Akiba, along with others, tried to prove from separate sentences like "Hamman spoke in his ears" that the Book of Esther was dictated by the Holy Spirit. The Spirit, it was believed, rested upon a prophet. Every biblical book allowed into the canon by the Jews (cf. T. B. Baba Bathra 14b) was, therefore, held to have been written by a prophet. If the Book of Esther was dictated by the Holy Spirit and since it could be shown from it that Esther wrote it (Esther 9:29), then Esther was a prophetess, and her book was holy writ within the canon. The attitude to the Book of Esther was unsettled for a long time. Simeon (c. 150 A.D.) held Esther to be canonical, but Samuel of the 3rd century denied that it was. T. B. Meg. 14a gives a Baraitha which states that of all the canonical books none took from nor added anything to the Law, except the reading of *Megillath Esther*. Of all the claims made for Esther, the most far-reaching is that all the books of the Prophets and Writings shall pass away[47] except Esther which, along with the Law, will remain. The Mishnah leaves us in no doubt as to the keeping of Purim in the Synagogues with the reading of the *Megillath Esther*. We have no evidence as to the keeping of the Feast of Purim in the Temple. This does *not* rule out the identification of the unnamed feast with Purim. The Fourth Gospel does not say that it was kept in the Temple. It is unlikely that the Sadducees would have allowed this non-Pentateuchal feast to be kept in the Temple, for whatever their faults the Sadducees were *not* innovators. In Adar there was the collection of the half Shekel in the Temple for its upkeep. After the destruction

of the Temple, this was associated with alms at Purim. Josephus
Ant. XI, 295 claims "the Jews still keep the forementioned days,
and call them days of *Phruraioi* [Purim]". However by the time
he had written *The Antiquities of the Jews* in the last decade
of the 1st century A.D., Purim was kept. But his claim tells
us nothing of earlier in the century. Güdemann in *Das IV
(Johannes) Evangelium und der Rabbinismus* (Frankel's Monats-
schrift 37 Jahrgang, p. 298) suggested not only that the unnamed
feast was Purim but that Jesus' command in Aramaic to the man
to take up his bed and walk contains the word "bed" which is a
punning allusion to Purim. פורייא in Aramaic means either
"bed" or "Purim". In the *Megillath Esther* 9:24 Purim is explained
as "lots". The paralytic typifying the Jewish people had been
waiting for something to happen and somebody to carry him. It
is up to him and the people he typifies to do something about
their lot. Esther is supposed to have been written in the time[48]
of the Maccabees to hearten the people by relating a deliverance
in what was then quite recent times as compared with the Exodus
from Egypt. This story, which does not mention the name of God
once,[49] was put almost on the same level as the Law. Our evidence
for the popularity of Esther is from the period after the destruction of the Temple. In fact the Tannaim of the end of the
1st century had to argue that the *Megillath Esther* could legally
be written down, i.e. that it should be on the same level as
scripture. It is significant that R. Akiba had declared Esther
was inspired and therefore canonical. These discussions about
Esther do *not* belong to the first half of the 1st century A.D.
but to the later part of the second half. If the writer of the
Fourth Gospel means Purim by "a feast of the Jews", then he is
reflecting the developments and emphases in Judaism at the end
of the century.

The charges and countercharges between the Jews and Jesus, when they condemn him for healing on a Sabbath, leads on in Jn. 5:18 to "Therefore the Jews sought all the more to kill him, because he not only had broken the Sabbath but also said that God was his Father making himself equal with God." Thereupon Jesus makes an important statement on the relation of the Son to the Father and reminds them of the witness of John the Baptist. However for our immediate purpose in Jn. 5 verses 39-47 are most important especially verses 46 and 47 which appear to condemn their handling of the written law.

There can be no doubt that the Fourth Gospel speaks of Jesus in the Temple at the time of the Feast of the Dedication. This was Hanukkah. Unlike Purim, this feast of the Jews is *not* given a tractate in the Mishnah. In fact it is in 1 Macc. 4:36 that we learn of the altar fire being kindled anew on the altar and the lamps of the Menorah being relit and are told how this dedication of the cleansed altar by Judas Maccabee and his brothers was celebrated for eight days amid sacrifices and songs. It was also the purification of the sanctuary (2 Macc. 1:18). The Maccabees resolved (2 Macc. 10:8) that it be kept each year in memorial of this rededication. This was a non-Pentateuchal feast, modelled on the lighting of lamps and torches which formed part of the eight day Feast of Tabernacles in the Second Temple. Whether Hanukkah was celebrated in the Temple we really do not know. Josephus (Ant. XII, 325) is more definite about the apparently unbroken continuity of the observance of this feast from its institution than he is about Purim. He says: "And from that time to this we celebrate this festival, and call it lights." Again Josephus may be merely reflecting the usage at the end of the 1st century A.D. He does not say how it was kept. The Pharisees turned early against the Maccabees and were it not for the Books of the Maccabees, preserved by the Christian Church,

and Josephus himself is here largely dependent on these same
sources, we would know little about them and the historical
reason for the Feast of Hanukkah from the Talmud and Midrash.
In early rabbinic sources there is, on the one hand, a playing
down of the Maccabean achievement and, on the other, a merging
of Hanukkah with an earlier rededication of the altar, e.g. the
story is told by Nehemiah that the relighting of the altar fire[50]
was due to a miracle which occurred on 25th. Kislev, and this
was the reason for the selection of that date for rededication
of the altar by Judah Maccabeus. Hanukkah was indeed older than
the Maccabees and was a popular celebration of the winter solstice
With the extension of the Law to cover all life, some customs
which were of longstanding existence and which were on the fringe
of Judaism were brought in under the aegis of the Law. For after
all was not 25th. Kislev by tradition the date of the dedication
of the altar in the time of Moses? (cf. M. Ex. R. LII, M. Num. R.
XIII,4) The Maccabees might be blurred over, but Moses, the one
shepherd, came through.

What emerges from the fact that the Fourth Gospel includes
the Feast of the Dedication, i.e. Hanukkah as a feast of the
time of Jesus, is that the writer is projecting back from his
time the celebration of a feast which was not kept during the
Herodian period. If the unnamed feast of Jn. 5:1 is Purim, the
same would apply to it also. True, in neither case does it say
the feast was celebrated in the Temple, though in the case of
the Feast of the Dedication, Jesus was in the Temple. In the
case of the Passover (Jn. 2) and the Feast of Tabernacles (Jn. 6)
it is also stated that Jesus was in the Temple, but it does not
say that the celebration of either of these feasts was in the
Temple. One may think it reasonable to suppose that the writer
of the Fourth Gospel meant that the Feast of the Dedication was
likewise celebrated in the Temple and presumably also the unnamed
feast of the Jews (Purim) in Jn. 5:1.

Other than the Dedication, the feasts mentioned in this
Gospel are called by him feasts of the Jews. Who are the Jews?
Often this has been taken as a sign of a late date, of the writer
not knowing the divisions at the time of Jesus, or of his being
from outside Palestine. If, as has been suggested earlier,
Sadducee and Pharisee are nick-names given by one to the other,
it might be significant that the name Sadducee does not occur
in this gospel. But the term "the Jews" occurs very frequently.
The name "Jew" was a proud title and antedated the division of
the community into what the New Testament and Josephus call the
Sadducees and Pharisees. The Maccabean coins[51] know of the
community of the Jews. The Fourth Gospel knows of the Jews,
Pharisees, and the multitude. It looks as if the Jews in the
Fourth Gospel are "the establishment" centering round the Temple.
Most of the Jews would be Sadducees, but some of the priestly
establishment had Pharisaic leanings. Sadducee and Pharisee in
the time of Jesus probably had much common ground, otherwise how
could the Temple have operated. The last *Segan* or governor of
the Temple is mentioned in the Mishnah[52] as being one of the
rabbis. Other priests probably became Christians after the destruction of the temple. If the writer of the Fourth Gospel
were himself of high priestly stock, it might have been natural
for him to call the temple feasts, the feasts of the Jews. The
Mishnaic rabbis do not call themselves Jews, but Israel.[53] This
may be a protest to the claims of the early Christians to be the
true Israel. But the writer of the Fourth Gospel--speaking of
the regnant group of his time, the rabbis, whom most of the
former priests joined--may have transferred the proud name of
"the Jews" to them. He is writing for his own time, a time when
the Temple was no more. The rabbis were perpetuating the celebration of the feasts in the Synagogue and bringing non-Torah
feasts, such as Purim and Hanukkah, into the Synagogue. Both of

these latter told of deliverance and fostered national pride.
The deliverance wrought by Jesus, he had to show, was greater
than that by Esther, Judas Maccabeus or even Moses. Moses'
deliverance of the people from Egypt was celebrated at Passover
and his leading them in the wilderness at Tabernacles. But
Moses never brought them into the promised land. The deliverance
by Moses was long, long ago. The deliverances wrought by Esther
and by Judas Maccabeus were nearer in time. The leading rabbis
of his day had brought them into the cycle of feasts celebrated
in the Synagogue, and they were proving just what the people
wanted. The writer of the Fourth Gospel had to bring them into
the cycle of the feasts whether they had been officially celebrated in Jesus' time or not. R. Akiba and the rest of the
establishment had approved of them. Purim which was gaining on
Passover and Hannukkah, was the winter Tabernacles. Not to have
shown Jesus as towering over them, over feasts so important for
the Jewish establishment of the writer's own time, would, by its
very omission, have commented unfavourably on his Lord. The
tendency in Judaism was to see everything that was important
in the religious life of the people as always having been central
in religion. Jubilees knew of the antedelivuians keeping the
Mosaic feasts. The Fourth Gospel is quite right in calling even
the Pentateuchal feasts the "feasts of the Jews", because, as
kept in the 1st century, they were not exactly in the written
Torah. New elements were grafted on and hallowed by their
association with the old elements. The Targum on Gen. 35:14
tells of Jacob pouring wine and water on his safe return to the
rock pillar at Bethel--the site, according to the Targum, of
the future altar at Jerusalem--thereby justifying the late
practice of the water-pouring ritual.[54] If Purim and Hanukkah
had not been celebrated in the Temple, the rabbis, like Josephus,
implied that they ought to have been. The writer of the Fourth

Gospel agrees with them in this. If Jesus was to fulfill and transcend all the types provided by the Temple and its institutions, he had to fulfill all the types including those engrafted by the rabbis of the time following the destruction of the Temple. The writer of the Fourth Gospel interprets Jesus for his time, just as R. Akiba was interpreting the Torah for his day and age. What Akiba achieved by his biblical exegesis, the writer of the Fourth Gospel claimed he received from the Paraclete, the Christian version of the Spirit of prophecy. There is a distinction made in the Fourth Gospel between the Word of God and the Law written by Moses. The Word is alive in Christ, the Law *is* in Christians, and the self-declared disciples of Moses are dead. It is as if with all their efforts at reinterpretation, they can never get away from the dead letter of the law.[55] This reminds one of Jacob's vow on leaving Bethel (Gen. 20:20, 21): "If God will be with me, and will keep me...then the YAHWEH shall be my God." In Targum Onkelos this is rendered--"If the Word of *Yeya* will be my help...the Word of *Yeya* shall be my God." The Word of *Yeya*, for those who heard the Targum, was the Torah and it is as if it was Jacob's God.

CHAPTER 3

I. The Immanence of God: The *Shekinah* and *Memra*

The biblical expression "and Yahweh came down" had great significance for Jewish as well as Christian theology. In the first place, the rabbis found ten occurrences of this expression or ones like it and, on the basis of such, worked out a short sketch of the Lord's dealing with men. The Targums changed the verb *yarad* "to come down" to "was revealed", so the descents were not only divine contact with men but divine self-revelation to men. The complete schemes of the ten descents are found in Aboth de Rabbi Nathan and Pirke de Rabbi Eliezer.

According to Aboth de Rabbi Nathan,[56] the Divine Presence (*Shekinah*) made ten descents upon the earth. The first descent was in the Garden of Eden, as it is said: "And they heard the voice of the Lord God walking in the garden" (Gen. 3:8). Again in the generation of the Tower of Babel, it was said, "And the Lord came down to see the city and the tower" (Gen. 11:5).

Again in Sodom, it was said, "I will go down now and see whether they have done altogether according to the cry of it" (Gen. 18:21). Again in Egypt, it was said, "And I am come down to deliver them out of the land of the Egyptians" (Ex. 3:8). Again at the Red Sea it is said, "He bowed the heavens also and came down" (2 Sam. 22:10; Ps. 18:10). Again at Sinai, it is said, "And the Lord came down upon Mount Sinai" (Ex. 19:20).

Again in the Temple, it is said, "And the Lord said to me: This gate shall be shut, it shall not be opened...for the Lord the God of Israel hath entered by it" (Ezek. 44:2). Again in the pillar of cloud (or in the tent of meeting [another reading]), it is said, "And the Lord came down in the cloud" (Num. 11:25). And once more when He will come down in the future in the days of Gog and Magog, cf. Ezek. 38:2ff., it is said, "And His feet shall stand in that day upon the Mount of Olives" (Zech. 14:4).

The parallel passage to this is in Pirke de Rabbi Eliezer XIV. Ten descents[57] upon the earth were made by the Holy One, blessed be He, they were: (1) once in the Garden of Eden (Gen. 3:8); (2) once at [the time of] the generation of the dispersion (Gen. 11:7); (3) once at Sodom (Gen. 18:21); (4) once at the thorn-bush (Ex. 3:8); (5) once in Egypt (Gen. 46:4); (6) once at Sinai (Ex. 19:20); (7) once at the cleft of the rock (Ex. 34:5); (8) and (9) twice in the tent of assembly (Num. 11:25, Num. 12:5); and finally (10) once in the future. This, on the face of it, appears to be largely the same as the ten descents from Aboth de Rabbi Nathan. But there is one basic difference. The descents in Rabbi Nathan are those of the *Shekinah*, but in Pirke de Rabbi Eliezer, they are the descents of the Holy One, blessed be He. Only in connection with the third and the fourth descents, where they are respectively described in Pirke de Rabbi Eliezer XXV and XXXIV, is there any reference to the *Shekinah*.

In the case of the fourth descent in Pirke de Rabbi Eliezer XXXIX which was "when He descended in Egypt, as it is said, 'I will go down with thee into Egypt'" (Gen. 44:4), Jacob heard concerning Joseph that he was living, and thinking in his heart saying: "Can I forsake the land of my father, the land where the *Shekinah* of the Holy One blessed be He, is in its midst, and shall I go to an unclean land in their midst, for

there is no fear of heaven therein?" The Holy One, blessed be
he, said to him: "Jacob, do not fear: I will go down with you
into Egypt and I will also surely bring you up again." Note
that even here in this Midrash there is no mention of God sending
His *Shekinah*, nor is there in Targum Onkelos, on Gen. 46:4
"And He (the Lord) said, 'I am God, the God of your father, fear
not to go down to Egypt. I will go down with you into Egypt
and will surely bring you up.'" Targum Pseudo-Jonathan (*ibid.*):
"Do not fear to go down to Egypt on account of the servitude I
have decreed with Abraham...I am He who in My Word will go down
with you into Egypt: I and My Word shall bring you up from
thence, and cause your children to come up."

Incidentally in the ten descents of the *Shekinah* in Aboth
de Rabbi Nathan, in the first descent to the Garden of Eden
(Gen. 3:8) the Targums Onkelos and Jerushalmi have "Word of *Yeya*".
Targum Pseudo-Jonathan has "the voice of the Word of *Yeya*". In
the second descent in connection with the Tower of Babel (Gen.
11:5) while the Hebrew text had "And the Lord came down", this is
rendered in the Targums Onkelos and Pseudo-Jonathan: "And *Yeya*
was revealed". In Gen. 11:7 the Hebrew texts have "Go to, let
us go down" which is rendered by Onkelos, "Come We will be manifest". In Targum Pseudo-Jonathan this appears as "And *Yeya*
said to the seventy angels which stand before Him, 'Come, we
will descend'. And the Word of *Yeya* was revealed against the
city and with Him seventy angels..." In the third descent, that
to Sodom (Gen. 18:21), the "I will go down now" of the Hebrew
text is omitted by Targum Onkelos. The sentence there reads
"I will now see and will judge whether". In the Targums
Jerushalmi and Pseudo-Jonathan this is rendered: "Now will I
appear and see whether". In the fourth descent to Egypt (Ex.
3:8) in the Hebrew text, Yahweh says to Moses: "And I am come
down to deliver them." In Targum Onkelos this is rendered:

"And I have appeared to deliver them." Whereas in Targum Pseudo-Jonathan this is: "And I have revealed Myself to you this day that by My Word they might be delivered."

In the descent on Mt. Sinai (Ex. 19:20) the Hebrew text has: "And Yahweh came down upon" which in the Targum Onkelos is rendered: "And *Yeya* was revealed upon Mount Sinai." In Targum Pseudo-Jonathan this appears as "And *Yeya* revealed Himself." In Ex. 19:18 the Hebrew text had "Yahweh descended upon it [Mt. Sinai] in fire." In Targum Onkelos this was rendered "from before the revelation of *Yeya* upon it [Mt. Sinai] in fire". In Targum Pseudo-Jonathan this appears as "and He was revealed over it [Mt. Sinai] in flaming fire". Targum Jerushalmi, however, has "because the glory of the *Shekinah* of *Yeya* was revealed upon it in flame of fire".

With the descent of Yahweh in a cloud (Num. 11:25) in the Hebrew text, this is "And Yahweh came down in the cloud, spoke to him, took the spirit that was upon him, and put it upon the seventy elders." In Targum Onkelos this is: "And the Lord was revealed in the cloud, and spoke with him, and he made enlargement of the Spirit that was upon him, and imparted it to the seventy men, the elders; and it came to pass that when the Spirit of prophecy rested upon them they prophesied and did not cease." In Targum Pseudo-Jonathan this is: "And *Yeya* was revealed in the glorious cloud of the *Shekinah* and spoke with him. And he made enlargement of the [Spirit of] prophecy that was upon him, so that Moses lost nothing thereof, but he gave it to the seventy men, the elders. And it was when the Spirit of prophecy rested upon them that they prophesied and did not cease."

The Targum knows the term *Shekinah*, but it is not as widely used as it is in Midrash and Talmud. The basic text in the Targum Onkelos is Gen. 9:27. In the Hebrew text this read:

"And let him dwell in the tents of Shem." Targum Onkelos
rendered this: "And he shall make His *Shekinah* to dwell in
the tabernacles of Shem."

Ex. 17:16 (the Hebrew text) runs: "Yahweh has sworn;
Yahweh will make war with Amalek from generation to generation."
In Targum Onkelos this becomes "With an oath has this been
declared from before the Fearful One whose *Shekinah* is upon His
glorious throne, that war shall be waged with the house of
Amalek to destroy it from the generations of the world."

In Targum Pseudo-Jonathan we have: "Because the Word of
Yeya has sworn by the throne of His glory that He will fight
by His Word against those of the house of Amalek and destroy them
for three generations: from the generation of this world, from
the generation of the Messiah, and from the generation of the
world to come." Targum Jerushalmi has: "The oath has come
forth from beneath the throne of the Great One, the Lord of
all the world; the first king who will sit upon the throne of
the kingdom of the sons of Israel, Saul, the son of Kish, will
set the battle in array against the house of Amalek and will
slay them; and Mordecai and Esther will destroy those of them
that remain. *Yeya* has said by His Word that the memory of
Amalek shall perish to the age of ages."

There are two different ideas even in the Targums about
the *Shekinah*. The first is the immanence of Yahweh. Usually,
where the word "dwell" occurs in the Hebrew applied to Yahweh
or His Name (e.g. Dt. 14:23), "*Shekinah*" is substituted for the
divine name. The Hebrew text has: "in the place where He
will choose to cause His Name to dwell" which becomes in the
Targum Onkelos: "to make his *Shekinah* dwell there". Dt. 6:15
where the Hebrew has "for Yahweh your God in the midst of you",
becomes in Targums Onkelos and Pseudo-Jonathan: "whose *Shekinah*
dwelleth in the midst of you". In this sense, the *Shekinah* is

associated with Tabernacle and Temple. But there is another
use of *Shekinah* (Ex. 33:20): "You can not see My face" for
which Targum Onkelos has "see the face of My *Shekinah*". Or
Ex. 33:23 "You shall see My back, but My face shall not be
seen", while Targum Pseudo-Jonathan has: "And I will make
the host of angels who stand and minister before Me to pass
by, and those shalt see the handborder of the *tephillah* of
My glorious *Shekinah*; but the face of the glory of My *Shekinah*
thou canst not be able to see." Targum Jerushalmi has: "And
I will cause the hosts of angels who stand and minister before
Me to pass by and will make the oracle known for thou art not
able to behold the glory of My *Shekinah*."

The *Shekinah* and "the face" of God seem to be linked, cf.
also Num. 6:25: "Make his face to shine upon you" which in
Targum Onkelos becomes "*Yeya* will make His face to shine upon
you, when occupied in the Law, and reveal to you its secrets."
Num. 11:20 "Because that you have rejected Yahweh who is among
us", becomes in Targum Onkelos "because you dislike the Word of
Yeya whose *Shekinah* dwells among you".

But where does God's *Shekinah* actually dwell? Dt. 3:24
"for what God is there in heaven or earth" becomes in the Targum
Onkelos "for Thou art God whose *Shekinah* is in the heavens above
and Thou rulest in the earth".

Rabbinic Judaism made frequent use of the *Shekinah* concept
as equivalent to the Holy Spirit and related it to study of the
Law, cf. Targum Pseudo-Jonathan, Num. 6:25. This usage of it
is parallel to the Johannine view of the Paraclete which Christ
sends. It is as if rabbinic Judaism were saying that the Holy
Spirit comes through the Torah to a man. But the Targum seems
to know two almost diametrically opposed views of the *Shekinah*:
one, the *Shekinah* dwelling in Tabernacle and Temple; the other,
"the *Shekinah* of My glory cannot go up among you, nor My majesty

dwell in the habitation of their camp", Targum Jerushalmi on
Ex. 33:3; or again on Ex. 33:5 "were the glory of my *Shekinah*
to go up with you, in one little hour, I should destroy you".
This latter is of course fairly faithful to the Hebrew which is,
"If I go up in the midst of you for one moment I shall consume
you." One is left wondering whether there were two types of
Shekinah. Indeed the rabbinic doctrine of the *Zimzum* seems to
try to explain such a view. *Zimzum*[58] means the concentration
of the deity into one small spot.

Kabod glory is not identical with the Targumic and Midrashic
concept of the *Shekinah*; however *Doxa* in the N.T. (translated
"glory") may, especially in the Fourth Gospel, sometimes refer
to the *Shekinah*, although "light" more certainly does. The
pillar of the cloud in Ex. 33:9, 10 is very significant: "And
it came to pass, when Moses entered into the tent, the pillar
of cloud descended and stood at the door of the tent and spoke
with Moses." Targum Onkelos translates the Hebrew text literally.
Targum Pseudo-Jonathan renders it thus: "And it came to pass
when Moses had gone into the tabernacle, the column of the cloud
of glory descended and stood at the door of the Tabernacle; and
the *Memra* of *Yeya* spoke with Moses." Even in the Hebrew M.T.
it is the pillar of the cloud which speaks with Moses. The pillar
of cloud is as it were Yahweh descending. In Targum Pseudo-
Jonathan He (*Yeya*) communicates by word with Moses. Also in the
same Targum He is "the cloud of glory". This refers to what is
elsewhere called the *Shekinah*. One is reminded of Ex. 40:35
where, at the dedication of the Tabernacle, the "glory of the
Yahweh filled the Tabernacle (*Mishkan*) and the 'cloud' dwelt
(*Shakan*) over it". Whereas Targum Onkelos follows the M.T.
text closely, Targum Pseudo-Jonathan has "Then the cloud of
glory overspread the Tabernacle of ordinance, and the glory of
the *Shekinah* of *Yeya* filled the Tabernacle." Even so the normal

habitation of the *Shekinah* was in the heavens. Targum Onkelos (Dt. 33:26) has: "There is no [God] like the God [*El*] of Israel, whose *Shekinah* in the skies is your help, and whose power is in the heaven of heavens. The habitation of God [*Eloha*] is from eternity and the world was made by His Word." Targum Pseudo-Jonathan has: "There is no God like the God of Israel, whose *Shekinah* and chariot dwell in the heavens. He will be your helper. He sits on His glorious throne in His majesty, in the expanse of the heavens above. The habitation of *Eloha* is from eternity; by the arm of His power beneath, the world is upborne."

Targum Jerushalmi has: "There is none like the God of Israel whose glorious *Shekinah* dwells in the heavens and His magnificence in the high expanse. In His abode has the *Shekinah* dwelt before they were, and he brings the world under His power."

The Targumic use of *Shekinah* seems to work two ways (a) to bring God nearer and (b) to keep Him at a distance that men can bear. It is customary to call the *Shekinah* God's intermediary. To do so is to read back post-Christian ideas of God into the text. Dt. 33:26 is very significant. The Hebrew text has *El*; Targum Onkelos introduces the *Shekinah* here and not just Targum Pseudo-Jonathan. *Shekinah* is normally associated with Yahweh. One would venture to suggest that Yahweh is the *Shekinah* of *El* on high. Yahweh is the immanent aspect of the transcendent *El* (God). The *Shekinah* on earth is the *Shekinah* of *Yeya* (Yahweh). In Targum Pseudo-Jonathan (Dt. 31:8) "And the *Shekinah* of the *Memra* of *Yeya* will go before you" is the rendering: "And Yahweh He is the one who goes before you." So even the *Memra* of *Yeya* has a *Shekinah*. In Targum Isa. 6:4 Isaiah is not allowed to claim that he has seen the King, Yahweh of hosts, but the *glory* of the *Shekinah* of the King of ages, *Yeya* of hosts. The glory stands in relation to the *Shekinah*/Yahweh as that *Shekinah*

stood to *El* in Dt. 33:26. But the *Shekinah* is Yahweh, just as
the *Memra* is Yahweh and Yahweh and *El* are one. R. Levi (M.
Pesikta 2b ed. Buber) illustrates the *Shekinah* in the Tabernacle
by the simile of a cave situated near the shore is not lacking
any water, cf. also M. S. of S. R. 3:8. This simile is used by
Aphraates[59] to show how Christ can be in a man's heart and also
in heaven.

In T. B. Sanh 39a R. Gamaliel is asked by an infidel how
many *Shekinahs* there are in existence, seeing that, according
to the Jews' belief, wherever ten men are gathered together there
the *Shekinah* is. Gamaliel's reply is to the effect that the
Shekinah is God, who is everywhere. There is one and one only
sun, which lights up every nook and corner of the universe. How
much more so is it the case that the only God makes His presence
known and felt everywhere. The same argument is used by Aphraates[60]
to answer the similar objection as to how many Christs and Holy
Spirits there must be to be in every believer's heart.

In the late Midrash Yalkut on the "Song of Songs" the
question is asked:

> Why does he compare the Holy One to a bundle of
> myrrh (Song 1:13)? Because the whole world is
> not large enough to contain Him and yet He can
> compress the *Shekinah* into the narrow space be-
> tween the two staves of the ark. You will find
> that God loves Israel more than the ministering
> angels for the latter can only approach God at a
> distance of 15 cubits, as it is said (Isa. 6):
> 'Seraphim stood above him', but the Israelites
> stood in the Tabernacle and not one among them
> was injured.

M. Gen. R. 4:5 deals also with "the world being too small to
hold God, while the space between the staves of the Ark was
large enough". R. Meir, M. Gen. R. 4 (mid-second century A.D.)
was asked by a Samaritan to explain Jer. 23:25: "Behold I fill

heaven and earth". How would God speak to Moses from between
the two divisions of the ark? R. Meir demonstrates this by
bringing large and small mirrors--that the figure of man changes
according to the size of the looking-glass. If that is possible
in the case of a human being, how much more likely is this with
God. Rabbi Meir's reply is doubtless indebted to the Cabbalistic
doctrine of *Zimzum* regarding God's concentrating His *Shekinah*
in a certain place.

Marmorstein (*The Old Rabbinic Doctrine of God*, I, *The Names
and Attributes of God*, Oxford, 1927, p. 103) regards the *Shekinah*
as the latest of God's names used in the last period before the
redaction of the Mishnah. Landau thought that R. Akiba was
probably the first to apply it. Abelson (*ibid*. p. 104) writes:
"It may be that the people popularized this name after the destruction of the Temple in order to indicate that in spite of
the loss of the Temple and land, the divine presence was still
in Israel. Its frequent occurrence in the Targumim is most
noticeable. It is by no means impossible that the *Shekinah*
stands in the Aramaic versions for *Makom*, both of which point
to the dwelling place of God." This last statement is to the
point. *Ha-Makom* is a Mishnaic name for God, and we have seen
above (p. 49) that the *Shekinah* is indeed introduced in the
Targum in Deuteronomy where reference is made to the place where
God shall chose to put His name. This may be the starting
point, but when the Temple was gone, the Law and the Land took
its place. In the Targum to Isaiah,[61] Palestine is called the
land of the house of my *Shekinah*. When two study the Torah
(M. Ab. 3:3) the *Shekinah* is present; this is especially so if
the Law is studied at night (T. B. Tam. 32b). The doctrine of
the *Shekinah* stresses the immanence of God and is largely
parallel to the Christian doctrine of the Holy Spirit but it is
centered on the Law.

T. B. Sot. 3b states that before the Israelites sinned
the *Shekinah* rested on every one, but when they did evil it
departed. Targum Onkelos (Dt. 32:20) renders "I will hide my
face from them" by "I will take away My *Shekinah* from among
them". This is parallel to the Samaritan concept of *Fanutha*,
i.e. the withdrawal of *Rahutha* or Divine Favour. There is the
rabbinic phrase *Mekabbel Pene Shekinah* to see the face of the
Shekinah. R. Meir maintained that those who observe the law of
wearing the fringes (*Zizith*) on the corners of their garments
exactly were to be regarded as if they had seen the face of the
Shekinah (P. T. Ber. 1. 4, cf. R. Simon b. Yohai T. B. Men. 43b).
Faithful observance of religious duties as laid down in the Law
enables a man to reach complete nearness to God (cf. Marmorstein
ibid. p. 105). To visit a scholar full of the Torah, was as if
one approached God (M. Tanhuma, ed. Buber, ii, 115).

However for God to be visible, Israel must be One (M.
Tanhuma, ed. Buber, v. p. 12). Yet the belief that wherever
Israel (the particular Jewish community) was there the *Shekinah*
was, made life tolerable for the Jew in the dispersion. The
general belief was that the dying saw the light of the *Shekinah*,
the beatific vision, which no mortal could see and live.

II. The *Shemoneh Esreh*--the *Kedushah* and the Sanctus

The first three benedictions of the *Shemoneh Esreh*, or
Amidah (the prayer of 1st century Judaism) are ascriptions of
praise. The fourth to the sixteenth are petitions. The last
three (i.e. the seventeenth to the nineteenth) are the offering
of thanksgiving. We have here a fixed framework of praise and
thanksgiving enclosing variable petitions.

The names used for God in the *Shemoneh Esreh* are *YHWH*, *El-ohim*, *ha-El* and *El-Elyon*, *Adonai*, *Ba'al* and *Melek* (King).

The first benediction[62] blesses *YHWH* (the Lord) as the shield of Abraham. *El Elyon* (God Most High), possessor *or* creator of all, whom *Meleki-zedek* (Gen. 14:18) (His priest at Salem) asked to bless Abraham, is identified with *YHWH* whom Moses (Ex. 6:1ff.) revealed to the people of Israel as the *El* (God) of Abraham, Isaac and Jacob, the *El* (God) who is great, mighty and terrible (Dt. 10:17). He brings a redeemer (*Go'el*) for their children's children for His name's sake in love. He is King, Helper, Saviour, and Shield.

The second benediction blesses *YHWH* (the Lord) as the quickener of the dead. In loving-kindness He is sustainer of the living; with great mercy He is quickener of the dead, and He is causer of salvation to spring forth. The emphasis is on the Lord's faithful providence in life and death (cf. Dt. 12:2). Thou dost keep faith with them that sleep in the dust.

The third benediction is "Thou are Holy, and Holy is Thy name and holy ones (i.e. the angels) praise Thee every day: Blessed art Thou, *YHWH*, the Holy God (*El*)." After this third benediction comes the *Kedushah* (Sanctification). Although this is not an integral part of the original *Shemoneh Esreh*, it seems to have been the pattern for the Sanctus in the Christian communion office, e.g. in the Anglican Prayer Book (1662) the liturgical framework surrounding the proper preface is the thanksgiving before the preface, then praise and the Sanctus. With the *Shemoneh Esreh* it is praise, Sanctus, and the special petitionary prayers varying with the Sabbath and feast, and then thanksgiving.

After the *Kedushah* or *Kedushath ha-Shem*, the Sanctification or Sanctification of the name is repeated by the cantor. He proceeds to say: "We will sanctify Thy name in the world even as they sanctify it in the heavens of the height, as it is

written by the hand of Thy prophet." And this one called to
this and said:

The congregation responds: "Holy, Holy, Holy, *YHWH* of
hosts, the whole earth is full of His glory" (Isa. 6:3).

The cantor says: "Those over against them say,
Blessed..."

The congregation continues: "Blessed is the glory of
YHWH from His place" (Ezek. 3:12).

The cantor says: "And in Thy holy Words it is written,
saying:"

The congregation: (Ps. 146:10) "*YHWH* shall reign forever, Thy God (*Elohim*), O Zion, all generations, Praise ye *Yah*."

The cantor ends with: "To all generations we will declare
Thy greatness, and to all eternity we will proclaim Thy holiness,
and Thy praise, O our God (*Elohim*) shall not depart from our
mouth for ever, for Thou art a God (*El*) [and] King great and
holy. Blessed art Thou O *YHWH* the holy God (*El*)."

There are three *Kedushahs* in Jewish divine morning service.
There is (1) that which is recited in the *Yozer* (or the benediction before the *Shema'*), and (2) that which is said in the
Shemoneh Esreh (in public prayers), and (3) that which is recited in the *Uba Le Zion* prayer as a doxology towards the end
of the service. But the basic element of all *Kedushoth* is the
verses from Isa. 6:3 and Ezek. 3:12.

The benedictions (four to sixteen) have been concisely
summarized by Y. Vainstein[63] following Yehuda Halevi's statement in the *Kuzari*: "This group begins by asking for understanding of the Torah, leads to prayers for the forgiveness of
sin, redemption, and health; and continues by invoking the
Almighty's aid for Israel's regathering, for the elimination of
the slanderers and the prosperity of the righteous. It is con-
cluded with the prayers for the rebuilding of Jerusalem and the

restoration of the house of David, and a final petition for the acceptance of our prayers."

The fourth benediction is worth quoting in full: "Thou dost graciously grant knowledge to men, and dost teach discernment to men; graciously grant from Thee, knowledge and understanding and discernment. Blessed art Thou, O *YHWH*, the gracious giver of knowledge." One should bear this benediction with its prayer for knowledge in mind. *Gnosis* in the Fourth Gospel could and should be seen in the light of this prayer. This benediction clearly uses *De'ah* where *hakmah* might have been used. The beginning of wisdom is fear of the Lord or religion. Wisdom is not so different from knowledge of the Torah. Actually the form of this benediction at the conclusion of the Sabbath or a festival makes plain what is the knowledge requested: Thou hast favoured us with a knowledge of Thy Law, and hast taught us to perform the statues of Thy will, etc. The statutes of the Law are the revealed will of God, a revelation of Himself. Knowledge of God in rabbinic Judaism is not only derived from but is knowledge of the Torah and *vice versa*.

The fifth benediction is: "Cause us to return, O our Father, to Thy Law: And draw us near, O our King, to Thy service; and bring us back in perfect repentance to Thy presence. Blessed art Thou, O *YHWH*, who delightest in repentance." It shows the application of the knowledge asked for in the fourth benediction as a return to the Law and the appropriate worship of God based on the Law. The *'Abodah* service was primarily a Temple service. On the basis of such a service, the worshipper would be brought into God's presence. Granted that after the Temple fell, *'Abodah* was used in the synagogue service, but this prayer (even in the revised form drawn up by Rabban Gamaliel II towards the end of the first century after the Temple had fallen) does look forward to the restoration of the temple service, cf. the seventh benediction called the *'Abodah*.

The seventh benediction is:

> Favourably accept (*rezeh*), O *YHWH* our God
> (*Elohim*), Thy people Israel and their prayer;
> and restore the service (*'abodah*) to the oracle
> of Thy house; and accept with favour the fire
> offerings of Israel and their prayer in love
> and may the service (*'abodah*) of Thy people
> Israel, forever find favour [with Thee] (or
> ever be according to [Thy] will). And may our
> eyes behold Thy return to Zion in mercy.
> Blessed art Thou, O *YHWH* who causest His
> *Shekinah* to return to Zion.

This benediction was spoken in the prayer-service in the "Chamber of Hewn Stones" in the Temple after the benediction "True and Sure" which follows the recital of the *Shema'*. In its original form it goes back to Temple times. It then asked for acceptance in love and favour of the prayer-service in the "Chamber of Hewn Stones", and likewise of the ensuing daily offering of the lamb offered for the sins of Israel.

The seventeenth benediction, like benedictions eighteen and nineteen, form the expression of thanks which are a part of the *Amidah* prayer every day of the year. Although here too additions are made at the appropriate festival. The eighteenth benediction is a wonderful expression of thanks to God for what He has done, now does, and what He is by nature.

> We give thanks to Thee for Thou art He *YHWH*
> our God (*Elohim*), and the God of our Fathers
> for ever and ever; rock of our lives, shield
> of our salvation. Thou art He from generation
> to generation (i.e. What He was to Abraham, He
> is to his descendants now). We will give thanks
> to Thee and recount Thy praises for our lives
> which are committed into Thy hand, and for our
> souls (*nishamoth*) which are in Thy charge, and
> for Thy miracles which are with us all the day,
> and for Thy wonders and Thy benefits which are

at all time, evening, morning and noon. The
good One art Thou for Thy mercies have not
failed (cf. Eccles. 3:22), and the merciful
One for Thy mercies have not come to an end.
From of old we have hoped in Thee. And for
them all, Thy name is to be blessed and
exalted O, our King, continually for ever and
ever. And all that lives shall thank Thee,
and praise Thy name in truth; O God (*El*) of
our salvation and our help. Blessed art Thou,
YHWH. The good is Thy name, and to Thee it is
fitting to give thanks. Because of what He
has done from Abraham's time to the present,
for His ever merciful providence, *YHWH* is to
be blessed and His name is the good One.

On Hanukkah there is inserted in this seventeenth benediction
a thanksgiving for "the great deliverance wrought by God in His
abundant mercy in the days of Mattathias son of Johanan the high
priest (the Hasmonean and his sons), (cf. *Singer Daily Prayer
Book*, p. 52). Likewise on Purim a briefer insertion is made in
this benediction (cf. *Singer*, *ibid*.) of how God "in the days of
Mordecai and Esther in His abundant mercy brought Haman's counsel
to not". It is God who acted on behalf of Israel, not the
Hasmoneans, nor Mordecai and Esther.

The nineteenth benediction called "the Blessing of the
Priests" (as spoken at the morning and additional services, also
on fast days, and at the afternoon service) is:

Grant goodly peace and blessing, grace and loving-
kindness and mercy upon us and upon all Israel,
Thy people. Bless us, O our Father all of us together, with the light of Thy countenance. Thou
has given to us, O *YHWH* our God, the Law of Life,
loving-kindness and righteousness, blessing, mercy,
life and peace; and it is good in Thine eyes to
bless Thy people, Israel, at all times, and in
every hour with Thy peace. Blessed art Thou, *YHWH*
who blesses His people Israel with peace.

Possibly it is the original nucleus of this blessing (and not
the actual *Birḵath Kohanim* of Num. 6:24, 26) that was said in
the Temple after the seventeenth blessing at the morning prayer
service for the priests in the Chamber of Hewn Stones.[64]   As
it stands, it is an interesting midrashic expansion of the
priestly blessing. This is the *third* time in the *Shemoneh
Esreh* that God is called "Our Father". We note that the fact
that they have been given the Law of Life is proof of the fact
that the Lord did lift up His countenance and shone on them.
It would be inconceivable for the composer of this benediction
to think of loving kindness and righteousness, blessing and
mercy, life and peace, as over against or existing separately
from the Law of Life. Without the Law of Life (known to others
as the Law of Moses), Israel could not possess these blessings.
But the special core of this benediction as in all the others
is in the last line: "Blessed art Thou, O *YHWH* who blesses
His people Israel with peace."

However, the petititons in benedictions four to sixteen had
first to be granted to obtain the crowning blessing of peace in
its fullest sense. We have looked at the fourth and fifth
benedictions above. The sixth benediction is a request to God
our Father and our King for the forgiveness of sin and transgression, because God pities and pardons. *YHWH* is blessed as
gracious and abundantly forgiving in the sure conviction that
God is true to His nature.

Two abstracts of benedictions four to sixteen exist, one
in T. B. Ber. 29a was made when the *Shemoneh Esreh* was quite
similar in form and order to what is known now as the *Shemoneh
Esreh*.

> Give us understanding, O *YHWH*, our God (bene-
> diction 4), to know Thy ways, and circumcise
> our hearts to fear Thee (benediction 5) and

do Thou pardon us (benediction 6) that we may
be redeemed (benediction 7). And remove from
us bodily pain (benediction 8) and fatten us
with the fertility of Thy land (benediction 9)
and our dispersed ones from the four corners
of the earth do Thou gather together (benediction 10) and they that go astray against the
knowledge of Thee shall be judged (benediction
11) and upon the evil-doers do Thou lift up
Thy hand (benediction 12) but may the righteous
(benediction 13) rejoice in the building of
Thy city (benediction 14) and in the refound-
ing of the Temple (benediction 17) and in the
sprouting up of a horn, unto David Thy servant,
and in the sprouting up of a horn for Jesse's
son, Thy messiah (benediction 15) before we
call Thou wilt answer. Blessed be Thou, O
eternal, who hearest prayer (benediction 16).

In the Palestinian Talmud (P. T. Ber. IV) there is an
abstract of the petitions, i.e. benedictions four to sixteen:

Give us understanding, O *YHWH*, our God
(benediction 4); and be pleased with our
repentance (benediction 5); pardon us, O
our Redeemer (benedictions 6 and 7) and
heal our sick (benediction 8); bless our
years with dews of blessing (benediction 9)
for the dispersed Thou wilt gather (benediction 10); they who err against Thee will be
judged (benediction 11); but upon the evil-
doers Thou wilt lay Thy hand (benediction
12); and they, (the *Zaddukim* are not specified) who trust in Thee will rejoice (benediction 13) in the rebuilding of Thy city (benediction 14) and in the restoration of Thy
sanctuary (benediction 14).

But the fifteenth benediction, the Davidic messianic one, is
omitted. "Before we call, Thou wilt answer (benediction 16).
Blessed be Thou, O *YHWH*, who answereth prayer."

A comparison of the former with the "sealing" of the blessing,[65] i.e. the last and most important phrase of the individual

benedictions, will show significant differences in order and
content.

1. Blessed art Thou, O *YHWH*,
    the shield of Abraham
2. Blessed art Thou, O *YHWH*,
    the reviver of the dead
3. Blessed art Thou, O *YHWH*,
    the Holy God (*El*)
4. Blessed art Thou, O *YHWH*,
    the gracious granter of
    knowledge
5. Blessed art Thou, O *YHWH*,
    who delightest in repentance
6. Blessed art Thou, O *YHWH*,
    the gracious One,
    who multiplieth forgiveness
7. Blessed art Thou, O *YHWH*,
    the Redeemer of Israel
8. Blessed art Thou, O *YHWH*,
    the healer of the sick
    of His people Israel
9. Blessed art Thou, O *YHWH*,
    who blessest the years
10. Blessed art Thou, O *YHWH*,
    the gatherer of the dispersed
    of His people Israel
11. Blessed art Thou, O *YHWH*,
    King, lover of righteousness
    and justice
12. Blessed art Thou, O *YHWH*,
    the breaker of enemies,
    and the humiliator of the
    arrogant
13. Blessed art Thou, O *YHWH*,
    the stay and trust of the
    righteous
14. Blessed art Thou, O *YHWH*,
    the builder of Jerusalem
15. Blessed art Thou, O *YHWH*,
    who causest the horn
    of salvation to sprout
16. Blessed art Thou, O *YHWH*,
    the hearer of prayer

17. Blessed art Thou, O *YHWH*,
            the restorer of His *Shekinah*
            to Zion
18. Blessed art Thou, O *YHWH*,
            The good is Thy Name,
            and to Thee it is seemly
            to give thanks.

Here we have a theology of Yahweh, and a future plan of
action for Him. The theology of Yahweh is not just found in
benedictions 1-3 and 17-19. It also occurs in the petitions
where *YHWH* is reminded of His nature that He may hasten to perform the requests.

A fragment of a Midrash on the *Shemoneh Esreh* now serves
as connecting links between different sections of the second
part of Pirke de R. Eliezer. This fragmentary Midrash on the
Amidah prayer is of interest in that it purports to give a
biblical reference and setting to the benedictions mentioned in
it. The first benediction (cf. Pirke de R. Eliezer XXVII)
refers to Abraham after his delivery from the kings (Gen. 14:18)
and his meeting with Melchizedek. Melchizedek here, as in the
Targum Jerushalmi and Pseudo-Jonathan in this place, is identified with Shem the son of Noah. Abraham ascribes the victory
to God and quotes (Ps. 3:3): "But Thou, O *YHWH*, art a shield
about me" in the world; "my glory and the lifter up of my head"
in the world to come. The angels answered and said: "Blessed
art Thou, O *YHWH*, the shield of Abraham." The angels' words
are the last sentence of the first benediction of the *Shemoneh
Esreh*.

The second benediction (cf. Pirke de R. Eliezer XXXI)
refers to Isaac bound and about to be sacrificed (Gen. 22:9).
When Jacob pours oil on the stone, the Holy One made the stone
the keystone of the earth, and the Jerusalem Temple was to stand
on it. The stone represents Israel, and Isa. 5:16 "And the Holy
God (*El*) is sanctified in righteousness", is cited. The angels

replied: "Blessed art Thou, O *YHWH*, the Holy God." It is the words of the angels which form the last sentence of the third benediction. The Midrash teaches that this third benediction of sanctification should remind us of Jacob.

The fourth benediction (cf. Pirke de R. Eliezer XL) refers to Moses at the burning bush and God making known His great and holy name: "I am that I am" (cf. Ex. 3:14). The angels on seeing that the Holy One had given Moses the secret of the ineffable name said: "Blessed art Thou, O *YHWH*, who graciously bestoweth knowledge." This is the last sentence of the fourth benediction of the *Shemoneh Esreh*.

The fifth benediction (cf. Pirke de R. Eliezer XLIII) refers to Elijah. Israel will not sincerely repent until Elijah comes. Mal. 4:5, 6 are cited, and then "Blessed art thou, O *YHWH*, who delightest in repentance" is spoken. This is the last sentence of the fifth benediction of the *Shemoneh Esreh*.

The thirteenth benediction (cf. Pirke de R. Eliezer X) refers to the sailors in the ship with Jonah. When they saw all the signs, miracles and great wonders the Holy One did to Jonah, they returned to Joppa, went to Jerusalem, and circumcised themselves. This is a comment on Jon. 1:16. Pirke de R. Eliezer, *ibid.*, says: "But this sacrifice refers to the blood of the covenant of circumcision, which is like the blood of a sacrifice." Our Midrash says, "And concerning them: 'Upon the proselytes, the proselytes of righteousness'." This is from the thirteenth benediction.

It is possible that the eighth benediction, "Blessed art Thou, O *YHWH*, who healest the sick of Thy people Israel", was handled in the Midrash, as these words are cited in the Venice edition 1544 in the contents of the chapters. The sixth benediction, "Blessed art Thou, O Lord, Who dost abundantly forgive",

could be illustrated by Pirke de R. Eliezer XLV but the words
are not cited. Here Moses is summoned the second time up the
mount on the new moon of Ellul and after forty days descends
on the Day of Atonement. The Midrash here gives a *panegyric*
on the atoning power of the Day of Atonement. But Pirke de R.
Eliezer XLVI is perhaps more likely, where Moses says to the
Holy One, "Pardon, I beseech Thee the iniquities of this people
in the affair of the calf." The reply is "Moses! Behold, let
it be according to thy words", as it is said, "And the Lord
said, I have pardoned according to thy word."

The seventh benediction: "Look upon our affliction and
plead our cause, and hasten to redeem us. For Thou art God
[King] Mighty Redeemer. Blessed art Thou, O Lord, the Redeemer
of Israel", although not quoted might be reflected in Pirke de
R. Eliezer, ch. Ll, which deals with new heavens and a new earth.
It begins: "Rabban Gamaliel said: 'Just as the new moons are
renewed and sanctified in this world, so will Israel be sanctified and renewed in the future world just like the new moons,
as it is said: 'Speak to all the congregation of the children
of Israel, and say unto them 'You shall be holy, for I the Lord
your God am holy'" (Lev. 19:2).

Ratcliff[66] sees the Sanctus as an intrusion in the East-
Syrian and also in the Roman rite. This is very interesting
for the *Kedushah*, following the third benediction of the *Shemoneh
Esreh* is also an intrusion; so also is the *Kedushah* in the *Yozer
Or* benediction before the *Shema'*. Ratcliff (*ibid.*) sees the
"Epilesis" as an interpolation too, and the basic form of the
Anaphora to have been:

(a) An address of praise to the name of the
Creator and Redeemer
(b) A thanksgiving for what he has done for men
(c) A solemn following of Christ's example and a

special commemoration of his redemptive death
and resurrection, for which again praise and
thanks are offered to the divine name.

Perhaps the most significant thing in the Anaphora of
Addai and Mari is that they say "amen". The saying of "amen"
in the *Shemoneh Esreh* also called the *ha-Tefillah* (the Prayer)
was the congregation's responsibility. Undoubtedly this Prayer
was *par excellence* the source of all prayer in the Church as in
the Synagogue. It was the common inheritance of the Synagogue
and Church until, in the last decade of the 1st century A.D.,
the *Bir̲kath ha-Minim* was introduced and Jews and Christians
could no longer pray together. The Lord's prayer is in the
nature of an abstract[67] from the *Telfillah*. In this Jesus
followed the practice of the other rabbis in producing an abstract for his disciples, as the rabbis did for theirs. The
hallowing of God's name is in the Lord's prayer and presumably
the *Kedushah* was part of the *Tefillah* or *Amidah* in the first
century. Note also that as the third benediction it is a part
of the fixed content of the *Tefillah*.

Oesterley and Box[68] maintained that the first three and
last three benedictions of the *Shemoneh Esreh* (i.e. the *Tefillah*
in reversed order) provided the pattern for the *Sursum Corda*
to the *Sanctus* in the order of Holy Communion. This is impres-
sive but they based it only on the evidence of the Anglican
Book of Common Prayer. MacLean,[69] however, shows how the part
of the Eucharist from the *Sursum Corda* to the consecration is
attested and outlined in the early church orders. Their evidence precedes that of the liturgies by several hundred years.
So we are thrown back on the *Tefillah* (the Prayer) especially
the first three and the last three benedictions. In the
Tefillah the last three are thanksgivings and the first three
are praises ending in the hallowing of God's name. Actually
Isa. 6:3 is *not* quoted in it, but it is quoted in the *Kedushah*

which is introduced after the third benediction. There may not
have been a Sanctus in the original core of the Eucharist--if
that was based on the *Tefillah*. However it surely is significant that despite Christian and Jewish prayer going their
separate ways, there is a Sanctus in both the present *Tefillah*
and the Christian Eucharist.

The ninth benediction of the *Tefillah*, the blessing of
the years, seems to have left its mark not only on the liturgy
of Addai and Mari[70] but also in a fifth century Syriac fragment
of a Persian anaphora.[71]

While not denying the undoubted influence of the *Tefillah*
on the Eucharist, one would venture to suggest that the *Tefillah*
has to be seen in its context. The *Shema'* is central. There is
early evidence for the benedictions before and after the *Shema'*,
especially for the *'Emeth we Yazib* (True and Sure) which is also
known as the *G^eullah* redemption prayer. It is immediately after
the latter that the *Tefillah*, i.e. the *Shemoneh Esreh* is said.
This order goes back beyond the Synagogue to the Temple prayer
service during the Tamid offering (cf. M. Tam. 5:1). As pointed
out above it is possible that the phraseology of the *Yozer Or*
(the creator of light), and the *Ahabah Rabbah* ([with] great love)
or *Anabath 'Olam* ([with] everlasting love) which are the benedictions before the *Shema'*, may have influenced the vocabulary of
the Fourth Gospel. But this would not be a direct influence.
Perhaps the Fourth Gospel mirrors the liturgical language of
the Church, which was borrowed from the prayers of Temple and
Synagogue. In fact, on the one hand, John 1:1-18 reminds one
of the *Yozer Or*[72] ("The Creator of Light" prayer), and, on the
other, also the first part of an anaphora without the intrusion
of the Sanctus. While we cannot perhaps argue back from a fifth
century anaphora, which may itself have been influenced by John 1,
it is still possible that the writer of the Fourth Gospel, who was

concerned to teach the meaning of the sacraments of baptism and
of the body and blood, did quote part of his own anaphoral prayer
as an introduction to his gospel.

III. The Name of God: *YHWH* Savior God, the *Memra* and *Kaddish*

A name in Hebrew thought is integrally connected with the
person who bears it. He not only answers to the name, but he
is like it. To know the name is to know its bearer's character.
For the worshipper to call on his god by his name meant that he
felt certain the god would answer and that he would answer
according to his true nature.

By listing the epithets which are applied to God in the
Old Testament, one could form a conspectus of Old Testament
theologies in brief. The name *par excellence* of God in the
Old Testament is Yahweh. The revelation of the name Yahweh
is associated with Moses at the burning bush. In Ex. 3:6 God
says to Moses: "I am the God of your fathers, the God of
Abraham, the God of Isaac and the God of Jacob." Yahweh (v. 8)
says: "I have come down to deliver them out of the hand of the
Egyptians, and to bring them up out of that land to a good and
broad land...." In Ex. 3:12 Yahweh assures Moses, "But I will
be with you; and this shall be the sign for you: when you have
brought forth the people out of Egypt, you shall serve God upon
this mountain." On Moses' demurring (v. 13) "If I come to the
people of Israel and say to them 'The God of your fathers has
sent me to you' and they ask me 'What is his name?' what shall
I say to them?" (v. 14), God said to Moses, "I AM WHO I AM."
And he said, "Say this to the people of Israel, 'I Am has sent

me to you.'" In the following verse it is stated that God also said to Moses, "Say this to the people of Israel, 'Yahweh the God of your fathers, the God of Abraham, the God of Isaac and the God of Jacob, has sent me to you': this is my name forever and in this way I am to be remembered throughout all generations." In Ex. 6:2ff. a distinction is introduced: while He was the God (*El*) who appeared to Abraham, Isaac, and Jacob and covenanted with them, He did not make His name Yahweh known to them. Ex. 6:3:

> I appeared to Abraham, to Isaac and to Jacob, as God Almighty (*El Shaddai*) but by the name Yahweh I did not make myself known to them (v. 4). I also established my covenant with them, to give them the land of Canaan, the land in which they dwelt as sojourners (v. 5). Moreover I have heard the groanings of the people of Israel whom the Egyptians hold in bondage and I have remembered My covenant (v. 6). Say therefore to the people of Israel, 'I am Yahweh, and I will bring you out from under the burdens of the Egyptians, and I will deliver you from their bondage, and I will redeem you with an outstretched arm, and with great acts of judgment (v. 7) and I will take you for My people, and *I will be* your God; and you shall know that I am the Lord your God, who has brought you out from under the burdens of the Egyptians (v. 8), and I will bring you into the land which I swore to give to Abraham, to Isaac and to Jacob; and I will give it to you for a possession. I am Yahweh.'

The name Yahweh is here firmly associated with the revelation of God not only as the fulfiller of the covenant with the fore-fathers, but as the deliverer and redeemer of Israel. Further it is indeed the case that in Gen. 17:1 God revealed Himself to Abram as *El Shaddai*:

When Abram was ninety nine years old Yahweh
appeared to Abram, and said to him, 'I am *El
Shaddai*; walk before Me, and be blameless (v.
2). And I will make My covenant between Me
and you and will multiply you exceedingly.'

In v. 8 the promise is made of the land of Canaan to his
descendants: "And *I will be* their God." However in Gen.
15:1 the word (*debar*) of Yahweh had appeared to Abram in a
vision, and in v. 2 Abram had said, "Lord Yahweh what wilt
Thou give me, for I continue childless...?" Then the promise
of descendants as numerous as the stars in heaven was made
(cf. v. 5). In Gen. 15:7 God declares Himself as "I am Yahweh
who brought you from Ur of the Chaldeans, to give you this land
to possess." Thereafter follows the covenant between the
pieces, the prediction of slavery in Egypt, and their possession
of the land of the Amorites.

Is it really one thing to recognize different sources in
the Pentateuch and another to hold the unity of the Torah? The
first century Jewish Christians doubtlessly accepted the Mosaic
authorship of the Torah, or as Jn. 1:17 puts it: "For the Law
was given through Moses." Just what the connotation of the Law
exactly was is another matter. There was a tendency in the
Targum and in the Book of Jubilees to show parts of the legis-
lation (e.g. on festivals) which was given to Moses as already
having been in operation at the time of the patriarchs, if not
indeed of the antediluvians. On the other hand, it is not likely
that they were so concerned as we are with apparent inconsistencies.
The Law (Torah) was Mosaic and the Torah admitted that God's name
(Yahweh) was known to the antediluvians of the generation of Enosh
and later that God had said to Abram (Gen. 15:7) "I am (*'Ani*)
Yahweh." If one wished to stress that Abram knew the name of
God as Yahweh long before Moses' day, one quoted the Torah for
this. At least one was on as good ground as another who stressed

that the name was a new revelation given to Moses at the burning bush. True, God had appeared as *El Shaddai* to Abram, but He had also appeared as Yahweh. In any case, the Targum Jerushalmi to Gen. 49 makes the sons of Jacob/Israel recite the *Shema'* (cf. Dt. 6:4) to their father Jacob.

The first of the Ten Commandments begins with the statement "I am Yahweh your God, who brought you out of the land of Egypt, out of the house of bondage." The basic part of the *Shema'* is Dt. 6:4, "Hear, O Israel: The Yahweh our God is one Yahweh; and you shall love the Yahweh your God with all your heart, and with all your soul, and with all your might." With the occurrence of the name Yahweh in these basic statements of Judaism, there could be no doubt that *YHWH* was *the* name of God. There were other names of God. T. B. Shebuoth 35a, b states that some names of God may be erased (by the scribe), while others may not be erased. The names *El, Eloheka, Elohim, Elohehem,* I AM THAT I AM, *Adonai, YHWH, Shaddai* and *Zebaoth* may *not* be erased. But names like the great, the mighty, etc. may be erased. This provides a rough and ready guide as to the degree of sanctity attached to these names.

Zech. 14:9 states, "In that day the LORD shall be one, and his name one." T. B. Pes. 50a asks: "Is His name not one now?" Rab. Nahman bar Yitzhak replied: "In the world to come it will be different from what it is in this world. Here the name of God is written *YHWH*, but is read *Adonai*; in the world to come it will be read as it is written." The comment refers to the practice of reading "MY LORD" instead of pronouncing the Tetragrammaton. It is hard to say how early this practice started. Certainly the later MSS of the LXX have 'o Κυριος though Theodotion has *IABE*. The Aramaic Targum, at least, wrote the Tetragrammaton (although in contracted form). The expression *Memra* was *not* a surrogate for the *writing* of the

Tetragrammaton. In the (Jerusalem) Temple the priest pronounced
the name of God as it was written, but in the provinces he
pronounced it "*Adonai*" (T. B. Sotah, 37b). In T. B. Kidd, 71a
Rabbi Yohanan said that *YHWH* used to be verbally communicated
by the sages to their disciples every week [Rashi's comment is
that they would deal with its proper pronunciation, orthography
and meaning]. Raba was once about to expound the Tetragrammaton
in a public discourse when an old man reminded him that in Ex.
3:15 it is written "This is My name for ever"-- לעלם without a
waw (so not לעולם - for ever) but *'allem* - to hide could be read.
In the Fourth Gospel Jesus says (Jn. 17:6), "I manifested Thy
name unto the men whom Thou gavest me out of the world", and
Jn. 17:26, "I made known to them Thy name and will make it known,
etc."

It is also stated in T. B. Kidd, 71a, in a *Baraitha* that
they formerly used to impart the divine name consisting of twelve
letters to every man. But, since the lawless abounded, they
restricted the knowledge thereof to the discreet ones among the
priests, and these used to repeat it hurriedly, while the other
priests chanted the blessing of the people. Here we are dealing
with a tradition about the state of affairs when the Temple
still stood. The beginning of the tradition, however, points
to a time when the name of God is not in general use but is
already a (priestly) secret and mystic views have had time to
grow up about what was the real name. Here it is a twelve
letter name. One mystery breeds another, and all this arises
out of pronouncing a surrogate instead of plainly saying Yahweh.
Can it be this state of affairs that Zec. 14:9 is referring to?
It is recorded of Rabbi Tarphon that he once followed his maternal
uncle to the porch in front of the Temple, where the priests
blessed the people (e.g. at the daily Tamid sacrifice). Tarphon
heard the high priest hurrying over the name of God consisting

of twelve letters, while the other priests chanted the blessing.
Rab Jehudah said in the name of Rab:

> The name of God consisting of forty-two letters
> is imparted only to one that is discreet and
> meek, who has reached middle life and who is
> not given to anger and to intoxication and is
> not vindictive. Whoever knows that name is
> circumspect with regard to it and keeps it in
> purity. He is beloved above and cherished
> below. He inspires men with feelings of awe
> and inherits both worlds (T. B. Kidd. 71a).

But the forty-two letter name was not the longest. There
was a seventy-two letter name. The Cabbala, which goes back in
its origins to priestly mysticism, knows of the power attaching
to knowledge of the more recondite of the names of God, which
could be called the *Shem ha-Meforash*, i.e. the name properly
interpreted. All these forms of the name with 12, 42, 72, etc.
letters are primarily surrogates for Yahweh, but eventually
they become the center of attention. A rabbi explained Dt. 32:3
thus: Whenever I shall call upon, or mention the name of the
LORD, do you ascribe greatness to God" (T. B. Yoma 37a). This
would presume mention of the LORD in worship in the Temple or
Synagogue and a response like "Blessed be the great and glorious
name of the LORD from His place."

The Samaritans, who did not use *Tefillin* like the Jews, had
Qame'in. The *Tefillin* are little cubes of leather with sub-
divisions into which little rolls were inserted on which were
portions of scripture basically the same as those of the *Shema'*.
There was a *Tefillah* for the hand and one for the head. The
Tefillin could be compared with the *Mezuzah*; again basically
the same portions of the scripture were written on one roll in
this case and enclosed in a small oblong box which is affixed to
the lintel of the door. Both *Tefillin* and *Mezuzah* are associated

with an interpretation of certain words in Dt. 6:4-9, the
Shema' section which they are seen as implementing. The
Tefillin, however, are also worn when one says the *Shema'*
morning and evening in private. The Samaritan *Qame'a* were
worn, it would seem, over the arm. It was an oblong piece of
parchment with seven columns of *ketafim*--or in this case extremely abbreviated digests of the Torah. One wearing the
Qame'a was, as it were, wearing the Law in brief. On the
Qame'a were squares with the name of God written so that it
could be read vertically, horizontally, or diagonally, i.e.
automatically as it were multiplying itself. In addition, the
letters of the alphabet from Aleph to Taw were written out in
such a square. Some of the letters formed the name of God, but
all the letters of the alphabet were in the Torah which the
Samaritans, like the Jews, believed had existed before creation
and indeed was used in creation. And so the letters of the
alphabet were behind the word and Torah. The *Shema'*, of course,
appeared on the Samaritan *Qame'a*, although it was usually written
backwards. Incidentally, the *Qame'a* was for the Samaritan the
Shem ha-Meforash. It contained the Torah in digest form, and
the Torah was the fully explained name of God.

We learn that much was made of (a) the name of God, (b) the
Shema', and (c) the knowledge of the forms of the name, originally
to disguise it, later, allegedly to squeeze its full power out of
it, (d) the use of the *Shema'* not only in prayer in the Temple
and Synagogue, but written on a "Phylactery" (properly *Tefillah*)
or *Qame'a* (for the Jews had such as well as the Samaritans) or
Mezuzah as a protection against the devil and his evil spirits
and their fell works.

But there was another aspect to this. Centering round the
concentration on the divine name, it is possible that we find
two things. First, there was a belief that if one properly

understood the name, one would know the nature of God. To the
rabbis this was revealed in the written and oral law. In 2 Sam.
6:2 we have "the ark of God, upon which the name, even the name
of the Yahweh of Hosts was called". T. B. Baba Bathra 14b says
of this, "What is it that is written (in this statement?", and
Rab Huna said: "It (the repetition of the word "name") shows
that both the tables of stone and the fragments of the first
tables were deposited in it." Here we have something like the
Samaritan identification of the name of God and the Torah.
Simon ben Yohai (beginning of the second century A.D.) adds:
"It (i.e. the quotation from 2 Sam. 6:2) shows that the essential
and the appellative names of God were deposited therein." It
is indeed true that the 1st commandment has the statement, "I
the Lord your God", and *Anoki*, *YHWH* and *Eloheka* could be meant
by Simon ben Yohai in his remark. But secondly (Ezek. 38:23),
"So (in the apocalyptic Cataclysm which befalls God and Magog)
I will show My greatness and My holiness and make Myself known
in the eyes of many nations. Then they will know that I am
(*Ani*) the LORD (*YHWH*)." This is interpreted by the rabbis as
a further revelation of His name. Just as the first redemption
(that from Egypt) was preceded by a revelation of the name *YHWH*,
so the last redemption will be accompanied with a further revelation of the name of God. In Ezekiel the *Nasi* (or Messiah) has
no part in this deliverance. It is by God alone. But it was so
in a way with the Exodus: God was the One who wrought redemption,
not Moses.

In T. B. Baba Bathra 75b it is said that three are called
by the name of the Holy One, blessed be He! viz.: the righteous,
Messiah and Jerusalem. Of the righteous it is said (Isa. 43:7):
"Everyone that is called by My name"; of the Messiah it is said
(Jer. 23:6): "This is His name whereby He shall be called:
The LORD (*YHWH*) our righteousness." And of Jerusalem it is

written (Ezek. 48:35): "And the name of the city from that day
shall be: The LORD is there." Read not *Shamma* ("there") but
Sh^emah ("her name"). There are plenty of examples in the O.T.
where one syllable of the Tetragrammaton forms part of an
Israelite's name, e.g. Jehoshua (cf. Yahu as saviour). More
interesting is the quotation from Jeremiah of the Messiah
being called by a name of which the full Tetragrammaton (the
divine name) is a part. It is noteworthy (Lk. 1:31) that it
is Gabriel at the annunciation who tells Mary "and you shall
call his name Jesus (v. 32). He will be great, and will be
called 'The Son of the Most High' [as the messiah] and the LORD
God will give to him the throne of His father David." In v. 35
the angel said to her, "The Holy Spirit will come upon you, and
the power of the Most High will overshadow you; therefore the
child to be born will be called holy, the Son of God" (i.e. his
sonship on the divine side).

As to Jerusalem's name being "the LORD is there". This
could be a reference in Ezekiel to the return of the divine
Kabod (or glory) to the Temple. "The LORD is her name" is more
difficult. Jerusalem was the place where God chose to put His
name. The rabbis in the Mishnah refer to God as *ha-Makom*, the
place. This statement about the name of Jerusalem being "the
LORD is her name"--even if it applied to the heavenly Jerusalem--
rather confuses God with His chosen place and blurs the distinction between God and His Temple.

In examining ancient Jewish attitudes to the name of God,
it is surely relevant at least to allude to the Zohar, although
it is mediaeval. The Zohar says (vol. IV, p. 55 Soncino, London
1949):

> At the time of the recitation of the *Shema'* a
> man has to be prepared to proclaim the unity
> of the divine name and to accept the yoke of

the kingdom of heaven. On the head of him who
thus recites the *Shema'*, to accept the yoke of
the kingdom of heaven--the *Shekinah* rests--a
witness to testify of him before the Holy King
that twice daily does he declare the unity of
the name, and thus, consciously, united the
above and the below. Therefore is the letter
'ain of the *Shema'* written large, and also the
daleth, of the *ehad* (one), which when put together make the word *ed* (witness): a witness
before the Holy King.

The mystery contained in the words "The Lord our God, the Lord",

the mystery of the unity in three aspects (lit. "in three sides")

has often been referred to by the Holy Lamp (R. Simeon [ben

Yohai]) and we are not permitted to enlarge upon what he has

said. However, it is certain that the *Shekinah* descends to

rest upon the head of the man who unifies the name of the Holy

One above and below and bless him with seven blessings and

proclaims concerning him: "Thou art my servant, Israel, in whom

I am glorified!"(Isa. 49:3). The Zohar (*ibid*. p. 56) says that

after the Israelites had been shown the signs and wonders

connected with the crossing of the Red Sea, etc.

'And by and by the Torah was given to them, and
gradually they learned the ways of the Holy One,
blessed be He', until, eventually they reached
that point when the words quoted (Dt. 4:35) were
said to them. Moses said, in effect: 'Till now
I had to teach you as little children are taught;
you have been shown to know and you have learnt
by now to know and penetrate into the mystery of
faith, namely, this, that "the Lord (*YHWH*) He is
God (*Elohim*)" which is no small matter, since
concerning this it says "know therefore this day
and consider it in thine heart that the Lord He
is God in heaven above and upon the earth beneath,
there is none else"' (Dt. 5:39). The whole
mystery of faith depends upon this; the knowledge
of the mystery of my stories and the secret of
secrets comes from this. *YHWH ELOHIM* is a

full name and the whole is one. Herein is a
mystery of mysteries the masters of the esoteric
knowledge. And indeed blessed are they who en-
deavor to comprehend the Torah.

- - - - - -

The above extracts from the Zohar show (a) the centrality
of, and the importance attached to the *Shema'* and its recitation
in Jewish worship. The interpretation of the large ש of the
word *Shema'* and of the large ד of Ehad as *'ed* witness is important.
One wonders if the stress on witness in the Fourth Gospel could
not be at least in part a reference to the witness of the unity
of God found in the *Shema'*. We postulate that the Fourth Gospel
is an exposition of the name of God, i.e. the personality of God.
The Zohar sees the *Shema'* also as concerned with witnessing to
the unity of the name of God in three aspects. The Zohar is
obviously attempting to emphasize that *YHWH Elohim* is one full
or complete name. We must remember that a name for the Zohar
is not just a label any more than it is for the Talmud or the
Old Testament. It corresponds precisely to the essence behind
it. The Zohar sees man's chief end as to know God and to understand that *YHWH* is *Elohim*; and the study of Torah is for that
end (cf. Zohar *ibid.* p. 58). The Zohar insists that to grasp
that *YHWH* is *Elohim* is the sum of the whole mystery of faith
and of the written and oral law. "This knowledge that *YHWH* is
one with *Elohim* is indeed the synthesis of the whole Torah."
Nay more it adds later, "This is the essence of all things, and
it is necessary that man should perceive it in this world."
There had been considerable thought among the first century
Jews as to what was the essence of the Law (cf. T. B. Shab. 30a).

And Hillel's definition is so like Jesus' answer to the lawyer
in the Temple (Mk. 12:31) and his selection of the second
commandment like to the first. The first for both was the
Shema'; the second for Jesus was to love one's neighbour as
one's self (Lev. 19:18). For Jesus that was all; for Hillel
the (written and oral) law was essentially commentary. Hillel
(T. B. Shab. 31a) gave the Golden Rule in its negative form--
what is hateful to you, do not do to your fellow (Israelite).
This is the whole Law; the rest is commentary. One should not
emphasize that one is negative and the other (Jesus' version)
positive. The thing to notice is that Jesus brings the second
command into conformity with the first. You shall love your
God ... You shall love your neighbour. The Jews had seen the
first command as the necessary prerequisite of the second which
for them was part of the yoke of the Law. Actually in M. Ber.
2:2, Dt. 6:4ff. (the [first part of the] *Shema'*) is the yoke
of the kingdom of heaven and Dt. 11:33ff. is the yoke of the
Law. Dt. 11:18, 20 provide a basis for the commands as to
wearing *Tefillin* and having *Mezuzoth* on one's doors. This
really is a long way from making "loving one another" the new
commandment, and saying, as in I John 4:20, that if one does
not love one's neighbour one cannot love God.

    With the rabbis the emphasis seems to have been put on
"Hear, O Israel the LORD our God is one LORD", cf. T. B. Pes.
56a: Our rabbis taught: "How did they (the men of Jericho)
read the Shema? They used to say: 'Hear, O Israel, LORD our
God ONE LORD' (Dt. 6:4) without a pause: (presumably as Rashi
explains, the pause between the word *'Ehad* ['one'] and the next
we-Ahabt ['And you shall love'] may be disregarded). So says
Rabbi Meir. Rabbi Yehuda says:

They continued to make the pause; only they
omitted the response: 'Blessed be the name of
His glorious kingdom for ever.' Presumably they
did say: 'And you shall love', etc.; but compare the following passage (*ibid.*). But why
do *we* repeat this response? 'Because,' said
Rabbi Simon ben Lachish, 'Jacob called his
sons, and said, "Gather yourselves that I may
tell you," etc. Jacob, namely, wished to
reveal to his sons the end of the right hand
(which God "has drawn back from before the
enemy" (Lam. 2:3), the end of the captivity,
in fact, and the advent of the Messiah), when
the *Shekinah* departed from him. Is there,
God forbid, he exclaimed, any defect in my
conjugal bed, as there was in that of Abraham,
who had Ishmael: and in that of my father
Isaac, who had Esau? "Hear, O Israel," cried
all the sons, "the LORD our God the LORD is
one;" as there is in your heart only One, so
there is in ours also only One. In that hour
Jacob our father opened his mouth and said:
"Blessed be the name of His glorious kingdom
for ever."'

It is noteworthy that this is almost precisely what is in the
Targum Jerushalmi to Gen. 49. The rabbis (*ibid.*) said: "What
shall we do? Shall we repeat this response? There is Moses who
never said it. Shall we not repeat it? There is Jacob who did
say it, so they ordained that it should be said in a subdued
voice." The Talmud (*ibid.*) tells us that Rabbi Abbahu of the
3rd century states that later it was ordained that it should be
repeated in a loud voice because of troubles caused by the Minim
(i.e. Jewish Christians who probably added some Christian formula).
The Talmud (*ibid.*) adds that at Nehardea in Babylonia where
there were no Minim, they repeated it to this day (i.e. fifth or
sixth century) in a subdued voice. Two things emerge from T. B.
Pes. 56a--that the rabbis were concerned with how to say the first
sentence of the *Shema'* and how to respond so as to protect the
declaration of the unity of God. Or to put it in another way,

they were concerned with the declaration of the name. So
also was the Zohar. It is very likely that the men of Jericho
did not make any pause in "Hear, O Israel, the LORD our God
one LORD" just because they were worried by Minim. On the
other hand, Meir and Jehudah respectively testify to the
fact that this change was not acceptable to the rabbis and
that formerly there had been pauses.

Two things seem to emerge in all that has been cited
above: (a) the centrality of the divine name in Judaism, and
(b) concern for the honour of the divine name. Men were convinced of the power of the divine name because of the association of the divine name with the redemption of Israel from
Egypt proclaimed in the Ten Words or Commandments and in the
Torah. Their hope for a future redemption was in that name or
a better understanding of it. On the other hand, there was the
other commandment which forbade taking the name of God in vain.
The Arab, who swears by Allah (God), is not necessarily taking
the name of God in vain—at least, in the sense of the commandment, not all the time. The ejaculation may be a prayer. If
it were a false asseveration, it would be taking it in vain,
however. As pointed out above, what may have begun as respect
for the name of God, ended up, in the case of Jewish mystics,
with giving respect not only for the power of the name itself
but for all its various surrogates. In fairness, some of these
latter were a statement of God's nature and were possibly derived from attributes He had shown in the stories of His dealings with men. The attributes though were contracted to
syllables or letters. The letters of the alphabet made up the
name, and they made up the Torah, the record of His dealing
with men. So the letters of the alphabet each had their significance. One may think of Jesus Christ described as the Alpha and
Omega in Rev. 1:8, etc., the Beginning and the End, or *ICHTHUS*

as a secret name for Christ (i.e. the initials of *'Iesus Christos Theou huios, Sōtēr*). These Christian expressions are a Christian application of Jewish Gematria and Notarikon. On the Jewish side, we have what is known as the alphabet of Rabbi Akiba. This work has no real connection with R. Akiba ben Joseph. In the form we have it, it is later than his time, though it claims him as its author--probably because of Gen. Rabba R. I. Akiba and R. Eliezer, as youths, are said to have shown how to derive higher meanings from the double form of the letters מנצפך. Compare also in M. Gen. Rabba I and M. Song. R. on 5:11, according to which *Aleph* complained before God that *Beth* was preferred to it as the letter used to begin creation (i.e. as the initial letter of *Bareshith* [= in the beginning]). God, however, assured *Aleph* that the Torah of Sinai, the object of creation, would begin with *Aleph* (*Anoki*:[73] [I am] the LORD your God). In the Midrash of Rabbi Akiba, all the letters, beginning with the last, *Taw*, and ending with *Beth*, assert their claim to priority. First *Taw*, as being the initial letter of the Torah. It is told that it will be *the mark* on the forehead of the wicked (Ezek. 9:4). Whatever else this may testify to, it shows concern not only with names but also with nouns (i.e. words; *Shem* means both) and their spelling. This led, at least, to a meticulous concern for establishing a fixed text of the Hebrew Bible and faithfully transmitting it (and explains R. Akiba's interest therein).

YHWH, the Saviour God of the Old Testament and the *Memra* (Ex. 20:1) says: "And God (*Elohim*) spake all these words, saying". Verse 2 continues with: "I am the LORD your God (*YHWH Eloheka*) who has brought you out of the land of Egypt, out of the house of bondage." Verse 3 adds: "You shall have no other gods (*Elohim*) before Me."

In Targum Onkelos verse 1 has: "And *Yeya* (*YHWH*) spake all these words."

Elohim was not a proper name in the way *YHWH* was. While in Ex. 20:1 *Elohim*, in view of the statement in v. 2, is the God of Israel. The use of *Elohim* in v. 3 could refer to other gods or god. Dt. 4:36 *YHWH hu' ha-Elohim* (*YHWH*) (= "He is the God") shows how even in Deuteronomy it was not enough to say *YHWH* was *Elohim* but that he was *the Elohim* (God). But there is added "there is none beside Him".

One is not quarrelling here with the Pentateuchal Documentary Hypothesis when one remarks that in Ex. 3:2ff. the E Document reveals that *YHWH* and the *Elohim* of Abraham, Isaac and Jacob are one and the same. Actually in Ex. 3:14 *Elohim* gives His name as *Ehyeh asher Ehyeh* (I AM THAT I AM). The P Document in Ex. 6:2 states that *Elohim* said He was *YHWH* and v. 3 states that while He had appeared to Abraham, Isaac and Jacob by the name *El Shaddai* (God Almighty), that "by My name of *YHWH* I was not known to them". Nevertheless, the point is the same; *YHWH* and *El Shaddai* are one; though a revelation of a new name implies a further and new revelation of the Divine Nature.

The P Document is later than the D Document. P provided the general framework for the first four books of the Pentateuch. P was apparently not satisfied with E's official version of the new revelation of God's personal name to Moses and felt that it must specifically state that the Patriarch had not known God as *YHWH*. E and P are basically doing the same thing, viz. they are identifying *YHWH* as He now reveals Himself more fully, as the God of the Patriarchs. In the Semitic world, a name was and is important. It denotes character and personality, if not indeed entity. The Deuteronomist had been faced before P with the union of the J and E traditions and the consequent merging of the names *YHWH* and *Elohim*. We are indebted to the

Deuteronomist for the *Shema'* which has become the classic formulation of the unity of God: "Hear, O Israel, the LORD *YHWH*, Our God (*Elohenu*) is one LORD (*YHWH*)" *or* "Hear, O Israel, *YHWH Elohenu*, *YHWH* is One (*Ehad*)." This has been hallowed by the martyr Akiba as a declaration of faith in *YHWH* as the one God over against the many gods of the Romans. Before him, Hillel and Jesus alike had said that this was the basic commandment of the Torah. Maimonides in his Thirteen Principles of Faith had specifically stressed the unity of *Ehad* (One). It could have been, however, that the Deuteronomist was concerned to stress that *Elohenu* (Our God), the *Elohe Yisrael*, and *YHWH* were and are One, *or* that *YHWH Elohenu* and *YHWH* are One. For before the burning bush episode, the J Document uses *YHWH* as the name of God, and the E Document uses *Elohim* as the name of God. After the burning bush episode, E does use *YHWH Elohenu* instead. To some it would be a difficulty. Is *YHWH Elohenu* and *YHWH* the same? Significantly enough, the Targum Onkelos does not use the Aramaic equivalent of *Elohim* in Genesis I but *YHWH*. The Hebrew prophets too claim that it was the word of *YHWH* that came to them. While the Zohar, as we have it, is late, yet a constantly recurring concern of that work as stated above[74] is to prove that *Elohenu* of the *Shema'* and *YHWH* are One.

Elohim besides meaning God, god, or gods can mean: rulers or judges (cf. Ex. 21:6, Ps. 82:6; angels, Ps. 97:7; godlike one, Ex. 4:15, 7:1, [of Moses]; I Sam. 28:13 [the ghost of Samuel]; Ps. 45:7 [of the Messianic King]). In the Targum, *Memra* is used along with *YHWH*. It permeates everything, brings everything into the realm of being, and conditions everything. It is the immanent manifestation of God in the world of matter and spirit. Divine wisdom, divine power, divine love, and divine justice, all these do not abide in the highest heavens isolated, unapproachable, and unknowable. They are imbedded in

the scheme of things that we can see, feel, touch, and know.
They are a part of the constitution of man and the world. Man
and the world are a fragment of them. The *Memra* comprises and
expresses these teachings.[75] But even if *Memra* and *Torah* are
not identical, they overlap.[76]

In the past there has been too much effort expended on
seeking to show that the *Memra* is a personality, as it were,
in its own right either as an agent of God or as a mediator
between God and man. The present writer believes both sugges-
tions are wrong. The *Memra* and *Yahweh* are one. Yahweh was and
is the God who cares enough to come down to His people.

For the purpose of this study, we will concentrate on the
evidence of the Targum of Isaiah. Our primary reason for this
is that in the Fourth Gospel (Jn. 12:41) after a citation from
Isa. 6:9, 10 the following is said in Jn. 12:40: "These things
Esaias said when he saw His glory, and spake of Him." "His
glory" must refer to Jesus' glory. The incident of Isaiah's
vision (Isa. 6) is rendered thus in the Targum:

> In the year in which King Uzziah was smitten
> (with leprosy) the prophet said, I saw the
> glory of the LORD sitting upon a throne, high
> and lifted up in the highest heavens, and the
> temple was filled with the brightness of His
> glory. Holy ministers (stood) in the height
> before Him, each one had six wings, with twain
> he was covering his face that he might not see,
> and with twain he was covering his body that it
> might not be seen, and with twain he was minis-
> tering. And they were crying one to another
> and saying, 'Holy in the highest heavens the
> house of his *Shekinah*, holy upon earth the work
> of His might, holy for endless ages is the LORD
> of hosts: the whole earth is full of the
> brightness of His glory.' And the doorposts
> of the temple trembled at the sound of the
> speaking, and the sanctuary was filled with
> thick darkness. And I said, 'Woe is me! for I

have transgressed, for I am a man deserving of
rebuke, and I dwell in the midst of a people that
polluted with transgressions, for mine eyes have
seen the glory of the *Shekinah* of the king of
ages, the LORD of hosts.' And there flew unto
me one of the ministering (angels) and in his
mouth was the speech which he had received from
before Him, whose *Shekinah* is on the throne of
glory in the highest heaven, high above the
altar; and he placed it in my mouth, and said,
'Behold I have set the words of my prophecy in
your mouth, and your transgressions shall be
taken away, and your sins expiated.' And I
heard the voice of the *Memra* of the LORD which
said, 'Whom shall I send to prophesy, and who
will go to teach?'

The Hebrew rendered by the Targum "the voice of the *Memra* of the
LORD" is *qol Adonai* (the voice of My Lord). At the beginning
of the vision the glory of *the LORD* which Isaiah saw is *Adonai*
(my LORD) in Hebrew. *Adonai* is doubtless Yahweh, but here instead of the *qere perpetuum* the consonants of the Tetragrammaton
are also changed, along with the vowels, to *Adonai*. That the
episode of Isaiah's vision should be referred to by the writer
of the Fourth Gospel is interesting in more ways than one.
First, because in the Synoptics the assurance that the people
cannot hear or cannot see is also given (cf. Isa. 6:10).
Secondly in particular, Jn. 12:41 shows that the Fourth Gospel
writer identifies Jesus his Lord with the LORD on the throne
whose glory Isaiah saw. There is the question of the relation
of the *Memra* to the LORD. This comes out more clearly in other
citations in the Targum of Isaiah which latter the Targumist of
course regarded as one book. The significant thing that emerges
in a study of the occurrence of *Memra* in the Targum of Isaiah
is that *Memra* is primarily put in place of the first or second
personal pronoun (unless otherwise noted) referred to the Lord
(e.g. Isa. 1:2; Isa. 25:9; Isa. 26:3 [2nd pers.]; Isa. 26:13;

Isa. 27:3; Isa 33:2 [2nd pers.]; Isa. 37:29; Isa. 41:11; Isa.
41:13; Isa. 41:14; Isa. 43:5; Isa. 46:12; Isa. 48:16; Isa.
49:15; Isa. 51:1; Isa. 51:4; Isa. 51:5; Isa. 51:7; Isa. 52:6;
Isa. 55:2; Isa. 55:3; Isa. 57:6; Isa. 60:9; Isa. 63:8 [3rd
pers.]; Isa. 66:13; Isa. 66:24). In the following, *Memra*
stands for "My (the LORD's) soul" (Isa. 1:14; Isa. 42:1); "My
(the LORD's) eyes" (Isa. 1:16; Isa. 49:5); "the mouth of the
LORD" (Isa. 1:20; Isa. 40:4; Isa. 58:14; Isa. 62:2); "zeal of
the LORD" (Isa. 7:6; Isa. 37:32); "His [the LORD's] tongue"
(Isa. 3:27); "breath of the LORD" (Isa. 30:33); "His spirit"
(Isa. 4:4; Isa. 34:16; Isa. 41:16; Isa. 48:16; Isa. 59:19; Isa.
63:10; Isa. 63:11; Isa. 63:14); and "My hand" (Isa. 48:13).
Regarding Isa. 63:10, 11, the "Holy Spirit" of the M.T. is
rendered the *Memra* of his holy prophets by the Targum. In
Isa. 5:25 *Memra* in the Targum translates *'imrath* the "word"
of the Holy One of Israel. In Isa. 28:23 *My Memra* translates
'imrathi which is parallel to *Qoli* My (God's) Voice. In Targum
Isaiah 11:4, speaking of the Messiah, it is said that he will
smite with the *Memra* of His mouth. The M.T. has "rod". The
remaining occurrences of *Memra* in the Targum of Isaiah fall
into the category of Isa. 6:8 where *Memra* is put between voice
and the LORD (i.e. the voice of the *Memra* of the LORD). This
mainly takes the form of the *Memra* of the LORD (e.g. Isa. 10:20;
Isa. 21:17; Isa. 22:25; Isa. 25:8; Isa. 26:4; Isa. 36:7; Isa.
36:15; Isa. 59:13). In Isa. 61:10 the *Memra* of the LORD
renders "My God" of the M.T. Is this not significant? Is it
not bringing God nearer? First He is *YHWH* the God of Israel,
who has revealed Himself and His will by communicating in speech
with the lawgiver and prophet. Later on, the rabbis did regard
the scriptures as the proof of the Holy Spirit's existence and
activity. As proof of the personalization of *the Memra of YHWH*,
let us see how the Targum handles Isa. 12:2. The M.T. (as

translated by R.V.) runs: "Behold, God (*EL*) is my salvation. I will trust, and will not be afraid; for the Yah Yahweh is my strength and song; and He is become my salvation. Therefore with joy shall ye draw water out of the wells of salvation." The Targum renders this thus:

> Behold in the *Memra* of the God of my salvation do I trust and shall not be dismayed because my strength and my glory is the terrible One, *Yeya* (*YHWH*). He has spoken by his *Memra* and has become my Saviour.

Not only is the source of one's trust specified, but *YHWH* is shown to be actively a Saviour and to have communicated this reassuring fact. The Targum Isa. 43:2 gives a historical reference to the waters which they pass through. The Targum has: "At first when ye passed through the Red Sea, My *Memra* was your support." The M.T. has: "I will be with thee" in Isa. 43:5. "Fear not for I am with thee", becomes in the Targum: "for my *Memra* is your support". These are two important verses showing the identity of the divine "I" and the *Memra* active alike in the Exodus and in the prophet's own time. A similar phrase occurs in Targum Isaiah 41:10, 13 and 14 with "My *Memra*" for I. While there is ample reference to the *Memra* of the LORD in the Targums to the Pentateuch, it does not occur in Gen. 1. True, the Targums read *YHWH* instead of *Elohim*, but the phrase *Memra de Yeya* does not occur there. Now the Fourth Gospel 1:1-3 says:

> (1) In the beginning was the Word, and the Word was with God, and the Word was God.
> (2) The same was in the beginning with God.
> (3) All things were made by Him, and without Him was not anything made that was made.

The Fourth Gospel did not get the information from the Targums
to the Pentateuch, though the Jerusalem Targum declares: the
Word of God created man in His likeness, in the likeness of the
presence of the LORD, He created him, the male and his yoke-
fellow, He created them.   However, the Targum to Isaiah 44:24
says: "I am *Yeya*, the maker of all things, and I suspended
the heavens by My *Memra*" (instead of the M.T. "that stretches
forth the heavens alone").   Again in Isa. 48:13 the Targum has:
"Yea, by My *Memra* I founded the earth; by My might, I suspended
the heavens."   The M.T. has instead of "My *Memra*", "My hand".
The *Memra* of *YHWH* was active in all creation, including that
of man (cf. Targum to Isa. 45:12:   "I have made the earth by
My *Memra*, and created man upon it.").   Important too for
definition of "My *Memra*" is surely Isa. 48:11, 12.

> (11) For Mine own sake, for Mine own sake, will
> I do it; for how should (My name) be profaned?
> And My glory will I not give to another.   (12)
> Hearken unto Me, O Jacob, and Israel My called;
> I am He: I am the first, I also am the last.

In the Targum to Isaiah this reads:

> (11) For My name's sake; for My *Memra*'s sake
> [i.e. *Lema'ani* which occurs twice in the
> Hebrew is once rendered in the Targum 'for
> My name's sake', and the next time, 'for My
> *Memra*'s sake'] and My glory wherewith I was
> revealed to you I will not give to another
> people.   (13) Hearken unto My *Memra* [M.T. Me]
> you that are of the house of Jacob, and Israel,
> mine appointed one: I am He, I am He that is
> from the beginning; Yea, the everlasting ages
> are Mine, and beside Me there is no god.

While taking the opportunity of stressing the unique revelation
of the glory of God to Israel, the Targum does not in the least

diminish the claim made in the Hebrew at the end of v. 13 that
Israel's God is the only God but inserts it with great effect
at the end of v. 14. God's *Memra* cannot be separate from God.
It is on an equal footing with His name, if not indeed identical
with it.

The Targum on Isaiah like the Hebrew Isaiah shows the
Lord as Redeemer as well as Creator. In the Targum to Isaiah
29:22; 41:8ff.; 43:12; 48:15; 51:2; and 63:16, reference is
made to Abraham. In the Hebrew Isaiah the important references
to Abraham in Targum Isa. 43:12 and Targum Isa. 48:15 do not
occur. Isa. 43:11: "I, even I, am the LORD; and beside Me
there is no saviour", is translated literally by the Targum.
Yet Isa. 43:12 which in the Hebrew reads: "I have declared,
and I have saved, and I have showed, and there was no strange
(god) among you: therefore you and My witnesses, saith the LORD
(god), and I am God" becomes in the Targum in the passage: "I
have declared...I have showed": "I have declared to Abraham
your father that was about to come; I delivered you from Egypt,
as I swore to him between the pieces: I caused you to hear,
the instruction of My law from Sinai: while you were still
alive." Isa. 48:15 in the Hebrew Bible is:

> I, even I, have spoken: yea, I have called him
> Israel: I have brought him, and he shall make
> his way prosperous. (16) Come near to me, hear
> this; from the beginning, I have not spoken in
> secret; from the time that it was, there am I:
> now the LORD *Yahweh* has sent me and His spirit.
> (17) Thus says *Yahweh* your redeemer the Holy One
> of Israel: I am the *Yahweh* your God, who teaches
> you to profit, who leads you by the way that you
> should go.

Verses 16 and 17 in the Targum are significantly different:

> I, even I, did make by My *Memra* a covenant with
> Abraham your father. Yea, I appointed (or
> called) him. I brought him into the land of
> the house of my *Shekinah* and made him prosper-
> ous. (16) Draw near unto My *Memra*, hear this:
> from the beginning I have not spoken in secret:
> from the time that the nations separated them-
> selves from fear of Me, there did I bring Abraham
> to My service. The prophet says, 'And now *Yeya*
> *Elohim* has sent me and His *Memra*.'

The passage "I, even I, did make by My *Memra* a covenant with
Abraham your father" from the Targum is as it were an explanation
and amplification of the M.T. "I, even I, have spoken." The
Targum shows the LORD in action communicating with Abraham. The
Memra is not separate from God, it is with God, and it is God
(cf. Jn. 1:1). If Jesus is the LORD's *Memra* (cf. Jn. 12:41)
then Jn. 8:58, if not v. 56, falls into place. Targum Onkelos
and Targum Pseudo-Jonathan to Gen. 15 should be taken into
account: "After these things the word (*pithgama*) of the LORD
came to Abram in prophecy, saying: 'Fear not Abram: My *Memra*
shall be your strength, and your exceeding great reward...' and
he believed in the *Memra de Yeya* and He reckoned it to him for
justification" (T. Onk. Gen 15:1f.).

The first of the Hallel Psalms (Ps. 113) in v. 2 contains
a doxology which was part of the Temple Festival Liturgy. The
form is to be noted. "Blessed *be the name of the LORD*." In v. 1
we have "praise the name of the LORD". The words *praise* and
bless are here synonymous. The *name* of the LORD is the LORD as
He really is and as He has revealed Himself to be. In v. 4 *His*
(the LORD's) *glory* is parallel to the LORD, and like the name
of the LORD, it cannot be separated from the LORD. His *glory*
is both His revelation of Himself as it is in the Theophanies
at Sinai to Moses, Isaiah in the Temple, and Ezekiel at the river
Chebar, and the total fullness of Himself not then revealed.

The name of God that is to be blessed is the Tetragrammaton (cf. Jb. 1:21: "Blessed be the name of the LORD."). In Ps. 72:19: "Blessed be His glorious name (or name of His glory) for ever, may his glory fill the whole earth, Amen and Amen" is parallel to "Blessed be the LORD, the God of Israel, who alone does wondrous things." Just as "the name of the LORD" and "LORD" are synonymous, so "who alone" and "his glory" are also synonymous. "His glory" is "He who is alone". Further we should note that *"Shem Kebodo"* explicitly indicates the Tetragrammaton in Dt. 28:58--"that you may fear this glorious and awful name (*ha-Shem ha-Nikbad we-ha-Nora*) the LORD your God." In Neh. 9:5 we have the Levitical injunction to bless the Lord: "Stand up and bless the LORD your God from everlasting to everlasting. Blessed be the glorious name *Shem Kebodeka* which is exalted above all blessing (*berakah*) and praise." "The name of Thy glory" is clearly a reference to the Tetragrammaton (cf. the following verse Neh. 9:6 when Ezra addresses God thus: "Thou art the Lord, Thou alone"). Ps. 24 is important here for its designation of Yahweh as the King of glory (Ps. 24:7, 8, 9, 10). This along with Ps. 72:19 may have helped to give rise to the later formula which was used in the Temple: "Blessed be the glorious name of His kingdom for ever and ever" (M. Tam. 5:1; 7:2; M. Yom. 6:2; T. B. Yom. 39b; T. B. Taan. 16b). *"Malkutho"* (kingdom) is a paraphrase for God (*Elohim*), just as *"Shem Kebodo"* is a synonym for Yahweh.

The *Kaddish* (holy) is the name of the doxology recited with responses by the congregation either at the end of a section of the service *hatzi Kaddish* (half *Kaddish*), or the *Kaddish Shalem* (the full *Kaddish*) at the conclusion of the service.

The *Kaddish* is in Aramaic. The opening words are reminiscent of the two Hebrew words at the beginning of Ezek. 38:23 which reads thus: *We-hithgadalti we-hithkadashti* "So I will show My greatness and My holiness and make Myself known in the eyes of many nations. Then they will know that I am the LORD." The *Kaddish* itself starts with *Yithgadal we - Yithkadash Shemeh Raba* ("May his great name be exalted and sanctified"). The following is the translation of *Kaddish Yithkabbal* said by the minister in the Sephardi Sabbath morning service[77] before the Torah is taken from the ark.

> May His great name be exalted and sanctified throughout the world which He created according to His will; may He establish His kingdom, cause His redemption to spring forth, and hasten the advent of His anointed in your lifetime, in your days, and in the lifetime of the whole house of Israel, speedily, and at a near time, and say ye, Amen.
> May His great name be blessed, and glorified for ever and ever. May His hallowed name be praised, glorified, exalted, magnified, honoured and most excellently adored; blessed is he, far exceeding all blessings, hymns, praises and consolations that can be uttered in the world, and say ye, Amen.
> May the fulness of peace from heaven with life plenty, salvation, consolation, deliverance, health, redemption, pardon, expiation, enlargement and freedom be granted unto us and to all His people Israel, and say ye, Amen. May He who established peace in His high places, bestow, through His infinite mercy, peace on us and on all Israel, and say ye, Amen.

The customary congregational response to the *Kaddish* is: "Let His great name be blessed and unto all eternity." This is to be taken to be equivalent to the response made by the people to the benedictions and prayers in the Temple. The name of His glorious kingdom there being rendered here as "His great name". In the *Kaddish* too there is a prayer for

the coming of the Messiah. The first words of the *Kaddish*
about God's great name being exalted and hallowed recall the
words of God in Ezek. 38:23 in connection with the apocalyptic
battle with Gog and Magog. The *Kaddish* was a doxology centering
on the name of God which had been revealed at Sinai before the
first redemption of Israel from Egypt. The common belief was
that the last redemption was to be like the first. But the
Kaddish sees the significant thing centering on the great name.
The last redemption to which Ezek. 38:23 refers is seen as being
brought about by a further self-revelation of not only the greatness and holiness of God but of Himself. This they understood
as summed up in His great name. The emphasis was put on the
congregational response "May His great name be praised for all
eternity!!" (cf. Sifre Deut. 306). T. B. Sotah 49a states:
"Since the destruction of the Temple the world has been sus-
tained by the *Kedushah* of the liturgy and the "*Yehe shemeh
rabba*" (i.e. May His great name be praised [the response to the
Kaddish]). In T. B. Shab. 119b (cf. Mishle X:10; XIV:4) R.
Joshua, A. Levi and R. Johanan assert that "Joining loudly and
in unison in the congregational response '*yehe shemeh rabba*'
has the power of influencing the heavenly decree in one's
favour or of obtaining for one forgiveness."

In the *Othiyoth de R. Akiba*, it is said under the letter
zayin:

> ...at the time of the Messiah, God shall sit
> in paradise and deliver a discourse on the
> new Torah before the assembly of the pious
> and the angelic hosts, and that at the close
> of the discourse on the new Torah, Zerubbabel
> shall rise and recite the *Kaddish* from one
> end of the world to the other: to which all
> mankind will respond 'Amen'. All souls of
> Jews and Gentiles in Gehenna will respond
> with 'Amen', so that God's mercy will be

> awakened and He will give the keys of Gehenna
> to Michael and Gabriel, the archangels, saying:
> 'Open the gates, that a righteous nation which
> observeth faith may enter.' [Isa. 26:2
> '*shomer emunim*' being explained as 'one that
> says Amen'.] Then the 40,000 gates of Gehenna
> shall open, and all the redeemed of Gehenna,
> the wicked ones of Isreal, and the righteous
> of the Gentiles shall be ushered into paradise.

What is the relevance of all the above to the Fourth Gospel?
First of all there is in the Fourth Gospel an emphasis on the
name of God. He has come (Jn. 5:43) "in My Father's name"; the
works He does are done "in My Father's name" (Jn. 10:25). He
has manifested "Thy (God's) name" to Me (Jn. 17:6). He has
kept them in "Your (God's) name" (Jn. 17:12). He has declared
to men "Thy (God's) name" (Jn. 17:26). At the same time,
emphasis is put in John's gospel on Jesus Christ's name, e.g.
"that you might have life through His (Jesus') name" (Jn. 20:
31). But belief in Jesus' name is (as Jn. 3:18 makes clear)
belief "in the name of the only begotten son of God". This has
to be seen in the context of the emphasis placed in the Fourth
Gospel on the oneness of the Father and the Son. So the references in Jn. 14:13, 14; Jn. 15:16; Jn. 16:23, 24 about asking
in My (Christ the only begotten Son's) name also have to be
seen in the context of the union of Father and Son. The same
would apply to the Paraclete "whom the Father will send in My
name" (Jn. 14:26). There is no alteration in purpose as Father
and Son are one in purpose and the Son is in the bosom of the
Father before incarnation, during incarnation, and after incarnation eternally. Likewise the evil which men do to the disciples, "for My name's sake", is as if they did it against God
(cf. Jn. 15:21). In short, in John's gospel we have redemption
linked with the supreme revelation of God's name in Christ.
With the revelation of God to Moses at the burning bush there

was the revelation of His name. Thereafter the Exodus followed
culminating in the manifestation of God's glory at Sinai. With
the incarnation there was both the fuller revelation of the
name of God in that of Jesus the redeemer and saviour, and a
fuller revelation of God's glory in the life, words, and work
of the incarnate Son of God (especially in His crucifixion,
resurrection and giving of the Holy Spirit).

The *Kaddish* testifies to the hope men had of a future,
further revelation of the name of God. The Fourth Gospel,
written after the Temple fell, and when Jews were clinging to
a hope in the efficacy of the response to "may His great name
be blessed" showed that it had already happened--had they had
the eyes to see--in Christ. The haggadic story about the
effects of the people's saying "May His (God's) great name be
blessed" to the *Kaddish* read by Zerubbabel (as Messiah) after
God proclaimed the new Law can help us to understand the Fourth
Gospel. By recognizing the glory of God in Christ and that he
has come in the Father's name (not just as an emissary but
actually in and with His name), if we can say "May His great
name be blessed", we raise ourselves from the dead freeing
ourselves from Gehenna. But in the Fourth Gospel the decision
and redemption and revelation of the new Law takes place now.
We might recollect that the third benediction[78] of the *Amidah*
prayer (*Shemoneh Esreh*) is called the *Kedushah* and is referred
to in M. Rosh ha-Shanah 4:5 as the "Hallowing of the name".
The term *Kedushah* is applied to the contents of the third benediction of the *Amidah* and the congregational responses which
are firstly: "Holy, Holy, Holy is the LORD of hosts: the
whole earth is full of His glory" (Isa. 6:3); "Blessed be the
glory of the LORD from his place" (Ezek. 3:12). "The LORD
shall reign for ever, even your God, O Zion to all generations.
Praise the LORD for ever, even your God, O Zion to all generations.

Praise the LORD" (Ps. 146:10). To these two further responses
on Sabbaths are added: "Hear, O Israel, the LORD your God, the
LORD is One" and "I am the LORD your God". Whether these
responses go back to Temple times is not certain. After the
destruction of the Temple, the *Ḳedushah* like the *Ḳaddish* was
emphasized more and expanded. However, they are important to
us as showing how the theme of holiness, His glory, and His
name are linked together. Isa. 6:3 was important to Jews as
a Theophany in the Temple and was later taken by Christians
(cf., e.g. Theodore) as prefiguring the Christian revelation
of the triune God. Jews would hardly have inserted it later.

CHAPTER 4

The Fourth Gospel and the Book of Esther

In the Fourth Gospel two biblical feasts stand out clearly
from the others--Passover (3 times) and Tabernacles (once). It
should be noted that in its third and final occurrence Passover
shares some of the features of Tabernacles (e.g. the palms, the
Hallel (sung by day), the water and the blood (Jesus' blood) instead of the wine being poured out at the altar of the new
Temple (Jesus). Passover was the remembrance or memorial of
the national deliverance from Egypt. While recalling the wilderness days, Tabernacles from the time of Zech. 14:16 had been
given an eschatological direction and also an international
connotation. Two other feasts are mentioned: a Feast of the
Jews and the Feast of the Dedication. As we have earlier remarked, the feast of the Jews of Jn. 5:1 has presented a continuing problem of identification. Purim, Passover, Pentecost,
Rosh ha-Shanah, Yom Kippur, and Tabernacles have all been
suggested at some time, even though Rosh ha-Shanah and Yom Kippur
are not Temple feasts in the ordinary sense. Purim like Hanukkah
(Dedication) is not a Pentateuchal feast. However Hanukkah is
mentioned in the Fourth Gospel, so the fact that Purim is not
one of the three feasts of the Pentateuch cannot be fairly urged
against the unnamed feast being identified as Purim. Gudemann[79]
pointed out that the Fourth Gospel was aware of developments in
Judaism in the last part of the 1st century A.D. He suggested
that Hanukkah and Purim belonged to this period. While it is
true that Purim has a tractate in the Mishnah, it is not under

that name and deals with the reading of the Scroll (of Esther).
We have seen that in the discussions on the canon held at
Jamnia,[80] Esther would have been excluded from the canon had it
not been for the advocacy of R. Akiba. Since the Scroll of
Esther is central to Purim, it is unlikely that Purim was
celebrated with the approval of Pharisaic Judaism before the
Synod of Jamnia. This does not rule out a consideration of
Purim for the title of the unknown feast of the Jews (Jn. 5:1).
Esther was probably written at the time of the Maccabean Revolt,
and it is a very nationalistic work. It may be significant
that the term "the Jews", rare in the Old Testament as a designation for the nation and people, occurs in Esther with great
frequency. According to Josephus, it is also the term used by
the Maccabees and I and II Maccabees use it to signify themselves
and their state. The term "the Jews" occurs frequently in the
Fourth Gospel and there too it seems to have a technical[81] sense
probably referring to a member of the Sadducean priestly aristocracy.

Hanukkah does not get a tractate in the Mishnah, nor were
any of the Books of the Maccabees included in the Jamnia biblical canon. This latter fact may have determined the former.
Actually Hanukkah is mentioned only a few times in the Mishnah.
Especially significant is M. Meg. 3:6 which gives special Torah
readings for both Purim and Hanukkah. I Macc. 4:59 tells of the
institution of Hanukkah or rather the Feast of the Dedication,
as it calls it. On the occasion of the rededication of the
temple altar after the defeat of the Seleucids, II Macc. 10:8
tells how it was ordained that this feast was to be kept each
year in perpetuity. This does not mean more than a pious wish
and does not prove that it was kept from 165 B.C. on to the
present, anymore than that Purim was kept from the time of
Ahasuerus, although in Esth. 9:20, 27 it is also laid down that

the deliverance of the Jews wrought by Esther was to be commemorated each year in perpetuity. Incidentally, Purim in II Macc. 15:36 is called Mordecai's Day and had not then attained the name Purim. The references to Hanukkah in the Mishnah belong to the end of the 1st century A.D. at the earliest, but they are mainly second century. It is quite conceivable that the original institution of Purim and Hanukkah being associated with the Maccabees later led to their neglect during the Herodian period. If they were still celebrated, it was not by all parties. "A feast of the Jews" would designate a feast authorized and approved by the then ruling group. In the time of Jesus it could mean a feast instituted by the authorization of the Sadducees. But by the time of the writing of the Gospel at the end of the century, it would refer to an authorization by Akiba and his followers or the Patriarch Gamaliel II. The Fourth Gospel is working on different levels of time. It purports to tell of the time of Jesus, but it is actually dealing with the last part of the century and the Christianity and Judaism of that period. Judaism had changed and so the Church's Christ must be shown to have an answer relevant to the new situation.

The two Maccabean feasts were Nicanor's Day[82] and Dedication (Hanukkah). It is true Nicanor's Day was the day before Mordecai's Day (according to II Macc. 15:36), but considering that in M. Megillah 1:1, 2 various days are given for the reading of the Scroll of Esther in cities, large towns, and villages too much should not be made of the one day's difference between Nicanor's and Mordecai's Day, the latter being known as Purim. Michaelis thought that Nicanor's Day was the origin of this latter feast. This suggestion, while brilliant, cannot be accepted quite in that form. II Macc. 15:36 does mention both Nicanor's Day *and* Mordecai's Day. The Maccabean struggle did call forth the Book of Daniel. In the latter we have an adaptation of what purports to be tales of the oppression of Jews by Nebuchadnezzar and the deliverance therefrom by God. These are followed by visions and apocryphal angelic communications up to the writer's own time, but this is clearly before the rededication of the altar in the Jerusalem Temple. The Book of Esther, like the first part of Daniel, recalls tales of the exile. Mordecai provides a direct link with the captivity of Judah--he is impossibly old at 130.[83] Not only so, he is shown to be the descendant of Saul and a Benjaminite.[83a] But Haman, his adversary, is a descendant of Agag and is, therefore, an Amalekite. Mordecai and Haman represent, as it were, Israel and the Amalekites, who were the agelong enemies. It is Mordecai's mission, with the help of his niece Esther, to work out vengeance on Haman, his family, and followers thus fulfilling the doom pronounced on Amalek in Exodus 17:14. Haman as a descendant of Agag the Amalekite stands for all the foes of the Jews, including the Greek oppressors of the Maccabees, and the tale shows what Jews ought to do to their oppressors. Unlike Daniel, Esther is a tale of self-help without waiting or hoping for divine intervention. Judith is another tract for the same times, but it goes further than Esther in showing what a Jewess, unaided by a Jewish male, can do to liberate her people. In the shorter recension B, Seleucus and not Holofernes is the oppressor. In other words, it is an updating of the tale from Babylonian times to the nearer time of the Maccabees (cf. how the Greek Esther makes Haman, a Macedonian, actually work against Persia's real good).

It is possible that such a tale as the book of Esther did produce a Mordecai's Day[84] before Nicanor's Day. After all from its very appearance and reception, its insistence on keeping an anniversary of the deliverance of the Jews in Susa would surely find a response. In a way, Nicanor's Day, all the events leading up to the rededication of the altar, and the eventual setting up of the Judean Kingdom of the Maccabees were responses awakened by such a book as that of Esther.

But were Purim and Hanukkah celebrated annually from Maccabean times and by whom? Josephus (*Ant*. XI:199-289) relates the story of Esther with its insistence that Purim be kept, then adds that it is kept in his days. Remembering, as we must, that he wrote his *Antiquities* at the end of the 1st century A.D. and that Akiba had by then had the Book of Esther declared canonical, there is no doubt that Purim was celebrated in his days. But Josephus is no real guide as to the whole period between the Maccabees and the end of the 1st century. As to Hanukkah, it is plain from II Macc. 1:9 that even by the time of John Hyrcanus propaganda had to be made to encourage its observance. Whereas it could be that Nicanor's Day was observed by the Sadducean priests and Mordecai's Day (or Purim) by the Pharisaic populace, so it was only after the fall of the Temple in 70 A.D. that rabbinic Judaism, while now recognizing Nicanor's Day (cf. *Megillath Ta'anith*) elevated Purim as the more important one. The case may have been different with Hanukkah. This may well have been purely a temple feast, and even if it were celebrated in the Herodian period, it may not have evoked any response from the Pharisees. It could be that only after the destruction of the Temple when some of the former temple's hierarchy joined ranks with the rabbis that the popular attitude to Hanukkah changed. But this probably took some time to make headway. One might suggest that the period after the destruction and before the Bar Cochba Revolt was, in some ways, parallel to the Maccabean situation after the desecration of the altar. Hopefully the Jews would call to mind the Maccabean feast commemorating its rededication and regard it as having a new significance for them. Certainly we have synagogical lections

in M. Megillah (Meg. 3:4, 6) for both Purim and Hanukkah. To
date these are not only difficult but well nigh impossible.
They are important as being no later than the second century A.D.,
but they could conceivably belong to the last quarter of the 1st
century A.D.

According to M. Meg. 3:4, if the first day of the month
Adar fell on a Sabbath, they read the section in the Torah en-
titled Shekels (i.e. Ex. 30:11-16). But if the first day of
Adar was not a Sabbath, it was read on the preceding Sabbath.
On the second Sabbath they read "Remember what Amalek did" (Dt.
25:17-19), while on the third Sabbath they read the section
"The Red Heifer" (i.e. Num. 19:1-22). On the fourth Sabbath
they read "This month shall be to you" (i.e. Ex. 12:1-20).
Thereafter they reverted to the set order of the reading of the
Torah, explained by Danby (*The Mishnah*, Oxford, 1933, p. 205-
210) as the ordinary cycle of Sabbath readings from the Pentateuch. The Mishnah notes here that on the first days of the
months, at the (Feast of the) Dedication (25th. Chislev) at
Purim, on days of fasting, at the set feasts, at *Maamads*, and
on the Day of Atonement "they break off from the set order in
the reading of the Law".

M. Meg. 3:6 states: "At the (feast of the) Dedication
(they read the section) 'the Princes' (i.e. Num. 7:1-89), at
Purim, 'Then came Amalek' (Ex. 17:8-16)." In this latter
section, Joshua and Israel prevailed over Amalek as long as
Moses held up his hand (Ex. 18:11). In Ex. 17:14 Yahweh tells
Moses: "Write this for a memorial in a book, and rehearse it
in the ears of Joshua: that I will utterly blot out the remembrance of Amalek from under heaven." The reference to *a book*
was later used as an argument for the inclusion of the book of
Esther in the canon dealing, as it was supposed to do, with the
destruction of descendants of Amalek. Ex. 17:16 states: "Yahweh

has sworn:[85] Yah will have war with Amalek from generation to generation." This, presumably, gave the writer of the Book of Esther the idea of identifying Haman as an Amalekite. However, Dt. 25:17-19 read on the second Sabbath of Adar ends with the statement that when they were settled in the land of their inheritance, "You shall blot out the remembrance of Amalek from under heaven: you shall not forget." This Saul the Benjaminite (I Sam. 15:9) did forget in dealing with Agag, and so the Book of Esther shows Mordecai finishing the task. The job had to be done and done by the Jews themselves. One could argue that the Book of Esther's lack of overt mention of God or seeking God's help is an example of this. It is *not* irreligious. Only if Esther fails her people in their hour of need, will deliverance come "from another place". "Place"[86] is a metonymy for God. Mordecai (Esth. 4:14) is not so much warning Esther, as demanding that she do her duty and reassuring her that if she does her best and fails, God will help His nation.

But what grounds have we for identifying "a feast of the Jews" (Jn. 5:1) with Purim? We do not get much information from that title "a feast of the Jews". In Jn. 2:13 Passover is called "the Passover of the Jews", while in Jn. 6:4 it is called "the Passover, the feast of the Jews". Whereas Tabernacles in Jn. 7:2 is introduced thus: "Now the feast of the Jews, the Feast of Tabernacles...", in Jn. 11:55 the Passover is again called "the Passover of the Jews" though later in the same verse it is merely referred to as "the Passover". In Jn. 2:23 it is "the Passover" whereas in Jn. 2:13 it was qualified by "the feast of the Jews". Again in Jn. 12:1 it is "the Passover" whereas in Jn. 13:1 it is "the Feast of the Passover", but in both cases *without* "of the Jews". Jn. 18:28 "that they (i.e. those who took Jesus to Caiaphas) might eat the Passover" and Jn. 18:39 (Pilate speaking) "that I should release to you one at the

Passover" are likewise unqualified. One might have expected
"the Passover" in both these cases to be qualified by a
possessive pronoun, i.e. "their" and "your". Jn. 19:14 "Now
it was the Preparation of the Passover" is a temporal notation
before Jesus is led off to be crucified. It could be that the
Fourth Gospel "whose Christ is the Paschal Lamb" scrupulously
refrains from qualifying the last Passover, at least after
Jn. 11:55 so as not to give ground for any to cavil as to its
validity on sectarian grounds.

In Jn. 4:43 the Passover is called "the feast" as it is
also called in Jn. 12:12 and 12:20. In Jn. 13:29 Jesus is
reported as having said to Judas: "Buy what things we have
need of *for the feast*", i.e. the Passover. But in Jn. 7:8
Tabernacles is called "the feast" too, as also in Jn. 7:10, 11,
14, 17. One cannot go further than to say that either Passover
or Tabernacles could be called the feast. Further the Fourth
Evangelist, having made his point that the feast in question is
a feast of the Jews, can then refer to it as the feast. It is
odd, however, that in Jn. 10:22 Hanukkah is introduced merely
as "the Feast of the Dedication" without any addition such as
"of the Jews". True, it does add "at Jerusalem" which was not
put after Tabernacles when that feast was introduced in Jn. 7:2.
Now too, for the Feast of the Dedication (Hanukkah) one did not
need to go up to Jerusalem. For Passover, Pentecost, and
Tabernacles one was expected to go up to Jerusalem. Whatever
be "the unknown feast", it need not be one of the three biblical pilgrimage feasts, i.e. Passover, Pentecost and Tabernacles.
It is therefore no argument against it to say that one did not
need to go to Jerusalem at Purim. But the Fourth Gospel makes
Jesus go to Jerusalem even for the other Maccabean feast Hanukkah.
If so, he could do the same for Purim.

The Fourth Gospel gives great prominence to Passover and its season. He also includes the Feast of Tabernacles. Passover and Tabernacles were the two poles of the biblical festival year. They were not just the feasts of spring and autumn--the former with lambs and the first-fruits of the barley harvest, the latter with its sacrifices of 70 bullocks in eight days and the celebrations of the grape-gathering. We should remember that Passover recalled a national deliverance in the distant past. The other, Tabernacles, had acquired an international concern. Both Passover and Tabernacles were thought by various rabbis to be the anniversary of creation, and both looked to the end time: Passover to the coming of a national deliverer, the messiah of the stock of David; Tabernacles to the ingathering of the Gentiles and their worship of Yahweh, the God of Israel, as the One Most High God in His Temple at Jerusalem.

Actually there were probably attempts in the Maccabean times to update these two basic feasts. In the case of Tabernacles, elements were brought in which were not represented in the Torah. One thinks of the illumination[87] of the Temple and the ritual of the water-pouring.[88] This last, a mimetic rite to induce rain, may be very old. At least we can say that the connection of Tabernacles and the subsequent rains or drought is mentioned by Zech. 14:17. The three old biblical feasts were being altered in various ways. One could say that they were not the feasts of the Jews. As kept by the Jews, they were not the feasts of the Samaritans. As regards both Passover and Tabernacles, there are many differences in ritual between Jews and Samaritans. As to Tabernacles, the Samaritans know nothing of the water-pouring, rain-ensuring ritual. Yet the phrase "feasts of the Jews" is hardly used in a pejorative sense when the same Gospel writer also says (Jn. 4:22) that salvation is of the Jews. The phrase "feasts of the Jews" seems merely to describe the

feasts as those authorized by the authorities of that time.
The question is *what* time. The authorities concerned could
and did change with the times. On the face of it, the gospel
of John purports to be describing events in the ministry of
Jesus. But if we allow that he has altered the teaching of
Jesus to make it relevant to the position in which the nascent
Christian Church found itself at the end of the century, vis-a-
vis Judaism--a Judaism which itself had altered to meet changed
circumstances--then perhaps we must also allow the possibility
of the gospel writer adapting the feasts which Jesus would
attend. Basically the feasts were as they were in Maccabean
times. The term "Jew" comes to the fore with the Maccabees.
Presumably even till the ministry of Jesus, the high priests
regarded themselves as the abiding core of the Jewish people.
But, by the end of the first century, the expression "feasts
of the Jews" would have all the more the ring of authority for
that period in particular was seeking to rally the Jews and
remove schism and schismatics.

Esth. 2:5 states: "There was a certain Jew in Shushan,
the capital, whose name was Mordecai." Pirke de R. Eliezer
commenting on this says:

> Rabbi Shema'iah said: 'Was there then no other
> Jew in Shushan, the capital, except Mordecai
> alone? Lo! it is written "And the Jews that
> were in Shushan" (Esth. 9:15). But because he
> was a Jew and a direct descendant of the patri-
> archs and also of the royal seed, and he was
> engaged in (the study of) the Torah all his
> days, and he was not defiled by any forbidden
> food in his mouth, therefore was his name called
> "a Jew".'

The above shows that "Jew" was a very honourable title and
doubtless the Book of Esther, which uses the term more than any

other book of the Old Testament, held it to be such. But the
Book of Esther did not belong merely to the Maccabean Age. It
was introduced to the canon at the end of the 1st century.
Later some were to put it on the same level as the Torah itself.
Judaism was changing at the end of the 1st century. The Temple
had gone, but the feasts remained. An attempt was made to
collect priestly traditions of Temple practice but Akiba, with
his exegetical methods, could improve on tradition. And the
Law, as interpreted by him, was as it always had been or should
have been. It is in such a setting that we must see the Fourth
Gospel's references to the feasts of the Jews. If Purim only
became an (authorized) feast of the Jews by the time of Akiba,
well it had been or should have been all along. If Hanukkah
also became an (authorized) feast of the Jews only by the time
of Akiba, it ranked like Purim as part of Judaism's ancient
festival cycle. The Torah covered feasts too. Akiba knew the
Torah better than Moses. What was good Torah had always been
good Torah. The Temple was no more, but the feasts of the Jews
went on. The writer of the Fourth Gospel had to face the contrast of what he believed his Christ stood for and could offer
men with what the festivals stood for and inculcated. In a
very real way, the festivals of Judaism acted out the ideals
and hopes of the Jews in general.

CHAPTER 5

The "Unknown" Feast of John 5:1
and Esther and Purim

There are temporal indications in various parts of the
Fourth Gospel. Perhaps from the deputation of the priests and
Levites from Jerusalem Jn. 1:19ff. to the wedding at Cana (of
a maiden on a Wednesday, but of a widow on Thursday) is the
clearest example apart from the week preceding the crucifixion
and resurrection. We do know that before Passover, lambs were
selected. With the Samaritans it is on the Sabbath before Passover which is still called *Sabbath ha-Gadol* by the Jews that the
lamb is set aside. It is significant that Jesus is designated
twice by John the Baptist (Jn. 1:29 and 35) as the Lamb of God,
and then in Jn. 2:13-23 Jesus is at the Passover of the Jews
at Jerusalem. Presumably the writer of the Fourth Gospel wants
to show that Jesus is the true Paschal Lamb, and that John the
Baptist had so designated him to be the lamb before the priests.
The question is how long was the period between the designation
of Jesus as the Lamb of God and his going up to the Passover?
Four days are mentioned in Jn. 1:19-43, i.e. the priests and
Levites are coming and three 'morrow's, vv. 29, 35, 43, on the
last of which Jesus goes to Galilee. In Jn. 2:1 we have the
temporal indication: "And the third day there was a marriage
in Cana of Galilee." The plain sense of "the third day" would
be Tuesday.[89] If we then counted the time indications back
from this then John the Baptist first designated Jesus as the
Lamb of God on the Sabbath[90] (v. 29) and on a Sunday (v. 35).

It could be that the two occasions of designation are clearly marked as falling on two separate days so as: (a) to fulfill the old Jewish custom of designating the lamb for the Passover on the Sabbath before the Passover, and (b) to have John the Baptist testify to the first disciples of Jesus and possibly (cf. v. 40) to the writer of the gospel that Jesus was the Lamb of God on the Sunday the future day of the Eucharist. There would just be enough time after Tuesday (if the wedding at Galilee fell on that day) for Jesus to go (Jn. 2:12) to Capernaum ("He and his mother, and his brethren and his disciples: and there they dwelt not many days") and then go up to the Passover, if it fell at the end of the week. We should remember that the Passover Festival lasts seven days. But before he went up he had not only been designated as the true Lamb of God to the priests and Levites who had visited John, but also to two of John's disciples who had then followed him. These latter two formed the nucleus of his disciples who acknowledged his messiahship. In addition, he had manifested his glory at Cana of Galilee and had shown that the Messianic age had begun with the Marriage Feast. At the Passover at Jerusalem, he had shown that his body was the true Temple of God. During this period he had also received the approbation of Nicodemus (Jn. 3:12) as being a teacher come from God, and he had taught the necessity of baptism by water and the Spirit (Jn. 3:5) and hinted at who he was (Jn. 3:13) and his crucifixion to come (Jn. 3:14) and why he had been sent by God (Jn. 3:16). Thereafter Jesus and his disciples tarried (Jn. 3:22) at Aenon where they baptized and where again John testified of him as to his mission and who he was (Jn. 3:27-36).

No indication is given of the time Jesus spent baptizing in Judea. Jn. 4:3, 4 tells us of his resolve to go to Galilee and his going through Samaria. This seems to be the one real gap in the temporal indications of the Fourth Gospel. It could be that the Evangelist had no information for this period. Certainly he had not received any from the Synoptic Gospels which make the ministry of Jesus start only after the imprisonment of John the Baptist. On the other hand, he may have wanted to separate the Passover of Jn. 2 and the events surrounding it from the festival cycle that follows. To say this cuts across the grouping together of chapters 2, 3 and 4, all of which deal with water. But we might point out that the water symbolism in Jn. 3 and 4 is not the same. One might argue that Jn. 4 shows Jesus' acceptance by the Samaritans as over against Nicodemus' mere inquiry. This would not be fair to Nicodemus who as "a ruler of the Jews" privately testifies to Jesus' right to teach as having been sent by God and that God is with him (Jn. 3:2). No, Jn. 4 should rather be contrasted with Jn. 5. Jn. 3 is similar to Jn. 1, both having the testimonies of John the Baptist to Jesus, first to the priests and Levites and then to two of his own disciples (who became the nucleus of Jesus' disciples) and then again to his own disciples.

We could have a significant temporal indication in connection with the visit to Samaria in Jn. 4:35: "Don't you say, 'There are yet four months, and then comes the harvest'." We are aware, however, that it could be regarded as a proverbial statement. But even if it were, it does not need to be an old proverb but a proverb coined by Jesus or by the writer and put into his mouth. Even so, the relevance of "four" is odd unless it points to something. The grain harvest would end at Pentecost, having started at Passover. It seems to the present writer that the Fourth Gospel writer may well have given the time of the arrival of Jesus at Jacob's well in Sychar some special temporal significance, not only in his overall temporal sequence but also in the Samaritan festival year. Samaritans kept Passover,

Pentecost, and Tabernacles as did the Jews. He was not writing
for folk who knew only the Old Testament feasts. The fact that
he included Hanukkah shows that. But Hanukkah was a Jewish
feast. And he was not writing for Jews alone, nor even for
Christians who had been Jews. The Samaritans were an important
element in Palestine and also in the Diaspora. Now the Samaritans had two semi-feasts: the *Zimmuth Pesaḥ* and the *Zimmuth
Sukkoth*. These were important for determining respectively the
dates of their *Pesaḥ* and their *Sukkoth* which usually fell at
different dates respectively from the Passover of the Jews and
the *Sukkoth* of the Jews. The Samaritan *Zimmuth Pesaḥ* and *Zimmuth
Sukkoth* were the vernal and autumnal equinoxes or to be more
specific the conjunctions of the sun and the moon near the vernal
and autumnal equinoxes. The *Zimmuth Pesaḥ* and the *Zimmuth
Sukkoth* were each sixty days before *Pesaḥ* and *Sukkoth* respectively. They were and still are the occasions when the Samaritan
high priest issued the calendar for the ensuing six months. Now
four months before the grain harvest would bring one back to the
Zimmuth Pesaḥ. The *Zimmuth Pesaḥ* was, if anything, the more important of the two since it was understood as celebrating the
coming of Moses from Sinai after having been commissioned to redeem Israel by Yahweh at the burning bush and his meeting with
Aaron. The conjunction of the sun and moon were interpreted as
Moses meeting Aaron preparatory to their campaign that led up
to the first Passover. Jesus and the woman meet at Jacob's well.
The woman's reference to "our father Jacob" in her question (Jn.
4:12) "Are you greater than our father Jacob"[91] may well be
deliberate in order to stress that Jacob was common father of
the Jews and Samaritans. Our Lord's reference to the woman's
five husbands (Jn. 4:18) may well be an allusion to the five
heathen nations (cf. 2 Kgs. 17:24) with whom the northern
Israelites intermarried, for the woman is representative of

the Samaritans in general. The woman's statement in Jn. 4:25 "I know that Messiah cometh....When he is come, he will declare unto us all things" is not a vague statement if it is seen in the context of the *Zimmuth Pesaḥ*. The Samaritan Taheb was either a returning Moses or one like to Moses (cf. Dt. 18:18). It was at *Zimmuth Pesaḥ* that Moses had come to prepare to redeem Israel. So when Jesus said (Jn. 4:26) "I who speak to you am he", the woman was prepared to be receptive. This is an *Ego Eimi* statement. She thought that he had identified himself with the Messiah whom she mentioned. But her category of thought about him was too small. It was the Samaritans, who heard Jesus for themselves when he stayed there two days, who said (Jn. 4:42): "We believe...and know that this is indeed the Saviour of the world." The title "Saviour of the world" was given to Moses by the Samaritans.

The story of the healing of the nobleman's son (non-Jewish) who was sick at Capernaum, while Jesus (Jn. 4:46) was in Cana of Galilee, resulted in the nobleman and his whole family believing in Christ. Here we have the extension of a faith in Jesus beyond the half-Jews or Samaritans to the heathen. But until now, it is not said that the Jews, not even Nicodemus, believed in Jesus. We do not include his disciples who, after the manifestation of his glory at Cana, believed on him (Jn. 2:11) in the term "the Jews". If Nicodemus had acted on his statement (Jn. 3:2): "Rabbi we know that you are a teacher come from God", he would not have stopped there. Dt. 13:1-5 warn against the giver of signs who leads astray. Jn. 3:2 makes Nicodemus deny the Beelzebul controversy before it is raised but quite pointedly makes him refrain from proceeding to make the positive deduction that he is the one like Moses (cf. Dt. 18:18). It is left to the Samaritans to do this. Nor do we include many who "believed on his name" when he was in Jerusalem at the Passover (Jn. 2:23).

In view of the fact that the Samaritan encounter lends itself to a date sixty days before Passover, one could quite
logically expect "a feast of the Jews" practically immediately
following to be before the Jewish Passover, even allowing
that the latter tended to come before the Samaritan Passover.
If this assumption is correct, "a feast of the Jews" at this
period would be Purim. The pool with the five porches could
refer to the Law and the five volumes of the Torah. As interpreted by the rabbis, the sick, blind, halt and withered could
be those who hoped for help from it. The man who had been there
thirty-eight years is singled out as representative of Israel
in the wilderness. That he had no man to help him to the pool
underlines the lack of help given by the rabbis as doctors of
the Law. If we stress that the event took place on Purim when
Jews were accustomed to give gifts to one another and gifts to
the poor, the episode is the more significant. Even among the
sick and disabled it is everyone for himself (cf. Jn. 5:7).
"Another steps down before me." Jesus tells the infirm man to
take up his bed (*krabbatos*) and walk. In Aramaic this could be
rendered קום טול פוריא דלן וטייך. It should be noted that
פוריא means either bed or Purim. The difference is merely in
the vocalic pointing, פוריא bed or פוריא Purim. *Phoreion*
("litter") occurs in Greek. Our case for this feast being
Purim does not rest on a possible Aramaic pun on bed and Purim,
but on this Jewish feast falling between the Samaritan *Zimmuth
Pesaḥ* (cf. Jn. 4:35) and the Jewish Passover (cf. Jn. 6:4).
However if that is accepted, the possible Aramaic pun between
bed and Purim is illuminating. Purim was a nationalistic updating of the Exodus celebrating a deliverance nearer their own
times. In a way Purim was more real to the Jews than Passover
and the Exodus. It is significant that after the fall of the
Jerusalem Temple and the disastrous Roman War the Book of Esther's

admission into the canon as the inspired Word of God was
championed by no less than R. Akiba. The nationalist spirit
of the Book of Esther was further encouraged by the festival
of Purim. It was not that Purim was divorced from the Torah.
With the Torah readings about the command to exterminate
Amalek, and the statements in Esther that Haman was an Agagite and therefore descendant of Amalek, Purim and the Pentateuch were brought together for the Jew. In other words the
Jew rested on his bed at Bethesda with its five porches, but
sick as he was, he never managed to get up and reach the healing influence of the pool which was the real Torah. And yet,
though the spirit of the Book of Esther is courageous self-
help, Purim had become a palliative. Jesus does not carry
him to the pool. He tells him to get up, carry his bed, and
walk. In a way this was in the spirit of the Book of Esther
itself, i.c. it encourages self-reliance. To say this is not
to underestimate the fact that Jesus healed the man with his
very presence and word, but even he had (Jn. 5:6) to ask the
man if he wanted to be made whole. When the man gives the
excuse that somebody always gets there first, when the pool
shows healing properties, Jesus tells him to be self-reliant.
The man at Jesus' word acted in the spirit of the Book of
Esther. He became whole and immediately fell foul of the
religious authorities. "Now (Jn. 5:9) it was the Sabbath on
that day. (v. 10) So the Jews said to him that was cured, 'It
is the Sabbath and it is not lawful for you to take up your
bed'."

Purim could fall on the Sabbath (M. Meg. 1:2):

> If it [the 14th. Adar being Purim] fell on the
> Sabbath, villages read it (the *Megillath
> Esther*) earlier on the day of assembly (i.e.
> Thursday the 11th. Adar), large towns on the
> day itself, and walled cities the next day.

Massekta Soferim 17:4 says:

> If Purim falls on a Sabbath, seven read [the
> section] of the Sabbath while the eight reads
> 'Then came Amalek' (i.e. Ex. 17:8-16) which
> is read on the second Sabbath of Adar and on
> Purim itself, before the reading of the
> *Megillah.*

While Purim could fall on a Sabbath, we must admit that since
Jerusalem was a walled city the reading of the *Megillah* on the
Sabbath was postponed till the next day (cf. M. Meg. 1:2b).
Nowadays the 13th. Adar is a minor fast day called *Ta'anith
Esther.* *Massekta Soferim*, however, tells us that the three
fast days (i.e. in commemoration of the three days of fasting)
ordained by Mordecai and Esther (Esth. 4:16) are not observed
on consecutive days but are separated and observed on Monday,
Thursday and the following Monday. It adds that in the land
of Israel the rabbis had the custom of fasting after Purim, i.e.
not as others, before it, on account of the victory over Nicanor
and his associates (which occurred on the 13th. Adar, the day
before Purim [cf. I Macc. 7:49, II Macc. 15:36, Jos. Ant. XII:
407, 409] because of which feasting was prohibited) and also
since the commemoration of sad events is postponed rather than
antedated.

The *Megillah* is held in great respect. The *Megillah* (i.e.
the *Megillath Esther*, called "the *Megillah*" by the Mishnah)
Scroll is read on Purim Eve at home and at the Synagogue morning
service on Purim itself. The reading of the *Megillah* and Ps.
22 are closely associated, e.g. *We-'attah ḳadosh* ("But Thou art
holy") is said[92] after the Megillah is read (cf. Ps. 22:3). In
fact, the justification for the practice of reading the *Megillah*
both on the eve and the next morning is found in Ps. 22. R.
Joshua b. Levi said (T. B. Meg. 4a): "Every man must read the

Megillah in the night, and repeat it in the day, for it is written (Ps. 22:2): '0 my God, I cry in the daytime, but You answer not; and in the night season and I am not silent'."

There were and are special benedictions before and after reading the *Megillah* or Scroll of Esther in the Synagogue on Purim. As regards the reading of *Megillath Esther*, the *Massekta Soferim* 14:5 points out that the rabbis decreed that the benediction on the season [of Purim] must be said. And after the conclusion of the reading he who read must say, "Blessed art Thou, O Lord our God, King of the Universe: O God who dost plead our cause, judge our suit, and avenge our wrong: Who redeemest and savest us from the hands of all tyrants: Blessed art Thou, O Lord our God, Helper and Saviour." We are told that this benediction is said on account of the humiliation of the Torah, while others maintain that it is said on account of the humiliation of Israel who was affronted by Haman's plot against God's people. Instead of the Torah, another reading is *Shekinah*. The relationship between Torah, *Shekinah*, and Israel could be significant. *Massekta Soferim* (14:6) adds that the rabbis further enacted that it is also necessary to offer praise and thanksgiving for redemption and release (from threatened destruction) in the benediction. So one includes: "Blessed art Thou, O Lord, God of vengeance, Who dost requite enemies according to their deeds, but art a shield to the righteous and savest Thy people from the hands of their adversaries." After that the righteous are lauded: "Blessed be Mordecai, blessed be Esther, blessed be all Israel." *Massekta Soferim* (*ibid.*) adds that the Amora Rab (a famous Babylonian rabbinic scholar of the mid 3rd century A.D., i.e. the period of the Amoraim) however declared that one must say: "Accursed be Haman and accursed be his sons."

After the reading "Then came Amalek..." (Ex. 17:8-16) at Purim, the Scroll of the Law was put back in its place and Ps. 113:2: "Blessed be the name of the Lord from this time forth and forever" and the *Kaddish* were said (so *Massekta Soferim* 21:6). The reason given is (*ibid.*):

> Because neither on new moons, nor fast days, nor Mondays and Thursdays, nor on the inter-mediate days of a festival, nor the eight days of Hanukkah nor Purim is *Kaddish* said until after the Torah Scroll has been re-stored to its place, while the people stand and respond 'Amen, let His great name', etc. with devotion and [still] standing. Further-more you have no reading that requires a *Kaddish* before [the scroll of the Law] is put back except that of Sabbaths and festivals alone [when it is said] before the *haftarah* is read in the Prophet.

This is important for showing that according to *Massekta Soferim*, Purim did *not* rate as a full festival. However, the *Kitzur Shulḥan Aruḥ* (142:8) says:

> No labour may be performed on Purim, and who-ever performs any labour on that day will never derive any benefit from it. But it is permissible to have work done for us by a non-Jew. It is also permissible to attend to business, to write even a social letter, to make a note of debts due and to do any-thing that does not require much concentra-tion. Especially is it permissible to write something of a religious nature or do some work for the performance of a precept. For the requirements of Purim it is permissible to perform any labour.

The *Kitzur Shulḥan Aruḥ* (vol. III, ch. 98:1):

> Any work which is forbidden on the Sabbath, is
> also forbidden on a festival....The festival
> differs from the Sabbath only with regard to
> the preparation of food. As it is written
> (Ex. 12:16): 'Only that which every one must
> eat, that only may be prepared by you.' Thus
> kneading, baking, slaughtering and cooking
> are permitted on a festival. Carrying objects
> from one place to another and kindling a fire
> are also permitted on a festival, even when
> not needed for cooking but for some other
> purpose. Our sages, of blessed memory, re-
> ceived this rule by tradition that 'cer-
> tain labors are permitted for other purposes'.

This last would not apply on Purim, and yet in other respects
(see also above) Purim was not kept as strictly as the major
festivals. The reading of the *Megillah* was important. The
Midrash on Psalms, Ps. 57 on v. 3 says: "I will cry to God
Most High; to God that approves the cause I have in hand."
R. Simon taught in the name of R. Joshua ben Levi: "Concerning three things--tithes, greeting with God's name and reading
the Scroll of Esther--the Holy One, blessed be He, approved
the decree of a court on earth..." (*ibid.*, cf. also T. B. Meg.
7a).

And what is the proof that God approved the decree concerning the reading of the Scroll of Esther? It is written:
"They ordained what the Jews took upon them" (Esth. 9:27)--
that is, they decreed in heaven what the Jews took upon themselves on earth. Dr. Y. Vainstein in *The Cycle of the Jewish
Year* (Jerusalem, 1953, p. 114):

> The reading of the Torah applicable to Purim
> takes place on the 14th., and on that day
> alone *Al Hannissim* in the *Shemoneh Esreh* is

recited. The *Mishloach Manot*,[93] however, and
the *Se'udah* [i.e. the meal or dinner itself]
take place on both days (i.e. 14th and 15th
Adar). It may even happen, as in 1951, that
in Jerusalem a פורים משולש is kept, observing, on three consecutive days the different
Purim laws and customs. Thus if the 15th of
Adar falls on a Sabbat we read the *Megillah*
on Friday, the 14th (M. Meg. 1), recite *Al
Hanissim* on the 15th, and hold the festive
meal on Sunday, the 16th since the Sabbat
meals must not be mixed with the Purim *Se'udah*
(T. J. Meg. 1, 4).

This last is illustrative of the fact that technically Purim
could be on Sabbath though the actual reading of the Scroll of
Esther was on the Friday, and the Purim *Se'udah* or festive
meal was on the Sunday. Light is a characteristic of the
Purim meal and candles are lit even though the meal takes
place during the day. One is encouraged to study the Torah
for a while before commencing the feast. This practice is
based on Esth. 8:16 "the Jews had light" and the "light" is
interpreted as meaning the Torah. The *Ḳitzur Shulḥan Aruḥ*
(142:6) says:

Since the whole miracle of Purim was occasioned
through wine: Vashti met her fate at the wine
feast and Esther took the crown in her stead,
the downfall of Haman was due to wine, therefore the sages, of blessed memory, made it
obligatory on everyone to become drunk and
ordained: 'One is obliged to regale himself
on Purim, until one is unable to differentiate
between "Cursed be Haman" and "Blessed be
Mordecai".' At least to commemorate the
great miracle, one should drink more than he
is accustomed, until he falls asleep, and
while asleep, he will be unable to differentiate between 'Cursed be Haman' and 'Blessed
be Mordecai'.[94] However if one has a delicate
constitution likewise if one knows that drunk-
enness may cause him, God forbid, to slight

> some precept, a benediction or a prayer, or
> that it will lead him, God forbid, to levity,
> it is best for him not to become intoxicated
> for all our deeds must be for the sake of
> Heaven.

Nowadays it is customary on Purim night to give the half
Shekel as charity to the poor before reading the *Megillah*.
While this is not mentioned in the Book of Esther, the "sending
of portions one to another and gifts to the poor" (Esth. 9:22)
are. However, the Sabbath before the new moon of Adar is called
Shabbath Parshath Shekalim, i.e. the Sabbath of the Section of
the Shekels. This refers to the additional reading from the
Torah of the section (Ex. 30:11-16) dealing with the precept
of giving half a shekel for the Temple. It is interesting to
see how after the destruction of the Temple, old Temple dues
not only were passed on to the poor, but were now associated
with Purim celebrations.

Purim from Mishnaic and Talmudic times was a day of feasting and gladness. In addition to the special rejoicings engaged
in by the sages on Purim (cf. T. B. Meg. 7b, T. B. Pes. 68b),
there was the custom of hanging Haman in effigy. In the Middle
Ages the Church sometimes interpreted this as a scurrilious
attack on Christ. Whether this was ever intended cannot be
ascertained. What is interesting is the fact that Ps. 22, which
in all four gospels is referred to in the crucifixion narrative
and on which the Johannine version is almost a Midrash, is applied
in the Midrash on Psalms (Ps. 22) principally to Esther. In fact
it is the words from that Psalm that Jesus quoted on the cross
(Mt. 27:46; Mk. 15:34).

Esther in the Midrash on Psalms (Ps. 22:2) is called "His
(God's) Holy One" and in M. Ps. 22:3 she is called "the light of
Israel" and a darkness for Gentiles. Actually the scriptural
basis for this is Esth. 8:16. M. Ps. 22:3 says that Mordecai

and Esther were a darkness for the Gentiles, whereas they were
a light for the Jews because it is said in Esth. 8:16 that on
account of Mordecai and Esther: "the Jews had light and gladness, and joy and honour." "Light" here probably does not
refer to the Torah but to Esther while (according to M. Ps. 22)
crying out "My God, my God, why hast Thou forsaken me?" before
she went in unannounced to King Ahasuerus, reminded God that
she had kept the three precepts of the Law specifically given
to women. Yet M. Pirke de R. Eliezer (ch. L) says that when
Esther (Esth. 4:16) asked Mordecai to go and gather together
all the Jews in Susa, and fast with her for three days, that
Mordecai agreed even though it meant transgressing the Torah.
As M. Pirke de R. Eliezer says:

> These (days) were the thirteenth, the fourteenth,
> and fifteenth of Nisan. Mordecai said to her:
> 'Is not the third day (of the fast) the day of
> Passover?' (on which, like any Sabbath or festi-
> val, one was forbidden to fast). She said to
> him: 'You are the elder in Israel. If there
> be no Israel, wherefore is the Passover?' Morde-
> cai hearkened to her words and he agreed with
> her. So Mordecai transgressed [R.V. "went his
> way", but the word also means "to transgress"]
> (Esth. 4:17).

What is the meaning of the expression "So he transgressed" asks
the Midrash? M. Pirke de R. Eliezer's explanation is that he
transgressed the festivals and Sabbaths. The first editions
have "teaching that he transgressed the law of the first day of
Passover by not eating the unleavened bread, as prescribed by
the Torah" (Ex. 13:6). However the same Midrash Pirke de R.
Eliezer ends that chapter (in which the above statement is made
about Mordecai) by saying:

> Because he was a good man, a man of peace and
> seeking the peace of his people, as it is said:
> 'For Mordecai the Jew was next to King Ahasuerus,
> and great among the Jews' (Esth. 10:3) concern-
> ing him the scripture says: 'Mark the perfect
> man and behold the upright: for the latter end
> of (that) man is peace' (Ps. 37:37).

M. Ps. 22:15 commenting on the title to Ps. 22 which it understands here as: "For the leader; upon the hind of the morning",
says that the phrase (Isa. 9:2) "The people that walked in
darkness have seen a great light" applies to the generation
of Mordecai. The Midrash tells us that no day was more dark
or evil for the Jews than that referred to in Esth. 3:13 when
it was sealed (with King Ahasuerus' ring) "to destroy, to slay
and to cause to perish, all Jews, both young and old, little
children and women in one day". It was they who saw a great
light. A redeemer rose up for them and saved them. Who was he?
It was Mordecai. About him it is written: "And Mordecai went
forth from the presence of the king in royal apparel of blue and
white" (Esth. 8:15). M. Ps. 22:5, however, interprets "For the
leader; upon the hind of the dawn" on the basis of Gen. 15:12.
As in M. Gen. R. XLIV.17, this verse is seen to refer to the
various exiles which Israel will undergo. The "great darkness"
which fell on Abram is Media, which darkened the light in the
eyes of Israel, till the Holy One in the days of Esther and
Mordecai restored the light (cf. Esth. 8:16). M. Ps. 22:5 (cf.
M. Gen. R. XLIV.17) sees "fell" (i.e. a great darkness *fell*
upon him [Gen. 15:12]) as referring to Edom. But M. Ps. 22:5
states that Edom is to *fall* by the hand of Israel, when the
Holy One will give light to Israel, saying (Isa. 60:1): "Arise,
shine, for your light is come." So the title to Ps. 22 is here
made to refer to the divine deliverer. But M. Ps. 22:5b specifically states that "the hind of the dawn" in the title refers to

Esther who brought the morning forth from the darkness. M. Ps.
22:10, after identifying Esther with the dawn in Ps. 57:9,
explains why Esther was likened to the dawn. One explanation
was that when Esther ("the dawn") awakened, the stars of Haman
and his sons set. Another statement by R. Benjamin bar Japheth
(in the name of R. Eleazar, though a *non sequitur*) is worth quoting *vis-a-vis* the canon. "As the dawn ends the night, so all
miracles ended with Esther." "But," adds the Midrash, "what of
Hanukkah?" The answer is: "We speak, however, only of the
miracles which are recorded in scripture." Esther and Purim
had the advantage over both Pesaḥ on the one hand and Hanukkah
on the other. It was more up-to-date than Pesaḥ and was in the
canon of scripture whereas Hanukkah was not.

The same Midrash states three times (M. Ps. 22:6, 16 [twice])
that Esther said: "My God, my God, why hast Thou forsaken me?"
(Ps. 22:2). It was only after she cried in a loud voice: "Why
have You forsaken me?" that her cry was heard (cf. v. 6).

> *My God*, You were at the Red Sea; *my* God, You
> were at Sinai, *Why have You forsaken me?* God
> acted there for His people. He had acted for
> Sarah, who was but one night in Pharoah's house
> and 'the LORD plagued Pharoah and his house
> with great plagues because of Sarah, Abram's
> wife' (Gen. 12:17).

But she tells Him He works no miracles for her (Esther). The
Midrash (*ibid.*) notes that Esther said "My God" (*Eli*) three times
in Ps. 22 (i.e. twice in v. 2 and once in v. 11). Why three
times? By this repetition of "My God" Esther (so the Midrash
informs us) was hinting that she had kept the three laws given
to her as a woman (i.e. the three laws 1) relating to monthly
purity, 2) to the priest's portion of bread, and 3) to the lighting of the Sabbath lamp) even though she was in the house of
Ahasuerus who was a heathen.

M. Ps. 22:6 has an interesting midrash on Ps. 22:2-5a, and M. Ps. 22:18 comes back to the same theme: "My God (*Elohai*), I cry in the daytime, but You do not answer: and in the night season, and am not silent", which was the verse used as a scriptural warrant for the reading of the Scroll of Esther on both Purim Eve and the Day of Purim (see above p. 121). According to the Midrash, Esther says to God (Ps. 22:4, 5): "Our fathers trusted in You. They trusted and You delivered them. They cried to You and were delivered." She is referring to the Exodus. She tells the Holy One that He did not deal with Esther and the Jews of her day as he did with their fathers in Egypt. As soon as their fathers in bondage to the Egyptians cried, the LORD heard their cry and came down to deliver them (cf. Ex. 3: 7-8). Esther says to the LORD: "Yet which is a greater trial, this one or the one in Egypt?" And to make it perfectly clear to Him, she compares Pharoah's decree to have the first-born sons cast into the river (Ex. 1:22) with Haman's ordering the destruction of young and old, little children and women in one day (Esth. 3:13). Pharoah had a man who did not finish his work immured alive. But the man who finished his work was not ill-treated. Haman, however, gave an order "to destroy, slay and cause to perish, all Jews" (Esth. 3:13). God heard the Jews in Egypt at once when they cried out. But Esther tells God: "You do not reply" to Esther and the Jews of Shushan who had been fasting three days and praying and crying incessantly. "Well," she concludes, "assuming that there are no good deeds in us, at least deal mercifully with us for the hallowing of Your name." (So the M. Ps. 22:6 end) this is when she says: "For You are holy, O You who are enthroned upon the praises of Israel" (Ps. 22:4).

Two things are apparent: (a) that Esther acted on her own, unaided, and (b) that she and the Jews of Shushan faced a greater threat than Israel in Egypt. The deliverance she wrought with Mordecai was therefore greater than the Exodus.

Whereas M. Ps. 22:20 (cf. also v. 6) interprets Ps. 22:4, 5 as referring to the deliverance from Egypt, there is another interpretation in v. 21. There (v. 21) it is stated that "Our fathers trusted in You" (Ps. 22:4) refers directly to Mordecai and to Esther. According to this interpretation there is no reference to the Exodus. So also Ps. 22:5, "They cried to You, and were delivered", refers to Esth. 9:31 which in the Midrash reads: "to confirm these days of Purim in their appointed times, according as Mordecai the Jew and Esther the queen had enjoined them and as they had ordained for themselves and for their seed, in the matter of the fastings and their cry." Likewise, "They trusted in You" (Ps. 22:6) refers to Esther's brave statement (Esth. 4:16): "And so I go to the king, which is not according to the law." "And they were not ashamed" (Ps. 22:6) refers to Esth. 8:16: "The Jews had light and gladness, joy and honour." Compare Ps. 22:8: "All they that see me laugh me to scorn: they shoot out the lip, they shake the head" to the Midrash which refers to the sons of Haman who laughed at the Jews, scorned them, stuck out their lips at them, and shook their heads saying: "Tomorrow these will be slain or hanged." In the Synoptic pictures of the crucifixion there is the same use of Ps. 22:7 in the mocking of Jesus by the chief priests, the scribes and the elders (Mt. 27:41).

The Midrash on Ps. 22:24 applies many verses of the Psalm to Esther (e.g. v. 12): "Be not far from me; for trouble is near; for there is none to help." Esther, we are told, said this when letters were sent with the authority of King Ahasuerus "to destroy, to slay and to cause to perish all Jews" (Esth. 3: 13) and she went and stood in the inner court of the king's house (Esth. 5:1). For the Midrash Ps. 22:25 Ahasuerus is the lion of Ps. 22:14: "They gaped upon me with their mouths, as a ravening and a roaring lion." Likewise Haman's sons are the dogs that are mentioned in Ps. 22:17: "For dogs have compassed me." Of more interest to us is the fact that Ps. 22:18 ("They part my garments among them, and upon my vesture do they cast lots"), which is cited *verbatim* in the Johannine crucifixion narrative, is in the Midrash on Ps. 22 applied twice to Esther. Firstly (*ibid.* v. 7): when Esther said (Esth. 4:16) "And so I go in to the king, which is not according to the law", those belonging to the palace said: "The king will be wroth with Esther and death will be decreed for her." Then each said: "I will take Esther's garments." Another said: "I will take her ornaments", and another said: "I will take her earrings", and yet another said: "I will take her royal vesture." This, the Midrash assures us, is known from Ps. 22:18: "They part my garments among them, and upon my vesture do they cast lots." Similarly, M. Ps. 22:27 applies Ps. 22:18 to Esther, although it dresses her in a different fashion. According to it she wears armour! R. Huna explains the phrase "and cast lots upon my vesture" by saying that they cast lots for her royal cloak, because it was not fitting for commoners to use it.

The incident of the dividing of the garments and casting lots for them features in the crucifixion narrative in all four gospels, but Ps. 22:18 is cited as fulfilled only in the Fourth Gospel. This latter gospel does not, as do Matthew and Mark, cite Ps. 22:2.

We might wonder whether the Jewish interpretations of this Psalm were known to the Gospel writers? They obviously have given it an interpretation of their own. It is not really a Messianic Psalm among the rabbis, though the late Yalkut on Isa. 40 applies Ps. 22:7 to the messiah of Ephraim. Yalkut also applies Ps. 22:15 to the messiah. Simonsen (*R.E.J.* XXII, pp.

283-285) cited by Louis Ginzberg (*The Legends of the Jews*, vol. VI, pp. 272-273) explained "the typological interpretation" of Ps. 22 in the crucifixion story as due to the fact that this Psalm was recited in the Temple and Synagogue on the 14th. Nisan, the original fast of Esther,[95] substituting for the suffering of Esther the passion of Jesus, which took place on the very same day. Ginzberg rejects this hypothesis on the grounds that the day the paschal lamb was sacrificed was not a fast day but a festival day. However, one would suggest that this overlooks the fast of the first-born then (*Massekta Sopherim* 21,3). Very much later the *Shulhan Aruh* (*Orah Hayyim* 470,18) brought in a *Se'udat Mizwah* to exempt them from fasting (cf. J. Vainstein, *The Cycle of the Jewish Year*, p. 121). According to M. Pirke de R. Eliezer (ch. L), Esther's fast days were the thirteenth, fourteenth, and fifteenth of Nisan. J. Van Goudoever (*Biblical Calendars*, Leiden: Brill, 1959) points out (p. 93) that "the story which is read on 14 and 15 Adar tells how Esther saved the people in the Passover season". He remarks (p. 94) that the Esther story has the character of a Passover story telling of deliverance from death and would be for the writer a "modern" Passover story not to be read at Passover itself, but in preparation for Passover, the story itself being set in the Passover season. With Segal, he sees (p. 93) it having significance in in the system of calendar prognostication. The fundamental thing is that the Scroll of Esther had to be read one month before Passover and so, if the year was intercalated, they read the scroll not in the first of Adar but on the second of Adar. From the point of view of calendar calculation, this means that Purim stands in the same relationship to Passover among the Jews as *Zimmuth Pesah* stands to Passover among the Samaritans. It was essential for Jews as well as Samaritans to keep their respective Passovers on what was the valid date for them.

It is of interest that the Karaites observe the fast of Esther on the three days preceding Passover. And this could point to an early usage when it was celebrated in Nisan, prior to Passover. But since, as Pirke de R. Eliezer recognizes, the story told in Adar tells of her fast in Nisan there is no reason why Psalm 22 (if it was associated with the fast of Esther which was observed in Adar) could not be utilized by the early Christians in connection with the passion of Jesus in Nisan. All the more so if Purim and Passover were closely associated in the minds of the Jews.

It ought to be noted that it is not only in the Midrash on Psalms but also in T. B. Megillah 15a-15b that it is assumed that Ps. 22 is what Esther prayed before she appeared before Ahasuerus.

The Scroll of Esther (see T. B. Meg. 16b) must be written in lines as though it were the Torah. It, as well as the Torah, requires a *minyan* for its reading in Synagogue. T. J. Meg. 1, 70d states that the Hagiographa and the Prophets will pass away, and only the Torah and the *Megillath Esther* will remain. M. Mishle 9, 61 states that only Purim and the Day of Atonement will be celebrated in the world to come.[96] It is plain enough that Purim and the *Megillath Esther* could seem to rival Passover and the Law in popularity.

To return to Jn. 5 and "a feast of the Jews" which fell on a Sabbath. As we have seen, it could have been Purim and an actual Sabbath. It would be a breach of the Sabbath to carry a bed. But with Purim being a joyful, happy season and the remembrance of the salvation of the nation from death, the contrast is heightened all the more. The man has been delivered by Jesus from prostrating sickness and "the Jews" (v. 10) can only say "it is not lawful for you to take up your bed" though none had helped him to the pool of Bethesda when he was laid out on his bed. Indeed when the man told them that it was Jesus who had

made him whole, Jesus was persecuted by them for healing on
the Sabbath. Jesus' reply, "My Father works[97] even until now
and I work" (Jn. 5:17), has in view not merely God's sustain-
ing His creation on a Sabbath as well as a weekday nor His
general providence, but His delivering His people from trouble.
This is all the more apposite if the feast is Purim, a sort of
updating of Passover. The Evangelist makes his point in in-
structing us that God is Jesus' own Father by making the Jews
seize on Jesus saying "My Father". Thereafter follows a very
important doctrinal discourse on the relationship between son
and Father, Father and son, and the authority and powers of the
son. Then the witness of God the Father and of John the Baptist
(as to his mission) are adduced. But the works which he does
are greater than John's witness. Jn. 5:35 describes John the
Baptist being "the lamp that burns and shines: and you were
willing to rejoice for a season in his light". When one remembers that both Mordecai and Esther were many times called
"the light of Israel", that lights were lit during the day at
the Purim festival meals, and that Purim was a season of re-
joicing and light, one wonders if the description of John given
here is not meant to point to the season at which they were pur-
ported to have been uttered.

Likewise, in v. 39 he says: "You search the scriptures,
because you think that in them you have eternal life; these
are they which bear witness to me." "Scriptures" here should
be taken in the sense of a division of the Jewish canon, the
Kethubim, i.e. the Hagiography which includes both the Psalms
and Esther.

CHAPTER 6

The Fast of Esther,
the Death of Jesus and the Death of Haman

The writer of the Fourth Gospel is patently very interested in the Passover. He mentions it more than the other feasts (e.g. Tabernacles and Hanukkah), and he shows it against the piercing light of Jesus' presence not once but three times. He does not use and discard it but reintroduces it not once but twice. The first time, Jesus the attested lamb of God is present at the time of Passover at the Temple. The priestly suppliers of authorized sacrificial animals are too busy raising money for the upkeep of the Temple to be aware of who he is, even when he upsets their stalls and tables. And yet in Jn. 1, we know that a priestly and Levitical delegation had heard John the Baptist testify as to who he was (Jn. 1:29). Nothing is said of the Passover itself in Jn. 2, though the Temple organization which made the Passover and other sacrifices possible is clearly discredited.

The visit to the well of Sychar near Samaria takes place four months before the grain harvest. This would put it in Shebat,[98] the month in which the Samaritans celebrated their *Zimmuth Pesaḥ* which recalled the meeting of Moses (after the burning bush where he had been commissioned by God) with Aaron, the representative of the Israelites in bondage in Egypt. Moses' commission was to tell Aaron and (through him) the Israelites of the coming redemption of Israel by God. At the well of Sychar, Jesus meets the Samaritan woman who had five husbands. She is a representative of the Samaritan community whose stock and religion were anything but pure. The Samaritans did hope for the *Taheb*, the one like Moses whom God would send.[99] In so far as she could, the woman recognized Jesus, the Jew that he was, to be possibly the *Taheb*, the long expected deliverer. At least she favourably aroused the attention of the Samaritan men in Jesus; and after Jesus had stayed with them two days, they believed in him and testified that he was the Saviour of the world, a term the Samaritans applied to Moses. Since the *Taheb* was supposed to be the "One like Moses", this was tantamount to declaring him to be the Samaritan "messiah".

After a short visit to Galilee, Jesus comes to Jerusalem to a feast of the Jews. It is *not* called a Passover. Passover is mentioned in Jn. 6:4 as being "at hand" when Jesus is again back in Galilee. If we take the chapters in the order in which they occur, the unnamed feast of Jn. 5:1 is before the Passover that is "at hand" in Jn. 6. Now the Jews had a preliminary feast of deliverance one month before Passover which was Purim on the 14th. of Adar. It had the same purpose as the *Zimmuth Pesaḥ* had for the Samaritans. The Samaritan *Zimmuth Pesaḥ*, sixty days before Passover at the lunar eclipse in Shebat, determined the date of the Samaritan Passover in Nisan. The Jewish festival of Purim in Adar was important for determining the date of their Passover, the Passover of the Jews. If by the 14th. of Adar it was essential to intercalate a second month of Adar this was signified by not reading the Book of Esther at the Purim in Adar, but by putting off the reading of Esther, the essential element in Purim, for thirty days. If Esther was read, it was known that Passover would take place at the end of another thirty days. Or to put it another way, the 15th. of Nisan, on which Passover was celebrated, would occur in another thirty days. The Book of Esther is recognized to be a product of the time of the Maccabean revolt, although it tells of a deliverance of the Jews in the time of the Persian King Ahasuerus. The Book of Esther tells of the dire plight of the Jews brought about by Haman the Agagite, i.e. the descendant of Agag, the king of the Amalekites, whom Saul, son of Kish the Benjaminite, spared (but Samuel hewed him to pieces), thus breaking the divine commandment to Israel given through Moses to wage an unremitting war with the Amalekites[100] until the latter were blotted out. And so the Jews of Esther's time found themselves almost blotted out. The Book of Esther tells of Mordecai, a Jew--the son of Kish the Benjaminite--on whom the responsibility fell for the welfare of the Jews. Actually the undoubled principle character in the Book of Esther is the heroine Esther. Although she acts in co-operation with Mordecai, the latter--though he becomes close to King Ahasuerus who ruled over the Persian empire, and sees that vengeance is thoroughly exacted from Haman, his sons, his family and all his people--could not have succeeded had it not been for Esther. It is she who, having replaced Queen Vashti in Ahasuerus' affection, risked everything when Haman had already obtained King Ahasuerus' decree against the Jews. The date of this persecution in relationship to the liturgical calendar is significant. It took place in Nisan. Esther fasted three days, namely the 13th., 14th., and 15th. of Nisan,[101] before confronting Ahasuerus on the third day, as it were, in his den. It is therefore a story about a modern deliverance of the Jews which took place at the time of Passover but was celebrated in Adar a month before Passover. But the celebration of Purim and this deliverance were related to Passover in that the reading of this story determined the day (i.e. thirty days later) for the Passover of that year.

The fast on Esther originally fell on the 13th. of Nisan, but it was later moved to the 13th. of Adar. The Psalms Midrash

on Ps. 22 realizes that Mordecai, by obeying Esther's command
and example to fast on the 13th., 14th., and 15th. of Adar,
was transgressing the oral law. *We-Ya'abor*, which is translated
by the R.V. as "and Mordecai went his way", can have the meaning "and he transgressed". So Amora Rab takes it (T. B. Meg.
15a) and says: "This indicates that he made the first day of
Passover pass as a fast day." (Technically it was a transgression to fast on a festival day, though, according to oral
law, it was mandatory for the first-born to fast on the day
before Passover. However in this latter case though, the
Shulḥan Aruḥ arranged that the first-born should study a section
towards the end of a Talmudic tractate and technically complete
it, which [by rabbinic usage] demanded a religio-legal repast
thus annulling the need to fast.)

Ps. 22:2 was associated (cf. the Midrash on Psalms, M. Ps.
22:6) with Esther's fasting. Indeed it was considered to be her
prayer (cf. T. B. Meg. 15b) before venturing in to the presence
of Ahasuerus unsummoned--the penalty for which was death.

The significant point is that here, as elsewhere in the
Book of Esther, it is Esther who takes the initiative. It is
she who arranges (Esth. 5:8) the little dinner party for the
king and Haman, after the king has graciously (Esth. 5:2) received her unannounced visit. Neither the king nor Haman knew
she was Jewish, she having concealed this. The result of this
generous treatment by Haman is that he overplays his hand (Esth.
5:12ff.). At the next little dinner party, again arranged by
Esther (Esth. 5:8) for the king and Haman his prime minister,
she (Esth. 7:3, 4) elicits the king's support for herself and
her people, and, on being asked who threatens them, denounces
Haman (Esth. 7:6).

Mordecai does play an important role however because indirectly he had led to Haman's advancement (Esth. 3:1). For

when Esther had been promoted from concubinage in the king's
harem to become the queen, Mordecai (Esth. 2:18) had told
Esther of Bigthan's and Teresh's plot against the king. On
being told to the king, this had led to their replacement by
Haman. Because of his refusal to pay respect to Haman (Esth.
3:2)(which was interpreted by the rabbis[102] as a refusal to
pay him divine honours), Mordecai incurred the wrath of Haman[103]
who decided to have the Jew Mordecai done away with. But on
reflection, Haman felt it was too little to ask the king for
the death of one man, and so he asked for a decree to destroy
all the Jews in the king's domains (Esth. 3:6).

When Haman had left Queen Esther's first dinner party
for the king and himself, he had seen Mordecai in the king's
gate. Mordecai neither stood up nor moved for him. The earlier
complaint was that Mordecai did not bow down (Esth. 3:2). On
hearing of this dishonour (Esth. 5:14) to her husband whom Queen
Esther had honoured, Mordecai's wife suggested the construction
of the gallows fifty feet high to Haman. The next morning her
husband was to ask the king that Mordecai be hanged on it, then
he could go merrily in to the banquet. However, it was brought
to the king's attention that night that it was Mordecai who had
saved his life by exposing the plot against him by Haman's
predecessors (Esth. 6:1-2). The king also learned that Mordecai had been unrewarded. And irony of ironies, the king asked
Haman, who was waiting outside, what should be done to the man
whom the king intended to honour. And Haman, who was so filled
with his own importance that he forgot his intended request to
hang Mordecai and told the king how he thought the king should
reward his favourite (cf. Esth. 6:6-9). He thought that the
man whom the king would honour was none other than himself; but
he was mistaken. It was Mordecai. So Haman had to lead the
horse on which Mordecai sat in royal apparel and with a crown

on his head (Esth. 6:10-12). Before Haman is actually *elevated*
(Esth. 7:10) on the fifty cubit pole, which he had intended for
Mordecai, a beam is added in the Targum which makes the mode
of death look like a crucifixion. At Haman's death (Esth. 8:1,
2; 8:15), Mordecai is *elevated* to the office that Haman had
held, and he receives all the extra honours and more that Haman
had suggested should be given by the king to the man he intended
to honour and whom Haman had thought was himself. It is Esther
and not Mordecai who asks for and obtains the death of not only
Haman's sons but also permission for the Jews to wreak vengeance
on all Haman's supporters throughout the king's domain (Esth.
9:13), while the Jews had feasting and gladness.

Thus the Book of Esther ends with a complete reversal of
what had been planned against them and furthermore their fortunes
were improved and they (cf. Esth. 8:17) were held in fear by the
peoples of the land. Although the name of God is not mentioned
in the Book of Esther it would be wrong to say that the rabbis
were unjustified in seeing the action of the book in a religious
context. We are not assuming that Mordecai's statement to
Esther (that if she failed, help would come from another *place*)
is an implied reference to God. It all depends on what one means
by religion. If it is loyalty to the Jewish community and its
welfare, to its religious practices, or at least to something
similar (e.g. fasting), Esther is a religious book. The terms
"Jew" and the "Jews" occur with great frequency in the Book of
Esther, and this in itself would imply that they mean not only a
nationality but a religio-ethnic identity similar to what the
terms "Jew" or "Armenian" or (modern) "Assyrian" connote in Iran
for the Iranian today. The quality of an individual's actual
religious faith may not be great, but the fact that he or she is
a Jew, an Armenian, or a (modern) Assyrian means that the individual is identified with the religious beliefs and way of life

of the community concerned by the outsider. As for the individual himself—provided he has not opted out—they have an identity in the community; and at great festivals of the community they can feel that they not only have a link with its glorious political past but also a share in its spiritual and political aspirations. In such a context it is wrong to set religion over against nationalism as if they were two separate things, since at that level they are but two different emphases of the same thing, namely group survival. Mordecai's gathering of information, Esther's personal heroism and use of Mordecai's information and her ruthlessness when she succeeded are all religious acts for they were all done for the sake of the survival of her community (the Jews) and their betterment. By fasting when he did at Passover, Mordecai transgressed the Torah, just as Esther concealed the fact that she was a Jewess. But as Esther said to Mordecai, (Pirke de Rabbi Eliezer, ch. L): "If there be not Israel, wherefore is the Passover?" One is reminded of the dilemma of the Maccabees, i.e. whether to be strictly loyal to the Sabbath and let themselves be slaughtered thereon as some of the strict Hasidim had been, or, if attacked, to fight on the Sabbath. It may have been that the Book of Esther was written with such situations in mind in the time of the Maccabees. With its stress on personal initiative and self-help, the Book of Esther represents a counterblast to the apocalyptism of Daniel, which was another Maccabean book, with its total dependence on God. However, while stressing and approving of self-reliant initiative and resolve, the Book of Esther does at least indicate that neither for the righteous, and certainly *not* for the wicked, does the individual's plan prevail. Instead there is an overruling providence that shapes our ends, no matter how we rough hew them. Mordecai's first plan for personal advancement failed. He had to wait a long time for his reward, and indirectly he

nearly brought destruction on his community and himself in the
interval. Esther succeeded, but was it not because she fasted
and acted on behalf of the community of the Jews, at no thought
of cost to herself? It is probably not surprising that the
Book of Esther was later regarded as on a level with the Torah,
though only in the narrow sense of the scriptures (i.e. in the
Kethubim). Of all the biblical books only the Scroll of Esther
and the Scroll of the Torah are to survive in the world to come.
Likewise, Purim and the Day of Atonement alone of the festival
cycle are to be celebrated in the world to come.

The unnamed feast in the Fourth Gospel, coming as it does
after the Zimmuth Pesaḥ of the Samaritans at Jacob's well and
before the Passover in Galilee (cf. Jn. 6), naturally seems to
be Purim. It is possible that the half-Shekel given to the
Temple in Adar did lead to favourable regard from the Temple
authorities to this feast. Certainly later, after the Temple's
destruction, the half-Shekel is closely associated with Purim
and becomes a mandatory gift to the poor at Purim. What the
position of the Book of Esther was vis-a-vis the canon at the
time of Jesus and whether there was a public reading of it in
the synagogue worship at Purim is uncertain. It must have been
known and cherished. However when the Fourth Gospel was written,
the position of the Book of Esther and Purim were secure. We
are really concerned only with the situation at the end of the
first century. The Fourth Gospel is comparable, in one way, to
the Book of Esther. Like the Book of Esther, the Fourth Gospel
claims to be written contemporaneously with the events it describes, although it was written much later with later situations and needs in view. True, there not as long a space
of time between the Fourth Gospel and the events it describes
as between the Book of Esther and the events it describes. But
both Esther and the Fourth Gospel are tracts for their respective
times.

By the end of the first century Purim was an important feast and Esther had been hallowed by Rabbi Akiba. Not everyone had been in favour of the inclusion of Esther in the canon of holy writ, but Akiba had indeed championed it (cf. T. B. Meg. 7a). One must remember that Akiba, the great Torah scholar and father of what became the "normative Judaism" of the Mishnah, Talmud, and codes, was the champion of the Book of Esther. He was a halakic scholar and also a messianist, and his messiah was the gallant Bar Cochba. There is no contradiction here. Doubtless he saw the oral law (as developed and expounded by him) as the constitution of the Messianic Age (cf. Targum to Isaiah 53, or Targum Jerushalmi, Gen. 49, "The Blessing of Judah").

It is in the light of the Judaism of the time of Rabbi Akiba that we must interpret the Fourth Gospel. It is not merely opposed to the Law as Mark's gospel was, but I suggest that it was also opposed to the Book of Esther. It is opposed to nationalism as well as legalism in religion. The Law's divine origin as the "Word of God" is set aside in the prologue. This is in itself an answer to Akiba who held that every word of the Torah is the word of God, contradicting Rabbi Ishmael who held it was only those sections in the Torah where God spoke directly to Moses saying "Thus you shall say to the children of Israel"; Rabbi Ishmael said that all the rest were merely Moses' words. Jn. 1:17 also contradicts Rabbi Ishmael: "For the Law was given by Moses but grace and truth came by Jesus Christ." In Jn. 5: 39 Jesus says to his Jewish accusers: "Search the scriptures; for in them you think you have eternal life; and they are they which testify of Me." One need not take this as referring to the Law, although in the *Amidah* prayer (19th benediction) the Law is called "the Law of Life". Scriptures in its technical sense means the Hagiographa, the third part of the canon finalized in Akiba's time. In fact, Akiba did much to reduce the

size of the *Kethubim*. He saw to it, however, that Esther was
retained. Just what were the scriptures were a burning issue
in the last decade of the century. Though reduced, they and
the *Nebi'im* ("the Prophets") were brought into a closer relation to the Law. There seemed to be a good argument for
the inclusion of the Book of Esther because Moses had mentioned
Amalek, and Esther dealt with Haman, the Agagite and descendant
of Amalek. The Book of Esther told how, in killing Haman and
his family, etc., Esther and Mordecai carried out the divine
command in the Law to root out Amalek. Furthermore, according
to the Law (Ex. 17:14), this was to be written in a book. Since
Amalek was not extirpated in the wilderness, it could not be
the Torah that was meant by "a book". But the Book of Esther
told of Amalek's overthrow as Haman. But one might ask how
does the Book of Esther testify of Christ? One could point to
the fact that Mordecai's words to Esther that if she failed in
her brave resolve "help would come from another place", which
was interpreted by the rabbis as from God. But Esther did not
fail, nor did the Maccabees fail; but when the Fourth Gospel
was written, a quarter of a century earlier, the Zealots had
failed. The rabbinic interpretation of Mordecai's astonishing
age (i.e., 115, as implied in Esther) was that he who had seen
the First Temple was spared to help raise funds for the Second
Temple. After Herod's Temple fell in 70 A.D. whatever popular
favour the Book of Esther had enjoyed before, the new establishment represented by Gamaliel II and Akiba now gave it whole-
hearted approval. They and their colleagues are "the Jews".
This is no vague term; it is the Fourth Gospel's term for "the
establishment". It could be that he has taken it directly from
the Book of Esther, though I suspect that the Book of Esther
itself showed its own true milieu in the use of this term, the
term we find in the books of the Maccabees. The latter used

it on their coins and edicts[105] to describe their state. We
might presume that the term was used in the time of Jesus, if
we can trust the wording of the title on the cross in the
Synoptics as well as in the Fourth Gospel. We are in no doubt
that the term was used to describe the nation at the time of
Josephus' *Roman War* which was written not very long before the
Fourth Gospel. Though Paul had used the term "Israel" for the
Christian Church, it was only with the introduction of Gamaliel
II's *Birkath ha-Minim* as the 12th benediction in the *Amidah*
prayer that Christians could no longer pray with Jews. Presumably the term *"the Jews"* was used thereafter in contradiction to the Christians (who were designated in that benediction
as *Minim* and *Nozrim*, depending on whether they were of Jewish
or non-Jewish origin). There is no reason to believe that the
writer of the Fourth Gospel did not know the sectarian divisions
among the Jews in Jesus' time. By the end of the century, there
were no more Pharisees and Sadducees, nor even Beth Hillel and
Beth Shammai. Although, as we have seen above, "Pharisees" and
"Sadducees" may only have been the names which the Synoptics
and Josephus gave to the Beth Hillel and Beth Shammai. It is
not certain that anyone other than Paul the Apostle called *himself* a Pharisee. That was a nickname which Sadducees and others
called them. It is not likely that the Sadducees of the Jerusalem Temple called themselves such. After all, there were the
Essenes who called themselves the *Bene Zadok* or Zadokites, and
they were on the outside. The "in" people, the Sadducees of
the Jerusalem Temple, would be most likely to call themselves
"the Jews". After they were displaced when the Temple fell,
those of them that were left who did not go over to the Christian Church, joined the former Beth Shammai or priestly supporters of the Pharisees. Presumably they continued to call themselves "the Jews". Then, when the divisions between Beth Shammai

and Beth Hillel were controlled (cf. Tos. and M. Eduyoth),
both wings of the former Pharisaic movement could call themselves by the proud title "the Jews". However the priestly
writer of the Fourth Gospel, writing "historically" about events
ca. 30 A.D., rightly speaks of the Pharisees in contradistinc-
tion to "the Jews", i.e. the title by which the Sadducees are
referred to. Yet we must admit that when speaking of "the Jews"
he does mean not only "the establishment" when the Temple was
standing, but he projects back opinions which the new establishment held at the end of the century. The same thing is true of
his doctrine of and speeches of Jesus. He starts with the Christ
of faith, i.e. his and the Church's faith. His Christ's message
is directed to the Jews of his (the writer's) own day. He is
speaking to their Judaism. The Temple had fallen, but its
festivals went on. They had to be shown to be as finished as
the Temple where they had been celebrated. So the Temple is
discredited at the beginning of Christ's ministry so that he
could the more expeditiously discard the feasts. The Samaritans
had lost their Temple in the time of John Hyrcanus, but their
feasts still continued. They had "that mountain", i.e. Gerizim.
While dismissing their mountain, the Johannine Christ, while
saying that salvation was of the Jews, also dismisses Jerusalem
(Jn. 4:21). As long as the feasts went on, even with no Temple,
Jerusalem was central for the Jews (cf. the Shema' benedictions).
So the feasts had to go; they were not to be discredited but
transcended. The Church (at the end of the 1st century and
until the 4th or 5th centuries) kept only one feast--the Christian Passover. This was largely due to the influence of the
Fourth Gospel, for its final Passover has elements taken from
the Feast of Tabernacles and the Day of Atonement. The Church's
Passover (*Pasch*) is therefore a denationalized Passover. But by
the end of the 1st century, the saving death of Christ was

celebrated not just once a year but at least once a week. The
Tamid[106] or daily whole offering of the lamb, which had been
offered in Temple times for the sins of Israel and which could
no longer be offered under the Old Dispensation, was by the
writer of the Fourth Gospel's time merged with Christian thinking on Christ as the new Passover offering. It was not merely
a deliverance from the bondage of the Law and a forgiveness of
sins that Christ could offer, but a new life not only for Jews
but also for Gentiles. However the Jew as much as the Gentile
had to be born anew in baptism as a member of the new international community. The concept of the new convert to Judaism
being like a newborn child was not foreign to Judaism, which
demanded both baptism by total immersion as well as circumcision
for the male convert. However, there is evidence that at least
one prominent rabbi at the time of John's gospel did regard
either baptism or circumcision as sufficient in itself. In the
Fourth Gospel there is no trace of circumcision being required
for the new convert to Christ; the Pauline fight against circumcision had long been won. Emphasis on the action of the
Holy Spirit in baptism is stressed in the Fourth Gospel. The
Spirit's active presence is fundamental along with the water of
baptism. The emphasis in Johannine baptism is on the new life,
the possession of eternal life here and now, and the passage
from death to life (death being the life in which one is now).
There is no Pauline concept of entering into the death of Christ
in the Fourth Gospel, unless that be seen in the water which,
along with the blood, flowed from the dead Christ's side on the
Friday before the resurrection. In Johannine thought the death
of Christ is essential before the life (which the Christ possessed
in himself while tabernacling with men) could be made available
for mankind. Men are in reality sick, blind, deaf, and dead,
although they think they are alive. It is up to men to realize

that they are sick, blind, and dead before they are ready to
recognize Christ for what and who he is.

Jesus says in Jn. 5:39: "Search the scriptures; for in
them you think you have eternal life: and they are they which
testify of me." In what way did the Jews of the writer of the
Fourth Gospel's time think that they had eternal life in the
scriptures? It all depends on what is meant by eternal life
here. Could it be that eternal life has a different meaning
in this context than it has elsewhere in this gospel? In other
words, the Jews of that time were hardly looking for Johannine
eternal life in their scriptures. What sort of eternal life
could they be looking for in their scriptures? Does not eternal
life here mean the *'Olam ha-Ba*, the life of the age to come,
i.e. the Messianic Age? Remember Jesus is speaking to the Jews,
i.e. "the establishment" which represents the community. The
individual does not think that he has eternal life for himself
but for the community. If this feast were Purim, they would
have read the *Megillath Esther*—if not on the Sabbath then on
the preceding Thursday. They would be reliving the overthrow
of Haman the Agagite, the descendant of Amalek the age-old enemy
of the Jewish people. They would have rejoiced in how his fell
plans were overruled.[107] As God had helped Mordecai and Esther
to save the community at that time, so He will do so in the
future. Rome's yoke on the Jews would be broken, as the Messiah
Bar Cochba was to seek so bravely to do, and they would enjoy
peace and joy. Their temple could be restored; and the (divine)
service of His people Israel would become acceptable with the
fire-offerings (cf. 17th benediction of the *Shemoneh Esreh*).
But in Jn. 5:39 Jesus says: "And they [the scriptures] are
they which testify of me." If the *Megillath Esther* was the
scriptures, where does this book testify of Jesus? It could be
that the reference is to Mordecai's words to Esther that if she

failed, relief and deliverance would arise to the Jews from
another place (Esth. 4:14). Esther was the cousin of Mordecai,
and the latter was a descendant of Shimei who was a descendant
of Saul. M. Pirke de R. Eliezer (ch. 50) explains that Mordecai was called a Jew because he was a direct descendant of the
Patriarchs and also of the royal seed. Pirke de R. Eliezer
(*ibid.*) continues: "He [Mordecai] was engaged in the study of
the Torah all his days and he was not rendered unclean by any
forbidden food in his mouth, therefore was his name called 'a
Jew'."

T. B. Meg. 12b commenting on the latter part of Esth. 2:5
gives a *Baraitha* on the meaning of the statement: "Mordecai,
the son of Jair, the son of Shimei, the son of Kish."

> I say: They are all designations of Mordecai.
> 'The son of Jair' means that he enlightened
> the eyes of Israel by his prayer. 'The son
> of Shimei' describes him as the one whose prayer
> God listened to. 'The son of Kish' tells us
> that he knocked at the gates of mercy and they
> were opened to him.

In a way Mordecai was a messiah though he was not a Davidic
messiah. But was Bar Cochba of Davidic stock? Mordecai and
Esther are both called "the light of the world" in the Midrash
on Psalms Ps. 22, a phrase which Jesus applies to himself in
the Fourth Gospel. In the *Megillath Esther* we have emphasis
placed on the survival of the Jewish community.[108] We must face
it that the Jewish messianic hope was always a nationalist hope,
and the Messianic Age was to be an age such as Mordecai and Esther
seemed to usher in, or one as is depicted in the blessing of
Judah[109] in the Targums Yerushalmi and Pseudo-Jonathan.

The one thing that is certain is that the Johannine conception of the messiah and the Messianic Age was *not* that of the

Jews at the end of the first century. If the unnamed feast
was Purim, Jesus (Jn. 5:39) could be referring to the help
that was to come from another place. Did the rabbis consider
this reference to "another place" to refer to God? For Philo
ὁ τοπος, as with the Mishnaic rabbis המקום, is another name
for God.[110] To the Johannine writer Jesus was God and knowing
the meaning given to המקום he could see Jesus mentioned in
Esth. 4:14. The M. Esth. R. VIII 6 on this verse says: "And
do you imagine that the Holy One, blessed be He, will abandon
Israel? In any case He will raise up a deliverer for them, as
it says: 'Then will relief and deliverance arise to the Jews
from another place.'" But we must admit M. Esth. R. VIII 6
probably does not understand God by "place" here.

We must remember that the Psalms were in the *Kethubim*
(i.e. the scriptures) and that Ps. 22 is said to be Esther's
prayer on the third day of her fast before confronting King
Ahasuerus. In fact, as we have seen, the words "My God, God,
Why have You forsaken me?" were said by Esther according to
the Talmud and Midrash. We further saw that the Midrash on
Ps. 22 applies most of that Psalm (midrashically) to Esther
and the events in her campaign for the redemption of her people.
This Psalm is applied to Jesus in the Synoptic Gospels and also
in the Fourth Gospel.

In view of the fact that the Fourth Gospel does make use
of Ps. 22 to a considerable extent in his narrative of the
crucifixion, it is very possible that he has Ps. 22 in mind
here when he has Jesus speak at Purim to the Jews of the
scriptures as testifying of him.

Jn. 5:40: "And you will not come to me, that you might
have life." They turned instead to the *Megillath Esther* which
they read annually on Purim just as the Torah was read, and
they kept Mordecai's and Esther's injunctions, e.g. Esth. 9:20-22

and 26-29, to keep Purim. Indeed they saw to it that these
days of Purim should not fail from among the Jews, nor the
memorial of them perish from their seed. Looking to Mordecai
and Esther, they recognized them as saviours of the world and,
unlike the Samaritans, they did not see Jesus Christ as such.
The Christ says (Jn. 5:42): "But I know you, that you have not
the love of God in you." This is a weighty charge to direct
at the Jewish establishment of his day and presumably the
writer's own day. After all, twice a day a Jew recited the
Shema' (Dt. 6:4, 5), the latter verse demanding total love of
God. Jesus states in Jn. 5:43 that though he who has come "in
my Father's name" (i.e. on his authority) he is not received
by the Jews. If anyone came on his own authority they would
receive such a one. We have to remember the Purim setting.
Mordecai and Esther were not sent by God to deliver the people;
they took it on themselves. Moses had been sent of God and
Jesus (Jn. 5:37) in this encounter with "the Jews" has emphasized that he was sent of God. John the Baptist, the works
which he (Jesus) does, yes and God the Father Himself, each
and all bear witness, says Jesus, that God the Father had sent
him (Jn. 5:35-37). Jn. 5:44 does seem to be an attack on the
whole rabbinic establishment of the writer's day. It could
even be Akiba whom the writer of the Fourth Gospel has in his
sights; because, as he says, they received glory one from
another, they cannot believe in one sent from God and (cf.
v. 41) who does not accept honour from men. His claim for the
Megillath Esther having been verbally inspired had been accepted.
Or it could be that Jn. 5:44 likens the Jews who receive glory
from one of another to Haman. It was because Mordecai refused
to give the honour due to God to Haman that the latter sought
to kill Mordecai.

Jesus informs them that he will not accuse them (i.e. the Jews) to the Father. Moses, however, the one in whom they trust is the accuser. One suspects that it is suggested that Moses will accuse them because they "the Jews" had accepted the story of Mordecai and Esther and virtually put it on the same level as the Law (of Moses). But Jn. 5:46 maintains that Moses wrote about the Christ; and if "the Jews" had believed Moses (= Torah), they would then have believed in Jesus. "For Moses wrote of me" (Jn. 5:46). The argument therefore is that if they do not believe in Jesus, it is because they do not believe Moses. Jn. 5:47 asks, "But if you do not believe his writings, how shall you believe my words?" One was not to add or subtract anything from the Law and yet the *Megillath Esther* was given the honour of the Law by man's authority thereby seriously encroaching on the Torah. This being so and their apparent disbelief of the strictures against addition (and diminution) of the Torah (cf. Dt. 4:2 and Dt. 12:32), if they cannot believe Moses' writings can they be expected to believe in Christ's words (Jn. 5:47)? The argument here is not against the Law but states that the Law is being ignored in what the Johannine Christ says it wrote of him. The argument proceeds that if such people do not believe Moses' words about him, how can they believe Jesus' words. We are faced here with the fact of different exegetical methods being used by Synagogue and Church. The latter sees references to his Christ in the Torah, which are real to him; the Jew does not and does not accept the biblical findings of the Christian, and *vice-versa*. And yet the Samaritan did find a Mosaic messianic promise in Dt. 18:18. The accusation which occurs in the Synoptics against Jesus is that he is not sent by God but that he does what he does by the help of Beelzebub (Mk. 3:22, Mt. 12:24; Lk. 11:15, 18); and therefore he should be destroyed, because he led men away from the Law. This recurs in the Fourth

Gospel despite Nicodemus' (the ruler of the Jews) saying that
(Jn. 3:2): "Rabbi, we know that you are a teacher come from
God; for no man can do these miracles that you do except God
be with him." Dt. 18:20 says: "But the prophet who shall
presume to speak a word in my name which I have not commanded
him to speak...that same prophet shall die." However Nicodemus
did *not* speak for everybody. Here in Dt. 13:1-5 it is stated:

> If there arise among you a prophet, or a dreamer
> of dreams, and gives you a sign or a wonder, (2)
> and the sign or the wonder come to pass, about
> which he spoke to you, saying, 'Let us go after
> other gods, which you have not known, and let us
> serve them', (3) you shall not listen to the
> words of that prophet, or that dreamer of dreams:
> for the LORD your God is proving you to know
> whether you *love* the LORD your God with all your
> heart and with all your soul. (4) You shall walk
> after the LORD your God, and fear Him, and keep
> his commandments, and obey His voice, and you
> shall serve Him, and cleave to Him. (5) But that
> prophet, or that dreamer of dreams shall be put
> to death: because he has spoken to turn you away
> from the LORD your God, who brought you out of
> the land of Egypt, and redeemed you out of the
> house of bondage, to thrust you out of the way
> which the LORD your God commanded you to walk in:
> so shall thou put the evil away from the midst
> of you.

Here we see why the Jews (Jn. 5:8) sought the more to kill him
(Jesus) because he not only had broken the Sabbath, but he also
said that God was his Father, making himself equal with God.
We see too why Jesus (Jn. 5:42) said they had not the love of
God in them, i.e. a reference to Dt. 13:3 where the appearance
of a prophet or dreamer of dreams, who works wonders and then
leads one away from God and his commandments. It is a test of
whether they love the LORD their God with all their heart and
with all their soul. There is irony in all this for at Purim

they were displacing the Scroll of the Law's uniqueness by
bringing in the Scroll of Esther, a work which had been allowed
into the canon of holy scripture only recently. And they were
celebrating a Feast of Deliverance which, doubtless, seemed more
contemporary and real than the Passover. But Jesus had *not*
spoken to turn them away from the LORD their God who brought
them out of the land of Egypt and redeemed them out of the
house of bondage. It was rather they with their man-appointed
feast (according to the T. B. Meg. 7a afterwards ratified by
God). The writer of the Fourth Gospel shows the basic inconsistency of Jesus' opponents "the Jews" in their alleged love
of God and loyalty to His Torah. At the very time they celebrated
a man-made feast and read in public worship a Megillah of a work
whose canonicity was questioned long after by some orthodox
rabbis, they started to work towards the death of Jesus as
being disloyal to the Torah. He said that God sent him; they
determined the dates of the feasts God celebrated and decided
what books were to go into the canon; and they had God ratify
their decision. Actually the fact that the *Megillath Esther*
had been declared canonical at this time would provide encourage-
ment to the Christians to try to include their gospels in holy
writ. There was, as yet, no New Testament but just one Bible.
Esther is known as the *Megillah* ("The Scroll"). In rabbinic
sources the gospel is termed the *avengilaion*, doubtless a pun
on *Evangelion*, but it has a possible reference to the gospel as
a scroll. As we will see, Jn. 5 is not the only indication that
the writer of the Fourth Gospel knew of contemporary developments in the elevation of Purim and the *Megillath Esther*.
Actually the Fourth Gospel could not have been written earlier
than the last decade of the 1st century, since its polemic and
apologetic is geared to counter and yet take advantage of the
new development in Judaism. We should note too that in the

clash with official representatives of the Jews at Purim (cf.
John 5) and their reaction to Jesus' calling God "my Father",
their decision to get rid of Jesus on the charge of blasphemy
and leading people astray is used by the writer of the Fourth
Gospel to provide the basic starting point for the central theme
of the gospel--an exposition of the *Shema'*. Dt. 13:5, in telling how to react to the wonder worker who led one away from God
and His commandments (i.e. the Torah), said that such a man
should be killed, and in the same context (v. 3) it quoted from
the *Shema'* about *loving* God. Furthermore, it should be noted
that Purim celebrated not only the deliverance of the Jews in
Persia. It also celebrated the slaughter of not only Haman and
his sons, but of all their would be opponents--both men, women,
and children throughout Persia as requested by Esther.

Jn. 5 is important as marking the time and occasion according to the Fourth Gospel when "the Jews" first decided to slay
Jesus.

If the unnamed feast (Jn. 5) is Purim and marks a significant stage in the ministry of Jesus, and if we remember also
that Ps. 22, the Psalm which the rabbis held was about Esther
and her ordeal, seems to be drawn on to provide some of the
action and details of the crucifixion narrative, it could be
that Purim did have hitherto undreamt of importance in the eyes
of the writer of the Fourth Gospel. In other words, the decision
to slay Jesus was first expressed at Purim and when they did slay
Jesus, the details of the passion at the crucifixion fulfilled,
as it were, or so it appeared to the Fourth Gospel, the words
of Ps. 22 which were by that time associated with Esther in her
passion and work of deliverance. But the whole tone of the
Fourth Gospel and its teaching is quite contrary to Purim and
what it celebrated and glorified. But this could be the very
reason why the intended action of the Jews against Jesus is

announced at Purim and why it is carried out in a manner that recalls Purim, though it was done at Passover. For it was traditionally on Nisan that Esther fasted and on the third day she went in to see the king and was accepted. Is the third day after the crucifixion of Jesus (when he has arisen) parallel to Esther's acceptance by the king, who in this case is God?[111] She did not say (Esther 4:16): "If I perish I perish on the third day, but on the first of these days." M. Ps. 22:5 compares Esther's three day fast to Jonah being delivered after three days in the belly of the whale (Jon. 2:11) and to Hosea 6:2: "After two days He will revive us, on the third day He will raise us up, and we shall live in His sight."

We must distinguish between the form and the content of the message, and we must remember that Christianity claimed to make all things new. In the Fourth Gospel the Law is demoted, but Moses is also pointed to as writing of Jesus and testifying to him. We can expect that the *Megillath Esther* was handled in the same way. But were Purim and Esther important enough for a gospel to give such attention to? Yes, very much so by the end of the first century. In fact if "the Jews" had heeded the Fourth Gospel there would not have been the disastrous revolt suppressed by Hadrian. The Christ of the Fourth Gospel declares (Jn. 18:36) to Pilate: "My kingdom is not of this world." This was important teaching for the Jewish-Christians and other Christians who had the Synoptic Gospels to guide them and looked for the second coming and establishment of his kingdom here on earth, which was in some respects very much like that of the Jewish messianic hopes.[112] The Fourth Gospel's realized eschatology was essential if the Church was not to be dragged into following some messianic hothead or to be suspected of taking sides with such a man in a clash with

Rome. R. Akiba who championed the Book of Esther also championed Bar Cochba.

How could Esther, which was now part of holy scripture, be defused? Now the *Megillath Esther* (cf. Esth. 9:1) does stress that what had been planned by the opponents of the Jews "was turned to the contrary". When the *Megillath Esther* had become part of the canon and was therefore held to be verbally inspired by the Spirit of God it is true that it could be seen as demonstrating God's overruling providence but also the divine irony. The Fourth Gospel stresses "the fulfillment of scripture", and Esther was now scripture. John's Gospel is in fact saying that Mordecai and Esther did *not* succeed and that enlargement and deliverance *did* arise for the Jews from another place (cf. Esth. 4:14). What they stood for and how they achieved it provides no guide to the present. But the Book of Esther not once but several times insists that Purim be kept as a memorial in perpetuity year by year and that all the words "of this letter" (i.e. *Megillath Esther*) be kept. (The rabbinic ruling is that the *Megillath Esther* must be read through in its entirety twice at Purim.) According to Maimonides, Esther will be read (along with the Torah) in the Messianic Age. Esther and Purim became at least as important as Passover. The latter was predominantly a religious feast, using religion in the modern western sense of the word, but Purim was a nationalistic feast. Yet Purim was also religious in the national-religious sense. And it was just this national-religious outlook that the Fourth Gospel was out to eradicate. In short, the Fourth Gospel wanted to disengage the universalistic religious teaching in the Old Testament and Judaism from the nationalistic and to develop the universalistic. Both are there, even in Second Isaiah. The Fourth Gospel, however, teaches that religion is not dependent for its survival on the existence of any one ethnic group or holy place.

If Esther and Purim presented such a challenge to the writer
of the Fourth Gospel, we might expect to see some evidence of
this in the form as well as the teaching of this gospel. Since
Esther was now holy scripture, he would have to act cautiously
but tellingly if he was to make his point.

One notes that there are six banquets or dinner parties in
the Book of Esther. First, there is that made by Ahasuerus in
the third year of this reign for all his princes and his servants
(Esth. 1:3) at which "he showed the riches of his glorious kingdom and the honour of his excellent majesty" (Esth. 1:4) (the
nobles and the princes of the provinces being before him). Immediately following, the banquet the king gave took place (Esth.
1:5) for all the people that were present in Susa the capital,
"both great and small". It was on the last day of this second
banquet that Vashti fell from favour, and the opening was left
for Esther to fill. It was as a result of Vashti's refusal to
obey the king that letters were sent to all the provinces that
(Esth. 1:22) "every man should bear rule in his own house".
Esther, having obtained the favour of the king was made queen
instead of Vashti (Esth. 2:17). The king (v. 18) held a great
feast for all his princes and servants, i.e. Esther's banquet.
(It took place seven years after the first two banquets.) Esther
herself gave two small dinner parties in the Book of Esther.
When she was favourably received by Ahasuerus after her three
day fast, and having learned from Mordecai what Haman had the
power to do to the Jews, she requested Ahasuerus and Haman, as
a favour, to come to a dinner party given by her (Esth. 5:5).
At this "banquet of wine" (Esth. 5:6) when the king asked her
for her petition, Esther invited the king and Haman to another
banquet the following day (Esth. 5:7, 8 and Esth. 7:1-5). It
is at the second dinner party that Esther, on being asked the
same thing by the king as at the first banquet: "What is your
request? It shall be granted even to half the kingdom" (Esth.

7:2, cf. Esth. 5:8) that Esther asks for life to be given to
her and her people. "For we are sold, I and my people, are to
be destroyed, to be slain, and to be annihilated. But if we
had been sold for bondmen and bondwomen, I had held my peace,
although the adversary could not have compensated for the king's
damage" (Esth. 7:4). This emphasizes the fact that the plight
of the Jews, from which Esther delivered them, was much worse
than the Egyptian bondage from which Moses delivered them. It
could be that in the period after the first Jewish war against
the Romans that such a comparison could and would be made by
many a Jew facing the wrath of Rome. When the king asked who
was the enemy to whom she referred, she denounced Haman. The
king was aroused in wrath against Haman, but he was also doubtless chagrined because he had given Haman (Esth. 3:10) his seal
ring to carry out Haman's destruction of the Jews with his
authority.

All this happened in Nisan (Esth. 3:7), and it should be
compared with the chief priests' council with the Pharisees as
to how to get rid of Jesus (Jn. 11:47f.) and Judas' betrayal
(Jn. 18:3) of Jesus to the agents of the chief priests and
Pharisees.

Haman had lots (*purim*) cast as to the best day to ask the
king (cf. Esth. 3:7) which reminds one of the continual references
from Jn. 5ff. of the Jews' desire to kill Jesus. The king goes
out into the garden and on returning found that "Haman was fallen
on the bed whereon Esther was". This sealed Haman's fate: "So
they hanged Haman on the gallows that he had prepared for Mordecai. Then was the king's wrath pacified" (Esth. 7:10). Still
there was no feasting by the Jews until Mordecai had obtained
the king's ring and Esther had Haman's decree against the Jews
reversed. "How," she said to Ahasuerus, "can I endure to see
the evil that shall come to my people? Or how can I endure to

see the destruction of my kindred?" And so she was told:
"Do you write also for the Jews, as you please, in the king's
name and seal it with the king's ring: for the writing which
is written in the king's name, and sealed with the king's ring,
can no man reverse." So the Jews were instructed by Esther to
stand up for themselves. Mordecai went out (Esth. 9:15) from
the presence of the king in royal apparel of blue and white and
with a great crown of gold and with a garment of fine linen
purple. While "the Jews had joy and gladness, a feast and a
good day" (Esth. 8:12), many of the people of the land became
Jews for the fear of the Jews fell upon them. (Cf. the expression
in John "because of fear of the Jews", Jn. 7:13; 19:38; 20:19).
The Hebrew Book of Esther (Esth. 10:3) ends thus: "For Mordecai
the Jew was next to King Ahasuerus, and great among the Jews,
and accepted of the multitude of his brethren, seeking the wealth
of his people, and speaking peace to all his seed."

Haman was hung in Nisan.[113] How early the crucifixions of
Jesus and Haman were compared by the Jews is uncertain. Certainly
the Esther Targum Sheni makes a direct comparison by making Haman
ask for a superinscription over his gallows to say that he was
king, and an indirect comparison by saying that Haman and Ben
Pandora (i.e. Jesus) shared the same lodging.[114] The word *Talui*
("the hung one") was later applied to Jesus in Mediaeval polemic.
Talah is the word used of what was done to Haman. But the Targum
Sheni uses words which show that it regarded Haman as crucified.
The detail in Aggadat Esther that the cross was not only 50 cubits
high but also 12 cubits wide might suggest this interpretation.
The last feast mentioned in the Book of Esther is that of the Jews
which took place after wreaking vengeance on those who had hoped
to massacre them (cf. Esth. 9:17 and 18). There are six feasts
or banquets in Esther. Three are given by Ahasuerus, two by
Esther, and one held by the Jews (their Purim).

Turning to the Fourth Gospel, there is (1) the wedding feast at Cana of Galilee, (2) the feeding of the five thousand, (3) the banquet at Bethany, (4) the meal with the disciples, and (5) the post-resurrection morning meal by the lake side. Thus here we have five meals. Actually there is a sixth meal, if we include the Passover meal which those that took Jesus to Pilate ate undefiled by refusing to enter his palace. It is somewhat parallel to the feasting of the Jews when Haman's decree was superceded by that of Esther and Mordecai against his followers. Just as the fear of the Jews fell on the people then (Esth. 8:17), it fell on Jesus' disciples (Jn. 20:19) before the risen Jesus came and stood in their midst. I suggest that this parallel in the matter of these dinner parties is not accidental, but is deliberately intended to indicate the similarity and show the contrast.

CHAPTER 7

The Feasts or Banquets in the Fourth Gospel
and in the Book of Esther

Looking at the feasts or banquets in the Fourth Gospel, we
note that great prominence is given to the wedding feast at Cana
of Galilee, the fact that the mother of Jesus was there (Jn. 2:1),
and that "Jesus also was invited to the marriage with his disciples". We note that when the mother of Jesus (Jn. 2:2) pointed
out "they have no wine", that Jesus snubbed her: "Woman, what
have you to do with me? My hour is not yet come." Jesus commands
to be filled with water (Jn. 2:7) up to the brim the six water
pots of stone (Jn. 2:6) "after the manner of the purification of
the Jews" containing twenty or thirty gallons apiece. Jesus next
(Jn. 2:8) commands them: "Draw out now and take to the governor
of the feast." The governor of the feast, when he had tasted
the water that was made wine, called the bridegroom and said
(Jn. 2:10): "Every man at the beginning sets forth good wine;
and when men have well drunk then that which is worse; but you
have kept the best wine until now." Jn. 2:11 states: "This beginning of his signs did Jesus in Cana of Galilee, and manifested
forth his glory; and his disciples believed on him." If we are
right in seeing a connection and implied contrast between the
six banquets in the Fourth Gospel and the six in Esther, the
wedding feast at Cana of Galilee (Jn. 2) seems to combine features
of both of the two banquets given by Ahasuerus in Esth. 1:5 and
2:18. We note the first of these (banquets) (Esth. 1:10) seems
to have lasted seven days. This would suggest a wedding feast
which lasted seven days. It is in connection with this feast that

Queen Vashti is mentioned, and because she disobeys his command, the law is promulgated that every man should bear rule in his own house (cf. Esth. 1:22). It is possible that Jesus' curt words to his mother are meant to recall this rule and make the reader think of the situation (familiar to all Jews who read or heard the *Megillath Esther* read every year) where it occurred.

We note that the Fourth Gospel is, however, careful to point out that the mother of Jesus said to the servants (Jn. 2:5): "Do whatever he tells you." In the Johannine account of the sign at the wedding feast at Cana of Galilee, the rather inexplicable detail about the water pots after the manner of the purification of the Jews may find explanation also if we see it as alluding to Esth. 1:8: "And the drinking was according to the law." The rabbis had been at pains to find evidence that the *Megillath Esther* was in conformity to the Law.[115] This verse (Esth. 1:8) is expounded in the Midrash on Psalms (Ps. 22) as showing that the Jews in Shushan kept the Law even at this banquet. The Fourth Gospel, in its story of the water made wine shows that the water which was made wine came from waterpots for Jewish purification. The resultant wine was truly kosher, like that drunk at the feast in Esth. 1:7. Esth. 2:8 is the feast King Ahasuerus gave for Queen Esther. Josephus calls it a wedding feast. It would appear that the Fourth Gospel brings the two wedding feasts in Esther together. If Esth. 1:5ff. is a wedding feast for Queen Vashti it is also the occasion of her dismissal. Yet it set in motion the train of events which led to the second wedding feast, that of Queen Esther. Esther is at least related to Vashti in that she is her successor in office as queen and as wife of the king. The wedding feast at Cana also deals with the motif "out with the old, in with the new". Who is the mother of Jesus? In the Fourth Gospel her name is *not* mentioned either here or at the cross. The mother of Jesus here in Jn. 2 typifies Judaism; the Synagogue, which was Jesus' mother [Church], like Vashti is set aside and her authority over Jesus and his disciples is taken away.

The governor of the wedding feast is not Jesus. Is he the bridegroom? Ideally yes, if the Church which includes his mother and disciples are his Bride. The immense quantities of fine wine produced when the water from the purification jars was turned to wine may remind one of Esth. 1:7: "and royal wine in abundance". This does not necessarily preclude the interpretation of the marriage feast as looking forward to the Messianic Age when wine, like all other good things, will be in super-abundance. But is this not precisely the messianic speculation that the Fourth Gospel is trying to avoid? Rather this is the marriage of the Lamb and his Church.

But it can also be a reference to the great King Ahasuerus' marriage feasts in Esth. 1:5 and 2:18 at which that king (Esth. 1:7) gave them royal wine in abundance to drink in fine vessels of gold (the vessels being diverse one from another). But even he, as rich and powerful as he was, could not make his wine out of water. In this way the disciples could see Jesus as manifesting his glory greater than Ahasuerus, the great king whose wealth and riches and power were described in the *Megillath Esther*. If we see the wedding feast in relation to Ahasuerus' feasts in Esth. 1:5 and 2:18, we have something with which to compare it and something which the writer of the Fourth Gospel wanted to bring to his readers' minds. They (the latter) often knew the *Megillath Esther* by heart. The Mishnah (Meg. 2:1) stresses that it is not enough to recite the Book of Esther; one must read it. It could be read either in Hebrew or Greek to fulfill one's religious duty. This being true, any verbal similarities in the LXX Esther and the Greek of the Fourth Gospel are indeed

significant, e.g. "for fear of the Jews"[116] in the Fourth Gospel
(Jn. 7:13; 19:38; 20:19; cf. LXX Esth. 8:17; 9:2).

The feeding of the five thousand, the second feast in the
Fourth Gospel, could be parallel to the first feast of Ahasuerus
(Esth. 1:4). Jn. 6 is a continuation of the manifestation of
his glory begun in Jn. 2, but now it is *not only* to the disciples.
When the five thousand had been fed we are told (Jn. 6:14-15):
"When the men saw the sign which he [Jesus] did, they said, 'This
is of a truth the prophet who is to come into the world.' When
Jesus therefore perceived that they were about to come and take
him by force, to make him king, he departed again into a mountain
alone." "The prophet that should come into the world" is the
prophet like Moses (cf. Dt. 18:18), i.e. the Messiah. Note that
in Jn. 6:15 it is indicated that the common concept of messiahship was kingship, and that Jesus rejected such a concept. In
other words, the Jewish and Samaritan concept of the Messiah as
a King was *not* according to the mind of Christ and therefore
should not be held by the Church. On the other hand the miracle
of the feeding of the five thousand was a sign which showed that
Jesus was greater than even Ahasuerus, who was famed for his
feasts. Ahasuerus could not feed five thousand with five barley
loaves and two small fishes or feed that number all at once. It
even took one hundred and eighty days to feed his princes and
servants (cf. Esth. 1:5). After the feeding of the five thousand
those present wanted to make him King.[117] To demonstrate that
Jesus is above anything they could have hoped for, the writer
of the Fourth Gospel shows Jesus walking a storm-tossed sea
(Jn. 6:18, 19). Ahasuerus or anybody that shared half his kingdom with him (like Mordecai) just was *not* in this class. When
the multitude find Jesus again, Jesus tells them (Jn. 6:26):
"Verily, verily, I say to you, you seek me, not because you saw
signs, but because you ate of the loaves and were filled. Work

not for the food which perishes, but for the food which abides
to eternal life, which the son of man shall give to you; for
him the Father even God has sealed." "The food which abides"
is his doctrine, his words. His words are approved by God in
this gospel; this is a claim not only for the acceptance of
Christ's words as given here but also for the canonicity of
their gospel. It is a claim that God and not men have approved
it. This could be casting a sidelong glance at the *Megillath
Esther* which is not only materialistic but became holy scripture
by the decision of men. When they ask (Jn. 6:28): "What must
we do, that we may do the works of God?" Jesus' answer is (Jn.
6:29): "This is the work of God that you believe on Him whom
He has sent (i.e. Jesus)." "Work" can mean worship as well as
labour. This is tantamount to having them ask "How can we
worship God properly?", and Jesus answering "Your worship of
God is in believing on him whom He has sent." Jn. 6:27 then
becomes: "Do not worship God for material ends but to understand and inwardly digest the doctrine which the son of man
gives." Then they (Jn. 6:30) asked him what sign he did "that
we may see and believe you". This provides the occasion for
explaining the sign of the feeding in relation to him as he
really is and *not just* as the prophet that was to come into the
world (cf. Jn. 6:14). There follows the catechetical sacramental
discourse of the body and the blood, just as the sacramental discourse on baptism to Nicodemus is given in the Passover setting
at Jerusalem. We must remember that the Passover is at hand
here in Jn. 6:4. Since the early Church, the time for baptism
was Easter eve, and the First Communion followed on Easter
Sunday itself. It is indeed fitting that such catechetical instruction is given in the Fourth Gospel in a Passover setting.

Following the discourses in Jn. 6, it is stated (v. 60)
that many of his disciples not only found it hard to accept but

(v. 64) that Jesus himself told them that some of them did not believe. He insists (v. 63) that his doctrine (words) is spirit and life. This is clearly a claim for canonicity. Jn. 6:64 states that Jesus knew[118] from the beginning who they were that did not believe and who it was that should betray him. In Jn. 6:70, on being assured by Simon Peter who was acting as a spokesman of the twelve:

> 'We have believed and known that you are the Holy One[119] of God.' Jesus answered, 'Did not I choose you the twelve and one of you is a devil?' (71) Now he spoke of Judas the son of Simon Iscariot, for he it was that should betray him, being [one] of the twelve.

Jesus' doctrine[120] not only causes division, as later among the people (Jn. 7:43), but also offence here among his disciples. But Judas is in a different category. Judas, in the Fourth Gospel, the son of Simon Iscariot, seems to be the equivalent of Haman in the Book of Esther. This view is strengthened by the singling out of Haman early in the Book of Esther (Esth. 3:1) and of Judas early in the Fourth Gospel (Jn. 6:71). In the Book of Esther King Ahasuerus learned from Esther (who had been informed by Mordecai) of a plot by Bigthan and Teresh, the king's chamberlains, on his life. This leads to Haman being brought into the narrative, apparently as a new chamberlain.

Between this second banquet (Jn. 6) and the third which is at Bethany (Jn. 12:1), Jesus is at first in Galilee (Jn. 7:1) "for he would not go about in Judea, because the Jews sought to kill him". In Jn. 5:16 it is in Jerusalem that the Jews first persecuted him, then in Jn. 5:18 it is stated that the Jews sought the more to kill him. Here in Jn. 7 Jesus is still in Galilee where he was after the Purim Feast (cf. Jn. 5), and the Evangelist takes the opportunity of reminding the reader why:

"because the Jews sought to kill him". Judas the son of Simon
Iscariot, "the one who is a devil" (Jn. 6:70), would betray
him (Jn. 6:71), but the gospel writer is pointing out that it
was the Jews who sought to kill him. The statement in Jn. 7:1
also explains why Jesus had not gone up to Jerusalem for the
Passover and did not seem to be going up to the Feast of Tabernacles. His reply to his brothers who urged him "to manifest
himself" to the world gives Jesus the opportunity of saying
"My time is not yet come" and in Jn. 7:8: "I go not up yet unto
the feast: because my time is not yet fulfilled." The mention
of his "hour" or his "time" which occurs in John is in clear
contrast to that reference in Esther about Haman who had lots
cast as to when to approach King Ahasuerus to get his assent
"to destroy all the Jews that were throughout the whole kingdom
of Ahasuerus, even the people of Mordecai" (cf. Esth. 3:6, 7).
Jesus' hour is determined according to the will of God with
which he agrees entirely. However the references are to the
Jews seeking to kill him, to stone him (Jn. 10:31), or to take
him (Jn. 10:39); and they could not. His enemies cannot lay
hands on him; as often as they set about to arrest him (Jn.
7:30, 44; 8:20, 59; 10:39; 12:36), or seek to slay him (5:16-18;
7:25, 32; cf. 7:19; 8:37, 40). The attempt fails (or when [Jn.
7:30] they sought therefore to take him, and no man laid his
hand on him because his hour was not yet come). Such references
are reminiscent of Haman's having lots cast before him (e.g.
Esth. 3:7; 9:24) as to when to take action against the Jews.
But here in John the hour is not astrologically determined; instead the Jews were powerless until his hour had come, i.e. it
was approved by the divine will of God. But the irony was that
his crucifixion was his glorification and he rose again. They
could not kill him. Jn. 7 shows the Jews seeking him at the
Feast (of Tabernacles), and at the same time it brings out the

fact that the multitude were divided, some in favour of Jesus
(Jn. 7:12): "Some said, 'He is a good man', but others said,
'Not so, but he is leading the multitude astray.'" Jn. 7:13
is important: "Nevertheless no man spoke openly of him for
fear of the Jews." This phrase occurs again in Jn. 20:19 on
the resurrection day "when the doors were shut where the disciples were, for fear of the Jews". It is all the more significant since the Greek here is exactly the same as the phrase in
LXX Esth. 9:2.

Although Jesus himself went up to the feast "not publicly,
but as it were in secret" (Jn. 7:10), he went into the Temple
and taught at the feast. The Jews marvelled because he had not
gone through their schools. Jesus' answer is that the teaching
is not his, but that of Him (God) who sent him. Then he explicitly states that one cannot understand that teaching unless one
wants to do the will of God. Thereafter he is making the same
charge as in Jn. 5:44 that "the Jews" seek their own and not
God's glory and that this makes it impossible for them to recognize that he is from God. The discourse in the Temple (Jn. 7)
is really a continuation of the defence of his action (Jn. 5)
by curing a man on the Sabbath when he was last at Jerusalem (at
Purim). For his part he says (Jn. 7:19) though Moses gave them
the Law, none of them keep it, and then he asks: "Why do you
seek to kill me?" Note it is the *multitude* here that answer
(Jn. 7:20): "You have a devil: who seeks to kill you?" This
I take to mean that the multitude (up for the feast) at this
stage do not know that "the Jews" were seeking to kill him and
are suggesting their own interpretation. In Jn. 7:21 Jesus
persists in directing their attention to the work which He had
done at Purim--it being a Sabbath (cf. Jn. 5:9, 10) which had
been the start of the Jews' persecution of him. It is apparent
that in John there is a reiterated insistence that Jesus has a

devil. The Jews (the establishment) held (Jn. 5) that he ought
to be killed because he broke the Sabbath Law and made himself
equal with God. According to the Law (Dt. 13:3) it would be
their way of showing their love of God. Here (Jn. 7) the
people say he has a devil. This is reiterated again in Jn.
8:48. It may serve two purposes. Already in Jn. 2 Jesus speaks
of his body as the Temple. The people say he has a devil. Does
this point to how the writer of the Fourth Gospel understood the
divinity in the man Jesus, i.e. that it possessed him like demon
possession? But, and this is the gospel's purpose in mentioning
those who called the Spirit (cf. God is a spirit) that possessed
him a demon, they who did so showed that their idea of God was
all wrong, and they were self-condemned. It was part of the
judging of themselves. All their values and attitudes are therefore wrong. One is not told much about the man Jesus in the
Fourth Gospel. But he is a real man. He has a mother (cf. Jn.
2:1, 3, 4, 5) whose name is not given. The Jews (Jn. 6:4) murmured concerning him because he said: "I am the bread which came
down out of heaven." They went on to say (Jn. 6:42): "Is not
this Jesus, the son of Joseph, whose father and mother we know?
How does he now say, 'I am come down out of heaven'?" In short,
they refused to accept the reality of God dwelling in Jesus and
totally possessing him. What applied to him is the saying in
the Epistle to the Colossians (2:9) that the whole fullness of
the Godhead bodily dwelt in him. And yet when an O.T. prophet
spoke, it was recognized that it was not he who spoke but the
Spirit of God in and through him. But the prophetic Spirit of
God only came on a prophet from time to time. With Moses the
Spirit of God had apparently continued, and God could take the
Spirit of prophecy that was on Moses and give it to the seventy
elders. John the Baptist (Jn. 1:32, 33) bore witness (presumably to the priestly and Levitical emissaries of the Jews)

that the Spirit descended on Jesus and abode in him, and (Jn. 3:34) that God had sent him, that he always spoke the words of God, for God had not given him the Spirit by measure. Philip (Jn. 1:45) could say to Nathaniel: "We have found him of whom Moses in the Law and the prophets did write, Jesus of Nazareth, the son of Joseph." The fact that he could call him "the son of Joseph" did not deter him. Perhaps (cf. Jn. 1:41) something like Andrew's words to Simon were in his mind: "We have found the Messiah (which is, being interpreted, Christ)." Jesus' words to Nathaniel ([Jn. 1:48]: "Before Philip called you, when you were under the fig tree, I saw you") is a claim to have been co-existent with Adam who was shown all his seed (cf. M. Gen. R. XXIV, 2). Incidentally, Adam is said to have seen Akiba.[121] Nathaniel's response: "Rabbi, you are the Son of God; you are King of Israel" could be merely a recognition that he was a messiah such as the one the Jews hoped for but it could imply a different sort of belief in the messiah--a pre-existent messiah. Jesus (Jn. 1:51) affirms to Nathaniel in a "verily, verily" pronouncement: "You shall see the heavens opened and the angels of God ascending and descending upon the Son of Man." The Targum (Jerushalmi, Gen. 28) tells us that Jacob was the *Ish Tam*[122] (Gen. 23:27), the perfect man, when he slept at Bethel and saw the heavens opened and the ladder on which the angels were ascending and descending. The angel in groups of angels pointed out that Jacob was like the one whose image was on the throne, i.e. the man on the throne-chariot of God, the image of God. If Nathaniel's eyes were opened, he would now see that Jesus, this son of the perfect man[123] Jacob, is the image of God in whose likeness Adam and Jacob were made. He is the Son of God but in a different way from the way Israel were sons of God and their representative the messianic king was the Son of God. This Nathaniel had yet to learn.

What is clear is that the Fourth Gospel does not deny the humanity of Jesus, e.g. he can weep (Jn. 11:35). The Jews who are always represented in this gospel as understanding Jesus wrongly say it was for the love of Lazarus. But (cf. Jn. 11:33) he is moved with indignation in the spirit, because he saw Mary and the Jews weeping. The tears of Jesus were caused by his anger at their unbelief in his miraculous powers (cf. v. 38 where the Jews ask: "Could not this man...have caused that this man [i.e. Lazarus] also should not die?"). He can thirst (Jn. 19:28), and be weary with his journey (Jn. 4:6). He is a real man with the feelings and passions of men. He had a father, a mother, and brothers (Jn. 7:3). But the latter (Jn. 7:5) "did not believe on him". Out of the Marcan Beelzebub controversy (which the Fourth Gospel does not gloss over but heightens) the Fourth Gospel in its typical manner is using the objections of antagonists to advance the argument, pass judgment on themselves, and inadvertently testify to the Christ.

The odd thing is that when the multitude (Jn. 7:20) say "You have a devil", Jesus ignores it and continues to hark back to the healing on the Sabbath in Jn. 5. Circumcision is not primarily of Moses, but goes back long before the Law to Abraham. The Sabbath laws derive their authority from the Mosaic Law and yet circumcision can override the Sabbath Law. He dwells on the clash between circumcision occurring on a Sabbath and the prohibition of any labour on a Sabbath, and he points out that the Sabbath can be pushed aside for circumcision. Actually this practice only occurred late in the 1st century[124] which in itself helps to date the gospel. He then argues that if they allow circumcision (which takes something away from a male) to override the Sabbath, why are they angry with him because he made a man completely *whole* on the Sabbath.

Then (Jn. 7:25) some "of them of Jerusalem ask, 'Is not this he whom they seek to kill?'". The further question is asked that since they say nothing to him against his teaching publicly in the Temple, can it be that "the rulers" actually know that this is the Christ (Jn. 7:26)? The Evangelist is thus subtly reminding one that in the first chapter of the gospel the representatives of the Jews had had the testimony of John the Baptist that Jesus was the Son of God or the Christ, but it was not what they expected. And yet (Jn. 7:27), they thought, since they knew all about "this man" Jesus, he could not be the Christ for that reason. Here they object because "when Christ comes, no one will know where he is from",[126] though in Jn. 7:42 some of the multitude hold the contrary view:[127] "The Christ comes of the seed of David and from Beth-lehem, the village where David was." These are *not* inconsistencies of the writer but lifelike *touches* reflecting two varieties of messianism. However Jn. 7:28, 29 takes up the point of their knowing where this man is from. For Jesus teaching in the Temple had called out: "You both know me, and know where I am from; and I am not come of myself, but He who sent me is true, whom you know not. (29) I know Him; because I am from Him, and He sent me." This is the sort of statement that Theodore of Mopsuestia, in his *Catechetical Lectures*,[128] delighted in saying was the man Jesus speaking, i.e. the man who was assumed as the Temple in which God the Word and God the Son tabernacled. I do not think it is possible to go through the Fourth Gospel saying--this is God the Word speaking, but that is the man Jesus, the man assumed speaking. Such a method is even impossible with the written prophets. Akiba was right not to follow Ishmael in differentiating some parts as the Word of God and the rest as the word of Moses in the Torah. It was all the Word of God. So too in the Fourth Gospel it is all the

Word or discourse of God, and the Christ who speaks in its
pages is one Christ. John the Baptist bore witness to the
Spirit descending and abiding upon him, a sign which God had
assured John would denote the Son of God. But it is as the
Son of God, the Lamb of God, and the Son of Man that he appears
in the pages of the gospel. It would be wrong to say there is
a Chalcedonian formulation in the Fourth Gospel, or even the
proto-Nestorianism of Theodore of two separate natures making
one *Prosopon*. The Fourth Gospel writer does not think in such
categories. He has clearly indicated that God the Word is in
the man Jesus, as Yahweh's *Shekinah* used to be in the Temple,
which truly makes that Temple the Temple of Yahweh. But by the
declarations Christ makes regarding himself and frequent references back to the witness of John the Baptist, emphasized with
the response of the Jews (from Jn. 5 on) that he makes himself
the equal of God, the intimate relation of Jesus to God is
clearly shown to be the burning issue in the Fourth Gospel.
His humanity is not denied, his divinity is proclaimed. By
their reacting against it, the Jews judge themselves and help
the reader stage by stage to see more clearly the essential relationship of Jesus Christ to God. In Jn. 7:31 "many of the
multitude believed on him" and asked: "When the Christ shall
come, will he do more signs than those which this mas has done?"
But many also had believed on his name at the first Passover in
Jerusalem (cf. Jn. 2:23).

It was obviously an imperfect belief, but it moved the
chief priests and pharisees to send officers to take him (Jn.
7:32). Jesus' statement (Jn. 7:33, 34) "Yet a little while am
I with you and then I go to Him Who sent me. (34) You shall
seek me and shall not find me: and where I am, you cannot come"
is misunderstood by the Jews. But the writer of the Fourth
Gospel makes the Jews unwittingly point to the future extension
of Christianity among the heathen world. The writer of the

Fourth Gospel has thus indirectly brought in the universalistic
note which from the time of Zech. 14 had been associated with
the Feast of Tabernacles in the messianic time. Jesus had (Jn.
7:33, 34) been alluding to his crucifixion and glorification.
In Jn. 7:36 the Jews take up the latter part (cf. Jn. 7:34):
"You shall seek me and shall not find me; and where I am you
cannot come." The Evangelist is making them, unbeknown to themselves, highlight the fact that they will have no part of him
(cf. Jn. 8:21) nor share in what he has to offer (cf. Jn. 7:39).
At the water-pouring ritual on the last day of the Feast of
Tabernacles when the water from Siloam and the wine were simul-
taneously poured through the two silver funnels at the end of
the altar, Jesus (Jn. 7:37) again makes the offer he had made
to the Samaritan woman at Jacob's well. But he goes further
here. He who believes on him could also provide living water
(cf. prologue Jn. 1:16). "For of his fullness we all received
and grace for grace." This (Jn. 7:39), we are told, was the
gift of the Spirit which those that believed on him were to
receive. For the Spirit was not yet given, because Jesus was
not yet glorified (Jn. 20:22). His glorification was his crucifixion (cf. also the breathing on the disciples and saying to
them, on the Easter Sunday evening [Jn. 20:19], after giving
the disciples his peace [Jn. 19:20]: "Receive the Holy Ghost
[Jn. 20:23]; whosesoever sins you forgive, they are forgiven
them; whosesoever sins you retain, they are retained.").

As a result of Jesus' words at the water-pouring at the
feast there is a division among the multitude. Some asserted
that he was "the prophet" (cf. Dt. 18:18, i.e. like to Moses)
and was therefore really sent by God. To the Samaritans this
had a definite messianic connotation. Others said he was the
Christ, meaning a Davidic messiah, and questioned his qualifications as to genealogy and place of birth. Some of the multi-

tude would have taken him, but none did. The officers sent by the chief priests and Pharisees returned without him, but they praised him. The Pharisees (Jn. 7:47) were worried by their apparent defection and comforted themselves by asking what they thought was a rhetorical question (Jn. 7:49): "Have any of the rulers or the Pharisees believed on him?", self-righteously stating (Jn. 7:49): "But this multitude [some of whom believed in Jesus] who know not the law are accursed." It is ironical, and deliberately so, that Nicodemus, a ruler of the Jews and a Pharisee (whom the reader of the gospel knows had come to Jesus secretly but is now reminded of this explicitly), shows that the Pharisees have prejudged Jesus, which was contrary to the Law. "The rulers" (cf. Jn. 7:48) were members of the high priest's temple council of which Nicodemus himself was a member.[129] The Pharisees presumably are Shammaites and like Nicodemus they are priestly members of that party. Both the chief priests, rulers, and the priestly Pharisees (Jn. 7) would constitute "the Jews", i.e. the establishment. One is aware that Jn. 8:1-11 is usually omitted as a later insertion. Some such encounter narrative is required here. There is a real hiatus between Jn. 7:53 and Jn. 8:12. The pericope of the woman taken in adultery *is* relevant. The Pharisees had said (Jn. 7:49): "This multitude who know not the law are accursed." Nicodemus shows them they do not know their Law so well. In the encounter narrative (Jn. 8:1-11), Jesus is teaching in the temple. The scribes and the Pharisees bring a woman to him taken in the very act of adultery. Then they quote the Law (Lev. 20:10 and Dt. 22:22, 24) at him to test him and trap him. Jesus is silent, stoops, and writes with his finger on the ground. When they continued asking, he got up and said to them: "He who is without sin among you, let him first cast a stone at her." Again (v. 8) he stooped down and with his finger

wrote on the ground. Then one by one from the eldest they all
went away. Jesus said to the woman, "Where are they? Did no
man condemn you?" And she said, "No man, Lord." And Jesus
said, "Neither do I condemn you: go your way; from henceforth
sin no more." This last phrase, "sin no more", is what Jesus
said to the paralytic whom he had healed on the Sabbath (Jn.
5:14). The style of the story, like that of the Synoptics,
is reminiscent of the Marcan encounter narrative in the Passion
week when he was teaching in the Temple. The story, however,
is frankly improbable. One can hardly expect an adulterous
woman to be stoned in the Temple. The story is parallel to
that of the Samaritan woman at Jacob's well. She, who had had
five husbands, represented the Samaritan mixed Israelite stock
who were supposed, according to II Kings 17:23, to have feared
the Lord and served their own gods, after the manner of the
nations from whom they had been carried away. Ezek. 16 likewise describes Jerusalem as of mixed stock and, despite what
Yahweh did for her, she also played the harlot. In Ezek. 16:46
Jerusalem's elder sister is Samaria, which had not committed
half of her (Jerusalem's) sins. Yet (v. 60), God will remember
his covenant with her in the days of her youth and He will
establish an everlasting covenant for her (cf. also v. 62, 63:
"And I will establish my covenant with you: and you shall know
that I am the LORD: (63) that you may remember and be confound-
ed and never open your mouth any more, because of your shame:
when I have forgiven you all that you have done, says the LORD
God.").

In Ezek. 16:44 we are told: "Everyone that uses proverbs
shall use this proverb about you, saying, 'As is the mother,
so is her daughter.'" It is possible the woman is Jerusalem
or the Jewish people. The implied accusation against the
accusing elders is that they have set a bad example. But one

wonders, if we allow that the Fourth Gospel is an attack on
the values of the Book of Esther, whether the woman taken in
the very act of adultery is not also symbolically Esther who
went to great lengths for her people. When she had denounced
Haman at her second dinner party (at which the king and Haman
were Esther's guests), this somewhat embarrassed the king who
went out into the garden. Haman, on his return, was caught in
a compromising situation on Esther's bed. The T. B. Meg. 13b
assures one that an angel had pushed him. This settled Haman's
fate. The case of the adulterous woman (in Jn. 8:6) is intended
to trap Jesus. In later times, Jesus was equated with Haman.
The tables may be turned here. Did he write two names, Esther
then Haman? Appearances could be deceptive here.

In Jn. 8:12 Jesus calls himself the light of the world.
One could say that this reference to light fits in with Tabernacles' illuminations. But in the Midrash Psalms (on Ps. 22:
2, 3) Mordecai and Esther alike are called the light of the
world. This is not to say that Jesus is a Mordecai. No, for
the burden of the complaint against the *Megillath Esther* would
be that nationalism and the promise of material reward bring
bitterness and disappointment. In the long run Mordecai was
anything but the light of the world for the Jews. This claim
of Jesus to be the light of the world is a divine claim. It
was YHWH that was the fountain[130] of life, and it is in His
light that we shall see life. The writer of the Fourth Gospel
is contrasting Jesus' code of life, not with that of Mordecai,
but with those of his own day who glorified Purim and the Book
of Esther and what they stood for.

In Jn. 8:13 the Pharisees are specified as saying: "You
bear witness of yourself; your witness is not true." This
specifically takes up the statement of Jesus in Jn. 5:31 where
he says: "If I bear witness of myself, my witness is not true."

He then (in Jn. 5) goes on to remind them that they had sent
John the Baptist and that he had witnessed to the truth. It
seems then as if the Pharisees have trapped him. However in
Jn. 5:34, Jesus then adds: "But the witness which I receive
is not from man: how be it I say these things, that you may
be saved." There (Jn. 5:36) he alreadys says: "But the witness which I have is greater than that of John: for the works
which the Father has given me to accomplish, the very works
which I do, bear witness of me, that the Father has sent me."
Then in Jn. 5:37 he goes on: "And the Father who sent me, He
hath borne witness of me." Already in Jn. 5 the witness of
John is being superceded. That his works are given by God for
him to do and testify of him is a continuing proof. But even
in Jn. 5:32 John's witness is not the primary one (cf. v. 32).
God is the "another". It is God's witness that is being emphasized. (Cf. v. 37 where he returns to it: "And the Father
which sent me, He has borne witness of me.") There (in Jn. 5)
the charge is already brought against the Jews that they (v. 37)
"have neither heard His voice at any time, nor seen His form"
(cf. also Jn. 1:18 and Jn. 6:46). (v. 38) "And you have not
His word abiding in you: for whom He sent, him you believe
not." The crux is believing acceptance of Jesus; that they do
not believe is proof that they have not heard God's voice nor
seen His form. This last statement is consonant with Jn. 1:18
at the end of the prologue proper. The writer of the Fourth
Gospel is not denying the revelation contained in the Torah
and the scriptures, perhaps not even in the Book of Esther,
if the "another" that is alluded to in Jn. 5:32 refers to
Mordecai's statement to Esther in her period of trial and test-
ing (cf. Esth. 4:14) that if she failed, then shall relief and
deliverance arise to the Jews from another place" (*Maḳom Aḥer*).
God being understood by the rabbis as the "another place".

If the feast of Jn. 5:1 is Purim this allusion to God as "the another" would be appropriate. In Jn. 8:14 there is a step forward. Jesus says: "Even if I bear witness of myself, my witness is true, for I know whence I came, and whither I go; but you know not whence I come, or whither I go." As to where he is going he had already (in Jn. 7:33) told the Pharisees that he would go to Him who sent him and they did not understand where he was going. They do not know whence he came, because they judge after the flesh, like the multitude in Jn. 7:41, who knew he came from Galilee, or the Jews (cf. Jn. 6:42): "Is not this Jesus, the son of Joseph, whose father and mother we know? How does he now say, I am come down out of heaven?" Here the validity of his witness is used to lead on to the rebutted charge of blasphemy. In Jn. 5:19ff. the charge of blasphemy is dealt with first, then his statement is made about the Father as his witness. Jesus (Jn. 8:16) claims his judgment, which is not after the flesh like theirs, is true. He is not alone, "but I and the Father that sent me" (cf. Jn. 5:36, 37). There is no mention of John's witness to the Jews to which he had also appealed, although he remarks they had sent a delagation to him and that John had witnessed to them. In Jn. 1:24 those who had been sent by the Jews were of the Pharisees. Is the writer of the Fourth Gospel wishing to distinguish between the Jews and those of the priestly establishment who were Pharisees and possibly Shammaite on the one hand, and the Hillelite Pharisees on the other? The writer of the Fourth Gospel (in chs. 7:43, 9:16; 10:19) shows how the fact of Jesus, his words (Jn. 7:43, 10:19), and deeds (Jn. 9:16) caused division among the multitude (the Jews) and the Pharisees respectively. Whereas the Jews in Jn. 5:17 had understood the reference to "my Father" this was not true of the Pharisees when Jesus uses the expression "the Father".

Jesus here (Jn. 8:17) refers to "your Law" where it is written
that the witness of two men is true. In Num. 35:30 it is said:
"If anyone kills any person, the manslayer shall be slain at
the evidence of witnesses; but no person shall be put to death
on the testimony of one witness." Dt. 19:15 has: "One witness
shall not rise up against a man for any crime, or for any sin,
in any sin that he commits on the evidence of two witnesses, or
at the evidence of three witnesses, shall a charge be established." This later part of Dt. 19:15 would appear to be the
passage referred to, but there is specific mention of two *men*
per se in the Hebrew. It is a peculiar passage to quote, for
how can one be one's own witness, and is the Father a man? In
fact, in Jn. 8:18, Jesus says: "I am he that bears witness[131]
of myself and the Father that sent me bears witness of me."
But the "I am" (*Ego Eimi*) is very significant. It may be a
proclamation that it is *YHWH* who is speaking. In Jn. 8:16
there is "I am (*Eimi*) not alone, but I and the Father that sent
me." This comes after a warning to the Pharisees not to judge
as they did "after the flesh". But not being able to see beyond what (it is alleged) their Law says, they judge after the
flesh and ask him, "Where is your Father?" When this gospel
was read to the believers (i.e. Christians) they would pity
such ignorance. The Jews are depicted as not knowing that
Jesus is talking about God and showing themselves ignorant of
God by their question. Jesus' retort is: "You know neither
me nor my Father; if you knew me, you would know my Father also."
The writer of the Fourth Gospel feels it is important to note
that these words were spoken by Jesus in the Temple treasury;
and he adds: "No man took him, because his hour was not yet
come." The reference to the Temple and the Pharisees in the
adultery pericope probably made it suitable for inclusion before Jn. 8:12-20. On the other hand, Jn. 8:12-20 (following as

it now does after Jn. 8:1-11) helps to undermine confidence in their judgment and their knowledge of God and the Law.

It is possible that the Fourth Gospel writer wants to distinguish between the two schools (in biblical interpretation) in the Judaism of his day. There was the literalist anthropomorphic school of Rabbi Akiba; alongside of which there was the allegorical school of Rabbi Ishmael. On the face of it, Rabbi Ishmael's approach was more what we mean by literal. The Talmud (i.e. Torah, Law) speaks in the language of men and therefore one cannot take literally an expression even in the Law. Rabbi Ishmael is remembered for his *Thirteen Middoth* or hermeneutical rules for interpreting the biblical text. *Middoth* also means "divine attributes". For by a proper understanding of the Bible, one can understand God's attributes. The school of R. Akiba was literalist in the extreme, if we understand by literalist a concern for the proper letters (textual readings) of the Law, because he and his school believed that the Law and every word of it was the very word of God. Only on the basis of an exact text, could he proceed to interpret the Law according to his special and (to us) highly fanciful method of exegesis. The Law, being the very word of God, and he, Akiba, having the key to its interpretation, he believed that the traditional (oral) law could be put to use giving the solid support of the written Torah and not only so, but that he could rediscover *halakoth* which were forgotten or waiting to be discovered. Even Moses could not recognize what was derived from his own Law when Akiba was teaching (cf. T. B. Men. 29b). Akiba's school was doggedly anthropomorphic and did not explain away anthropomorphic or anthropopathic statements. It is possible that the followers of R. Akiba's school were meant by "the Jews" of Jn. 5:1, 10, 15, 18. They are shown to understand Jesus' statement ("My

Father works even until now [the Sabbath] and I work") as referring to God's work in creation. They objected (Jn. 5:18) not only because he broke the Sabbath, "but also called God his own Father, making himself equal with God". Jn. 5:37: "You have neither heard His voice at any time, nor seen His form" could be directed against the anthropomorphism[132] of R. Akiba's school. The Pharisees in Jn. 8:13, 19, who did not know what he meant by "the Father who sent me" and who seemed to think it was his human father, could represent the allegorical school of Rabbi Ishmael. This school would *not* have taken any biblical anthropomorphic expression literally. If Jesus used one, it would be understood, since they understood the Torah according to the language of men.

In Jn. 8:21 it is not clear to whom Jesus is speaking unless "to them" specifically means the Pharisees. But "the Jews" appear in Jn. 8:22 and again in 48, 52, 57 where Jesus says: "I go away and you shall seek me, and shall die in your sin: whither I go, you cannot come." He had said something like this about going to the Pharisees (cf. Jn. 8:14) and to the Jews in Jn. 7:33. In Jn. 7:34 he had said, "You shall seek me, and shall not find me. And where I am, you cannot come." The new and significant clause is "and shall die in your sin". This new clause is reiterated in Jn. 8:24 (twice) but there it is "sins" not "sin". The Jews (Jn. 8:22) ineptly (as in Jn. 7:35) misunderstand him. This is a literary device used by the writer of this gospel to draw attention to his point. That they are made to misunderstand the point twice is not only intended to show their great ineptness but also to show how important he considers the point to be and to draw attention to it. The Jews (Jn. 8:22) ask if "whither I go, you cannot come" means he will kill himself. We have to imagine the early Christian readers' appreciation of the irony of this statement.

In Jn. 8:23 Jesus answers their question: "You are from
beneath (cf. Jn. 3:31); I am from above (cf. v. 31); you are
of this world; I am not of this world." The "I am's" are not
just a contrast to the "you's" but a statement of who he is,
for *YHWH* is from above. Jesus (Jn. 8:24) says it is because
they are of this world that he had said they would die in their
sins (in this verse the plural is used twice). Unless they
believed that he was "I am" (*Ego Eimi*), they would die for
their sins. One could say this is strongly gnostic. To be of
this world is to be in a state of sin. The only escape is to
believe in the gnostic saviour. But I think this is not the
case. In the great high priestly atonement prayer (Jn. 17:14,
reiterated in v. 16) Jesus prays for the Church: "They are not
of the world, even as I am not of the world." But in (*ibid.*)
v. 15 he does *not* pray that the Father should take them from
the world, but that He should guard them from the evil one.
Sanctified (v. 17) in the truth, Christ sends them (v. 18) into the world as the Father sent him into the world.

The Jews then (Jn. 8:25) ask him: "Who are you?", i.e.
the same question they had asked John the Baptist regarding
himself, but it is one which had not been put so far in this
gospel to Jesus. Jesus' reply is that he is as he has told
them from the beginning. This is the case, there is no development in the awareness of the divinity of Jesus in this gospel.
He always speaks in conformity with the doctrine set out in
Jn. 1:1-18,[133] which is probably the anaphoral prayer of the
Church (of Ephesus?) of the writer of the gospel's time. Jesus
tells them that he has many things to speak and judge concerning the Jews. He who has sent him is true. He had already
said that in the Temple when teaching the Jews (cf. Jn. 7:28).
In giving his last testimony about Jesus, John the Baptist had
said that he who received his (John's) witness had set his seal

to this: that God is true. This statement reminds one of the
prayer said immediately after the *Shema'*. The custom being to
avoid making a stop between the last word of the third section
of the *Shema'* and the first word of the benediction (the
Ge'ullah, "Redemption") which immediately follows after the
Shema'. We know that the *Ge'ullah* prayer was recited in the
Temple after the recital of the *Shema'* at the dawn prayer
service. To set his seal to it could be a way of saying "Amen".
During the Baptist's last testimony to Jesus, the Evangelist
said (Jn. 3:31):

> He who comes from above is above all (twice
> repeated at beginning and end of the verse,
> cf. Jn. 8:23); he who is of the earth, be-
> longs to the earth, and of the earth (cf. Jn.
> 8:23 "the world") he speaks. (Jn. 3:32) What
> he who comes from above has seen and heard,
> of that he bears witness; yet no man received
> his witness.

Jesus in Jn. 8:26 is referring back to his last testimony without mentioning John the Baptist. These things which he had heard
from Him who sent him, he claims are those that he speaks to the
world. Jesus (Jn. 18:20) told the high priest that he had also
spoken openly to the world and always taught in Synagogues and
in the Temple "where all the Jews come together". But the Jews
here in Jn. 8:27 did not perceive that he was speaking to them
about "the Father". True, he does not use the word in this
section. This, however, makes it all the more significant that
at the unnamed feast (identified here as Purim) the Jews had
seen the crux of the matter (though they had put a wrong interpretation on it) that by referring to God as "my Father" he was
making himself the equal of God. It is as if matters had come
to a head at the feast so that, looking back, one could see that
it was at Purim that the animosity towards and persecution of

Jesus began. Here, on the other hand, the Jews are shown as
most unperceptive, which gives the Evangelist the opportunity
of having Jesus expatiating and carrying the debate further
(Jn. 8:28): "When you have lifted up the Son of Man, then
shall you know that I am (*Ego Eimi*) he and that I do nothing
of myself, but as the Father taught me, I speak these things."
Here we have a clarification of his statement in Jn. 8:23: "I
am from above." It is also a reflection back to what he had
said to Nicodemus (Jn. 3:13), a ruler of the Jews: "And no
man has ascended into heaven, but he that descended out of
heaven, even the Son of Man, who is in heaven." In Jn. 8:23
he said that he was from above,[134] and not of this world. In
other words He was in heaven while in this world.[135] Jesus
declared to Nicodemus in Jn. 3:14: "And as Moses lifted up the
serpent[136] in the wilderness, even so must the Son of Man be
lifted up (v. 15) that whosoever believes in him may have eternal life.

John the Baptist states in Jn. 3:36: "He who believes in
the Son has eternal life." According to Jn. 20:31: "These
(things) are written that you may believe that Jesus is the
Christ, the Son of God; and that believing you may have life
in his name."

During Passion week Jesus, in Jn. 12:32, uses the same
metaphor: "And I, if I be lifted up from the earth, will draw
all men to myself." There the Evangelist adds v. 33: "But
this he said, signifying by what manner of death he should
die."[137] Here (Jn. 8:28) he is affirming that when he was
crucified they would know that he was *I am* (*Ego Eimi*) and that
he did nothing of himself, "but as the Father taught me, I
speak these things". This then is the answer to the Jews'
question (Jn. 7:15): "How does this man know letters, having
never studied?"[138] In Jn. 8:29 Jesus maintains that: "He who

sent me is with me; He has not left me alone" (cf. Jn. 8:16).
As a reason that He who sent him is still with him he states
(Jn. 8:29): "For I do always the things that are pleasing
him" (Greek, *Ta aresta*). In Hebrew *Raẓahas* the meaning "to
want", "to wish", "to will" and the noun *Raẓon* "wish", "good
pleasure", "will". So we might regard Jn. 8:29 as meaning the
same thing as Jn. 5:30b: "I seek not mine own will, but the
will of Him that sent me." The first part of that verse (Jn.
5:30a) states even more emphatically than Jn. 8:28 that he not
only does not, but cannot do anything of himself. Note how
Jn. 5 is alluded to here again in Jn. 8.

The Evangelist (Jn. 8:30) informs us that as he said these
things "many believed on him". This is parallel to the statement (Jn. 7:31): "But of the multitude many believed on him."
The next verse makes it plain that (Jn. 8:30) the reference had
been to the Jews. However when Jesus promises that by holding
fast to what he says, they will really become his disciples then
they will know the truth and the truth would make them free, they
refuse the need to be made free. Their assertion is just not
true that Abraham's seed had never been in bondage to any man.
What about the bondage in Egypt, Babylon, and Persia? Even if
the Exile was not bondage but merely a captivity, Egypt was the
house of bondage. At the time this gospel was written some Jews
captured by the Romans in 70 A.D. may still have been slaves.
Jesus (v. 34) explains the bondage of sin. He, the Son, could
make them free from their bondage to sin. He admits they are
Abraham's seed; they seek to kill him because his word has no
place in them. Again he asserts that he speaks the things which
he had seen with his Father (Jn. 8:38, cf. also Jn. 3:32, 5:19;
6:46), and he charges them with doing the things which they had
heard from their father. They bridle at this and say: "Our
father is Abraham." Jesus' retort (Jn. 8:39): "If you were

Abraham's children, you would do the works of Abraham" seems
to contradict the admission by Jesus in v. 37 that they are
Abraham's seed. But one should recall the scene in the Targums
Jerushalmi and Pseudo-Jonathan (Gen. 49) at Jacob's death bed.
Jacob is worried lest his children contain deviants like Abraham's son Ishmael and the descendants of his union with Keturah,
etc. or they be like Isaac's son Esau and his progeny. To re-
assure him, the twelve sons of Jacob led by Joseph say that
there is no impurity in their bed and recite the *Shema'*: "Hear
O Israel (Jacob's new name), *Yeya* our God is One *Yeya*" and Jacob
recites the Temple response to the *Shema'*: "Blessed be *Yeya*
from His Place." "But now," says Jesus (Jn. 8:40), "you seek
to kill me, a man that hath told you the truth which I heard
from God (cf. Jn. 8:26): this is not what Abraham did." To
what incident in Abraham's life can this refer? This probably
refers to Gen. 18:1 where Yahweh appeared to Abraham at the
oaks of Memra and v. 2 when Abraham lifted up his eyes he saw
three men and he ran to meet them. He (v. 3) addresses them as
my Lords (*Adonai* in the plural), offers to wash their feet, and
provides a meal for them, which (v. 8) "they did eat". Abraham
believed the promise of a son and that he (Abraham) should (v.
18) become a great and mighty nation (v. 12) and all the nations
of the earth should be blessed in him. Abraham received *YHWH*
in His manifestation as a man and believed Him. Jesus (Jn.
8:41) says that the Jews do the works of their father and he
does not mean Abraham. The Jews answer: "We were not born of
fornication; we have one Father, even God." The expression
"born of fornication" could refer to mixed stock. Inter-
marriage with the heathens led to the adoption of heathen
religious customs. The worship of other Gods was termed in the
O.T. as "a whoring after false gods". From the time of Nehemiah,
mixed marriages (cf. Mal. 2:10, 11) had been forbidden at

Jerusalem. Jesus is a Galilean and the Galilee of the Gentiles
had only become Jewish at the time of the Maccabee John Hyrcanus.
Implied in their statement "We were not born of fornication;
we have one Father, even God" may be the idea that only Jews
of pure stock, as descendants of Abraham through Jacob/Israel,
can have God as their one Father. But were they on the defen-
sive rather than on the offensive? One could be of the seed of
Abraham and not be a child of Abraham in the religious sense.
Esau/Edom (cf. Gen. 25:30; 36:11, 12), the grandson of Abraham,
was not only the ancestor of the Edomites but also of the Amalekites. King Herod, an Edomite, was of the seed of Abraham
through Esau. Haman, the Agagite and Amalekite, whose memory
was cursed every Purim when the *Megillath Esther* was read, was
a descendant of Abraham too, through the mixed marriages of
Esau and his son Eliphaz.

Jesus' reply (Jn. 8:42) is that "if God were your Father
you would love me". He emphasizes that he came from the Father
(cf. Jn. 16:28) as well as being commissioned by God. Jesus
(v. 43) asks the further question "Why do you not understand my
speech?" and then he answers it himself: it is "because you
cannot hear my word". (In essence his word is that God is his
Father, which is the very reason the Jews (Jn. 5:18) began to
plan to kill him.) The first thing required is to accept him
in faith, then one can begin to understand. But it is more
than that. They (v. 44) are of their father the devil (*Di-
abolos*); they copy the lusts of their father. By their father,
who "was a murderer from the beginning", Cain is probably meant.
However, according to the Samaritan *Malef*, Cain was the result
of Eve falling for the devil in the guise of a serpent under
the tree of forbidden fruit. The Samaritans believe in a pure
lineage (to which they belong) going back through Seth to Adam;
these are the children of light. There are also children of

darkness descended from Cain/the devil and the daughters of
the land. The two groups, sons of light and sons of darkness,
in the Dead Sea Scrolls' *Manual of Discipline* testify to a
similar belief. Sons of light could always fall away to become
sons of darkness. One does not doubt the presence of Iranian
influence here, but we do not think it is direct in the Fourth
Gospel. Instead it has been mediated over the centuries by the
constant influence of Iranian religion on the large Jewish
community in Iran which, naturally, had close religious links
with the Jewish brethren in Jerusalem and Palestine. These
latter could not help being influenced at second-hand by what
had influenced their brother Jews in Iran or for that matter in
Egypt too. Palestine was not shut off from the rest of the
Jewish world, and the Jews then were as cosmopolitan as they
have ever been. The gospel's argument seems to be as follows:
the reason why the Jews (Jn. 8:44) cannot believe Jesus when he
speaks the truth is because they are like their father in whom
there is no truth. Conditioned as they are to lies they cannot
believe because Jesus speaks the truth. Jesus is of God. He
that is of God hears the words of God. Because they are not
of God, they cannot hear them. The Jews' reply to this reason-
ing is that he is a Samaritan and has a devil. Jesus denies
he has a devil. At one stage I thought the Fourth Gospel was
written to present the gospel to Dosithean Samaritans who spoke
of Moses in much the same way as the Fourth Gospel does of
Jesus. I am not convinced now that there is any more significance in this allegation that Jesus is a Samaritan than a term
of abuse by Jews conscious of the purity of their genealogy.
That Jesus was called a Samaritan by Jews might have, along
with Jesus' encounter with the Samaritans (Jn. 4), have commended this gospel to the Samaritans, who would agree that the
Jews were descended from Cain. Jesus (Jn. 8:49) affirms that

he honours his Father, while they dishonour him (Jesus). Jesus
in a "Verily, verily" pronouncement (v. 51) says: "If a man
keep my word, he shall never see death." The Jews now feel
certain he has a devil. Abraham, good as he was, is dead and
the prophets are dead. "Are you greater than our father Abraham (Jn. 8:53)? Whom do you make yourself?" The writer of
the Fourth Gospel, as in the story of the Samaritan woman, is
here eliciting from his hearers the answer: "Yes. He is
greater than Abraham, just as he is greater than Jacob." One
might feel that in this chapter (8) it is Jesus the man speaking (cf. v. 29): "And He who sent me is with me. He has not
left me alone; for I do always the things that are pleasing to
Him." Also v. 50: "But I seek not my own glory; there is one
who seeks (it) and judges", and again in v. 54 Jesus' answer
to "Whom do you make yourself?". "If I glorify myself, my
glory is nothing; it is my Father who glorifies me, of whom
you say, that He is your God." But to make a distinction within the consciousness of Jesus is difficult. One might understand Jn. 8:55 as the human Jesus speaking of his mystic
experience: "And you have not known Him (God), but I know Him,
and if I should say I know Him not, I shall be like you, a
liar; but I know Him, and I keep His word." From the same
standpoint one might seek to explain Jn. 8:56: "Your father
Abraham rejoices to see my day; and he saw it and was glad",
taking it as referring to the promise of *YHWH* to Abraham (Gen.
22:18): "And by your seed shall all the nations of the earth
be blessed" (cf. Gal. 3:8). Although it is more likely to
refer to Abraham's answer to Isaac's question (Gen. 22:7):
"But where is the lamb for a burnt offering?" "God will provide (v. 8) Himself the lamb for the burnt offering, my son."
However with the Fourth Gospel, the writer uses the Jews'
apparent obtuseness to elicit the response of Jesus: "You

are not yet fifty years old (Jn. 8:57) and have you seen Abraham?" they said, judging like the Pharisees (Jn. 8:15) "after the flesh". Jesus (Jn. 8:58) said to them: "Verily, verily, I say to you, before Abraham was, I am." We cannot switch mechanically from Jesus the man to Jesus the Son of God. We must remember that this gospel starts with the Church's belief that Jesus Christ is the only begotten Son, who is in the bosom of the Father and that He has declared him (Jn. 1:18). We note the reaction of the Jews to this declaration of himself: "Before Abraham was, I am (*Ego Eimi*)" (Jn. 8:58). In view of this statement of himself, we do not believe the Evangelist meant that he hid himself (Jn. 8:59). He became, as it were, invisible to them, for it was not yet his hour.

The question is what does Jesus mean by "I am". It would appear to be that he is claiming to be *YHWH*. *Ani* and *Ehyeh* are divine names. In Ezek. 13:9; 23:49; 23:23; 28:24, and especially 29:16, "I" could be the name of God.[139] We note then in Gen. 4:26, in the time of Enosh son of Seth, then men began to call upon the name of *YHWH*. "I" or "I am" is specifically to be identified with *YHWH*, the name representing the revelation of the personality of God. It is with Cain and Abel that *YHWH* specifically deals with men, and from Cain's son Enoch down to Enosh when men began to call on the name of Yahweh (Gen. 4:1, 3, 4, 6, 9, 13, 15, 16, 26). In Gen. 5:29 He is mentioned again as having cursed the ground. The reference to Cain in Jn. 8:44 could show Jesus' dealings with this ancestor of theirs and show that before Cain as before Moses "I am". But we must also take the Targum and Midrash into account. When we take the Targum into account we find *YHWH* (not to speak of the *Memra*) even though in Gen. 1 it is *Elohim* in the Hebrew. However there are what the rabbis call the "ten descents" (of *YHWH*). Ten is a somewhat artificial number and the rabbinic enumeration

of them varies. They deal with cases where it is said in the
Hebrew O.T. that *YHWH yarad* ("came down"). It is always *YHWH*
who comes down. In the Targum it is rendered that the *Memra*
(Word) of *YHWH* revealed Himself or was revealed. In *Pirke de
Rabbi Nathan* these descents are ascribed to the *Shekinah*. It
is noteworthy that these descents of the *Shekinah* are *not*
identical with cases in the Targum where the *Memra* of *Yeya*
(*YHWH*) revealed Himself. It is taught by R. Simon B. Yehai
(cf. T. B. Meg. 29a) that the *Shekinah* became a captive with
Israel in every captivity and was in Egypt before the Lord
revealed Himself to Moses at the burning bush and had to be
redeemed along with His people.[140] Even in the Hebrew O.T.
YHWH is concerned for His people to such an extent as to come
down. This is heightened in the Targum and Midrash. As
pointed out earlier (pp. 14ff., 86ff.), it is not because
YHWH has become remote that *Memra* is inserted before the
divine name, and it is not because *Memra* becomes the mediator.
Often the *Memra* occurs in lieu of the personal pronoun referring to *YHWH*. The *Memra* is *YHWH* active in creation and among
men. The *Shekinah* is also found in the Targum, but *YHWH*'s
abiding presence among men is more common in Talmud and Midrash. Yahweh is the Saviour of His people (cf. Psalms and
Isaiah in particular). In talking of the ten descents of
YHWH the rabbis speak of his last descent in messianic times.

It is interesting that in *Pirke de R. Eliezer*, in relation
to the Midrash of the ten descents of *YHWH*, there is a Midrash
on the *Shemoneh Esreh*. This latter relates the various benedictions to the history of God's activity among men adumbrated
in the Midrash of the ten descents.

The healing of the man born blind (Jn. 9), like the healing of the paralytic (Jn. 5), is also on a Sabbath. The man
was born blind through no sin of his own or his parents, but

(v. 3) "that the works of God should be made manifest in him",
just as Lazarus' death was "for the glory of God, that the
Son of God my be glorified thereby" (Jn. 11:4). The miracle
is a sign that Jesus is the Light of the World. If the Fourth
Gospel is directed against the *Megillath Esther* and Purim it
has to be shown that he is greater than Mordecai or Esther,
both of whom the rabbis called (cf. Midrash on Psalms, Ps. 22)
"the Light of the World". We have Jesus making clay of dust
and spittle and anointing the blind man's eyes with the clay,
which is reminiscent of *YHWH (Elohim)* (Gen. 2:7) forming man
out of the dust of the ground. He sent the blind man to wash
in the pool of Siloam (*Shiloah* means "sent"). Designating himself (v. 5) as the Light of the World once had a Tabernacles
reference; but with the making of clay, the title now takes on
a reference to the creator who formed the light as well as the
eyes. The man is sent as Christ himself is sent (cf. Jn. 17:17).
The pool of Siloam was where the water was drawn for the water-
pouring ritual at the Feast of Tabernacles. The blind man
obeyed, washed, and saw. He too had trouble in establishing
his identity (cf. v. 9). When his neighbours at last accepted
that he was the erstwhile blind man and had heard of the details
of the cure, they brought him (v. 13) to the Pharisees. When
they had heard how he had received his sight, some of the
Pharisees said: "This man [Jesus] (v. 16) is not from God,
because he does not keep the Sabbath." Others (v. 16), apparently of the Pharisees, said: "How can a man that is a sinner
do such signs?" And now among the Pharisees (as among the
multitude, Jn. 7:43) there was a division because of him. And
so the blind man was asked (v. 17) what he thought of him "in
that he opened your eyes?". He said, "He is a prophet." The
reply was probably what set off the opposition of "the Jews"
because it would remind them of Dt. 13:1ff. and Dt. 18:20ff.

Here was a wonder-worker who was like the prophet, which these
sections of the Torah warned them against. He seduced the
people by his signs and by breaking the Sabbath. He turned
people away from the Law, and that was tantamount to turning
them away from God as they understood Him. By this disregard
for the Law on his part, as interpreted by them, they could not
recognize him as the prophet like to Moses (cf. Dt. 18:18). It
did not matter that Mordecai and Esther had broken the Law, as
interpreted by them, to save the nation. That was another
matter. The Jews (Jn. 9:18) at first denied the man had been
blind, then they called his parents who identified him as their
former blind son who now could see. But they did not answer
the Jews' question (v. 19) "How then does he now see?" but referred them back to their son. They denied responsibility for
him, he being of age and able to speak for himself. The Evangelist states (v. 22): "These things said his parents *because
they feared the Jews* (cf. Esth. 8:17; 9:2): for *the Jews had
agreed already*[141] that if any man should confess him to be
Christ, he should be put out of the synagogue." This actually
was the effect of the *Birkath ha-Noẓrim* in the *Shemoneh Esreh*
in which Christians were cursed; and no Christian could pray
their benediction in the *Amidah* prayer, and so he was excluded
from the Synagogue. Their fear of the parents is, as it were,
underlined (cf. Jn. 8:23). This then was the position to which
Mordecai and Esther (the Light of the World) had really brought
the Jewish community. It was not the Gentiles that feared the
Jews now but their own people.[142] The Pharisees called the man
a second time and said to him (v. 24): "Give glory to God:
we know that this man is a sinner." He declines to discuss
whether Jesus is a sinner or not, but he points out that one
thing he knows is that instead of being blind, he can now see.
When (v. 26) they ask him how Jesus opened his eyes, he points

out that he had already told them, and they would not listen.
Why do they want to hear it again? Do they also want to become his disciples? Then they assailed him: "You are his
disciple; but we are disciples of Moses" (Jn. 9:28). The
writer of the gospel is actually using the experience of the
former blind man at the hands of the Pharisees to show their
attitude to the followers of Jesus in general--"We know,"
they say (v. 29), "that God has spoken to Moses: but as for
this man, we know not whence he is." God, they may allow,
spoke to Moses, but God had to study His own Torah in His
heavenly *Beth Din* to keep up with the interpretations the
rabbis were giving it below and the new *halakoth* they were
promulgating. But the odd thing is that here again, as in
the previous chapter, they are citing the words of Jesus but
using them in what they fancy is his detriment: "We know not
whence He is" (cf. Jn. 8:14). The man found it surprising
that they did not know whence Jesus was, for he had opened his
eyes. In Jn. 7:26 the Jerusalemites asked if the rulers indeed knew that he was the Christ? However they added (Jn. 7:
27) that he could not be the Christ, because they knew whence
Jesus was "but when the Christ comes, no one will know whence
he is". One wonders if the reader is not being reminded of
this as an indirect testimony to Jesus being the Christ. "We
know," says the man (Jn. 9:31), "that God does not hear sinners,
but if any man be a worshipper of God and do His will, him He
hears." Now in the *Amidah* prayer the basic stock are the three
benedictions of praise preceding the intervening petitions
(benedictions 4-16) followed by the three benedictions of thanksgiving. In the last decade of the 1st century, the 18 (actually
19) benedictions were arranged in the order we have them now.
The *Amidah* prayer (the *Tefillah*, i.e. the prayer *par excellence*)
probably goes back to at least the beginning of the 2nd century

B.C., but the collection of petitions in the middle were
probably expanded after the sacrificial worship of the Temple
ceased. It is a Jewish community which had suffered much loss
and deprivation that shaped these petitions. These petitions
close with the 16th benediction:

> Hear our voice, O *YHWH* our God, have pity
> and mercy upon us and accept in mercy and
> favour our prayer: for Thou art God (*El*)
> the hearer of prayers and supplications:
> and from Thy presence, O our King, turn us
> not back empty. For Thou hearest in mercy
> the prayer of Thy people Israel, Blessed
> art Thou O *YHWH* hearer of prayer.

One of the previous petitions (the 14th) stated that God
will return to Jerusalem and speedily set up the throne of David.
The 15th benediction was the prayer for the coming of the Davidic
messiah: "Let his horn be exalted by Thy salvation, because we
wait for Thy salvation all the day." The 17th benediction was:
"Accept, O Lord, our God, Thy people Israel and their prayer;
restore the oracle of Thy house; receive in love and favour both
the fire-offerings of Israel and their prayer; and may the service of Thy people Israel be ever acceptable unto Thee." This
last had been said in the prayer service every morning in the
Chamber of Hewn Stones in the Temple after the *Ge'ullah* (Redemption Prayer) after the *Shema'* and before the offering of the
Tamid or whole burnt offering of the lamb, Sabbath or weekday
alike, for the sins of Israel. Obviously their prayers were *not*
being answered. The man (v. 31) pointedly states: "We know
that God does not hear sinners, but if any man be a worshipper
of God and do His will, him He hears." The erstwhile blind man
(v. 32) states that: "Since the world began it was never heard
that anyone opened the eyes of a man born blind." It was like

a new creation. When the man ends with (v. 33) "If this man were not from God, he could do nothing", they retorted (v. 36): "You were altogether born in sins and do you teach us?" And the writer of the Fourth Gospel says: "They cast him out." According to some, "born in sins"[143] means that the evil inclination enters the body at the time of conception; others said it was 40 days after conception. Most held that it enters at birth. However the good inclination does not appear until puberty. But does not this apply to all?

Jesus found the man and asked him: "Do you believe in the Son of God?" The man asked who the Son of God was, that he might believe in him? Jesus pointed out that he was the Son of God, and the man (v. 38) said: "Lord, I believe." Jesus (Jn. 9:39) really refers back to Jn. 5:22: "For neither does the Father[144] judge any man, but He has given all judgment to the Son (v. 23) that all may honour the Son, even as they honour the Father." Jesus is the judge, and people judge themselves on how they react to him. Jesus' pronouncement (Jn. 9:39): "For judgment came I into this world, that they which see not may see; and that they which see may become blind." This pronouncement is derived in part from Isa. 6:10 which belongs to the vision by Isaiah of the glory of Yahweh. This is later (Jn. 12:41) referred to by Jesus as when Isaiah saw "my glory". In the Targum to Isaiah the message is given by the *Memra* of *YHWH*.

CHAPTER 8

The Exegesis of the Fourth Gospel and R. Akiba

The Pharisees who heard him speak in this way to the erst-while blind man asked if they were also blind. Jesus' reply was that if they were blind they would have no sin. But because they said they saw their sin (of invincible ignorance) remained. In this chapter some of the Pharisees and all of the Jews are shown as being on the side of darkness and oppression rather than on the side of light and freedom, and they also appear as deliberately hostile to any attempt to free people from their power.

In Ch. 10 there is the similitude of the sheepfold. The robber does *not* enter by the door but climbs over. He who enters by the door is the shepherd of the sheep. The doorkeeper opens the door to him and the sheep recognize his voice. He calls his sheep by name and he leads them out. They will not follow a stranger but flee from him.

Since (Jn. 10:6) they did not understand what he was alluding to, he explains (Jn. 10:7) with all the authoritative emphasis of a "Verily, verily" pronouncement: "I am (*Ego Eimi*) the door of the sheep." In Jn. 10:11: "I am (*Ego Eimi*) the good shepherd." So he is both the door and good shepherd. It is hardly likely that he is comparing himself to Moses or David, when he says (Jn. 10:8): "All that came before me are thieves and robbers; but the sheep did not hear them." In Eccles. 12:11 we are told: "The words of the wise are as *goads*, and as nails well fastened are the words of the masters (*baale*)

of assemblies, which are given from one shepherd." The rabbis
(cf. M. Eccles. R. XII, 11) interpreted the one shepherd as
Moses. One could say that Jn. 10 is directed against this.
It is not only directed against Moses but also against "the
masters of assemblies", the rabbis, and their words, the oral
law. Jn. 10 is indeed an attack on the oral law as it was being
developed in the last part of the 1st century by R. Akiba in
particular.

But the key to this passage is the recognition, on the
basis of the "I am" statement in Jn. 9 (though indications of
the identity of Jesus had been given before throughout the
preceding chapters), that Jesus is *YHWH*. One naturally turns
to Ps. 23:1: "The LORD is my shepherd." The reference to
Jesus' sheep finding good pasture (Jn. 10:9) reminds one of
Ps. 23:2: "He makes me to lie down in green pastures." But
perhaps most of all we should think of Isa. 40:11: "He (*Adonai
YHWH*, v. 10) shall feed his flock like a shepherd..." This is
all the more significant in that Isa. 40:3, "The voice of one
proclaiming in the wilderness the way of the LORD (*YHWH*), make
straight in the desert a highway for our God (*Elohim*)", is
cited by John the Baptist (Jn. 1:23). Jesus says (Jn. 10:11):
"I am the good shepherd: the good shepherd lays down his life
for the sheep." "I am (*Ego Eimi*) the good shepherd" is again
repeated in Jn. 10:14. The "I am" has to be taken in the context of the "I am" utterances in Jn. 9. Jesus, who is Yahweh,
is the good shepherd. Earlier (Jn. 10:7) he has said: "I am
(*Ego Eimi*) the door of the sheep." This is again repeated in
Jn. 10:9: "I am (*Ego Eimi*) the door: by me if any man enter
in, he shall be saved, and shall go in and go out and shall
find pasture." "I am the door" can be explained by the Hebrew
text of Lev. 16:7 which refers to the Day of Atonement ritual:
"And he shall take the two goats and set them before the Lord

at the door of the tent of meeting" (R.S.V.). However the Hebrew could be rendered: "before the LORD the door of the tent of meeting" (i.e. the Tabernacle). This, I believe, is the origin of the "I am (i.e. *YHWH*) the door" reference. Yahweh is the shepherd (cf. Ps. 23:1), and here He is the door. "The fold of the sheep" (Jn. 10:1) is the Tabernacle, i.e. the community. But we should consider that the Synagogue (cf. Jn. 9:22) out of which the Jews put the erstwhile blind man and others who confessed Jesus to be Christ, was not just a building but a community. This makes the discourse on the good shepherd,[145] coming after the account of what the Jews did in Jn. 9, all the more relevant. They are the thief (cf. Jn. 10:10) and the hireling (cf. Jn. 10:12, 13). There may be a reference back to how Johanan ben Zakkai (with his disciples Eliezer ben Hyrcanus and R. Joshua b. Hananiah) left Jerusalem and the folk therein before it fell to the Romans with the consequent slaughter, and by so doing he was able to make a deal with Vespasian to get permission to set up his academy at Jamnia. "But," says Jesus (Jn. 10:14), "I am (*Ego Eimi*) the good shepherd..." and (Jn. 10:15) "I lay down my life for the sheep". Lev. 1:5 in the R.V. speaking of an atonement burnt offering says: "And Aaron's sons, the priests, shall present the blood and sprinkle the blood around about upon the altar that is at the door of the tent of meeting." Now this could be rendered: "upon the altar which is the door of the tent of meeting". It could be argued all the more so that in Lev. 1:3 "at the door" is a rendering of *el-ha Petah*--here just *ha-Petah*. This may seem to be odd exegesis, but it is answering the literalist school of Rabbi Akiba in its own kind.[146] By presenting Jesus in the age of Akiba, the writer of the Fourth Gospel can use similar exegesis for his Master's use. Also the same construction occurs in Lev. 17:6: "And the priest shall sprinkle

the blood upon the altar of the Lord at the door of the tent
of meeting" (so R.V.). This, according to the Hebrew, could
be translated: "upon the altar of *YHWH* the door of the tent
of meeting". So here we can see why the writer of the Fourth
Gospel (Jn. 10:11) makes the statement that the good shepherd
lays down his life for the sheep. This is repeated (in Jn.
10:15): "and I lay down my life for the sheep". We note the
pronoun "I" in Jn. 10:15. It would be unnatural to argue that
the first person "I" which referred to Yahweh as "the Good
Shepherd" (in Jn. 10:11) and as "the door" (in Jn. 10:9) is now
being used by someone else. In Lev. 1:5 the Hebrew text could
be taken as putting the altar in apposition to, and indeed as
identifying it with, "the door of the tent of meeting". Likewise Lev. 17:6 could, from the Hebrew text, be read: "upon the
altar of *YHWH*, the door of the tent of meeting". Jesus then,
like Yahweh, is laying down his own life on his own altar for
the sheep. One is reminded of Gen. 22:8 where Abraham, in reply
to Isaac's question as to where the lamb for the burnt offering
was, says: "God (*Elohim*) will see for Himself (provide himself,
R.V.) the lamb for a burnt offering." Although Gen. 22:1-13
uses only *Elohim* as the name of God, Abraham (v. 14) called
the name of that place *Yahweh Yireh* (*Yahweh* provides). *Yahweh*
and *Elohim* were one, cf. the *Shema'*.

Jn. 10:16 says: "And other sheep I have, which are not
of this fold; them also I must bring, and they shall bear my
voice; and they shall become one flock, one shepherd." This
has a much broader meaning than merely the bringing together
of Samaritans and Jews. In that connection one could turn to
Ezek. 37 and read how the stick of Joseph and the stick of Judah
become one stick (Ezek. 37:19), or Yahweh's statement to Ezekiel:
"And My servant David will be king over them; and they all shall
have one shepherd", or again (Ezek. 37:27): "My tabernacle also

shall be with them; and I will be their God, and they shall be
My people. (v. 28) And the nations shall know that I am Yahweh
who sanctifies Israel, when My sanctuary shall be in the midst
of them for ever." One might see this last statement as lying
behind Jn. 1:14: "And the Word became flesh and dwelt among
us and we beheld His glory..." But it is very far removed from
Jn. 1:14. The Fourth Gospel is not thinking of just Samaritans
and Jews. In Isa. 56:6 Yahweh speaks of

> ...the strangers who join themselves to the
> Lord, to minister to Him, and to love the
> name of the Lord, to be His servants...(v.
> 7) even them will I bring to My holy mountain
> and make them joyful in My house of prayer...
> for My house shall be called a house of
> prayer for all peoples. (v. 8) *Adonai Yahweh*
> who gathers the outcasts of Israel says:
> 'Yet will I gather others to him, beside his
> own that are already gathered.'

Jesus states (in Jn. 10:17): "Therefore the Father loves
me, because I lay down my life, that I may take it again." This
tells us of the Father's nature; He loves Jesus for his self-
sacrifice. In the light of Jn. 10:18, the betrayal, the arrest
and the crucifixion of Jesus are not events imposed upon him.
"No one takes it (his life) away from me, but I lay it down of
myself." That the Father loves the Son was already stated (Jn.
3:35) where it is claimed that He has given all things into his
hand. He has the power/right to lay it (his life) down. He
also has the power/right to take it again. In view of the
earlier identity of "I" (*Ego*) in Jn. 10, there is no reason to
regard the "I" (*Ego*) of Jn. 10:17, 18 as other than the same
person who earlier said: "I am the good shepherd." "This
commandment," says Jesus (Jn. 10:18), "received I from my
Father." Who then is his Father? Already (in Jn. 5:18) the

Jews had spotted his claim that God was his Father, but misunderstood it. A division (Jn. 10:19) again arises among
"the Jews" "because of these words". Presumably the whole
discourse is the cause of the dissension, but it is probably
the intention of the writer of the Fourth Gospel to highlight
the last sentence: "This commandment received I from my Father."
Many of them (v. 20) say: "He has a devil, and is mad; why do
you hear him?" In Jn. 7:20 the multitude in the temple at
Tabernacles had said: "You have a devil: who seeks to kill
you?" Here (in Jn. 10:20) the Jews seem to have gone beyond
the stage they had already reached in Jn. 5:18 where they sought
to kill him because he called God his own Father, thus making
himself equal with God, or in Jn. 8:58, where they took up stones
to cast at him because he said: "Before Abraham was, I am."
Now (Jn. 10:20) he is in their eyes only demon-possessed and mad,
so why listen to him. I do not think they are taking him seriously any more. The writer of the Fourth Gospel is showing us
the inadequacy of demon possession (even by a good demon) as an
adequate explanation of the phenomenon of Jesus. Demon possession had not been rejected in Mark. There the objection was
against the charge that he did his miracles thanks to Beelzebub.
Jesus' objection was that they called the Spirit in him evil.
But others (of the Jews) said (v. 21) that his saying in the
discourse on the good shepherd was *not* that of one possessed by
a devil and, in any case, "Can a devil open the eyes of the
blind?" It is worth referring to what Yahweh said to Moses
(Ex. 4:11): "And the Lord said to him, 'Who has made man's
mouth? Or who makes a man dumb, or deaf, or seeing, or blind?
Is it not I (*Anoki*) Yahweh?'" This sentence from the Torah,
known to them, would answer their question.

It is interesting that the clearest indications of who
Jesus claims to be appear in connection with the Feast of

Tabernacles (in Jn. 8) for presumably (Jn. 9) the Sabbath, on
which the blind man is given sight, was on the octave (eighth
day) of the Feast of Tabernacles. That being so, the events
in Jn. 8 would take place at this feast also. Jn. 10:1-21,
which has points of contact with Jn. 9 (e.g. Jn. 9:22), might
belong to this feast too. Jn. 10:22-39, however, though having
points of contact in content with Jn. 9:1-21, is several months
later at Hanukkah--which is in Chislew, while Tabernacles was
in Tishri. In Jn. 5:17 at Purim, which fell on a Sabbath, Jesus,
in defending his healing of the paralytic on the Sabbath, said
to the Jews who charged him with Sabbath breaking: "My Father
works *even until now* and I work." The Father is the creator
God, *Elohim*. In the Hebrew text, Yahweh is not mentioned before
Gen. 2:4. It is different in the Targum where *Yeya* (Yahweh) replaces *Elohim*. But in the Hebrew text (Gen. 1) *Elohim* (God) is
the creator. The point of Jesus' remark of God working "until
now" (this being said on a Sabbath) is that the Hebrew text of
Gen. 2:2 says: "And on the seventh day God finished His work
which He had made; and He rested on the seventh day from all His
work which He had made. (v. 3) And God blessed the seventh day,
and hallowed it; because *in it* He rested from all His work which
God had created and made." One gets the definite impression
from these verses that creation carried over into the seventh
day and that it was on it that God stopped and took His rest.
Here Jesus was but copying his Father. His Father is God (*El*).
The Jews (Jn. 5:18) say: "He is making himself equal with God,
Ha-Elohim." There was only one who could be described in this
way--Yahweh, the Redeemer, and Saviour (cf. Isa. 43:14; 44:6).

In Jn. 6 there is the next reference to "my Father".
Jesus (Jn. 6:28) in answer to the multitude's question, "What
must we do, that we may work the works of God?", tells them:
"Believe on him whom He has sent." They then ask for a sign

and cite Neh. 9:15 where "Moses your servant" could be taken
as the subject of v. 15, coming as it does immediately before
"and gave them bread from heaven". Jesus (Jn. 6:32) pronounces:
"Verily, verily, I say to you, it was not Moses that gave you
the bread out of heaven." Actually, according to Neh. 9:7, it
was *Yahweh Elohim*. "But," Jesus states (Jn. 6:32), "My Father
gives you the true bread out of heaven. (v. 33) For the bread
of God is that which comes down out of heaven, and gives life
to the world." Like the Samaritan woman (Jn. 3:15) saying:
"Lord, give me this water, that I thirst not, neither come all
the way hither to draw", they say: "Lord, evermore give us
this bread." Jesus (Jn. 6:35) tells them: "I am the bread of
life; he that believes on me shall never thirst." The Jews
(Jn. 6:41) murmur because of the saying: "I am the bread which
came down out of heaven", and (Jn. 6:42): "I am come down out
of heaven." The first quotation is drawn from Jn. 6:33, 35 and
38. They reject such a statement because they say they know
his mother and father. Jesus points out that no man can come
to him, unless the Father Who sent him draw him and such a one
he (Jesus) will raise up in the last day. Then he says (Jn.
6:45): "It is written in the prophets, 'And they shall all be
taught of God'." This is from Isa. 54:13: "And all your
children shall be taught of Yahweh." This is in the Messianic
Age in Isaiah. It is not Jesus' teaching but God's (cf. Jn.
7:16): "My teaching is not mine, but His that sent me."

The interesting thing is that this quotation from Isa.
54:13 (cited in Jn. 6:45) comes from a section which speaks of
Yahweh as Zion's *Bo'al* (cf. Isa. 54:5):

> For your Maker is your husband (ptc. *Bo'al*),
> the LORD of hosts is His name: and the Holy
> One of Israel is your redeemer; the God of
> the whole earth shall He be called. (v. 6)
> For the Lord has called you as a wife for-

saken and grieved in spirit, even a wife of
youth, when she is cast off, says your God.
(v. 7) For a small moment have I forsaken you;
but with great mercies will I gather you. (v.
8) In overflowing wrath I hid My face from you
for a moment; but with everlasting kindness
will I have mercy on you, says Yahweh your
Redeemer.

Isa. 54:5 has: "For your Maker *'Osaik* is your husband:
Bo'alaik.... [The plural of Majesty is used in both cases.
The pointing is odd because *Bo'al* means "lover", or "adulterer"
in later Hebrew, as Jastrow notes.[147] It must originally have
been your *Baal*.] Yahweh of hosts is his name; and the Holy One
of Israel is your redeemer, the God of the whole earth He shall
be called."

Jer. 31:32 shows that Yahweh could be thought of as fulfilling the role of a *ba'al* to Israel: "Although I was a husband
to them, says the LORD". The verb *ba'al* is used here. Hos.
2:16 has: "And it shall be on that day, says Yahweh that you
shall call Me *'Ishi* ("my Man") and shall call Me no more *Ba'ali*
("my *Ba'al*")." But it is not certain that people still did not
continue to think of Yahweh as *Ba'al*, cf. the occurrence of the
term as applied to God, the *Ba'al* of Battles, in the ancient
Jewish prayer *Yoẓer Or*.[148] *Ba'al* could also mean rain, cf.
T. B. Ta'an. 6b.

Further the term *Beth Ba'al* ("the house of *Ba'al*") was used
of a field sufficiently watered by rain which required no artificial irrigation. (See Tos. M. Ket. 1:1, *sede ha-Ba'al* = "the
field of *Ba'al*". M. Baba Bathra 3:1, Tos. Sukk. 2:7.)

There is also in the *Amidah* prayer the practice of adding
a second benediction, which was known as the *Geburoth* ("the
Powers") from the period from the eighth day of Tabernacles in
Tishri (i.e. the 23rd of Tishri) until the first day of Passover
(i.e. the 15th of Nisan): "Thou causest the wind to blow and

the rain to fall." This second benediction blesses God as He who quickens the dead and as He who is mighty to save.

In the ninth benediction, which blesses God as He who blesses the years (from the 4th of December until the first day of Passover), instead of the petition "give a blessing upon the face of the earth", the worshipper prays: "Give dew and rain for a blessing from the face of the earth."

The LORD (*YHWH*) was and is the giver of dew and rain, which the Canaanites and ancient Hebrews had thought were given by *Ba'al*.

It is interesting that the marriage feast at Cana of Galilee falls early in Nisan, certainly before the first day of Passover. Jesus is the real bridegroom. The water into wine assumes central significance. The Jews had been praying for rain for six months in the 2nd benediction of the *Amidah*, and from the beginning of December they had been praying in addition in the 9th benediction for dew and rain. He manifested forth his glory as one who could create wine from the water in abundance without having to wait for summer and autumn and the vintage and the pressing of the grapes. He was the LORD (Yahweh). but it was Yahweh in His Canaanite milieu who blessed the agricultural year. *Ba'al* never really disappeared. The Jews long became loyal followers of Yahweh, but their Yahweh, like the Yahweh of Hosea and Isaiah, had taken over some of the functions and with them some of the characteristics of *Ba'al*.

And *Ba'al*'s father was *El*. The name *El* appears as a divine name 226 times in the Hebrew Bible, 73 of which are in the Psalms. Sometimes *Elim*, like *Elohim*, can denote other deities. Sometimes *El* (especially in Deuteronomy-Isaiah) has the definite article just as *Elohim* does in the sense of the true God, e.g. Gen. 46:3. *El* is often used with some attribute, noun or adjective; perhaps the most frequent example is *El Shaddai* ("God

Almighty"). *El Elyon* occurs in Gen. 14:18-22 (four times),
Ps. 57:2; Ps. 78:56; but twenty-five times *Elyon* stands as a
divine name alone. In Ps. 7:17 and Ps. 47:2 it occurs in
combination with Yahweh. It is to be noted that Abram met
Melchizedek of Salem, the priest of *El Elyon*, and was blessed
by Melchizedek in the name of *El Elyon*. Abram also (Gen. 14:
22) swore by *El Elyon*. *El Elyon* is described in Gen. 14:19
as the "possessor/creator of heaven and earth". It is to be
noted that God is called *Elyonin* in Daniel (4 times: Dan.
7:18, 22, 25, 27) and *'Illai* ("most high") (9 times: Dan.
3:26; 4:17, 24, 25, 32, 34; 5:18, 21; 7:25). The Aramaic
equivalent *El* also occurs three times in Daniel (Dan. 9:4, 11,
36 [twice]). In the Maccabean period the *El Elyon* comes into
favour again as the name of God. The Maccabees, especially
John Hyrcanus,[149] seem to have favoured this name of God. We
must remember that this name denotes the concept of the personality in Hebrew thought. Just as *Elohim* seems to have been
used in some of the Psalms instaed of *Yahweh*, in fact replacing
original occurrences of *Yahweh*, *El* was used in others. Then
again *Yahweh* was identified with *El*. This was part of a movement to remove the apparent[150] nationalistic particularism of
their religion and of their God. There was universalism in
the Hebrew prophets, although they were primarily Yahwists.
Yet in view of Greek philosophic ideas of monotheism, there
certainly seems to be from the second century B.C. some diffi-
dence in using His name, "Yahweh". It is interesting that in
the *Amidah* prayer (the *Shemoneh Esreh*) the 1st benediction
"The Shield of Abraham" begins with God named as *El Elyon* ("God
Most High") and is at pains to identify Him with *Yahweh*. *El*
rather than *YHWH* occurs more frequently in the *Amidah*. We note
that *hupsistos* occurs thirteen times in the N.T. and that,
apart from Heb. 7:1 (which refers to Melchizedek, the priest

of the Most High God) and the Hosannas in Mt. 21:9, Mark
11:10 and Mark 5:7 (the Gerasene demoniac who calls Jesus Son
of the Most High God), it occurs mainly in Luke and twice in
Acts. It occurs twice in the annunciation in Luke 1:32, 35.
Jesus is to be called Son of the Most High. In the Fourth
Gospel the term "Most High" does not occur, but there is a
distinction between the use of the terms "God" and "Lord".
Jesus is the Son of God, Son of Man, and Lord. He is called
"my Lord and my God" only in Jn. 20:28.

As to the title Son of Man, it would appear in the Fourth
Gospel that this title is as much a divine title as Son of God.
The Son of Man was in heaven before (Jn. 6:62). The Son of Man,
even now, is in heaven (Jn. 3:13). He is really the heavenly
Man. One thinks of the man that Ezekiel saw: "Upon the likeness of the throne was a likeness as the appearance of a man
upon it above" (Ezek. 1:26). Ezekiel also saw (v. 28) the rain-
bow which was "the appearance of the likeness of the glory of
Yahweh" (Ezek 1:28). In Jn. 12:41, Isaiah (cf. Isa. 6) is said
to have seen Jesus' glory "and he spake of Him", i.e. when he
saw the Lord (Adonai) sitting upon a throne, high and lifted
up and His train filled the temple. It is significant that the
gospel says that no man has seen God at any time (Jn. 1:18)
and Jn. 5:37 says of the Jews: "You have neither heard His
voice [i.e. of the Father which sent me] at any time, nor seen
His form." The Jews sought to kill Jesus (Jn. 5:18) because
he called "God his own Father, making himself equal with God".
"The Father" is equivalent to God. No man has seen God. If
the Fourth Gospel means *El* by "God", we have no mention[151] in
the O.T. of anyone hearing the voice of *El* or seeing His form.
Names are important to the writer of the Fourth Gospel, just
as each divine name had a special significance for the rabbis,
e.g. Josh. 22:22: "The God of gods, The LORD, the God of gods,

He knows and Israel, He shall know." Here there are three names, i.e. *El, Elohim, Yahweh*, denoting three attributes of God.[152] They use the term *Middoth*, where the Christian would say (three) "natures". Actually *Middah* can mean "manner", "ways, "character", "nature", "condition" (cf. Jastrow, *Dictionary of Talmud and Midrash*).

But if "Son of Man" in the Fourth Gospel is Yahweh, how can one say of Jesus (= Yahweh) that He *qua* Yahweh is the Son of God, or even the Son of *El*? The expression "Son of God" is the Semitic way of designating one so named as being of the genus God. Similarly "Son of Man" means one of the genus Man, i.e. a Man. In the case of "the likeness as the appearance of a man" (Ezek. 1:26) above the throne, it is clear because of the qualifications before the word "man" that the Being only looked like a man. But, while the form of the statement that Jesus was Son of Man can be taken as actually being a man, what the gospel predicates of him is a divinity which shines through his manhood. It may be very significant that the Hebrew Bible, while stating "God (*El*) I am (*Anoki*) and not man (*Ish*)" (Hos. 11:9), does (especially in the Prophets) think of *YHWH* in anthropomorphic terms (e.g. Ex. 15:3, Yahweh is a man [*Ish*] of war). Yahweh is obviously active (e.g. He comes down [e.g. Gen. 11:5] and He goes up [e.g. Gen. 17:22]); *El*, on the other hand, is primarily passive. He possesses qualities. Yahweh is "I AM", He says of Himself; He will be. He causes to be. In the O.T. we find the following expressions: "God Almighty" (e.g. Gen. 35:11), "gracious God" (Jon. 4:2), "merciful God" (Dt. 4:31), "God of truth and without iniquity" (Dt. 32:4), "just (Dt. 32:4), the living God" (John. 3:10; Ps. 42:2; Ps. 84:2; Hos. 1:10), "the God of knowledge (2 Sam. 2:3), "God full of compassion and gracious" (Ps. 86:15), "God of salvation" (Ps. 68:20), "God that hides himself" (Isa. 15:45), and finally "the God of [the] glory"

(Ps. 29:3). These qualities or attributes are *El*'s. It matters not that in practically all the cases cited it is said that Yahweh is *El* with these attributes. Such a statement identifies Yahweh with, e.g. *El Rehum* (Merciful God). It is plain that *El Shaddai* ("God Almighty" who had appeared to Abram in Gen. 17:1, cf. Ex. 6:3) had to be identified with Yahweh, the God that Moses was bringing to the Israelites. One can say it was merely a new name for the same God, but, as we have seen, a name denotes character and for the ancient Hebrews a name was a personality. In Ex. 15:2 Yahweh becomes Israel's *El*. In Ex. 15:11 the question is asked who is like Him among the *Elim*. In Ps. 29:1 this class of deities is called the sons of *Elim*. *Elim* could be taken as a plural of majesty in the Phoenician usage, but even so, the sons of *Elim* are *Elim* in the general sense. Among this group Yahweh is outstanding. He seems to be identified with the *El* of glory in Ps. 29:3. Dt. 32:8 is very important as it seems to refer to a myth according to which *Elyon* (i.e. *El Elyon*) gave the nations their boundaries as an inheritance. Dt. 32:9 states: "For Yahweh's portion is His people; Jacob is the lot of His inheritance" (from whom? *Elyon*?). Yahweh may be identified with *Elyon* here and *vice versa*, though it points to a stage when they were not (cf. how the 1st benediction of the *Amidah* carefully identifies *El Elyon* the God of Abram with Yahweh). The Elohist and the Yahwist sources in the Torah were the first to seek to make plain the identification (cf. Ex. 3:6). Then the Deuteronomist in the *Shema'*, set in the context of the Sinaitic Revelation, stresses that *Elohim* and Yahweh are one Yahweh. The priestly source (Ex. 6:2ff.) seems specifically to be identifying Yahweh with *El* of the Patriarchs (e.g. *El Shaddai* is mentioned) but this is not true of Ex. 3:6 where the God of the Patriarchs is *Elohim*. Ex. 6:2, 3 is important

as showing that at the latest stage of the compilation of the
Pentateuch, it was essential in introducing Yahweh to identify
Him with *El*. This has become even more significant since the
emergence of the Ras Shamra material. No longer can *El* be
regarded just as a generic term for animistic style deities.[153]
El per se is the Father of *Ba'al*. Since Yahweh, in taking over
the functions of *Ba'al* assumes the status of *Ba'al*, Yahweh
found Himself in relation to *El*. We must not think of the Ras
Shamra material as influential on Israel only in the period of
the entry into the land. Eusebius in his *Praeparatio Evangelica*
1:10 cites Philo Biblus as showing that among the Phoenicians
Elioun (cf. *Aliyan Baal*) was still the name of God. There could
have been continuous influence from Phoenicia on Hebrew religion
right down to the time of Christ![154] Just as *Ba'al* took over
the functions and status of *El*, so did Yahweh take those of *El*.
And yet it could also work the other way around in Israel.
While Yahweh's close connection with the Jews made Him their
consolation and hoped for source of succour among the pious,
and hope of vengeance on the nations among the more militant
nationalists, there must have been doubts as to whether He was
the God Most High in their widening contacts with other nations
and in their experiences of political reversals. God Most High
(*El Elyon*), the creator/possessor of heaven and earth seems to
have in His own right made a come-back from the time of the
Maccabees and continued to be influential certainly through the
1st century A.D.[155] *El* became God transcendent and He continued
to possess many attributes which were historically His. Yahweh
was primarily the national and immanent God of the Jews, yet
because of His name being a proper name, attributes were not
adjectivally affixed to it. This may not have seemed to matter
when it was said by the P writer and the Psalmist that Yahweh
is *El Shaddai* or *El Rahman*, but when Jews began to get sensitive

about the personal proper name of their national God and stressed *El* and never mentioned Yahweh, the union of names and attributes brought about by the E writer (Ex. 3:6) and the union of Yahweh and Elohim by the P writer (Ex. 6:2, 3: Yahweh and *El* [*Shaddai*]) fell apart.

The writer of the Fourth Gospel identifies Jesus with Yahweh. Yahweh has made His long-awaited final descent in Jesus, which, as Pirke de Rabbi Eliezer expected,[156] would be in the messianic time. The Hebrew Davidic messiah was the only begotten/ unique/elected Son of God (cf. Ps. 2:7). Jesus the man may have been that, but it is not important for the writer of the Fourth Gospel. He is to all intents and purposes Yahweh saving. Jesus' consciousness is that of Yahweh the one like the likeness of the appearance of a Man (cf. Ezek. 1:26, 28). In short, he tells us that the Christ of faith who has been elevated to divinity is divine, and therefore any meaningful statement about his life must show him to be as he now is for the believer, facing the hostility and indifference of the world. But the Yahweh/Jesus relationship inherited the problem of the Yahweh/*El* relationship, i.e. a divine national[157] Redeemer, universal God. The Evangelist's Jesus has to break through the hostility and indifference of those whose God Yahweh was. He must go to the Greeks, but before he goes to the Gentiles he must come into relationship with the universal God idea of the philosophers who would not be impressed by a national God that saves only his own people. Yahweh's Law is the inheritance of Israel. Was Yahweh's supreme act of salvation in Jesus to be only national too? Yahweh's very anthropomorphic activity on the pages of the Old Testament was against Him. One could not make Him a supreme, impassible, immutable God. Creator He may have been, but it was all a mistake and a muddle as the gnostics were beginning to think. They actually thought Yahweh was the equivalent of a demon, cf. the

charge that was brought against Christ. The Christ of faith
must be identified with God. One way is to identify him with
Yahweh, but while that shocked the Jews, it did not really im-
press intelligent outsiders. "*Elohim*/God" has its handicaps.[158]
The writer of the Fourth Gospel explores the idea (cf. Jn. 10:
34). He does not completely reject it, but he does not stress
it for the relation of Jesus Christ to God his own Father. Instead he shows how it could be applied to those that are united
with Christ--those who recognize the glorified resurrected Christ
as LORD (*Yahweh*) and God (*El*) as Thomas did (Jn. 20:28) and love
him, can become one with him, like Yahweh is with *Elohim*. He
(Yahweh/the LORD/Christ) is the Son of God (*El*). Those who believe in him are reborn by the Spirit in the water of baptism
and receive the heavenly body of the risen Yahweh/Christ which
is his words and his very self can become children of God by
adoption. Just as Yahweh/the LORD/Christ is unique because He
is of His very essence. And who is *El*? He is the living God,
the merciful, gracious, faithful, and true God with whom Yahweh
is identified on the pages of the O.T. Well then is He Yahweh?
Yes, and no. It does not speak of the living Yahweh, the merciful and gracious Yahweh, and the faithful and true Yahweh. It
identifies Yahweh with the God who possesses all these qualities.
This may appear to be a minor point to us, but a solution had
to be found by the writer of the Fourth Gospel for the relationship of his Yahweh/Jesus to God the Father. He could identify
Yahweh with *El*. To say Yahweh is *El Hanun* ("Gracious God")
brings us face to face with the problem of names, and names
denote persons. Yahweh is one person; *El Hanun* is another person. Ex. 3:16 was obviously not very successful in establishing
the fact that Yahweh was one and the same God as *Elohim*, and the
God of your fathers, the God of Abraham, of Isaac, and of Jacob,
otherwise Deuteronomy would not have had to make it so prominent

in the *Shema'*. The obvious way out is to upgrade the concept of the messiah. Yahweh is *El*'s heir (cf. Dt. 32:8). Among the *Bene Elim* (the sons of God) he is the special, unique son. Like the Davidic messiah to Yahweh, or Israel corporately to Yahweh, he was the only begotten/unique Son of God, the Christ. So He, Yahweh, is Christ. Being the incarnation of *YHWH*, Jesus can be stated to be the only begotten Son of God and His Christ. The messiah concept is upgraded from the divine and human relationship to the purely divine level. The Word which was in the beginning with God (*El*) was Yahweh/Jesus. In the Targums to the Pentateuch (even Onkelos) Yahweh, not *Elohim*, is the creator God. One cannot argue from the Targums on Gen. 1 that the *Memra* created. The Word of *YHWH* creates in the Targum Onk. on Dt. 33:27 and that on Isa. 44:24; 45:12. As pointed out above, it is true that often His *Memra* stands for He, or Thy *Memra* for Thee in the Targum, the preposition in the Hebrew text referring to Yahweh. One could say that Yahweh is His Word. One can say, as did the Jews, that God created by the ten words (*Maamar*) ten times in Gen. 1. He said: "Let there be." Targum Jerushalmi says He created by wisdom. (This is an association of *Reshith* in *Bereshith* with *Reshith Hokhmah* in Prov. 1:7; 8:22, the beginning of wisdom.) Then, by identification of *Hokhmah* and *Torah*, God created with the use of the Torah. Whatever *Logos* (in Jn. 1:1f.) means, it does not mean *Torah*!

For Philo, Israel means "seeing God".[159] Philo holds that if one cannot become a son of God, the next stage to aim for is to be a son of God's first-born, who is variously called the Word, Israel, etc. Those who do so are the sons of God's invisible image (the Word) or the "sons of Israel".[160] The above statement is based on Philo's "The Confusion of Tongues" § 145-148:[161]

But they who live in the knowledge of the one
are rightly called 'Sons of God' as Moses also
acknowledges when he says: 'You are sons of
the Lord God' (Dt. 14:1) and 'God who begat
you' (Dt. 32:18) and 'Is not He Himself your
father?' (Dt. 32:6). Indeed with those whose
soul is thus disposed, it follows that they
hold moral beauty to be the only good, and
this serves as a counterwork engineered by
veteran warriors to fight the cause which
makes pleasure the end and to subvert and
overthrow it (146). But if there be any as
yet unfit to be called a Son of God, let him
press to take his place under God's first-
born, the Word, who holds the eldership among
the Angels, their ruler as it were. And many
names are his for he is called 'the beginning'
and the name of God and His Word and the Man
after His image and 'he that sees' that is
Israel (147). And therefore I was moved a
few pages above to praise the virtues of those
who say that 'We are all sons of one man'
(Gen. 42:11). For if we have not yet become
fit to be thought sons of God, yet we may be
sons of His invisible image, the most holy
Word. For the Word is the eldest-born image
of God (148). And often indeed in the law-
book we find another phrase, 'sons of Israel',
hearers, that is, sons of him that sees, since
hearing stands second in estimation and below
sight and the recipient of teaching is always
second to him with whom realities present
their forms clear to his vision and not
through the medium of instruction.

This citation from Philo is very important. First it
shows why Jesus called Nathaniel an Israelite. Indeed, in Jn.
1:47 he is not yet in the category of Israel, i.e. "seeing God"
and therefore a son of God in Philo's sense. Philo's advice is
that such should press to take his place under God's first-
born, the Word. "For," he says, "if we have not yet become fit
to be thought sons of God yet we may be sons of His invisible
image, the most Holy Word." Philo defines "sons of Israel" as

"hearers, that is sons of him that sees, since hearing stands
second in estimation and below sight". Nathaniel, because he
heard Philip's report of Jesus and came, is a son of Israel.
His testimony to Jesus (Jn. 1:49) is imperfect, "Rabbi, Thou
art the Son of God: Thou art the King of Israel", because he
uses "Son of God" in a Davidic messianic sense. Still he believes. And Jesus (Jn. 1:51) indicates that he will be able
to go on and see God and become a "Son of God", i.e. Philo's
higher stage. Jesus states what he will see: "the heavens
opened and the angels of God ascending and descending upon the
Son of Man". Rightly the parallel has been seen between this
and Jacob's vision at Bethel of the angels of God (*Elohim*)
ascending and descending upon the Son of Man. The Targum on
Gen. 28 here tells how one lot of angels report to the other
lot that Jacob, the *Ish Tam* ("Perfect Man"), has his likeness
on the throne of God. This refers to the "likeness as the
appearance of a Man (*Ish*) upon it (the throne) above", in
Ezekiel's vision of Yahweh's chariot throne (Ezek. 1:26).
One can then go on and deduce that Jesus was referring to Jacob's
vision and expecting him to associate it with the Targumic and
Midrashic reference to Jacob's likeness being on the throne of
God. Since he (Jesus) introduced the allusion to the Jacob/
Israel vision, there is a clear indication that Nathaniel (when
he saw) would appreciate Jesus' reference to it and see Jesus
as he really was. Jesus' claim seems to be that he is the one
who (after the flesh is Son of Jacob [Man]) is greater than
Jacob (cf. Jn. 4:12) and indeed that he is the Man on the
chariot throne in Ezekiel's vision. This is what Nathaniel,
when he really sees, will realize. Jesus is Yahweh come down.

In Philo it is with regard to the mind within the soul
that Adam, i.e. generic man, is sent to be made after the image
of God.[162] Usually the emphasis is on the likeness and prox-

imity to God. However in *Who is the Heir?* (§ 231),[163] Philo
explains "after the image of God" as meaning that the likeness
was at third hand.

Now if man is made after the image of God, the image
while like God must be like the man who conforms to that image.
Philo in *The Confusion of Tongues*[164] (§ 146) speaking of God's
first-born, the Word, says: "And many names are his, for he
is called 'the beginning' and 'the name of God' and 'His Word'
and 'the Man after His image'." The "Man after His image" may
seem to refer directly to Adam. One can expect therefore that
the image looks like man and therefore the "Man after His image"
(one of the names of the Word) could refer not only to the ideal
Adam, but to "the likeness of the appearance of a Man" (Ezek.
1:26) on the chariot throne. Be that as it may, what connection
can we see between what Jesus (Jn. 1:51) seems to be indicating
who he is, "a likeness as the appearance of a Man" on Yahweh's
chariot throne, and the Word of Jn. 1:1? Before leaving Ezekiel's
chariot vision, we should note its introduction.

There are two introductions to it. The first states the
year, month, and day when (Ezek. 1:1) "the heavens were opened
and I saw visions of God (*Elohim*)" (cf. Jn. 1:51 where Nathaniel
will see the heaven opened). The second introduction apparently
has the same date "the Word of Yahweh came expressly to Ezekiel
the priest...and the hand of Yahweh was there upon him. (v. 4)
And I looked..." Thereafter follows the vision which takes up
the whole of Ezek. 1:4-28. Only in Ezek. 2:1 is there a verbal
message which is introduced merely by "And He (the Man on the
throne) said to me". As the Hebrew text now stands, "the Word
of Yahweh" (Ezek. 1:3) *is* the vision, and the vision builds up
round one person the "likeness as the appearance of a Man (*Ish*)
upon it above it" (Ezek. 1:26). I venture to suggest that the
writer of the Fourth Gospel, who later could say (Jn. 10:7) that

Jesus said "I am the door" because the order of words in the
Hebrew (cf. Lev. 16:7) has identified the "likeness as the
appearance of a Man on the throne chariot" with the Word of
Yahweh which "came expressly" to Ezekiel the priest. One
can see the word of Yahweh (cf. Isa. 2:1). Further the[165]
hayoh hayah (Ezek. 1:3) is unusual in its emphasis as if to
remove our doubt that the Word of the Lord was what he saw.

If the writer of the Fourth Gospel understood that the
vision of the "likeness as the appearance of a Man on the throne
chariot" was the Word of Yahweh who came to him expressly, then
here we have the explanation of

> In the beginning was the Word, Yahweh/Jesus,
> and the Yahweh/Jesus was with *El* (God), and
> the Yahweh/Jesus was *El* (God) and the Yahweh/
> Jesus was in the beginning with *El* (*Elohim*).
> All things were made by Him [cf. Ps. 33:6,
> By the Word [*dabar*] of Yahweh were the heavens
> made]; and without Him was not anything made
> that has been made [cf. the Targum and Onkelos,
> etc. on Gen. 1, where Yahweh not *Elohim* is the
> creator].

The rest of the prologue (Jn. 1:4ff.) speaks of the incarnate
ministry.

Jn. 1:17 clearly implies that the Law was not given by
Yahweh, and it makes a distinction between *El*, whom man has not
seen at any time, and Yahweh, the appearance and likeness of
whom Ezekiel had seen as a Man on his chariot throne. The only
begotten Son is the Word (cf. Philo., *Conf.* § 146) who has the
appearance and likeness of the Man on the chariot throne and who
is in the bosom of *El* the Father (cf. the Ras Shamra concept of
El).[166]

The prologue is an essential part of the gospel of John,
and Jn. 1:51 helps one to understand who Jesus is, John's testi-

mony to him, and why the basic thing in coming to him is to
accept his words.

The Feast of the Dedication at Jerusalem ("and it was
winter" [Jn. 10:22]), Hanukkah,[167] falls on the 25th of Kislev,
three months after Tabernacles. Hanukkah commemorated the rededication of the Temple by the Maccabees after its desecration
by Antiochus Epiphanes, who (as his name shows) claimed he was
God made manifest. The feast was in origin a rededication of
the altar. Whether it was actually kept in Jesus' time we do
not know. It, like Purim, was a non-Pentateuchal feast and
came into its own after the Temple was destroyed in 70 A.D. It
was also known as the Feast of Lights, and, as kept by "the
Jews" from the end of the 1st century A.D. on, it commemorated
what God had done.

> In the days of the Hasmonean Mattathias son of
> Johanan, the high priest and his sons, when the
> iniquitous power of Greece rose up against Thy
> people Israel to make them forgetful of Thy Law
> and to force them to transgress the statutes of
> Thy will. Then didst Thou in Thine abundant
> mercy rise up for them in the time of their
> troubles; Thou didst plead their cause; Thou didst
> judge their suit; Thou didst avenge their wrong;
> Thou deliveredst the strong into the hands of
> the weak, the many into the hands of the few,
> the impure into the hands of the pure, the
> wicked into the hands of the righteous and the
> arrogant into the hands of them that occupiest
> themselves with Thy Law: for Thyself Thou
> didst make a great and holy name in Thy world
> and for Thy people Israel thou didst work a
> great deliverance and redemption as at this
> day. And thereupon Thy children came into the
> oracle of Thy hour, cleansed Thy temple, puri-
> fied Thy sanctuary, kindled lights in Thy holy
> courts and appointed these eight days of
> Chanukah in order to give thanks and praise
> unto Thy great name.[168]

Actually this is said as an addition to the 17th benediction in the *Amidah* prayer which asks *YHWH Elohenu* to look favourably on His people Israel and their prayer and to restore the service to the *debir* of His House (i.e. the Holy of Holies).

Originally the benediction had asked Him to receive the fire offerings of Israel and their prayer in love and with favour. This part of the benediction had been said in Temple times at the end of the prayer service in the Chamber of Hewn Stones before the offering of the *Tamid* or continual burnt offering of the lamb offered for the sins of Israel. The benediction went on: "and may the service/worship of Thy people Israel be always according to Thy will". Then the special thanksgiving for Hanukkah followed, which was cited above. The benediction proper closes with: "And for all of them, Thy name, O our King, shall be continually blessed and exalted for ever and ever." The Feast of Hanukkah seems originally to have been a non-Jewish celebration of the winter solstice. This explains the emphasis on lights which has been central in Hanukkah from earliest times. The rabbis brought the feast within the oral law. Like Purim, it helped to remind the people that all was not lost. Purim told of the deliverance of the Persian Jews from destruction and fostered national pride. Hanukkah commemorated the restoration of sacrificial worship of the Temple and thereby worship as ordained by the Law. If such were to be restored, God would be looking in favour on them again for His worship would be as He willed. Targum Sheni on Esth. 2:6 says: "Mordecai, after having been carried away by Nebuchadnezzar returned to Jerusalem and was again deported by Nebuchadnezzar in the second captivity." He who had been in Jerusalem before the first Temple fell helped to restore the Temple after he had turned the tables on Haman, saved the Jews, and came to power and influence in Persia.

Actually the Fourth Gospel almost seems to use the Feast of the Dedication as a temporal indication. Three months after the discourse on the good shepherd and the sheep, the debate between Jesus and "the Jews" seems to be continuing. They had been divided over him, some saying he had a devil and was mad, others feeling that his sayings and his opening of eyes of the blind could not be of a devil. The question in Jn. 10:19: "Can a devil open the eyes of the blind?" may deliberately be so phrased as either to refer to the miracle of Jn. 9 or to opening the eyes of those who refused to see. So (in Jn. 10:24) at Hanukkah the Jews surround him in Solomon's porch where rabbis usually taught and asked him not to hold them in suspense any longer. "If thou art the Christ, tell us plainly." This reminds us that earlier in Jn. 1 Andrew, along with "one of the two that heard John" (the Baptist) (v. 40) followed Jesus. Andrew had brought his brother Simon to Jesus after telling him (v. 41): "We have found the Messiah." This other one of the two disciples of John the Baptist (Jn. 1:35) is referred to in the same anonymous way that the writer of the gospel refers to himself. Was he among the Jews who refused to write Jesus off as one who was possessed with a devil, and as a result of their stand caused the others to put the question? But it would be safer to postulate rather that we have the continuing influence of Nicodemus here. However, if Nicodemus' influence had been seen here, the Evangelist most likely would have mentioned it. As much as anything, the point of the story is (Jn. 10:19): "There arose a division again among the Jews." Jesus (Jn. 10:25) in reply to their demand to inform them plainly whether he was the Christ or not, answered that he had told them and they did not believe. All one can say is that he had not told them he was the Christ, i.e. the Jewish messiah. What he had told them (Jn. 5:43) was: "I am come in my Father's name, and you

receive me not: if another shall come in his own name, him
you will receive." We must remember that this gospel was
written (cf. Jn. 20:31) "that you may believe that Jesus is
the Christ, the Son of God; and that believing you may have
life in his name". In Jn. 9 Jesus used the "I am" identifying
himself with Yahweh. Jesus is to Christ the Son of God as
Yahweh is to *El*. Jesus (Jn. 10:25) continues: "The works
that I do in my Father's name, these bear witness of me."
This verse (Jn. 10:25) seems to be referring back to Jn. 5
where Jn. 5:36b states: "For the works which the Father has
given me to accomplish, the very works I do, bear witness of
me, that the Father has sent me." Jn. 5:43 states: "I come
in my Father's name, and you receive me not." This is another
example of how important Jn. 5 is. It contains the doctrine
about himself because of which "the Jews" then sought to kill
him. It is important to remember when that teaching was first
given by Jesus to the Jews, namely at the Feast of Purim.
Jesus here (in Jn. 10:26) states that the Jews do *not* believe
because they are *not* his sheep. This is clearly the statement
of the Church at the end of the 1st century. Jn. 10:27 states:
"My sheep hear my voice and I know them and they follow me.
(v. 28) And I give them eternal life; and they shall never
perish and no one shall snatch them out of my hand." This
reference to the sheep links up with the good shepherd and the
sheep of Jn. 10:15. It is stated in that verse (and also in
Jn. 10:11) that the good shepherd lays down his life for his
sheep. The "laying down of his life" may be the second part of
this discourse or its continuation which is at the Feast of
Hanukkah. The dedication of the altar was the original fact
that the Feast of the Dedication commemorated.[169] The new
altar was dedicated on the same day three years after it had
been deserted. This is also assumed by the rabbis to be the

same date that the altar in the second Temple was dedicated
(the Temple which Mordecai is supposed to have helped rebuild).
Ezra 2:1 states:

> Now these are the children of the province,
> who went up out of the captivity of those
> which had been carried away, whom Nebuchad-
> nezzar the king of Babylon had carried cap-
> tive to Babylon, and who returned to Jerusa-
> lem and Judah...(v. 2) who came with Zerub-
> babel, Joshua, Nehemiah, Seraiah, Reelaiah,
> Mordecai, etc. [cf. also Neh. 7:7 where he
> is also mentioned].

According to Ezra 1:3 Cyrus granted permission to all of
the captivity who wished to go up to Jerusalem to build "the
house of Yahweh the God of Israel--he is the God who is in
Jerusalem". "Cyrus the king (Ezra 1:7ff.) brought forth the
vessels of the house of Yahweh which Nebuchadnezzar had carried
away from Jerusalem and put in the house of his gods." In Ezra
1:11 we are told that Sheshbazzar brought these back when the
exiles came back. According to Ezra, Mordecai (Ezra 2:2) was
present at least at the beginning of the reconstruction of the
Temple. Whether it was the same Mordecai as in Esther is not
important, nor is his age (it is even greater than in Esther).[170]
The name of Mordecai was a token of continuity.

In the earlier discourse (in Jn. 10, v. 9), Jesus had said
he was the door. Earlier[171] we saw this as alluding to Lev.
17:6 where the Hebrew text could be translated "Yahweh the door
of the tent of meeting". But (in Lev. 1:6) it is the altar
which is the door of the tent of meeting (translating *Petaḥ*
similarly as "door" and not "at the door"). So Yahweh/Jesus,
who is the door of the tent of the meeting, is also the altar.
In other words, the reference to the Feast of Dedication (in

Jn. 10:22) and the taking up again of the good shepherd and the
sheep theme would subtly remind us that Jesus who is the door
is also the altar, for he is prepared to lay down his life for
his sheep. Jn. 10:28 says: "I give them eternal life." It is
repeated in Jn. 17:2 in the great high priestly prayer of Christ
that the Father had given him authority over all flesh so that
he, Jesus, could give eternal life to those the Father had given
him. And there "eternal life" is defined (Jn. 17:3). It is
"that they should know Thee the only true God and him whom Thou
hast sent even Jesus Christ". In Jn. 10:16 Jesus had spoken of
the other sheep he had, who were not of this fold, which he must
bring. "The Jews" are some of these other sheep. They too have
an offer of eternal life, and this means that Christ must witness
to them regarding his Father and himself (cf. Jn. 17:3 and Jn.
20:31. This last reference gives the reason why this gospel was
written.)

However (cf. Jn. 6:37) *only* those that the Father gives him
shall come to him. Jesus (Jn. 10:30) states the basic principle
"I and the Father are one", which to know is eternal life, i.e.
to accept Christ in faith. The Jews (Jn. 10:31) took up stones
again (cf. Jn. 8:59) to stone him. Jesus asked them for which
of his many good words from the Father which he had showed them
were they stoning him? They told him that it was for no good
work but for blasphemy that he, being a man, made himself God.
This is virtually the same charge as in Jn. 5:18. There, however,
it was by calling God his own Father that he made himself equal
with God. Here it is said that he, a man, made himself God, not
equal with God, but God Himself. The question is did the Jews
here know whom he meant by the Father? It would appear that they
did now, but they still did not know who Jesus is. Jesus cites
Ps. 82:6 as being "in your law". In this Psalm *Elohim* (God)
stands in the congregation of *El* (God). He judges among the

Elohim ("Gods"). He castigates them for judging unjustly. In
v. 6 He (*Elohim*) says: "*'Ani* (I have said): You are *Elohim*
(gods) and all of you sons of *Elyon* (the Most High). (v. 7)
Nevertheless you shall die like men." Jesus cites only: "I
said 'You are Gods'." *Elohim* can mean "judges" and in the context of this Psalm it could be taken to mean "judges", and it
was probably so understood by the writer's contemporaries.[172]
The notable thing is the statement that "the scripture cannot
be broken". In other words, the Evangelist is insisting on a
literalist exegesis to counter that of R. Akiba and his colleagues.
The Psalms are holy scripture, and they are the inspired word of
God; therefore one can argue from the form of the individual words
that what he is contending is that *Elohim* means "gods". So holy
scripture here calls men (cf. the end of Ps. 82:6: "nevertheless
you shall die like men") gods. How then can "the Jews" say that
Jesus blasphemes? Notice Jesus' answer (Jn. 10:36): "Do you say
of him, whom the Father sanctified and sent into the world, 'You
are blaspheming', because I said, 'I am *the* Son of God'?" For
"Son of God" we are referring again back to Jn. 5:18: "but also
called God his own Father". That here (Jn. 10:36) Jesus said:
"I am the Son of God", whereas he said (in Jn. 10:30): "I and
the Father are one" is not an inconsistency; but it is the Evangelist's way of showing how Jesus as the Son of God and God as being Jesus' own Father[173] are to be understood, viz. there is an
essential unity between Jesus and God; but the Johannine Jesus
is Yahweh. So the Fourth Gospel is stating that Yahweh and *El*
are one God. The *Shema'* in Deuteronomy said our *Elohim* and
Yahweh are one Yahweh. That was nationalistic. This new version
of the *Shema'* is still Yahwist, but it is also universal. In any
case, Ex. 6:23 had said that Yahweh was the same god as the *El* of
Abraham. Note in Ps. 82:6 that the *Elohim* are gods, presumably
of the nations. They are all sons of *Elyon* (i.e. *El Elyon*) whose

congregation or council it was (cf. v. 1, the congregation of
El). This is obviously a relic of a pantheon of the gods
(*Elohim*) under *El*. The literal exegesis used by the Evangelist,
although *ad hominem*, partly uncovers what the early sense was.
The reference (in Jn. 10:36) to the Father having sanctified
Jesus, reminds one of Jesus' statement in his high-priestly
prayer before going from the room of the Last Supper to Gethsemane (Jn. 17:19): "And for their sakes I sanctify myself",
i.e. consecrate. Jn. 17:18, as well as Jn. 10:36 here, speaks
of God having sent Jesus into the world (cf. also Jn. 5:36, 37;
6:57; 7:29; 8:42, etc.).

Jn. 10:37 states that if he does not do the works of his
Father, they can then not believe him. The other side of this
is Jn. 15:24: "If I had not done among them the works which
none other did, they had not had sin; but now have they both
seen and hated both me and my Father." This is their passing
judgment on themselves (cf. Jn. 3:18: "He who does not believe
has been judged already, because he has not believed on the name
of the only begotten Son of God."). Jesus (Jn. 10:38) says if
he does good works (and the Jews had all but admitted that they
were good works, cf. Jn. 10:32, 33), even though they do not
believe him, they should "believe the works". From believing
the works, they may proceed to "know and understand that the
Father is in me, and I in the Father". This argument is used
again in the Last Supper room when Philip asks: "Show us the
Father" (Jn. 14:8). He replies: "He who has seen me has seen
the Father." In Jn. 14:11 he says: "Believe me that I am in
the Father and the Father in me; or else believe me for the very
works' sake." In Jn. 5:36 one of the witnesses Jesus cites is
"the very works which I do". "These," he said, "bear witness
of me, that the Father has sent me." Now (in Jn. 10:38 and Jn.
14:10) the works testify not just that the Father sent him, but
that the Father is in him.

Jn. 10:39 tells of the reaction of the Jews. They have judged themselves. They again sought to take him. Is this a parallel to Haman and his having lots cast to see when to go into the king to get permission to hang Mordecai? As in Jn. 8:59 when the Jews had cast stones at him, Jesus mysteriously passed out of their grasp. He was Yahweh/Jesus and would only let them take him at the time determined by God's plan of salvation which was also his own.

Jesus (Jn. 10:40) withdraws to the place beyond Jordan where John the Baptist had first been baptizing. There he remained and many came to him, and many (v. 42) believed on Jesus there. These many who came said (v. 41): "All the things that John said of this man were true." One is tempted to wonder whether those who said this had been in the deputation of priests and Levites, sent by the Jews (Jn. 1:19), when John had been baptizing there. John the Baptist's other testimonies cited in this gospel were: (a) to Andrew and an unnamed disciple of John (Jn. 1:35), and (b) (Jn. 3:27ff.) to some of John's disciples and an unnamed Jew (cf. v. 25). It would appear that those who cite John the Baptist (in Jn. 10:41) were either of the priestly Levitical delegation or some of John's disciples.

In Jn. 10 Jesus has declared himself to be the new altar on which he, the good shepherd, lays down his life for his sheep. Jn. 11 gives him the opportunity to sacrifice himself, even when (cf. Jn. 10:42) "many believed on him". Lazarus of Bethany, the brother of Mary and Martha, was sick. The sisters sent word to Jesus (Jn. 10:3): "Lord, behold, he whom you love is sick."

In Jn. 9 and 10 Jesus had made his identity plain, and he had declared his readiness for self-sacrifice for the Church. He made it plain that he would give his life for those outside the Church, e.g. in the Synagogue, so that there would be one

Church under himself, the one shepherd. In Jn. 10 he had again witnessed to the Jews and they had again sought to stone him.

But now comes the great confrontation.

CHAPTER 9

Jesus and Lazarus, Esther and Mordecai

In the story of Mordecai and Esther, Mordecai was known to be a Jew; Esther, at Mordecai's suggestion, did not disclose the fact. If we see the Fourth Gospel as telling us who Jesus was and is, and the major events about what he did and still does, but told in a story form, which is reminiscent of those of the Book of Esther, what stage in the Book of Esther is parallel to this? The "Jews" first persecuted Jesus in Jn. 5 when he did not agree with the Jews' interpretation of what was unlawful on the Sabbath, healed a man on it, and told the man to carry his bed. When Jesus went on by justifying his action to claim God as his own Father and making himself equal with God, the Jews sought the more to kill him. It is highly significant that this Sabbath fell on the unnamed feast which, by its position between the Samaritan *Zimmuth Pesaḥ*[174] and the Jewish Passover would be Purim. It would appear that the Fourth Gospel has made this incident parallel to Mordecai's refusal to bow down and do reverence to Haman (cf. Esth. 3:2, 3). In Esth. 3:3 the king's servants said to Mordecai: "Why do you transgress the king's commandment?", i.e. to do obeisance to Haman. It was when Haman heard that Mordecai had not bowed down, nor did him reverence that Haman was full of wrath. This incident is parallel to Shadrach, Meshach and Abednego refusing to worship the golden image that Nebuchadnezzar had set up (Dan. 3:12, esp. 19).

Haman decided not to lay hands on Mordecai alone but to destroy all the Jews. Haman's argument to King Ahasuerus was that "their laws are diverse from those of every people; neither do they keep the king's laws". Actually, as Caiaphas said in the case of Jesus (Jn. 11:50): "It is expedient for you that one man should die for the people and the whole nation perish not." The Fourth Gospel is certainly like Esther in that in it, as in Esther, things are not what they seem: e.g. Haman is impressed with Queen Esther's apparent honouring of him, only to be denounced by her; he builds a gallows only to be hung there himself, and the possessions and honours he had amassed went to Mordecai. The Jews, whom he had planned to destroy, destroy his people and have prosperity and peace. So too in the Fourth Gospel the man Jesus, whom the Jews plan to do away with, is the Living LORD and his followers have increased.[175] In Jn. 11:47 the chief priests and Pharisees convened a council. "What are we to do? For this man does many signs (v. 48). If we leave him alone all men will believe on him; and the Romans will come and take away both our place and our nation." But one of them, being high priest that year, said to them: "You know nothing at all (v. 50) nor do you reckon that it is expedient for you that one man should die for the people and that the whole nation perish not." In Jn. 18:13 Jesus is led to Annas who is identified as the "father-in-law to Caiaphas, who was the high priest that year". There is added (in v. 14) the reminder: "Now Caiaphas was he who gave counsel to the Jews that it was expedient that one man should die for the people." In Jn. 11:51 Caiaphas gives a reason "that the whole nation perish not". In the last resort it is the Romans of whom they are afraid. If one tried to make out a case that even in the Fourth Gospel the Romans[176] are the equivalent of Amalek, however, it will not work, for Pilate, the representative of the Roman power, is not represented as Haman. In Jn. 19:6 it is "the chief priests and the officers" who cry out "Crucify him, crucify him", but

Pilate says: "Take him yourselves, and crucify him: for I find no crime in him." It is the Jews (Jn. 19:7) who say: "We have a law and by that law[177] he ought to die, because he made himself the Son of God." The last part of this sentence recalls Jn. 5:17, 18 and 19 (for Son of God means God). The charge is the same as in Jn. 10:36 and refers to Lev. 24:16: "He who blasphemes the name of Yahweh, shall surely be put to death; all the congregation shall certainly stone him."

According to Midrash Psalms on Ps. 22, both Mordecai and Esther were each the light of the world. Jesus has already declared he is the light of the world. He is Yahweh. If the Fourth Gospel is written with the Book of Esther in mind and as a statement of the truth about Jesus, i.e. who he is and how he has come into the world to save all men (the Jews, the Samaritans and all mankind), the aim is to show that he has the monopoly on truth. Those who oppose him are not of the light, but of darkness and belong to the prince of this world. We must remember that this is the basic assumption with which the Fourth Gospel begins. In Jn. 12 the Greeks come to him. He had not gone to them, as the Jews earlier (Jn. 7:35) thought he would, but they had come to him. It is now that he stated (Jn. 12:3) that his hour had come. Confirmation came in the voice from heaven, and he said (Jn. 12:31): "Now shall the prince of this world be cast out." The work that Yahweh/Jesus was doing was cosmic salvation. The Fourth Gospel can have nothing to do with nationalism. Purim and *Megillath Esther* were the expressions of nationalism. If the Fourth Gospel is speaking to its time at the end of the 1st century, when *Megillath Esther* was admitted by the Jews to holy writ, it is quite feasible that it makes passing allusions to counter its influence. The first mention of the Jews seeking to kill him falls on the unnamed feast which, from the calendrical references

before and after it, seems to be Purim. Does that mean that the
Jews are Haman in the Fourth Gospel? Before answering that, one
has to take into account who Jesus is in the Fourth Gospel. One
must go back to the prologue. He is God of very God. It is not
the case that the Jews are Haman and the Church is the Jews.
Christ, the Son of God, is the true light of the world. As
noble patriots as Mordecai and Esther were, they were not the
light of the world, over against the real wicked one, the prince
of this world, Satan, who is the real cause of evil and not a
mere Haman. Although it is true that the rabbis sought to find
Haman mentioned in scripture as *he-Rasha* (cf. T. B. Meg. 11a),
they did not get to the root of the matter. The Jews (Jn. 5)
who sought[178] to kill Jesus because he said that God was his own
Father are, in the eyes of the Fourth Gospel, not merely Haman.
They had refused God and had passed judgment on themselves. The
Fourth Gospel is truly a terrible, absolutely uncompromising
book. If one does approach it and does not accept it and its
claims, it declares that we have passed judgement on ourselves.
It is not opposed to the Jews, any more than it is opposed to
the Christians for whom it was written. In fact the Christ of
its pages would now pass harsher judgement on Christians of today than Jesus did on the Pharisees when he said (Jn. 9:38):
"For judgment came I into this world, that they which see not
may see; and that they which see may become blind." "Are we
also blind?", asked the Pharisees. To them Jesus replied:
"If you were blind you would have no sin: but now that you say
'We see' your sin remains." And we must remember that "the
Jews" in the Fourth Gospel is a technical term for the religious
establishment. True, the Fourth Gospel says "the Jews" sought
to kill him (in Jn. 5:16; 10:31) and they sought to cast stones
at him (in Jn. 8:59) but they did not succeed, because as the
gospel says "his hour" was not yet come. "Hour" is an astro-

logical term; it reminds one that the rabbis said Haman was an
astrologer, and from the time Mordecai would not worship Haman
he kept on casting *"Purim"* (i.e. lots) to find the hour or
auspicious time to go in to seek permission from the king to
kill Mordecai and all the Jews. The gospel keeps on reminding
us (cf. Jn. 7:25; Jn. 8:37; Jn. 8:40) that the Jews were seeking to kill or stone Jesus, but it admits that there was a
division among the Jews, e.g. Nicodemus, a ruler of the Jews,
spoke up for Jesus and more or less told the Pharisees that in
prejudging him without a hearing they did not know their own
Law as they ought. The officers of the Jews at the Feast of
Tabernacles (Jn. 7) refused to bring him in (Jn. 8:45, 46) and
those who the chief priests and Pharisees sent to take him in
Gethsemane (after Judas betrayed him) fell down in awe when
Jesus approached them (Jn. 18:6). True, the Pharisees are
mentioned along with the chief priests here. This seems to
constitute the establishment, the Jews. But the Pharisees also
appear to be separated from the Jews. This could be an attempt
to indicate the historical division of the Sadducees (the priests
and the Shammaitic Pharisees) as over against the Hillelites
(the Pharisees in the New Testament and in Josephus' general
nomenclature). Although unconvinced, the Pharisees proper do
not seek to kill him (cf. Jn. 10:38). They sought again to
take him (cf. also Jn. 7:30, 44) not to kill or stone him. They
were reported to have threatened to put to the *herem*[179] those
who confessed him as Christ. The multitude as a whole are the
most tolerant, and many seem to be willing to believe him.
Yet they are the first (Jn. 7:20) to say that he has a devil.
This is said by some of the Jews (Jn. 10:19). It might be too
much to say that the Evangelist means that those who say this
of the Son of God are themselves devil-possessed. It is only
Judas, one of his disciples, who he said of Jesus (Jn. 6:70):

"And one of you is a devil." Jn. 13:2, in speaking of the
foot-washing, says: "the devil having already put it into the
heart of Judas Iscariot, Simon's son, to betray him". Who
then is Haman? This is like asking who is the anti-Christ.
Theodore of Mopsuestia rightly sees the anti-Christ as the
devil and the alleged candidates for the position as individual
men in their fallen state among the heathen emperors and even
in the Church (cf. *Mingana Woodbrooke Studies*, vol. VI, pp. 39,
490). One cannot even say that Caiaphas, the high priest, was
Haman, although he has a claim to this distinction more than
Judas Iscariot. Haman had thought that the death of Mordecai
was not enough and that his people should die with him. Caiaphas thought it expedient that one man die for the people, so
that the whole nation perish not. The rabbis (in T. B. Meg.
13b) pointed out that Haman had said in Esth. 3:8: "There is
one nation", which, according to them, implied that Mordecai
and the nation were one, and so they should die together. Esth.
3:6 shows that in Haman's eyes it seemed contemptible to lay
hands on Mordecai alone. However, Mordecai was not different
from the Jews (Jn. 11:51), but Jesus was. The Evangelist said
that Caiaphas, being high priest that year, prophesied that
Jesus should die on behalf of the nation and not for the nation
alone, but so that he might unite into one the children of God
that are scattered abroad. And by this statement the writer
of the Fourth Gospel meant that he should die for all mankind
who would accept him and be his sheep, i.e. hear his voice.

Basically it was the members of the establishment, "the
Jews", who, for the best part of a year, had been seeking to
kill Jesus. This reminds one of the time (12 months) Haman
had cast lots[180] as to when would be the auspicious moment to
get permission to crucify Mordecai and kill all the Jews. The
earlier attempt (cf. Jn. 7), when the chief priests and Pharisees

had tried to arrange for his arrest, had failed. The resurrection of Lazarus brought matters to a head; now the chief priests
and Pharisees in council were worried. If they left Jesus alone,
they said "all men will believe on him". (They now admitted that
Jesus did many signs.) They were chiefly worried as to what the
Romans, Edom/Amalek would do (Jn. 11:48): "The Romans will come
and take away both our place and our nation." The irony of this
statement is that the Romans did not do this because of Jesus or
his teaching but because of the political nationalism of latter
day "Mordecais". And even after 70 A.D., they took the example
of Mordecai and Esther as their guiding light. And worse was to
befall them in the Bar Cochbah Revolt. If Caiaphas said "the
Romans will come and take away both our place and our nation",
he showed he was more concerned about political expediency and
his position than about God and religious values. And yet his
cynical remark about it being expedient that one man should die
for the people was turned into God's glory; and by the time this
gospel was written, the chief priests and Caiaphas had lost both
their place and what vestige of individual nationality that Judea
had possessed under a Roman Procurator and a Judaized Edomite
puppet ruler.

But note although now the Sanhedrin "took counsel that they
might put him [Jesus] to death" (Jn. 11:53), they could do
nothing until Judas, being inspired by the devil, betrayed him.
In the Zohar, which is admittedly medieval,[181] Haman is the
devil.

If it is compared with the movement of the Esther story,
Jesus' going to raise Lazarus is parallel to Esther going in
unannounced to the king. For the raising of Lazarus brought
Jesus directly before Caiaphas' attention (cf. Jn. 11:49). As
we have pointed out above (p. 124), Jesus combines in himself,

as it were, for the writer of the Fourth Gospel the action
carried out in the Esther story by *both* Mordecai and Esther.
Esther was identified by the rabbis with the "Hind of the
Dawn" (cf. the title to Ps. 22) though a minority opinion
(cf. Midrash Psalms, Ps. 22) was that the "Hind of the Dawn"
was God Himself. It could be that Lazarus is a type of Mordecai. "Sick" (cf. Jn. 11:1) may mean that Lazarus, who had
once been a friend of Jesus, was no longer such a friend. We
must remember that for the Evangelist Jesus is Yahweh incarnate
and that Yahweh (the Lord) and God *El* (= *El Elyon* God Most High)
are closely related. Since *El Elyon* is universalistic in His
outlook, Yahweh/Jesus cannot regard patriotism as enough.
Whether it is the Samaritan woman speaking of our father Jacob
or the Jews (being of Abraham's seed) boasting of their father
Abraham, ethnic nationalism was no surrogate for a believing relationship with the living God (*El Hai*). Knowing who Lazarus
was helps to explain the sickness.

The Fourth Gospel introduces us to new characters not
found in the Synoptics: we know Martha and Mary from Luke's
gospel, but Nicodemus and Lazarus are new. Actually the Talmudic sources know of Nicodemus, Martha, and Mary. We may learn
much about Lazarus (or Eleazar) and perhaps even something about
Nicodemus and Mary from Josephus. These characters were all
apparently well-known at the time of the Roman War. This does
not necessarily mean that they were not alive around 30 A.D.
The active public life of a man can easily span 35 to 40 years
from maturity. This does not mean, however, that the writer of
the Fourth Gospel, by speaking of Lazarus or Nicodemus or Martha
and Mary, was necessarily describing events which happened to
them in Christ's earthly ministry. The Christ they knew was
already the Christ of faith, the Son of God, and the Son of Man
who is in heaven. He was the Christ speaking to them in their

desperate need, and their bitter disillusionment with nationalism and messianism which was allied to an ever-expanding legalism of the new establishment which was now dominated by the
rabbis.

As this present work sees it, the Fourth Gospel sets out
who Jesus was, is, and will be. He is the great I am. It compares him with Abraham, Jacob, Moses, and by implication Esther.
Since it was speaking for its own day, it contrasts Mordecai and
Esther and their work for the deliverance of the Jews with the
work of Jesus for not only the Jews but all mankind. It shows
him not only at the great Mosaic feasts of Passover and Tabernacles but at feasts such as Purim and Hanukkah, which were recent innovations even after his time. The Fourth Gospel is not
afraid to introduce people confronted by Jesus who lived after
his time. We think of Lazarus, Martha, Mary and Nicodemus. It
not only shows that the glorified Christ is the Christ of faith
but also that his gospel has a word for them as well as for the
people of his own incarnate ministry. When he recites the Passover Haggadah, the Jew rightly believes that he was present at
the Exodus and that what was done there was done for him. The
Christian believes that he was at the cross and that he, i.e.
the twentieth-century Christian, crucified Jesus and that Jesus
died for him. Christ the Son of God is his Saviour. In a very
real sense we celebrate his death, passion, and resurrection at
the altar. The Fourth Gospel by showing what Jesus does for
Nicodemus in answering his inquiries, by directing him as to
what he must do to obtain eternal life, by comforting Martha and
Mary, and by raising Lazarus is speaking to the Evangelist's own
time. Some of these individuals in the gospel are types of individual human beings, while others (like the Samaritan woman at
Jacob's well, the woman taken in adultery, the paralytic, or the
man born blind) are symbols of groups of individuals of all

periods. It is a timeless gospel which it preaches, and yet
it is ever timely and relevant. We were there and he heals me.
He creates sight in me which I never had. He raises me to a
new life here and now. And it is to a new type of life he
raises me. Since the Jesus of the Fourth Gospel is Yahweh,
the redeemer God of Israel, the creator and *El*, the God of all
mankind, and the one God, the message which the gospel imparts
is not only directed to the men and women of ca. 30 A.D.; but
the God revealed in it also speaks to men and women of the end
of the first century A.D. And when I recognize my plight in
theirs, when I realize my common humanity with them and accept
him for what he is, i.e. God of very God, I hear him speaking
to me and my fellowman in this and every age.

"Martha (Jn. 11:21) therefore said unto Jesus, 'Lord, if
thou hadst been here, my brother had not died'." A distinction
is made in Jn. 11 between the death of the body and the special
significance that the Fourth Gospel gives to the word "death".
The key statement for the understanding of what the Fourth
Gospel means by death is (Jn. 5:24): "Verily, verily, I say to
you, he that hears my word, and believes Him that sent me, has
eternal life and comes *not* into judgement, but has passed out
of death into life." We are driven back again to Jn. 5, the
chapter which contains so much of the central teaching of the
Johannine Christ which he delivered on the Feast of Purim. The
word of Jesus is the word of the Father. The Father has given
all judgement to the Son. Our attitude to Jesus the Son is
fundamental. Do we honour the Son as we honour the Father?
If we do, we hear the word of the Son as the word of God and
we believe not just that God sent him, but we also believe what
God says. Such a person has eternal life here and now. It
would appear that there is *no* future judgement for such a person.
He has now passed out of death into life. Even at the end, the

judgement is basically on our attitude of God. Realizing this, the Fourth Gospel sees no need to wait for a judgement at the end as far as the individual is concerned. This does not necessarily conflict with the idea of a general resurrection on the last day, but with a general judgement. In the Fourth Gospel, Jesus reverses the common early rabbinic[182] Jewish concept of the resurrection as being restricted to the righteous Jews or at the most to Jews. Jn. 12:47-49 is parallel to the statement in Jn. 5:24-29. Jn. 12:48 states: "He who rejects me and receives not my saying has one who judges him: the word that I spake, the same shall judge him in the last day." On the other hand, the man who has believed Jesus' word now has passed from judgement, and there is no future judgement for him. In Jn. 5:25 "the hour" is at hand when the dead shall hear the voice of the Son of God and they that hear shall live. The only physical resurrection of the dead in the Fourth Gospel is the case of Lazarus. He is not the only dead man referred to by this verse. The "now" of Jn. 5:25 is not restricted to the earthly ministry of Jesus. The Fourth Gospel is a literary gospel (cf. Jn. 20:31): "But these are written that you may believe that Jesus is the Christ, the Son of God, and that believing you may have life in his name." "The dead" must be those who have a wrong concept of God for "the Father has life in Himself" (cf. Jn. 6:57: "the living Father"). The Fourth Gospel stresses the oneness of the Father and the Son and of God and Jesus who is Son of God and Son of Man. One thinks in particular of Jn. 10:30 ("I and the Father are one"), but it is already declared in Jn. 1. This stress on the unity of God and Jesus is the Christian *Shema'*. The *Shema'* (Dt. 6:4) states: "Hear, O Israel: *YHWH* our God is one *YHWH*: (v. 5) and you shall love *YHWH* your God with all your heart, and with all your soul, and with all your might." The Fourth Gospel is a haggadic discourse or series of such discourses based on the life of the risen, glorified Jesus and his continued deeds of power within the Church up to its writer's own time.

The "now" of Jn. 5:25 is not just the "now" of Jesus' lifetime in the body. It is the "now", the existential moment, whenever his word (i.e. the word about him) is proclaimed. The fundamental demand made on the hearer of the Fourth Gospel is to declare the loving unity of God and Jesus Christ and to love God as shown in and by Jesus Christ. The old *Shema'* was the declaration of faith by Israel. It emphasized that *YHWH Elohenu* (the LORD *our* God) is one *YHWH* LORD. The Christian declaration, the Johannine Kerugma, is that Jesus (*YHWH* saves) is LORD (= *KURIOS* = *YHWH*) and is one with God. The old *Shema'*, which is not quoted in the Fourth Gospel, has a national emphasis. It does not say that the LORD our God is the one God, but that God is one *YHWH*, recalling the revelation of God as *YHWH* to Moses. While identifying Jesus with the incarnation of *YHWH*, the Fourth Gospel declares he is one with God (i.e. the God whom all men sought after or believed they knew) and that only Jesus had declared God as He really was. We must remember that the Fourth Gospel was speaking to Jews who twice daily recited the *Shema'* (the whole three sections of it) with the benedictions before and after it. It is saying to such people that they are dead, i.e. that they are not in contact with the living God. It could be that the emphasis on the Torah in the benedictions before and after the *Shema'* is under attack, but it is more likely that the gospel is attacking the interpretation of the scriptures by Rabbi Akiba and his school to support their development of the oral law. Hillel (T. B. Shab. 30b) had summarized the Torah with quotations of Dt. 6:4 and Lev. 19:18. This latter passage stressed love of one's neighbour in the Fourth Gospel. In Jn. 13:34 and 15:12 the new commandment is (Jn. 13:34): "You shall

love one another; even as I have loved you, that you also love
one another. (v. 35) By this shall all men know that you are
my disciples, if you have love one to another."

Jn. 15:12 reads: "This is my commandment, that ye love
one another, even as I have loved you. (v. 13) Greater love
hath no man than this, that a man lay down his life for his
friends." This new commandment goes much further than Lev. 19:
18 or its Matthean and Lucan parallels.[183] The extent to which
one is to go in loving one another is infinitely greater. It
is to the extent that Christ, the Son of God, loved mankind and
came into the world of men and died for them, so as to enable
them to love one another. If the Christians love one another
to that extent, then all men will know that they are disciples
of Christ. The rabbis of M. Ber. 2:2 said one had to declare
the *Shema'*, i.e. belief in God and His unity, before one could
take on the yoke of the Torah and its commandments. In Jn. 15:
13, after the second citation of Jesus' commandment, the example
of Christ's death for his friends is the means and inspiration
of how to fulfill that commandment.

The First Epistle of John 4:20 states: "If a man say I
love God, and hates his brother, he is a liar: for he that
loves not his brother whom he has seen, cannot love God whom
he has not seen." Whereas the later record of Christianity
has not been as good as that of Judaism, yet in the period before and during the Roman War, the Jews of Palestine were shock-
ingly divided, and the treatment of Jews by other Jews was almost as bad as they were treated by the Romans. One is not
thinking of the extortion and plundering of the Jewish farmers
by the sons of Hanan (Ananias?) or the ruthless murders and
robbing by the Sicarii[184] (to some extent with the connivance
of Procurators like Albinus[185]). It is rather the civil war
of Jew against Jew which went on from the time of Eleazar[186]

son of Ananias son of Nedebaeus which divided the Jews and incensed the Romans by forbidding the Temple officers to accept sacrifices from a foreigner. The civil war did not stop with the Roman War itself. Simon bar Giora[187] and John of Gischala are singled out in particular by Josephus for their fleecing and plundering of their fellow Jews. "As rivals for power they were divided, but in their crimes unanimous."

CHAPTER 10

Which Lazarus?

Jn. 11 is linked with the Esther allusions of the earlier
chapters. The Jews are much in evidence. When Jesus decides
to (v. 7) "go into Judea again" the disciples say to him:
"Rabbi, the Jews were but now seeking to stone thee; and are
thou going thither again?" This reminds us of Jn. 8:59 and
Jn. 10:31. Jesus' cryptic question in Jn. 11:9, "Are there
not twelve hours in the day?", is possibly a reference to it
not yet being his "hour". It could also be an allusion to Haman
casting lots for twelve months as to when it was appropriate to
get the king's assent to destroy the Jews in Persia (cf. Esth.
3:7). The second part of Jn. 11:9, "If a man walk in the day,
he stumbles not, because he sees the light of this world", is
reassurance to the disciples. He is the light of the world;
they will go safely because he is with them. Jn. 11:10 may be
a reference to his adversaries who stumble because the light
is not in them. The story of Lazarus is given an exact geo-
graphical setting--Bethany. In Mk. 14:3 and Mt. 26:6, it is
at Bethany in the house of Simon the leper that at a supper two
days before the Passover and his arrest that a woman anoints his
head. Here in the Fourth Gospel, Bethany is the village of Mary
and Martha her sister. Jn. 11:2 very carefully links the raising
of Lazarus in Bethany with the anointing by Mary of the Lord at
Bethany (Jn. 12:2). Mary and Martha are known by name to us in
Luke (10:38, 40, 41) but they are not of Bethany.

Lazarus is Mary's and Martha's brother. When he became
sick, they sent to Jesus saying: "Lord, behold he whom thou

lovest is sick." Jesus' statement (Jn. 11:4): "This sickness
is not unto death, but for the glory of God, that the Son of
God may be glorified thereby" reminds one of Jn. 9:3 where the
case of a man born blind evoked Jesus' statement: "Neither did
this man sin, nor his parents: but that the works of God should
be made manifest in him." Whatever "sickness" means, it is "not
unto death". And yet he did die before Jesus came. This is
significant. Death here is not physical "death"; it is something far worse. This incident is put in here "for the glory
of God, that the Son of God may be glorified thereby". "Glorified" in John means crucified. The raising of Lazarus is clearly
shown to be the immediate cause of this glorification (i.e. crucifixion). But it serves another but vitally related purpose; (cf.
Jn. 11:15) it is so that "you may believe". Jn. 11:11-14 are important as showing that the Johannine definition of physical
death is sleep (but cf. also Mk. 10:52). Thomas' demand (Jn.
11:16) to his fellow-disciples, "Let us also go, that we may die
with him", has to be seen in the light of Peter's boast (Jn. 13:
37): "I will lay down my life for thee." On the other hand,
"him" may not refer to Jesus, but to Lazarus.

If Lazarus is the Eleazar who held on at Masada after Jerusalem fell and encouraged the people besieged there with him to
commit mass suicide, then Thomas is made to voice the opinion
of those who died there with Eleazar. Josephus gives Eleazar's
two speeches. The first is the shorter of the two (B. J. VII
320-336; 337-339). Eleazar regards it as a favour granted by
God to them to die bravely and in a state of freedom. He is convinced "that the same God, who had of old taken the Jewish nation
into His favour, had now condemned them to destruction". And now
when they are openly deprived by God Himself of all hope of deliverance, and when many hung back from killing their wives and
children and destroying themselves, Eleazar tried again in a

speech (B. J. VII 341-388) which is partly philosophical, partly historical in tone. He gives discourses on the immortal soul imprisoned in a mortal body. When the soul is freed from the weight of the body which drags it down to earth, it goes to

> its own proper place and does then become a partaker of that blessed power, and those abilities, which are then in every way incapable of being hindered in their operations. The soul continues, invisible to be sure, to the eyes of men, as is God Himself: for certainly it is not itself seen while it is in the body; for it is there after an invisible manner; and when it is freed from the body, it is still not seen. It is this soul which has one nature, and that an incorruptible one also; but yet it is the cause of the change that is made in the body. For whatsoever the soul touches lives and flourishes; and whatsoever is removed from it withers away and dies; to the degree that there is immortality in it. Let me produce the state of sleep as a most evident demonstration of the truth of what I say: wherein souls, when the body does not distract them have the sweetest rest depending on themselves, and conversing with God, by their alliance to Him, they then go everywhere, and foretell many futurities beforehand; and why are we afraid of death, while we are pleased with the rest that we have in sleep? And how absurd a thing it is to pursue after liberty while we are alive, and yet to envy it to ourselves where it will be eternal! We, therefore, who have been brought up in a discipline of our own, ought to become an example to others of our readiness to die.

The reference to Lazarus as sleeping may be an allusion to the above comparison of the body sleeping and its death. However, it is indeed doubtful if the Fourth Gospel makes such a dichotomy between body and soul, and if it regards the body as the source of all ills, and every soul as incorruptible. In fact in the Fourth Gospel it is not the death of the body which automatically frees the soul. The whole man, awake in his body, can enjoy communion with God now.

Eleazar (Jos., *ibid.*) then goes on (after stating however that "we do not stand in need of foreigners to support us in this matter") to speak of Indian philosophers and their attitude to life in the body as a necessary servitude. They, he tells us, have such a desire of a life of immortality that they welcome death,

> and nobody hinders them, but every one thinks
> them happy men, and gives them letters to be
> carried to their familiar friends [that are
> dead]; so firmly and certainly do they believe
> that souls converse with one another [in the
> other world].

He knows of the body being burned on the ghat, but it would appear as if Eleazar thinks of them being burned alive. He says:

> For their dearest frineds conduct them to
> their death more readily than do any of the
> rest of mankind conduct their fellow-citizens
> when they are going on a very long journey,
> who at the same time weep on their own account,
> but look upon the others as happy persons, as
> so soon to be made partakers of the immortal
> order of beings.

Eleazar asks his audience if they are not ashamed to have lower notions than the Indians? If, however, they (his audience) had been brought up to believe that life is the greatest good which men are capable of, and that death is a calamity, then they ought to bear that calamity courageously. He goes on:

> Since it is by the will of God, and by necessity,
> that we are to die; for it now appears that God

> has made such a decree against the whole Jewish
> nation, that we are to be deprived of this life
> which [He knew] we would not make a due use of;
> for do not you ascribe the occasion of your
> present condition to yourselves, nor think that
> the Romans are the true occasion that this war
> we have had with them is become so destructive
> to us all; these things have not come to pass
> by their power, but a more powerful cause hath
> intervened, and made us afford them an occasion
> of their appearing to be conquerors over us.

Towards the very end of his speech Eleazar reiterates: "God Himself hath brought this necessity upon us." This attitude is totally different from that of the Fourth Gospel. God is not just the God of Israel. He loves all men equally, and so much did He love them that He sent His Son Jesus into the world to save them and to show them how to live in the world. By loving one another, they show how they really love God.

Josephus (B. J. VII, 401) points out that this mass suicide was on the 15th Xanthicus,[188] which is identical with Nisan. In Esther, Haman decides in Nisan to get rid of Mordecai and the Jews. Also it is on this day that Esther went in to the king. Her words (Esth. 4:16) had been: "If I perish, I perish." The fall of Masada was the very end of the (Palestinian) Jewish Revolt and War with Rome. It had all come to nothing. Yet Judaism continued thanks to Rabban Yohanan ben Zakkai who had left[189] Jerusalem before its fall and had obtained permission from Vespasian to set up an academy. He rallied Judaism, bereft of its Temple as it was. New prominence was give to the Torah, even though without a priesthood and Temple, the laws of sacrifice and purification could not be carried out. With R. Akiba at the end of the century, nationalism was encouraged by the admission of the *Megillath Esther* into the canon of holy scripture.[190] Relations between Judaism and Christianity were almost broken

off by the introduction by Gamaliel II of the *Birkath ha-Minim*
in the *Amidah* prayer. The Fourth Gospel is written within this
context, and seeks to give Jesus' word for the situation with
the Jewish community which in many ways resembled that of Jesus'
time. The calamitous defeat of 70 was sufficiently far away for
nationalist aspirations fostered by the particularism of the
Torah, and a desire for national revenge fostered by Esther.
Later, before the second revolt, a Messiah Bar Cochbah was to
epitomize all their hopes.

Now Josephus (B. J. VII, 399) does mention two women and
five children who survived.

> Yet was there an ancient woman, and another who
> was of kin to Eleazar, and superior to most
> women in prudence and learning, with five
> children, who had concealed themselves in
> caverns underground, and had carried water
> thither for their drink, and were hidden there
> when the rest were intent upon the slaughter
> of one another.

Josephus (*ibid.*, 403, 404) tells how the Romans, the next morning
after their surprise at the fire and absolute silence, shouted
and the women ventured out of their underground cavern. The
second one of them, the relative of Eleazar, told the Romans
what was said and done. Here we have two women one of whom is
related to Eleazar; they came out of a cave alive. Eleazar the
patriot has perished by his own hand; Eleazar, to use his own
terminology, is sleeping—the sleep of death. He may have
imagined that once their souls were released from their bodies
he and the others in Masada would converse with God. Lazarus
was to converse with God in the body.

Jn. 11:17 stresses that Lazarus was properly dead. He was
in the tomb "four days", not like Jesus' "three days" being only
a visitor there. The Jews come to console Martha and Mary con-

cerning their brother. Martha goes to meet Jesus to whom she
said: "If you had been here, my brother would not have died."
This is later paralleled in Jn. 11:3 when some of the Jews said:
"Could not this man, who opened the eyes of him that was blind,
have caused that this man should not die?"

We must take this whole story within the context of the
Fourth Gospel as a church book. So when Martha said "Lord if
thou had been here, my brother had not died", it means if he had
been a Christian, he would not have really died, he would only
have fallen asleep. However, though she did not realize the
implication of her remark, Martha is confident that even now
Jesus can do something. God will answer his prayer. Mary is
not as confident in this story. It is beyond his power now.
She weeps (Jn. 11:33) and the Jews weep. Jesus (Jn. 11:23) told
Martha: "Your brother shall rise again." Martha (Jn. 11:24)
states: "I know that he shall rise again in the resurrection at
the last day." This implies that his resurrection at the last
day was as automatic as her reply. Jesus declared himself to
be Yahweh (Jn. 11:25, 26). He said to her: "I am the resurrection and the life: he that believeth on me, though he die, yet
shall he live; (v. 26) and whosoever lives and believes on me
shall never die." Martha's reply to Jesus' question "Do you
believe this?" shows that she is on the way to understanding.
"I have believed that thou art the Christ, the Son of God, *even*
he who is coming into the world." The second part of the statement is a purely messianic statement like what the people said
at the feeding of the five thousand (Jn. 6:14). Jn. 6:15 adds:
"Jesus therefore perceiving that they were about to come and take
him by force, to make him king, withdrew again into the mountain
himself alone." In short, Martha's belief in Jesus is affected
by Jewish political messianism. Martha, however, sends her
sister Mary to Jesus. Jn. 11:28: Jesus "groaned in the spirit

and was troubled" at the weeping of Mary and the Jews. This
indicated their unbelief. When Jesus asks the Jews where they
have laid Lazarus, they reply: "Lord, come and see." Jesus
weeps (v. 35).[191] We can be sure that this is no mere overflowing of emotions. It is more likely that he wept in pity
at their implied lack of faith in him by asking him to come and
see. Martha's remark as they rolled away the stone underlines
her imperfect faith: "Lord, by this time he stinks: for he
has been *dead* four days." What was the glory of God which she
should see if she believed? It was what he had said in Jn. 11:
25: "He who believes on me, though he die, yet shall he live
and (26) whosoever lives and believes on me shall never die."
The believer would see Yahweh recreating that and more than
that. This chapter (Jn. 11) is concerned to show that Jesus
is God of very God. His prayer of thanksgiving (Jn. 11:41) is
explained in v. 42 as only said so that the multitude might believe that God had sent him. When Lazarus comes forth on hearing Jesus' voice, this is a single example of what is promised
in Jn. 5:28. Unlike the risen Jesus (Jn. 19:40; 20:7), the
risen Lazarus is still bound hand and foot with grave clothes,
and his face bound about with a napkin.

The resurrection of Lazarus leads some of the Jews (v. 46)
who had seen what he did to believe in Jesus. But some (v. 46)
went and delated on him to the Pharisees who wanted to seize
him. This then led to the chief priests and the Pharisees con-
vening a council (see above, p. 231-2) at which Caiaphas ruled
that Jesus should die that the whole nation perish not. Then
what they feared, namely, that the Romans would come and take
away "both our place and our nation", took place. Eleasar of
Masada is Eleazar the son of Jairus (B. J. II, 447; cf. also
B. J. VII, 253 where he is described as the head of the Sicarii).
He was apparently a grandson of Judas, a Galilean who is mentioned

in Gamaliel's speech in Acts 5:37. This Judas was the founder
of the Zealots. According to Josephus (B. J. II, 118 and also
B. J. VII, 253), he incited his fellow-countrymen to revolt.
He induced multitudes of Jews to refuse to enroll themselves,
when Quirinius was sent as a censor to Judea in the time of
Augustus (cf. Lk. 2:2). Josephus (B. J. II, 118) says that he
incited his countrymen to revolt by upbraiding them as cowards
for consenting to pay tribute to the Romans and tolerating
mortal masters, after having God for their Lord. On the doc-
trines of the Zealots (*Ant*. XVII, 23), Josephus says that
while they agreed in other respects with the Pharisees, they
have an invincible passion for liberty and take God for their
only leader and Lord. Even then the Sicarii banded together
against those who collaborated with Rome, plundered their
property, rounded up their cattle, and set fire to their homes
(cf. B. J. VII, 254). Eleazar of Masada had escaped to Masada
when the Zealots under Menahem, probably Eleazar's uncle, had
been defeated in Jerusalem in the struggle between pro-Romans
and the insurgents in the summer of A.D. 66. This sprang from
the refusal of Eleazar, the son of Ananias the high priest, and
a captain of the Temple (i.e. Segan), to allow the priests
officiating in Temple services to accept any gift or sacrifice
from a foreigner. Josephus (B. J. II, 409) points out that
this action laid the foundation of the war with the Romans for
the sacrifices which were offered on behalf of Rome and the
emperor were in consequence rejected. The chief priests and
the notables favoured its continuance, but the priests, as
numerous as they were and supported by the revolutionaries, held
to Eleazar's ruling. Josephus (B. J. II, 411-416) tells how the
chief priests and the leading Pharisees decided to convene a
mass meeting before the bronze gate, i.e. that of the inner
Temple (this was the beautiful gate of Acts 3:2 and the Nicanor

gate of the Mishnah).[192] They explained to the people that
this was a revolt and could lead to war. In any case, they
said, their forefathers had always accepted the gifts of
foreign nations and had never prevented anyone from offering
sacrifice there (i.e. through the duly accredited priests).
This was a strange and dangerous innovation to their religion
which they were now proposing and which besides endangering
the city was "laying it open to the charge of impiety, if Jews
henceforth were to be the only people to allow no alien the
right of sacrifice or worship" (B. J. II, 414, 415). The chief
priests and leading Pharisees said that they were afraid if
they refused the sacrifices for the Romans, they might not be
allowed to offer sacrifice for themselves (*ibid.*, 416).

However, because the revolutionary party would not listen
to them, the Jewish notables were afraid that they would be the
first victims of Roman displeasure and to exonerate themselves
from blame they sent two deputations, one to Florus the Procurator and the other to King Agrippa, requesting them both to
come with troops and crush the revolt. Josephus tells us that
Florus, as determined as he was to kindle the war, gave no reply.
Agrippa, who was "anxious that the Romans should not lose the
Jews nor the Jews their Temple and mother city", sent two thousand horsemen. With this reinforcement, the chief priests and
those of the citizenry who favoured peace with Rome occupied the
upper city, the lower city and the Temple being in the hands of
the insurgents. For seven days there was a full-scale battle
of Jew against Jew. On the eighth day during the feast of wood-
carrying (i.e. fuel for the altar) the Sicarii joined with the
rebels in the Temple and their combined forces took the upper
city, burnt the house of Ananias the high priest and the palaces
of Agrippa and Bernice, and left much of the city in flames.
Ananias the high priest, his brother Ezechias, and others fled

to the fortress palace of Herod the Great on the highest
terrace of the upper city which was invested the next day.
Now Menahem, who was the son of Judas the Galilean who in the
time of Quirinius "had upbraided the Jews for recognizing the
Romans as masters when they already had God" (Jos. B. J. II,
433), got into the king's armory at Masada and armed his body-
guard. He came to Jerusalem and directed the siege of the
palace fortress, and Ananias and his brother were caught in
the palace grounds and slain (Jos. B. J. II, 441). This turned
Eleazar and his followers against Menahem who with his followers
was attacked in the Temple (Jos. B. J. II, 445). His followers
in Jerusalem were massacred, except for a few like Eleazar the
son of Jairus and the nephew of Menahem who escaped to Masada.
Menahem, who sought concealment in Jerusalem, was tortured and
killed. The Roman garrison in the fortress retired to the forti-
fied towers. Hippicus, Phasaelus and Mariamne, and Metilius the
Roman commander of the garrison asked Eleazar, the son of Ananias, to spare their lives if they surrendered. The promise to
spare them was given by oath, but when Metilius marched his men
down and they laid down their arms, they were slain by Eleazar's
party. Only Metilius was spared by promising to be circumcised
and become a Jew (Jos. B. J. II, 454). This massacre took place
on the Sabbath. Eleazar, the son of Ananias, had coins struck
in his name with the inscription: "The First Year of the Liberation of Jerusalem". When this gospel was written there was a
double irony here. He had not only died for the nation but also
for all the children of God, and the Romans *had* come and taken
away their place. There was also an Eleazar of Macherus (cf.
B. J. VII, 196-209) whom Bassus was going to crucify in the
eyes of those in the citadel there. A cross was set up and the
young man was to be hung on it. Bassus was going to trade his
life for the surrender of the citadel. Eleazar besought them

not to disregard him and to surrender. Eleazar escaped but many died. By going to raise Lazarus, Jesus saved Lazarus but he himself was crucified. This incident may have been recalled by the writer of the Fourth Gospel, but it is principally the death of Eleazar at Masada that seems to have been in his mind. In a way Eleazar was a latter day Mordecai, like the one who escaped hanging at Macherus, but many died. He himself and the Jews who made the last stand at Masada with him died to be free. They died for their Law, the Law of Life, but they also died because they had lost confidence in life and felt that God Himself had deprived them of all hope of deliverance. They felt this, although as Eleazar states (Jos. B. J. VII, 331): "We have still great abundance of food, and a great quantity of arms, and other necessaries more than we want." This is where a national patriotism of the Mordecai type can lead. It was not the Romans who were their worst enemies, but they themselves, and not only themselves, but also Eleazar. His knowledge of God was very faulty; his nationalism had blinded him to what God was doing for his people and all mankind. The Christian Church was active in Palestine during the Jewish Revolt and War. It also had to reassess itself. It had shared the messianic nationalistic views of the Jews. It was having then and later to reassess its picture of its Saviour and what he saved them from. It had to reinterpret the positive connotation of salvation. It had to see the gospel as intended for all men. It had to learn more of the brotherhood of man under God the one Father. The Fourth Gospel showed that true religion can only remain true if those who claim to practice that religion show love to all men. The glory of God is seen in that "He so loved the world that He gave His only begotten Son to die that men should not perish but have everlasting life" and that the Son of God died for us so that we might live enabling us to love our fellowmen. It is also our bounden duty because it is the way we can show our love of God.

As far as the movement of the Fourth Gospel is concerned, when it is seen as parallel to the movement in the *Megillath Esther* and assuming Lazarus to be a sort of lay-figure modelled on Mordecai, the notice of his sickness marks the stage when Esther hears that Haman is going to act against Mordecai. Note in Jn. 11:6 the unexplained delay of Jesus when he heard that Lazarus was sick: "He abode at that time two days in the place where he was." "Then" (Jn. 11:7) "after this he said to the disciples, let us go into Judea again." This is parallel to Esther's fasting three days and then venturing to go in unannounced to the king on the third day. The writer of the Fourth Gospel makes it plain that the disciples felt that going into Judea was like going to certain death, just as Esther's statement, "If I perish, I perish", reveals the same consequence for going unannounced to the king. Jesus' going to raise Lazarus was in fact a story on the theme "Greater love has no man than this, that he lay down his life for his friend" (Jn. 15:13). That Jesus loved Lazarus is noted in Jn. 11:3 and 36. Lazarus is parallel to Mordecai as Jesus is to Esther. If Lazarus is really Eleazar the fighter for freedom, Jesus was the bringer of freedom who can also free the freedom fighter from himself, his own true enemy. In a way, as the chief priests and the Pharisees felt (Jn. 11:47), Jesus (as an innovator and as a leader of any great popular movement) was as dangerous, if not more dangerous, as the Sicarii and Zealots. Jn. 11:54 reminds one of Jn. 7:1. Here Jesus retires into the country with his disciples near the wilderness to a city called Ephraim. Obviously he could no longer walk openly among the Jews because the chief priests and Pharisees in council had taken counsel how they might put him to death. First they had to take him (cf. Jn. 11:57), and they "had given the commandment that if any man knew where he was, he should show it, that they might take him". Jn. 11:55 states that the Passover of the Jews was at hand and that many had gone up to purify themselves so that they might, like those that brought Jesus before Pilate (Jn. 18:28) and those who refused to enter the Praetorium, eat the Passover in the requisite state of ritual purity. Jn. 11:56 makes those at the Temple undergoing their purificatory rites ask one another whether Jesus would come up to the Passover, much as he had made the Jews at the Feast of Tabernacles wonder where he was (Jn. 7:11). John 12:1 states that Jesus, six days before the Passover, came to Bethany where Lazarus was, and it reminds us that this was the one Jesus raised from the dead. There is a supper at Bethany which stands in a relationship to the supper before his arrest just as the supper Esther arranged for the king and Haman (at which Haman thought he was to be honoured by Esther the queen) stands in relationship to the next supper (which Esther arranged for the king and Haman) at which she denounced Haman. Martha (Jn. 12:2) served the supper and she is here apparently the same character as in Lk. 10:40. It is emphasized that Lazarus sat at the table with him. Mary took a pound of very precious spikenard and anointed the feet of Jesus and she wiped his feet with her hair. This version of the anointing has definite points of contact with Lk. 7:37, 38 where Jesus' feet are anointed. Although in Luke, the woman stood behind at his feet, weeping. And she began to wet his feet with her tears, she wiped them with the hair of her head, then she kissed his feet and anointed them with the ointment. The event takes place in the house of Simon the Pharisee in Capernaum, and the woman who was in that city was a sinner. Mark has his own version of the anointing. It is in the house of Simon the leper in Bethany, and is two days before Passover. Who the woman was is not stated nor the fact that she was a sinner. While in the Marcan account Judas Iscariot went away to the chief priest *after* the anointing, "that he might deliver him to them" (Mk. 14:10), in the Fourth Gospel this does *not* occur after *this* supper but during the next one. Whereas in Mark "they" (indefinite) murmured among themselves about the waste, in the Fourth Gospel it is Judas who verbalizes the complaint. The same sum of money (for which it might have been sold) is mentioned as in Mark. That the money from its sale could have been given to the poor occurs in both Mark and the Fourth Gospel. John 12:6 points out that Judas said this "not because he cared for the poor, but because he was a thief and since he held the money box he used to take what was put into it". The Fourth Gospel (and also Mark 14:7) has the statement by Jesus in reply: "The poor you have always with you, but me you have not always." The Johannine form is the shorter (omitting "and whensoever you wish you can do them good"). Whereas Jesus says in Mk. 14:8: "She has done what she could; she has anointed my body beforehand for the burying", in the Fourth Gospel Jesus says: "Allow her to keep it against the day of my burying". This would appear to refer to what is left of the ointment. It would almost appear as if Judas wanted to appropriate what was left ostensibly to sell it for the poor. Whereas Jn. 12:3 states that the house was filled with the odor of the ointment, we have in Mk. 14:8 a saying of Jesus: "Wheresoever the gospel shall be preached throughout the whole world, that also which this woman has done shall be spoken of for a memorial of her." There may be some relationship between the two statements; a good odor and good name are associated ideas.[193]

The interesting thing is that the immediate outcome of this supper in the Johannine account was not the arrangements between Judas and the chief priests to deliver over Jesus to them. Rather the chief priests also took counsel to put Lazarus to death because

by reason of him many of the Jews went away and believed on
Jesus. Lazarus is being afforded the same attention as Jesus
by the same people. The entry into Jerusalem (Jn. 12:12-15)
is closely parallel to that in the Synoptics. Among the gospel
accounts, the branches of the palm trees mentioned in Jn. 12:13
are unique to the Fourth Gospel. They do feature in Simon
Maccabee's triumphant entry into Jerusalem (I Macc. 13:51).
Note that Jn. 12:16, "These things understood not his disciples at the first: but when Jesus was glorified, then remembered they that these things were written of him, and that they
had done these things to him", follows after the citation from
Zech. 9:9. This latter is itself, as it were, the scriptural
foretelling of the manner of his entry, but it is actually the
basis for the description which developed when Jesus was revered
as messiah in the Jewish Christian Church. The Fourth Gospel,
however, retains it for the entry of the incarnate Son of God.
As in Luke, the reference to David is omitted, yet he who enters
is the king of Israel. It is a royal entry: the note of meek-
ness (cf. Mt. 21:5) is missing. The raising of Lazarus is not
forgotten. It is specifically mentioned that the multitude,
which was with him when he called Lazarus out of the tomb and
raised him from the dead, bore witness, and as a result the
multitude that now welcomed him had gone out to meet him because
they had heard of the sign which he had done in raising Lazarus.
As a result the Pharisees (Jn. 12:19) said among themselves
(after the manner of the opponents of Jesus in the Fourth Gospel
who bore an unintentional but telling witness to him): "Behold,
how you can achieve nothing: lo, the world is gone after him."
In Jn. 11:48 the Pharisees had said: "If we let him thus alone
all men will believe on him." They were not letting him alone,
but the result was the same.

Jn. 12:20ff. tells of the Greeks that were among those who came up to worship at the feast. The Syriac naturally calls them Arameans. They are brought in here to typify the non-Jewish world coming to Christ. They come to Philip with their request, who tells Andrew and they both tell Jesus. It was Andrew who in the first chapter had brought Philip to Jesus. Jesus' reply (Jn. 12:23) is that "the hour is come, that the Son of Man should be glorified". This is a very significant statement coming at this specific juncture. It would appear to mark the climax of the mission. The Greeks represent the world which God sent His only begotten Son to save. Here it is plain that the Fourth Gospel, although historically set in a Palestinian Jewish milieu, is not primarily directed at the Jews. Certainly the gospel shows that the Jews had their chance, but their leaders rejected him, and in so doing judged themselves. Like Andrew and Philip in the beginning, the Greeks now come to Christ. He went time and again to the Jews and to Jerusalem, even when he knew they sought to stone him and kill him, so this gospel tells us. But now it tells us the Greeks came to seek him, just as the disciples had done.

The Jews (Jn. 7:35) suggested that he would go to the Greeks. And the Greeks came to him when he was amongst the Jews. He had not gone out to them. It was as the Pharisees (Jn. 12:19) had said: "Behold how you prevail nothing; lo, the world is gone after him." The glorification of the Son of Man is his crucifixion, his raising up which draws all men unto him. In Esther "the fear of the Jews" (i.e. of their supremacy), after Haman was hung and his decree reversed, made people become Jews. Here before the decree has been finalized against the deliverer, the Greeks came to Jesus.

Jn. 12:24 is a "verily, verily" statement in the illustration of the necessity of a grain of wheat falling into the earth

and dying (*qua* "grain of wheat") so it can produce much fruit.
Otherwise it just remains a grain of wheat. If one loves his
life in a possessive manner, one loses that life because one
cannot hold on to a life like that and have it remain life.
"He that hates his life in this world shall keep it to life
eternal." This is a very hard saying. I do not think we are
justified in setting "life in this world" over against "life
eternal" in any temporal or spatial sense since this would be
contrary to the Johannine usage. Nor is the contrast similar
to say a "business life" as over against a "Church life", see
e.g. in an obituary: "He found his niche in business life; he
was also active in Church life." And the reason why it is not
similar is that it would appear in the quotation that "business
life" and "Church life" are two separate spheres, and further
that they both can end with death. Life eternal can begin in
this world. He who gains it now has it forever. Hate is a
very strong word. It must mean to esteem lightly according to
the world's values. It is a question of values, and it is a
question of the desired aim to be attained.

But Jn. 12:26 provides the guiding principle, perpetual
devotion, and attendance on Jesus: "Where I am, there shall
also my servant be." God the Father bestows honours on the
servant of such a master. That transcends all worldly honours
for he who thinks he loves his life loses it. Serving Christ
is basically partnership with God in His work of redemption.

In Jn. 12:27 Jesus, the Son of God, says: "Now is my soul
troubled." The Fourth Evangelist shows Jesus as the glorified
Christ, the Son of God. In this verse he is not being inconsis-
tent and dropping back into the view of Jesus as merely a good
and saintly man faced with the prospect of death. Nay, he is
the same Christ the only begotten Son of God as throughout the
gospel, but the Evangelist is showing and daring to show that,

even for the Son of God, what he was about to do was no easy
matter. It is not make-believe; God the Son as Jesus Christ
was personally involved in mankind's struggle. The second part
of v. 27 says: "And what shall I say? Father save me from
this hour. But for this cause came I unto this hour." This is
the nearest this gospel gets to Jesus' prayer at Gethsemane in
the Synoptics. There is no request in the Fourth Gospel for
the cup to pass (cf. Mt. 26:42; Mk. 14:36; Lk. 22:42). In Jn.
12:28 Jesus' real prayer appears: "Father, glorify Thy name."
The glorification of the name of God is His martyrdom, but it
is not an ordeal to be grimly borne, but the means of glorifying
God's name. Then comes a voice out of heaven, a *Bath ḳol*, saying: "I have both glorified it and will glorify it again."
This is the time a heavenly voice appears in the Fourth Gospel.
In the Synoptics it occurs at baptism (e.g. Mk. 1:11: "Thou
art my beloved Son, with thee I am well pleased"). In the Fourth
Gospel (Jn. 1:30ff.) reference is made by John the Baptist to
what he saw and heard (cf. especially v. 33): "Upon whosoever
you shall see the spirit descending, and abiding upon him, the
same is he that baptizes with the Holy Spirit." But the following verse (Jn. 1:34) is the more important: "And I have seen
and have borne witness that this is the Son of God." In fact,
it is by John's witness that God glorifies Jesus in the beginning
of the gospel. The Baptist had described himself as the voice
crying in the widerness, "Make straight the way of the LORD as
said Isaiah the prophet" (Isa. 40:3). "LORD" here has to be
taken in the sense that the LORD is Jesus and He is Yahweh saving. But if it be argued that John the Baptist claims "to make
straight the way of the LORD", his various testimonies to Jesus,
and who he is, are an ascription of glory to him. Jesus' request (Jn. 12:28) was: "Father, glorify Thy name." What does
"Thy name" mean? Jesus does say (Jn. 5:32): "I am come in my

Father's name", and also in Jn. 10:25 he refers to "the works which I do in my Father's name". Does this use of "in my Father's name" mean just "by the authority of my Father"? That explanation does not cover all that is meant by "name" in the Jewish milieu of the past century. The Talmud[194] is nearer the mark when it says that Jesus worked the miracles by means of the *Shem ha-Meforash* (the fully explained, properly enunciated name of God) which he had written out and inserted under his skin. They however looked on him as a magician. But their own Cabbalists in the Middle Ages believed that if one only found the proper enunciation of the name of God, one could work amazing miracles like the Rabbi[195] of Prague and his Golem.

But when the Hebrews spoke of God's name, they meant His very personality and character. While it is true that theologically speaking when God is given a new name, it is tantamount to a new revelation of the character and personality of God. From the point of view of the historian of ancient Middle Eastern religious phenomena, when a god gets a new name it means his community has united with another community and the two communities have identified the other's deity with their own. *El* or *Elohim* may have been the God of the Patriarchs, but after Moses His name was Yahweh. But Yahweh is not just a name; He is a Being in His own right. *El* and *YHWH* are one the worshippers are told. How are they one? How can the worshippers know they are one? By telling them that *YHWH* is the name of *El*. The Fourth Gospel is speaking to a Gentile world as well as to a Jewish or Judaean Christian group who were both worried lest Gentiles thought their religion to be narrow and nationalistic. There had been hopes based on Ezek. 37:28 that at the messianic deliverance there would be, like that of the Exodus, a new name of God, i.e. a new revelation of His personality and character would be revealed. The Fourth Gospel writer holds fast to *YHWH*

the Saviour God of Israel.[196] But just as Moses explained
Yahweh as the new name of the God of the Forefathers, so also
the Fourth Evangelist sees Jesus as Yahweh (Yahweh saving) and
Jesus as the new revelation of the name of God. There is a
continuity between Yahweh and Jesus, not just in name but personality. Yahweh was a personality in His own right, as well as being the name of God; so it is with Jesus. Jesus is God's name.
"Glorify Your name" when said by Jesus to God means "glorify me".
The Fourth Evangelist actually explains the relationship of Jesus
to God as being as close as God's name to God Himself. In a
sense it is parallel to the concept of *Logos*, Word of God and
God, but name, i.e. personality and possessor of the name or
personality, was more equal and coterminous one with the other.
The theology of the Fourth Gospel is a *nomen* theology more than
a *Logos* theology. If so, does this run counter to the idea of
identity of will, or to put it in another way, the subordination
of the will of the Son to the Father? "Will" in English is a
hard, harsh word; even *Thelema* in Greek is not so hard. Certainly *Razon* in Hebrew has both the sense of "favour" and "will".
Sons in the ancient Middle East did the will of their Fathers
and were pleased to do it, nay they esteemed it a privilege so
to serve the wishes of their elders. The occurrences of "will"
in the Fourth Gospel show the harmonious relationship and the
identity of purpose between Son and Father, and Father and Son.
Actually the principal reference in Jn. 12:28 to the heavenly
voice's reply, "I have *both glorified* it" (the name), would be
the raising of Lazarus whose death was for the glory of God,
that the Son of God may be glorified thereby (Jn. 11:4; cf. also
Jn. 11:40). While in the raising of Lazarus, Martha saw "the
glory of God" and the Son of God was glorified thereby, if his
real glorification is the crucifixion, this latter is also a
revelation of the glory of God. The Fourth Evangelist (in Jn.

12:29), by making some of the multitude think the voice was
thunder, shows their spiritual deafness. The others who said
"An angel has spoken to him", while partly wrong, give Jesus
the opportunity of telling them: "That voice has not come for
my sake, but for your sakes." Thus the Evangelist reassures
his hearers that Jesus as divine is completely in control of
this and every situation. Jn. 12:31: "Now is the judgment of
this world: now shall the prince[197] of this world be cast out."
It is a cosmic drama. It is not just something happening at the
human level between a Jewish messianic miracle worker and the
Jewish authorities, or by implication between the followers of
such and the Jewish authorities. The Gentiles have come to him
who in any case is not a Jewish messianic miracle worker, but
the Son of God. Because he is who he is, it is not merely the
judgment of the Jews but of the world; nor is it merely the
judgment of the people of this world, but of the prince of this
world, Satan. It is he whom they all serve, thinking they are
serving God. It is not a Haman, or those who act the part of
Haman, whether they be the Jews, Caiaphas, or the Romans, but
the prince of this world, the prince of darkness with whom the
battle is. And Jesus is confident of the outcome. Jn. 12:32:
"And I, if I be lifted up from the earth, will draw all men to
myself" refers to his crucifixion. Haman had made a truly lofty
crucifixion gallows of 50 cubits for Mordecai; but Jesus' cross,
whatever its height, will lift him higher. The cross is not a
disaster, it is the predetermined climax of his ministry, and it
will take all men away from the Prince of this world. In Jn.
12:34: "The multitude answered him, 'We have heard out of the
law[198] that the Christ abides for ever.'" If they are referring
to Ps. 89:4, 29, it could be that they are interpreting "seed"
as referring to the Messiah who then could be understood as enduring for ever. Ps. 110:4 could refer to the (Davidic?) messiah

as a priest forever after the order of Melchizedek. In any case,
the multitude's concept of the Messiah was not that of the Fourth
Evangelist. The multitude then paraphrase the first part of Jn.
12:32 and ask what it means. "And how do you say, the Son of
Man [for "I", v. 32] must be lifted up? Who is this Son of Man?"
This occurrence of the term "Son of Man" reminds the hearer of
the gospel of what Jesus had himself said earlier about the Son
of Man; cf. Jn. 6:62: "What then if you should behold the Son
of Man ascending where he was before?", or Jn. 8:27: "When you
have lifted up the Son of Man, then shall you know that I am
he..." They have just now (Jn. 12:32) substituted Son of Man for
Jesus' "I". When they have lifted up Jesus, they will know who
"I" is, i.e. Yahweh the Man on the throne-chariot of Ezekiel's
vision. He being who He is, abides for ever. As in Jn. 7:3
Jesus tells them that he (here called the light) is but a little
while among them. They are to walk while the light is among them
so that the darkness overtake them not, for he that walks in the
darkness knows not whither he goes. While they have the light
(i.e. Jesus), they should believe on the light (Jesus) so that
they may become sons of light (v. 36).

In Jn. 8:59 Jesus withdrew in such a manner that they could
not find him. The Evangelist in Jn. 12:37-43 gives his comments
on the situation. Although Jesus had done so many signs before
them, they still did not believe him. Why? So that the word
of Isaiah the prophet might be fulfilled. It is surely significant that only the first verse is cited from Isa. 53. The reason
they could not believe was because Isaiah said (cf. Isa. 6:10):
"He has blinded their eyes and hardened their heart, lest they
should see with their eyes, and perceive with their heart, and
should turn, and I should heal them." Actually in the M. T.,
Yahweh on sending Isaiah commands him (Isaiah) to "make the
heart of this people fat, and make their ears heavy, and shut

their eyes, lest they see with their eyes, and hear with their ears, and understand with their heart, and turn again, and be healed." It is important to note that in the Johannine rendering of this Isaianic passage the "and [they] be healed" of the M. T. becomes "and I should heal them". What is the reference of the intrusive "I"? If the "he" of v. 40 refers to Isaiah whose commission it was to carry out the blinding and hardening, then the "I" refers to Jesus. On the other hand, if the first person is Isaiah in the earlier quotation (Isa. 53:1 in Jn. 12:38) and also in the next quotation based on Isa. 6:1 in Jn. 12:40, then the LORD is the one who has blinded their eyes and hardened their heart with the result that Isaiah could not heal them. This is more likely and leads on easily into Jn. 12:41: "These things said Isaiah, because he saw His glory; and he spake of Him." The reference here is to Isaiah's vision of the Lord (*Adon*) (Isa. 6:1ff.). One should refer to the Targum where Isaiah does not see the Lord, but only "His glory". The writer of the Fourth Gospel is identifying Jesus with Yahweh. When he calls Jesus LORD, He is the same LORD as Yahweh.

Jn. 12:42 admits, however, that some of the rulers believed on him; by "rulers" he must mean those like Nicodemus who were high in the hierarchy, i.e. rulers of the Jews (the establishment). "But because of the Pharisees they did not confess it, lest they should be put out of the synagogue." In Jn. 9:22 it was the Jews that the parents of the man born blind feared: "For the Jews had agreed already, that if any many should confess him to be Christ, he should be put out of the synagogue." Here the rulers (of the Jews) did not confess him because of the Pharisees for the same reason, viz. lest they should be put out of the synagogue (or community). But the basic reason is that of Jn. 12:43: "For they loved the glory of men more than the glory of God", which emphasizes what Jesus had said to the Jews

in Jn. 5:44: "How can you believe, who receive glory one from
another, and the glory that comes from the only God you seek
not." Jn. 12:44-50 summarizes and draws together much of the
doctrine of earlier chapters. The setting where Jesus cries
and uttered (Jn. 12:44) the statements in this section is not
given. The basic theme is the mutuality of Jesus and God (the
Father) which is reminiscent of Jn. 5:19-20. The emphasis here
is not as in Jn. 5:36 on the works of Jesus or the testimony of
John the Baptist as witnessing that the Father sent him, but
that believing on Jesus is believing on Him that sent him.
Likewise in Jn. 12:45, the emphasis is not, as in Jn. 6:40, on
the fact that beholding the Son and believing on him gives
eternal life to the beholder, but that the one who beholds Jesus
beholds Him that sent him. In Jn. 12:46 Jesus is the light of
the world as in Jn. 8:12: "Whosoever believes on Jesus does not
abide in darkness." To believe on him is the first essential
(cf. Jn. 3:36). It would appear from Jn. 12:47, 48 that to hear
Jesus' sayings and not to keep them is equated with the rejection
of Jesus as well as of the word which he spoke. But the word
which he spoke will judge him in the last day. It is not just
the word of Jesus, but the word of the Father. The word of the
Father, who sent Jesus and commanded him to speak it, is life
eternal. This is reminiscent of Jn. 5:24: "He who hears my
word, and believes Him that sent me, has eternal life, and comes
not into judgement, but hath passed out of death into life."
But there is a difference of emphasis. It is not Jesus' word
but God's word. Yet bearing in mind that belief in Jesus is
belief on Him who sent him (Jn. 12:44), one should *not* see any
real difference between the Word of Jesus and the Word of God.
What is more fundamental is the question of what distinction
if any the Evangelist sees between his word and the word of

Jesus. The answer would be none. His justification would be that Jesus had said (Jn. 16:12):

> I have yet many things to say to you, but you
> cannot hear them now. (v. 13) Howbeit when
> He, the Spirit of truth is come, He shall
> guide you into all truth: for He shall not
> speak from Himself; but whatsoever things
> He shall hear, these shall He speak, and He
> shall declare to you the things that are to
> come. He shall glorify me: for He shall
> take of mine, and shall declare it to you.

The Fourth Gospel is to the Marcan story of Jesus as the oral law of Rabbi Akiba is to the written law. And yet just as Rabbi Akiba saw his oral law not as an adjunct to the written Law but as its very essence (if the written law were to be understood aright), so what the Fourth Evangelist says of Jesus is not a later construction or re-interpretation of a gospel or gospels which were early interpretations of the personal ministry of Christ, but the real truth.

Jn. 13 is parallel to the second of Esther's dinner parties for the king and Haman, at which Haman is denounced. It is not the Passover Seder meal, nor is it intended to be understood as such. At last his hour has come, and it is now made plain that it is the hour of his departure. Very important is the statement (Jn. 13:1): "Having loved his own which were in the world, he loved them unto the end." Jn. 1:11 has: "He came to his own, and they that were his own received him not." Are "his own" (Jn. 13:1) the disciples? There is the possibility that at this stage there is not meant to be a clear-cut distinction between the Jews and the disciples. It is significant that according to Jn. 13:2 during the supper (the devil having already put into the heart of Judas Iscariot, Simon's son, to betray him) that Jesus rises, lays aside his garments, takes a towel, pours water in a basin,

and begins to wash and dry the disciples feet. This was done
by Jesus (v. 3) "knowing that the Father had given all things
into his hands, and that he came forth from God, and was going
to God". When Peter, the first to be approached, refused to
let Jesus wash his feet, Jesus says: "If I do not wash you,
you have no part in me." When Peter now asks to be washed all
over, Jesus says to him (v. 10): "He that is bathed needs not
to wash save his feet...." This is an allusion to the priests
in the Temple. In the morning before the officer on duty came,
they had to wash and vest themselves in readiness against his
coming. During the day on duty in the Temple, they need only
wash their feet. The Evangelist loses no opportunity of stressing the omniscience of Jesus. "You, the disciples, are clean,
but not all" (v. 11) "for he knew him that should betray him."
No mention is made of the washing of Judas' feet, but it is
presumed in v. 12. When he has robed himself again, he sits
down to the supper and asks them if they know what he had done
to them. What had he done? His remark to Simon Peter gives a
clear indication. He had made them his own, they had a part in
him, and one with the other through their common bond with him.
He had baptized them. This was not the usual baptism, but it
was recognized in the early Church as associated with baptism.[199]
Jn. 13:13: "You call me Master and Lord: and you say well, for
so I am." "Master", he is their Rabbi or Rabboni (cf. Jn. 20:
16). The Rabbi could expect his disciples (cf. Jn. 1:38, 49;
6:25) to carry out menial tasks for him. In fact it was said
(cf. Rambam, *Hilkoth, Talmud, Torah*) that the reason why the
Shekinah left Israel was because students offended their Rabbi![200]
The Rabbi and the LORD were almost synonymous in a pupil's
mind.[201] Jesus says "for so 'I am'". This is not just a statement that he is Rabbi like any other Rabbi. He is I AM, i.e.
Yahweh, and Yahweh is their Rabbi and LORD. *YHWH* by the end of

the 1st century was getting quite like the rabbis who regarded
Him in their own image, studying Torah like them, keeping their
rulings, meticulous in laying *Tefillin* (i.e. wearing Phylacter-
ies), keeping the feasts on the dates calculated by them. Jesus
(Jn. 13:14) drives home the lesson that if he who was then their
LORD and the Master, washed his disciples' feet, they ought to
wash one another's feet. He has given them an example of how
they should treat one another. Jn. 13:16 with all the force of
a "verily, verily" statement enunciates that "a servant is not
greater than his lord; neither is one that is sent greater than
he that sent him. (v. 17) If you know these things, blessed are
you if you do them." This is not only the basis of true Christian
humility, but of true Christian service. Our pattern should be
Jesus our LORD and Master. The ethics like the theology of the
Fourth Gospel is in terms of personal relations, not abstract
statements logically set out. Jesus states that he knows whom
he has chosen and that it is so that the scripture may be fulfilled that there is an ingrate in their midst. The scripture
to be fulfilled is Ps. 41:9: "He that eats my bread lifted up
his heel against me." One is left with the impression that the
supper setting is intended to provide the opportunity to fulfill
this scripture. Jesus (Jn. 13:19) tells his disciples that
henceforth he will tell them before it comes to pass so that
when it is come to pass they may believe that I am *He*. Again
the "I am" emphasizing that he is Yahweh. Jn. 13:20 is a
dominical dictum on hospitality showing the custom of the early
Church and its high regard for hospitality. Jesus (Jn. 13:21)
"was troubled in the spirit"[202] and testified and said: "Verily,
verily I say unto you, that one of you shall betray me" (cf. Jn.
12:27: "Now is my soul troubled"). Jesus felt sorely the in-
gratitude. At the table (Jn. 13:23) reclining in Jesus' bosom
was one of his disciples, whom Jesus loved. Lazarus is the only

individual in the Fourth Gospel, apart from Martha and Mary, of whom it is said that Jesus loved. Simon Peter asked this disciple of whom Jesus spoke. The beloved disciple leaned back and said: "Lord, who is it?" Jesus' answer was: "He it is for whom I shall dip the sop, and give it to him." This he did and gave it to Judas, who is here called the son of Simon Iscariot. It was then "after the sop" that Satan entered into Judas. Jesus (v. 27) told him: "What you do, do quickly." The Evangelist tells us that no one at the table knew why he said this to Judas. Some (Jn. 13:29) thought that Jesus had told Judas, who had the money bag, to buy something for the coming Passover Feast or to give to the poor. After receiving the sop, Judas went out into the dark; and it was night.

CHAPTER 11

Judas and Haman

While it is true that Judas is parallel to Haman in
Esther's second dinner party, it is really the devil that is
the true Haman. Judas is his tool. According to the Fourth
Gospel, one fears that the Jews, and Caiaphas as well, because
of their opposition to Jesus have passed judgment on themselves
and are possessed, or at least they are under the same influence
as Judas. In Jn. 8:44 Jesus calls the Jews "sons of the devil".
One fears what judgement the writer of the Fourth Gospel would
pass on most, if not all, of his commentators. At her dinner
party, Esther asked the king for her life and that of her people.
The king said: "Who is he, and where is he, that dares presume
in his heart to do so?" Esther (Esth. 7:6) said: "An adversary
and an enemy even this wicked Haman." There is a parallel to
this in Jn. 13:22 when Jesus says: "One of you shall betray me."
There is also a parallel when Jesus thus indicates Judas. In
Esther it was the king who went out into the garden, and it was
Haman who stood up to request his life from Esther the queen.
When the king returned, he found Haman in a compromising position
on Esther's couch. In the gospel dinner party, Jesus is parallel
to Esther. Simon Peter may be parallel to the king.

When Judas went out, Jesus said (Jn. 13:31): "Now is the
Son of Man glorified, and God is glorified in him; (v. 32) and
God shall glorify him in Himself, and straightway shall He glorify him." This reference to the Son of Man being glorified refer
back to Jn. 7:39: "For the Spirit was not yet given because

Jesus was not yet glorified." Jesus in Jn. 7:37 had said:
"If any man thirst let him come to me and drink." Then in v.
38 he had promised: "He who believes on me, as the scripture
said, 'out of his belly shall flow rivers of living water'.
(v. 39) But this spake he of the Spirit, which they who believed on him were to receive." Water and the words of the
Torah are equated in haggadic statements. Spirit and prophecy
were closely associated in Jewish sources.[203] Jesus (Jn. 6:63)
says: "The words that I have spoken to you are spirit and are
life." The Fourth Evangelist may be indicating that Jesus is
now going to be in a position to convey to the disciples the
special teaching such as follows in Jn. 14-17. The disciples
that remain after Judas is gone are his Church. His words are
drink to them (cf. also Jn. 6:35b: "he who believes on me shall
never thirst"). The Son of Man is glorified because of the
faith of the disciples. The coming of the Greeks to ask to see
Jesus was the sign that the Son of Man should be glorified (Jn.
12:23). God is glorified in him by the faith of the disciples
in the efficacy of prayer to Jesus (cf. Jn. 14:13: "And what-
soever you shall ask in my name, I will do it, that the Father
may be glorified in the Son"). God is also glorified in the
disciples' lives. "Herein (Jn. 15:8) is my Father glorified,
that you bear much fruit; so shall you be my disciples." Jn.
17:1-5 shows how God glorified Jesus in Himself, and how He
glorified him. God had given the Son authority over all flesh
that to those given him by God, he should give eternal life.
Eternal life is defined in Jn. 17:3 as knowing the only true
God and him whom He sent, Jesus Christ. Jesus (Jn. 17:4)
glorified God on earth by accomplishing the work which He had
given him to do. Now (Jn. 17:5) Jesus asks the Father: "Do
You glorify me with Your Own Self with the glory which I had
with You before the world was?" Because eternal life is knowing

the only true God and him whom He sent, Jesus Christ, we now
understand how, in the testimonies of John the Baptist and in
Jesus' confrontations with the Jews, the acceptance of the
witness as to who he was was fundamental.

Jesus (Jn. 13:33) announces his imminent departure to the
disciples. He tells them: "You shall seek me, and as I said
to the Jews, whither I go, you cannot come." This is what he
had said in Jn. 7:33 and the Jews said among themselves (Jn.
7:35): "Whither will this man go that we shall not find him?"
Now he says the same to his disciples. But to them he gives a
new commandment: to love one another, as he has loved them;
they are also to love one another. By this all men shall know
that they are his disciples, if they love one another. If we
remember when this gospel was written, we will appreciate all
the more the full significance of this new commandment. During
the first century the Palestinian Jewish community was torn
with religio-political divisions which engulfed the Jewish
people in the revolt and Roman War, in which it was not only
Roman against Jew, but Jew against Jew.[204] In the period of
reconstruction after 70 A.D., the rabbis with the development
of the oral law divided the Jews into the learned and the un-
learned. The intolerance of the *Talmide Hakamim* for the *Am ha-
Arez* was only matched by the hatred of the *Am ha-Arez* for the
Talmide Hakamim. The Johannine Jesus makes love for one another
not only the ideal but norm of religious practice and the basic
test of orthodoxy. Further Jesus did not expect, in fact he did
not want, his followers to die with him as Eleazar of Masada
did, but to live, and live in harmony with one another.

When Simon Peter said, "Lord, where are you going?", Jesus
(Jn. 13:36) told him: "Whither I go you cannot follow me now;
but you shall follow me afterwards" (cf. also Jn. 20:18, 19).
Simon Peter wanted to know why he could not follow him now, and

he said that he would lay down his life for Jesus. Jesus queried
that statement and predicted: "Verily, verily, I say to you,
the cock shall not crow till you have denied me thrice" (Jn. 13:
38).

(Jn. 18) After the discourses in the place where they had
supped, ending with the great high priestly prayer of Christ,
Jesus went with his disciples over the Kidron and entered a
garden there, where apparently Jesus and his disciples often
went. Judas knew the place, and a band of soldiers and officers
from the chief priests and the Pharisees came thither with lan-
terns, torches, and weapons. Jesus knew this as he had detailed
prescience of what was coming on him (cf. Jn. 18:4, and also
Jn. 13:1 and Jn. 13:19). This foreknowledge is connected with
his being *I AM*, i.e. Yahweh. Judas was with them, and when Jesus
(Jn. 18:6) said to them, "I am he", they drew back and fell to
the ground. This is not just surprise on the would-be captors'
part on their being taken unawares. The Evangelist wants us to
see that his saying "I am" backed also by his presence had something to do with it. We must remember that Judas is now possessed
by Satan (cf. Jn. 13:27). When it says in Jn. 18:2 that Judas
knew the place, would it be going too far to see "the place" as
a rabbinic metonymy for God? But when Jesus said "I am", the
Evangelist is very careful to mention: "And Judas, also, who
betrayed him, was standing with them" (Jn. 18:5). This is the
confrontation of Jesus/Yahweh with Judas/Satan. And Judas/Satan
with his minions from the chief priests and the Pharisees is
thrown down.

CHAPTER 12

John's Gospel: Christianized <u>Megillath</u> <u>Esther</u>
Superimposed on a
Christianized Passover Haggadah Pattern

One may ask about the gospel modelling its plot on that of
Esther. Must one allow that the Fourth Gospel had to conform
to certain points already fixed by previous gospel form since
Mark's gospel? Fixed points of this form were: the witness of
John the Baptist before or at the beginning of the ministry, the
betrayal by Judas, the trial, the crucifixion, and the resurrection. All these were open to reinterpretation but they had to
be dealt with. Apart from John the Baptist, the other fixed
points in the tradition allowed themselves to be fitted into
the Esther pattern. In fact, Ps. 22, which was traditionally
associated with Esther's ordeal, had suggested the form of the
crucifixion narrative. However, since the Fourth Evangelist
was the first to design his gospel after the pattern of the
Megillath Esther, he was faced with adapting an already established gospel pattern which basically was a Christianized Passover Haggadah. What our author has done is to produce a Christianized *Megillath Esther* which is superimposed on top of the
Christianized Passover Haggadah pattern, some of whose fixed
points could not be omitted although they were thoroughly re-
dressed and reinterpreted. But even with the parallels with
Esther, the writer of the Fourth Gospel is transcending the
events, causes, and ideals of the *Megillath Esther*, as well as
making a greater use of divine irony than the Book of Esther

ever dreamt of. The Fourth Gospel is universalistic whereas the *Megillath Esther* is nationalistic. This difference affects the doctrine of God and the doctrine of man; for in the Book of Esther there is by implication a doctrine of God. And certainly the *Megillath Esther*, as interpreted by the rabbis and because of that allowed in the canon, had a doctrine of God. It could not have obtained entry into the canon of scripture had it not been inspired by the Spirit.[205] It could be that the doctrine of the Spirit in the Fourth Gospel is an answer to the rabbinic doctrine of the Spirit which had led to the canonization of the Book of Esther. The Spirit in the Fourth Gospel leads one into all truth (Jn. 16:13). Even with the fact of the revelation of *the truth* in and by Jesus, the full implications of this truth as it was and is in Jesus had yet to be grasped by men.

Judas the betrayer was Haman,[206] but Judas as the betrayer of Christ was Satan just as Satan had been in Haman. The Fourth Gospel is not looking at earthly things and stopping there. It is seeing beyond appearances to the real forces which are in conflict. Therefore the Jews in the *Megillath Esther* who were the would-be victims of Haman's guile and malice are playing the role of Haman in this gospel along with Caiaphas and Judas, Herod, and Pilate.[207] Lazarus (Eleazar) is the epitome of the ideals of Mordecai and Esther, and he has to be rescued, nay even brought back from the death to which his ideals had brought him. He is rescued by Jesus who now seems to the Jews to be Haman, but in reality Jesus is the help from (Esth. 4:14) the other place (God). The Fourth Gospel then is the struggle between light and darkness, good and evil, God and Satan. And God is victorious. The characters in the drama like the institutions of the Temple and festivals represent what had been good and virtuous in Jewish life and history and worship. But they are shown not to be good and virtuous enough. It is the case of

the good being the enemy of the best. More than that, it shows
how if men try to preserve old traditions and attitudes dear to
them, they can be seduced into coming to terms with the Evil
One. They may think they are still serving God, but in reality
they are the tools of Satan. All change is not necessarily
good, but holding on to the past at any price may be positively
evil, and it may result in getting one's values mixed. One may
then call good evil and evil good. There is a warning in the
Fourth Gospel for the Christian Church. It is now the Jews of
the Fourth Gospel, the religious establishment, that is coming
to terms with Haman of nationalism and secularism for the sake
of the survival of religion as the establishment know it, until
in the end it plays the part of Haman's master, the devil. No
institution, however good in its day, is immune from decay. Nor
are ideals such as nationalism the supreme good. To cling to
such ideals in the face of new and nobler ideals is to make what
once was a good a positive evil.

Again Jesus (Jn. 18:7) asked his would-be captors who are
now prostrate: "Whom do you seek?" And they said: "Jesus of
Nazareth." In Jn. 18:8 Jesus answered: "I told you that I am
he: if therefore ye seek me, let the disciples go their way."
Jn. 18:9 states that this was done by Jesus so that the word
which he spake (cf. Jn. 17:12) in his high priestly prayer might
be fulfilled: "Of those whom you have given me I lost not one."
According to this, Jesus was determined to make the sacrifice
alone. He did not want to involve his disciples in death with
him. Unlike Haman, Judas is not going to act as Haman did with
Mordecai (Esth. 3:6): "But he thought scorn to lay hands on
Mordecai alone, for they had showed him the people of Mordecai."
Jesus is not like Eleazar of Masada, the deliverer who made his
people die before killing himself. So when Simon Peter drew a
sword and cut off the high priest's servant's ear, Jesus said

to Peter (Jn. 18:11): "Put up the sword into the sheath: the cup which the Father has given me, shall I not drink it?" The sword as a means of salvation is clearly shown to be ruled out.

The band, the chief captain, and the officers of the Jews (here the Jews are clearly identified with the chief priests, cf. Jn. 18:3) seized and bound Jesus, and they brought him to Annas, who is identified as the father-in-law of Caiaphas who was high priest that year. The gospel (Jn. 18:14) reminds us that Caiaphas was the high priest who had counselled the Jews (cf. Jn. 11:50; but Jn. 11:47 shows that the Jews here could include the chief priests and the Pharisees gathered in council). Annas is the redoubtable high priest who, in addition to having been high priest himself, had five sons and one son-in-law, Caiaphas, the high priest. He was a sort of *eminence gris* as long as he lived. The tomb of Ananus, as Josephus calls him, is mentioned in Jos. B. J. V, 506 when speaking of the wall that Titus built round Jerusalem to block every exit and starve the Jews out. It could be that this tomb was not that of the elder Ananus, son of Seth = Annas, but of his son the younger and more famous Ananus who was murdered by the Idumaeans (Jos. B. J. IV, 314-318). Ananus, Jr., the son of Ananus Sr., was a Sadducee and had been appointed high priest by Agrippa II and was deposed after three months on account of his highhanded action in punishing James the brother of "Jesus called Christ" with death (*Ant.* XX, 197ff.). In his *Antiquities*, Josephus ascribes a harsh character to him; whereas in the wars, Josephus shows him to be the leader of the moderate party, opposed to the Zealots, betrayed (Jos. B. J. IV, 126-127) by John of Gischala. In dealing with his murder by the Idumeans, he adjudges him as Thackeray.[208] The corpse of Ananus (Jr.) was cast out without burial. Ananus (Jr.) was not a pacificist: he incited the citizens to attack the Zealots. In his speech to the people, Ananus said of the

Temple seized by the Zealots (B. J. IV, 173): "Well, they [the Zealots] have mastered the strongest point in the city,...for henceforth the Temple must be spoken of as a mere citadel or fortress....(§ 174). Will you wait for the Romans to succour our holy places?" Ananus in the same speech (*ibid*, § 180-184) says:

> Now that I have mentioned the Romans, I will not conceal from you that thought which struck me while I was speaking and turned my mind to them. I mean that even should we fall beneath their arms--God forbid that those words should ever be our lot!--we can suffer no greater cruelty than what these men have already inflicted upon us. Is it not enough to bring tears to the eyes to see on the one hand in our Temple courts the very votive offerings of the Romans, on the other, the spoils of our fellow countrymen who have plundered and slain the nobility of the metropolis, massacring men whom even the Romans, if victorious, would have spared? Is it not lamentable that, while the Romans never overstepped the limit fixed for the profane (i.e. the limit of the unhallowed ground), never violated one of our sacred usages, but beheld with awe from afar the walls that enclose our sanctuary, felons born in that very country, nurtured under our institutions and calling themselves Jews should freely perambulate our holy places, with hands yet hot with the blood of their countrymen? After that, can any still dread the war with the foreigner and foes who by comparison are far more lenient to us than our own people? Indeed, if one must nicely fit the phrase to the fact, it is the Romans who may well be found to have been the upholder of our laws, while their enemies were within the walls.

It was indeed because of the fighting going on in Jerusalem, and in which Ananus (Jr.) had been involved, that the Roman generals

urged Vespasian to attack Jerusalem when he did. "Divine providence," (*pronoian theou*) they said, "has come to our aid by turning our adversaries against each other; but changes come rapidly
and the Jews will quickly return to unanimity through weariness
or repentance of civil strife" (B. J. IV, 366, 367). It is
possible in reading Josephus' *Jewish Wars* to confuse the Ananus
there mentioned with the Ananus of the time of Jesus (as this
is even done in the index to *The Works of Josephus*, trans.
Whiston, London, 1866, which considers the eulogium in B. J. IV,
319-322 to be that of Ananus [Sr.]). It is quite possible that
Annas is deliberately mentioned by the Fourth Evangelist to relate the capture of Jesus with a notable high priest whose influence directly or indirectly was felt in the Civil War that
preceded the war with Rome proper, at least as far as Jerusalem
was concerned. The high priesthood of Caiaphas, however, ties
the event of Jesus' capture to the same year as in Matthew and
Luke. (Mark does not name the high priest of the trial of Jesus.
Luke does mention Annas along with Caiaphas in giving the date
of John the Baptist's call [Lk. 3:2].)

Simon Peter (Jn. 18:15) followed Jesus, and so did another
disciple, who was known to the high priest. We do *not* know who
the other disciple was, but at the Last Supper Simon Peter asked
the disciple whom Jesus loved to ask Jesus whom he was alluding
to as the betrayer. Apart from Andrew who brought Simon Peter
to Jesus (Jn. 1:41), there was the unnamed other who, having
heard John the Baptist's testimony, had been the first to follow
Jesus. In Jn. 21:20, 21, Peter, having heard how he will die
and seeing the disciple whom Jesus loved following, asks Jesus:
"Lord, and what shalt this man do?" It might appear that "another disciple" (cf. Jn. 18:15) is the disciple whom Jesus loved,
since Peter on two recorded occasions seems to be particularly
associated with him. That disciple (Jn. 18:15) "was known unto

the high priest" and entered in with Jesus into the courtyard
of the high priest. Jn. 21:24 seems to claim that the writer
of this gospel is the disciple that Jesus loved. Since he
claims first-hand knowledge of all that went on in the high
priest's house (cf. Jn. 18:19ff.), it is quite likely that he
means himself by "that disciple" (Jn. 18:15) who was known to
the high priest. It appears on internal[209] evidence that the
disciple whom Jesus loved is Lazarus. If Lazarus were Eleazar,
the first son of Annas to be high priest, it would not be surprising that he was known to Annas. The problem of identifying
the resurrected Lazarus with John the Elder is another matter.
It is not insuperable. There is the tradition that John the
Elder wore the *Petalon*, i.e. the *Ẓiẓ* or high priestly plate
which was holy to Yahweh. The *Petalon* was the prerogative of
the high priest or presumably a past high priest. If the disciple whom Jesus loved was Lazarus, and he was entrusted with
the Lord's mother, and Mary lived in Ephesus with John, it is
possible that Lazarus had changed his name after he was raised
from the dead. One thinks of the old Jewish custom of one's
changing a personal name[211] when he is seriously ill, or of the
baptized Saul changing his name to Paul. On the other hand,
there is no need to take literally the *after the flesh* statements of this spiritual gospel. It is the latest of the gospels.
Jerusalem had fallen, the Temple had gone, not only so but the
Megillath Esther was almost rivalling the Law in the canon.
Christians were shut out of synagogues as there was the *Birkath
ha-Minim* and the malediction on Jewish Christians *et al.* in the
Amidah. The tone of this gospel, which knows Purim and Hannukah
among the Jewish religious feasts (a mark of its lateness), is
designed to emphasize that Jesus is not just an historical figure
of the first third of the first century. But Jesus is speaking
about Judaism after the Temple was destroyed, and not just that,

he is speaking about the contemporary (for the writer of that gospel) Judaism at the end of the first century. There had been several Lazaruses since Eleazar, the son of Annas, had been high priest for a year or two years before Caiaphas. The fact is that, apart from Acts 4:6, and except for the gospels in the N.T., we do not know the names of any high priests of the first century. From the rabbinic literature, we learn little of the names of individual[212] high priests. In short, we are dependent on Josephus (especially the *Jewish Antiquities*), if we are to reconstruct a list of high priests in the last seventy years of the Temple's existence. If the Fourth Gospel was written in the last decade of the first century, it is possible that only the *Jewish War* and not the *Jewish Antiquities,* was available to the writer. If the *Jewish Antiquities* was not available to the writer, then he could not have known of Eleazar the son of Ananus who is only mentioned in the *Jewish Antiquities* (XVIII, 34). In the *Jewish War* the high priest Ananus (Jr.) does not appear apart from a reference to Ananus as father of high priest Jonathan (B. J. II, 240). If one only knew of Annas' (Ananus) son, one might think that any reference to the high priest Ananus in the *Jewish War* referred to the one and only Ananus (Annas) of whom one had heard.

There are numerous[213] Eleazars mentioned in the *Jewish War*. Ananias the high-priest (the father of Eleazar and captain of the Temple) doubtless knew of Eleazar (the son of Jairus) because Eleazar (the son of Jairus and nephew of Menahem the Zealot) was in Jerusalem at the time when his uncle and his brigands joined forces with Eleazar (the son of Ananias) and his followers in the Temple fighting against Ananias and the more pacific of the citizenry in the upper part of the city.

Ananus (Jr.) certainly knew Eleazar (the son of Simon), who was at first the leader of the more pro-Roman forces, but then later was the most influential leader of the Zealots (B. J. II, 566) to whom John of Gischala denounced Ananus. Ananus would also certainly know Eleazar (the son of Ananias [B. J. II, 566]) when he became general for Idumea as the revolt became structured.

Since there can be a confusion between Ananus Senior and Junior, or Ananias (the high priest) and Ananus (the son of the latter (B. J. II, 243), it is possible that Eleazar, the son of Ananias, can be mistakenly thought to be the son of *either* Ananus. In which case Eleazar, the son of Ananias, would be thought to be the son of Annas. Ananus, the son of Ananias, was the captain[214] of the Temple in *Ant.* XX, 131 just as his brother Eleazar was later. One could be excused for thinking, if one had not Josephus' *Antiquities of the Jews*, that Annas and a son Eleazar were active in the early days of the revolt. If a confusion is possible with Ananias, Annas, and Ananus, it is likewise just as possible with Eleazar. In fact Eleazar (the son of Ananias), Eleazar (the son of Jairus), Eleazar (the son of Simon), and Eleazar of Machaerus could become mixed up and a composite Eleazar (the son of Annas) could be produced whose patriotic activities stretched from the time of Annas to Masada. One might the more easily expect the writer of the Fourth Gospel to have written from the standpoint of such a composite Lazarus (Eleazar) who had come to Jesus as his LORD and his God. Could we expect to hear of him in the gospel if, after he had been raised by Jesus from the dead, he had reverted to militant political nationalism? The difference between Pharisaism and Zealotry was only in the degree of national activism. Lazarus (Eleazar) of the Fourth Gospel is a type, and represents all the Zealot nationalists, i.e. the Mordecais of

their time. What he stood for would be recognized by his name.
The Fourth Gospel shows what Jesus' attitude to these patriots
is and how he recreates and uses them, to such an extent that
this "Gospel of Freedom" was written by Lazarus. But did the
writer of the Fourth Gospel know Jesus after the flesh? He
knew Jesus Christ, the Son of God. In his gospel there is
much talk of death and life, but it is plain that the real
death is spiritual death, and the real life is knowing Jesus
Christ the Son of God. The risen Christ says to Thomas (Jn.
20:29): "Because you have seen me, you have believed: blessed
are they that have not seen and yet have believed." If one
takes the witness of this disciple (Jn. 21:24) as meaning that
he was an eye witness and put all the emphasis on that, one
does less than justice to the writer of this gospel. The Jews,
the Pharisees, and the multitude all saw and heard Jesus; and
yet they did not see him as he really was or understand what
they heard him saying. The writer of the Fourth Gospel was
not a witness like that. He knew Christ with the discerning
eye of faith. He knew his LORD and his God. He need not have
met Christ in the flesh; Paul probably had never met Jesus
either. But he knew *him*. The writer of the Fourth Gospel is
almost certain to have been a priest because of his knowledge
of the Temple and its ceremonial. He had most probably not
only lived through, but taken an active part in the trouble
in Jerusalem from the time of Eleazar, the son of Ananias.
He may have been one of the Eleazars, either the Eleazar of
Macherus (if he is different from the Eleazar of Masada) or
even Eleazar of Masada (who was supposed to have killed himself). Or again he may have seen himself as typifying the
Eleazar of Masada, identifying himself with Eleazar of Masada
--in the sense of, "There but for the grace of God go I".
But he himself had found Christ, and he thought he had been

sick, nay dead, in the worst sort of death, the spiritual death. In baptism he had been raised to life by the word of Christ. Christ had died because of him, because of what he did for him. Lazarus is central in the Fourth Gospel, central in the way in which a soul commences with Christ and meditates on what facts of Jesus' life he knows. But the facts have been given to him in the preaching and liturgy of the believing community. They are the spiritual realities which he heard as a catechumen, i.e. a hearer, which he learned in a credal statement and which he made his own both before and after, but especially after baptism, when he felt he had the gift of the Spirit. It was the Spirit who led him as it were, leading other baptized Christians into a deeper knowledge of Jesus Christ and assurance that in his light we see God. In the word as preached by believers, he met Jesus. "Sir, we would see Jesus," the Greeks said to Andrew, and it is the cry sometimes despairing, always heartfelt, though often inarticulate, that the worshipper directs at the preacher. In the sacrament of the body and blood (the central worship of the Church) the writer of the gospel had found sustenance and had grown in grace on the bread of heaven. He knew that Jesus' words were spirit and meat indeed. He knew that the Spirit works in the sacrament of the altar and presents the heavenly body of Christ to the believer, just as the same Spirit which proceeds from the Father and the Son recreates the believer, raises him to life, and gives him eyes that see spiritual realities and ears that hear and understand the word of God. The writer of the Fourth Gospel sees himself as a very Eleazar of Macherus or Masada, or if not actually him, at least his type, and realizes that patriotism and nationalism are not enough, that hatred of the foreigner turns to hatred of some of one's own. We must love one another, not just as we love ourselves, for most often we do not really love ourselves. We must

love one another, even as Jesus loved us. And so the writer
of the Fourth Gospel after learning to know God through Christ
which is life eternal, in the sacraments, in prayer and preaching, in all these things discerning the Spirit of Christ, set
out his witness to the spiritual reality which he had experienced.
In his meditations he had been with Jesus, the lamb of God at the
Jordan. He had been with him when he had witnessed to the Jews,
at Purim, at Passover, at Tabernacles, and at Dedication. But
had he come to Christ late? Yes indeed, for the writer of this
gospel had witnessed for Christ to the Jews. The Spirit Paraclete had spoken through him as he preached. And when he thought
of the cause of the death of Christ, he preached his own conver-
sion and his own raising to life. He knew the opposition he (a
man destroyed, a *Meshummad*) faced from his former coreligionists.
He realized that many would have confessed Christ but were afraid,
not just of losing their seat in the synagogue, but of being put
beyond the pale as far as the community was concerned. He knew
the tensions in the community and the politics. He had seen what
fear of authority could do to a man and a community. He had been
a Zealot, and he knew Jesus had sympathy with the Zealots' whole-
hearted devotion to God as the only King. But he realized that
whole-hearted devotion to God was not to be shown by looting,
plundering, and killing, but by seeking to love each other, the
Roman included, as Jesus had loved him and eleven men. The story
of Mordecai and Esther being lauded by Akiba seemed hollow to
one who had been in the siege of Jerusalem, in Macherus or in
Masada. Masada was the end of the line. Haman/Edom had the
last word there, or had he? Eleazar had made a brave stand, but
he should have given himself for his people; but would Haman/
Edom have accepted his life and his alone? But the Minim and
the Nazarenes held that their Messiah had done just this, not
only for the Jews, but for all men.

Peter, on the word of the disciple who was known to the high priest, is brought in and immediately Peter denies Jesus to the maid at the door (Jn. 18:16). While Simon is standing, warming himself by a fire along with the servants, etc. of the high priest, the latter was asking Jesus about his disciples and his teaching. Jesus pointed out that he had spoken publicly and taught in synagogue and temple "where the Jews come together". He had spoken nothing in private. Jesus asked the high priest why he asked him; he should ask those that heard him; they knew what he said to them. One of the officers (v. 22) slapped Jesus for answering the high priest thus. Jesus asked for an explanation but got none except that he was sent bound to Caiaphas. The picture switches to Peter warming himself. The servants ask him if he is one of Jesus' disciples. He denies this. Then a kinsman of the man whose ear Peter had cut off in the garden asks if he is not the man he had seen in the garden with Jesus. Peter makes his third denial as the cock crew. In Mark the cock crows (Mk. 14:68) after the first denial. Then Peter denies Jesus a second time to the maid who tells the others. When the others take the matter up, Peter begins to curse and swear as he makes his third denial, as the cock crows (Mk. 14:72) the second time, fulfilling the Marcan version of Jesus' prediction that he would deny him thrice before the cock crowed. In Mt. 26:62-75, as in the Fourth Gospel, Peter makes his third denial before the cock crew. The details of Peter's behaviour are however closer to one another in Matthew and Mark than to those in the Fourth Gospel. In Mark, when the cock crowed the second time, Peter thought on what Jesus had said, and "he wept" (Mk. 14:72). In Matthew 26:75 Peter remembered the word which Jesus said and he went out and wept bitterly. Luke 22:54-62 resembles the Matthean and Marcan accounts but omits the cursing and swearing. However, like the

Fourth Gospel, the prediction fulfilled there is that he will deny Jesus thrice before the cock crowed. Luke 22:61 has an unique detail of the Lord turning and looking at Peter as the cock crew. Luke like Matthew ends the account by Peter going out and weeping bitterly. The Johannine Peter is apparently unrepentant. Nothing is said in the Johannine account of what transpired at Caiaphas' palace where, according to the Synoptics, there was some sort of examination before the council centering round whether he claimed to be the Christ, the Son of God. The alleged charge was blasphemy. In Jn. 18:28 the Jews being purified for Passover would not enter the impure palace of Pilate, so Pilate comes out to them. It is all the more striking that in their answer to the impure Pilate, the representative of Edom and Amalek, the accusers of Jesus say to Pilate: "If this man were not an evil-doer we should not have delivered him up to you." "Evil-doer" in this context is ironical; they meant it as an euphemism for anti-Roman political messianistic and/or revoltuionary activity about which high priests were very nervous lest it would disturb the *status quo*. (For frequent examples of this giving of information to the Procurators by the high priests see Josephus' *The Jewish War*.) Even the poor "prophet", who kept crying out "Woe to Jerusalem" a few years before the war, was handed over to the Romans by the Jewish establishment as a spreader of alarm. But Jesus was not political; he had not been impressed by authority as represented by "the Jews", i.e. the establishment. In fact he questioned it. Nor had he shown the grovelling respect to Annas which was probably expected (cf. Jn. 18:22). This was the charge that Haman had laid against Mordecai to the King Ahasuerus. Pilate had to be careful with the Jewish authorities, lest they report him to Caesar as being highhanded and interfering in cases that the Jews felt were within the jurisdiction of their

Law. So Pilate (v. 31) said to them: "Take him yourselves [this alleged evil-doer] and judge him according to your law." Now it comes out. They wanted his death (cf. Jn. 12:50 especially, but also Jn. 5:18, etc.): "It is not lawful for us to put any man to death." Jn. 18:32 sees this as fulfilling the word Jesus spoke (Jn. 12:32, 33) as to what manner of death he should die. The Jewish means of execution would have been stoning; the Roman method, crucifixion.

Pilate (Jn. 18:32) entered his palace and called Jesus in. He asked him: "Are you the king of the Jews?" The Greek could be taken as an ironical statement and not a question. Jesus asked him if he was saying this of himself, or did others tell him. It is clear from Pilate's answer that the fact that the chief priests had delivered him over was enough to suggest to his mind that he was a messianic claimant. But Pilate wants details: "What have you done?" (Jn. 18:35). Jesus' answer is a statement about his kingdom, i.e. it is not of this world: "If my kingdom were of this world, then would my servants fight, that I should not be delivered to the Jews." Pilate (Jn. 18:37) says: "Are you a king them?" (This could be taken in the Greek as a statement and not quite so ironical as the first.) Jesus' answer to that is: "You say that I am a king." It was important for the writer of the Fourth Gospel to have Pilate, the representative of Rome, say that Jesus was a king, even if the leaders of his own people would not admit it. It is comparable to the Greeks who came asking to see Jesus (Jn. 12:20ff.). Jesus expatiates on his mission (Jn. 18:7): "To this end have I been born, and to this end am I come into the world that I should bear witness to the truth." "Truth" is here a synonym[215] and title for God. The benediction after the *Shema'*, which is spoken in the Temple in the morning prayer service in the Chamber of Hewn Stones (cf. M. Tamid 5:1), starts with the phrase *Emeth we Yazib*, "True and Firm". Actually the very old Jewish custom is *not* to make a break between the last phrase of the third[216] part of the *Shema'* (which is I am [*'Ani*] YHWH [the Lord] your God [*Elohehem*]) and the first word (*Emeth*) of this benediction, so that the phrase then runs: "I the Lord your God am truth." The last sentence of this section of the *Shema'* also starts with "I (*Ani*) am YHWH (the LORD) your God who brought you out of the land of Egypt to be to you for God (i.e. to be your God). I the LORD (YHWH) your God am truth." Jesus referring to himself as "I am", as we noted earlier, is his claim to be Yahweh, or it is a self-identification with Yahweh. There also he must be alluding to this third part of the *Shema'*. There is reason to think that the third section[218] of the *Shema'* was a late addition. If it appeared in Temple times, it must have been in the last days of the Temple. Yet this section of the *Shema'* is known to the Fourth Gospel writer, which is another indication of the late date of this gospel and also shows again how this Evangelist is presenting Jesus as speaking to Jews of the writer's own day.

The benediction immediately before the *Shema'* is that which starts, among the Askenazim, in the morning with *Ahabah Rabbah*: "With abounding love hast thou loved us O LORD (YHWH) our God (*Elohenu*)." Among the Sephardim, it begins with *Ahabath Olam*: "With everlasting love Thou hast loved us O LORD (YHWH) our God." This benediction ends: "Blessed art thou O LORD who has chosen thy people Israel in love." When their prayers are said privately, one adds *El Melek Ne'eman*, i.e. God (*El*) faithful king. This usage was known as early as the Talmud,[252] and on the basis of it *Amen* was explained as a notarikon of this phrase.

The benediction after the *Shema'* (I the LORD [YHWH] your God is):

Truth or true and firm, established and
enduring, and right and faithful and beloved
and dear, and desired and pleasant; revered
and mighty and well-ordered and acceptable and
good and beautiful is *this word* over us for
ever and ever. Truth or true (it is) the
Eternal God is our King, the rock of Jacob,
the shield of our salvation God; to all generations He endures and His name endures; His
throne is established and His kingdom and His
faithfulness endure for ever. And His words
are life and endure; faithful and desired (are
they) for ever and to all eternity over our
fathers and over us, over our children and
over our generations, and over all the generations of the seed of Israel thy servants.
Over the first ones and over the last ones (it
is) a word good and enduring for ever and ever.
Truth and faithfulness or true and faithful is
a statute and it does not pass away. Truth or
true it is that Thou art He the LORD (*YHWH*)
our God and the God of our fathers, our King,
the King of our fathers, 'our redeemer, the
redeemer of our fathers, our creator, the
rock of our salvation, our deliverer, and our
Saviour from everlasting, He (*hu'*) is Thy
Name. There is no god (*Elohim*) beside Thee.'

Help of our fathers Thou art He from of
old. Shield and Saviour to their children
after them in every generation. In the
height of the world is Thy seat, and Thy
judgments and Thy righteousness are to the
ends of the earth. Blessed is the man who
hearkens to Thy commandments, and lays Thy
Torah, and Thy word (*dabar*) upon his heart.
Truth or true Thou art He LORD (*Adon*) of Thy
people, and mighty king to plead their case.
Truth or true Thou art He first, and Thou art
He last. And beside Thee we have no King,
Redeemer and Saviour. From Egypt Thou didst
redeem us, O LORD (*YHWH*) our God and from the
house of slaves Thou didst deliver us; all
their firstborn Thou didst slay, and Thy first-
born Thou didst redeem; and the sea of reeds
Thou didst divide, and the proud Thou didst
submerge, drown; but the beloved ones Thou
didst make pass through while waters covered
their adversaries, not one of whom was left.

For this the loved ones praised and exalted God
(*El*), and the dear ones offered hymns, songs,
praises, blessings and thanksgivings to the
King God (*El*) the living and enduring high
and exalted, great and revered, subduer of the
haughty, raiser up of the lowly, bringer out
of prisoners, deliverer of the meek, helper of
the poor, answerer of His people when they cry
to Him; praises to *El Elyon* (to God Most High).
Blessed is He and (ever) to be blessed. Moses
and the children of Israel sang to Thee a song
with great joy, and all of them said:
> Who is like to Thee, O LORD (*YHWH*)
> > among the *Elim* (gods)
> Who is like to Thee glorious in
> > holiness, revered in praises,
> > doer of marvel(s).

A new song the redeemed offered as praise to
Thy name on the shore of the sea. All of them
united gave thanks, and proclaimed Thee as
King, and said:
> The LORD (*YHWH*) shall reign for ever
> and ever. Rock of Israel, arise to
> the help of Israel, and deliver
> according to Thy word (*ne'umeka*)
> Judah and Israel. Our Redeemer,
> the LORD (*YHWH*) of Hosts is His
> name, the Holy One of Israel,
> Blessed art Thou O *YHWH* who hast
> redeemed Israel.

This benediction shows that *YHWH* is the truth, but since
Jesus is Yahweh in the Fourth Gospel we should understand that
in that gospel the truth is Jesus, e.g. Jn. 4:23: "Worship the
Father in spirit and in truth." Truth here is Jesus. In Jn.
5:33 John the Baptist bears witness to the truth, i.e. to Jesus.
Jn. 8:32 reads: "You shall know the truth and the truth shall
make you free." Read Jesus for truth. Jn. 14:6 reads: "I am
the way, the truth, the life." Truth here is a title of Jesus.
Note also that "life" (*Hayim*) could be "living" as in the above
benediction, "His words are life (or 'living')". The Spirit of
truth in the Fourth Gospel is obviously the Spirit of Jesus.

But it also comes from God the Father,[220] because in the last
phrase of the 3rd section of the *Shema'* and in the first word
of the benediction *'Emeth we-Yaẓib* ("I the LORD [YHWH] your
God am truth"), *I AM* is not just *Yahweh* but *Yahweh* in union
with *Elohenu*. Likewise it is *Yahweh Elohenu*, i.e. Yahweh in
union with *Elohenu*, which is truth. So Jesus as Yahweh is
truth, but he can also tell the truth about God (*Elohim* or
El, cf. Jn. 8:40).

"The LORD (*YHWH*) our God is truth, but also this Word is
true and firm, established and pleasant and revered and mighty
and well ordered and acceptable and good and beautiful over us
for ever and ever." What is this Word that is truth? Is it:
I AM the LORD (*YHWH*) your God? Later in the second part of
this benediction "Thy *Torah* and Thy Word", though side by side,
are not on the face of it the same. Is "Thy Word" the *Shema'*?
The LORD (*YHWH*) our God (*Elohenu*) is one *YHWH*. Both deal with
witnessing to the name of God, and knowing His name as one.

Again what is the Word which is good and enduring over
the first ones and the last ones. Is it *'Emeth we 'Emunah*,
truth and faithfulness? But *'Emeth* (Truth) is the LORD your
God. Is *'Emunah* another name, i.e. an attribute of the LORD
your God? We note that in Jn. 1:14 it is stated that the
"Word became flesh, and dwelt among us...full of grace and
truth." Though grace is usually associated with *Hesed*, there
does seem to be the possibility of an allusion to the statement in this prayer about the word which is good and is truth
and faithfulness.

This use of *Dabar* in this benediction reminds one of
Ezekiel's vision of Yahweh, the Man on the chariot throne, who
is described as the Word (*Dabar*). Note that after speaking of
the word which is truth and faithfulness the benediction passes
on to its description of the truth. "His LORD *YHWH* is *Elohenu*

our God, our King, our Redeemer, our Maker, the Rock of our Salvation, our Deliverer and Rescuer from Everlasting, such is Thy name." All of these statements make up the name of the truth. The benediction closes with the line, "Blessed art Thou O LORD *YHWH* who hast redeemed Israel." This benediction from its ending is called the *Ge'ullah*, a redemption prayer, and Yahweh is the redeemer. As in the *Shemoneh Esreh* (*Amidah*) (the first benediction), care is taken to identify the LORD (*YHWH*) our God (*Elohenu*) with *El Elyon* (God Most High). When He, the LORD (*YHWH*) our God (*Elohenu*), redeemed them from Egypt and took them through the Sea of Reeds, the beloved people praised and exalted *El* (God) and offered hymns, songs, praises, blessings, and thanksgivings to the King and to *El hai we-Qayyam* (God, living and enduring). He is then called *El Elyon*, "ever praises to the Most High God, blessed is He, ever to be blessed".

Jesus is the truth, and he is witness to the truth, himself in union with God. To believe this and to know this, as he stresses elsewhere (Jn. 3:32, 33, 36), is eternal life. Jesus maintains to Pilate that everyone that is of the truth "hears my voice". Yes, if they have accepted Jesus (i.e. they are of the truth), they hear (obey) his voice. Pilate (Jn. 18:38) said to him: "What is truth?" At least he asked the question, but it is put wrongly here, according to the Fourth Gospel and even according to the benediction after the *Shema'*. To them the right way to ask the question is: Who is the truth? Although the Fourth Gospel and the benediction *'Emeth we-Yaẓib*, which is also known as the *Ge'ullah* (Redemption), seem to answer the question differently, they are in greater agreement than is realized. The LORD our (or your) God is the truth. The benediction means *YHWH* our God by that, whereas the Fourth Gospel means by it both Yahweh, the Word of God, and Yahweh, the Redeemer God who did frequently come down from heaven to visit His people and who especially came in Jesus. Thomas has the definition of the risen Jesus: "My LORD and my God." And Jesus in his ministry had shown in the Fourth Gospel that he is the "I AM" and "the truth". If Pilate had said: "Who is the truth, their God as understood by them or by you?", he would have been near the mark. However, Pilate did go out and say to the Jews (Jn. 18:38, Jn. 19:4, Jn. 19:6): "I find no crime in him." He then offered to release Jesus, whom he called the king of the Jews, under a custom whereby he said he released someone to them at Passover. They (the Jews) cried out: "Not this man, but Barabbas." The gospel states (Jn. 18:40): "Now Barabbas was a robber." This is not an ordinary robber but one of the *sicarii*, the brigands who robbed, burnt and killed those they thought were pro-Roman. The high priests, for all their protestation of concern for Roman law and order, found it wise to keep on good terms with the Zealots. Jesus was denounced to Pilate as an evil-doer, i.e. as a messianic agitator, because the high priests and his colleagues along with the Pharisees (Jn. 11:47) had become worried that if all men believed on him, the Romans would come and take away their place and their nation. And so, being more concerned for their own welfare, their national pride, and also the esteem of the Romans, than for who Jesus was and what he stood for, they denounced him to Pilate. Pilate could find no fault in him and would have released him, but they chose Barabbas, the robber Zealot and the proven enemy of Rome, instead. They paid heavily for this sort of conduct as Ananus, Annas' son, and Caiaphas' brother-in-law, was to realize when the Zealots got power. Ananus, himself a high priest, then tried to stand for moderation, but he was murdered (cf. B. J. IV, 314-318). Actually the Jews were acting on the same sort of values as inculcated in the *Megillath Esther* when they chose Barabbas. Barabbas in a way is their Mordecai.

In Jn. 19:1 Pilate had Jesus scourged. This scourging by
the Romans could bare the bones as Josephus says (B. J. VI,
304-309)[221] in speaking of the Prophet who cried "Woe, woe to
Jerusalem" and whom "some of the leading citizens" (possibly
the chief priests) handed over to the Romans as a messianic
agitator. The soldiers placed a crown of thorns on his head,
arrayed him in a purple garment, saluted him (Jn. 19:3): "Hail,
king of the Jews", and slapped him. Pilate (v. 4) went out and
announced to the Jews that "I bring him out to you, that you
may know that I find no crime in him". Then Jesus came out,
crowned with thorns and robed in purple. Pilate said to them:
"Behold the man!" This is parallel to Jn. 1:1f. and the Word
which is the Son of God, Jesus. This "the man" is Jesus equated
with the man that Ezekiel (1:26) saw who is the Word which expressly came to Ezekiel. This is Yahweh/Jesus. This is the
help from the other place that Mordecai had said would come if
Esther failed, i.e. those failed who followed the example of
Mordecai and Esther and whose aims were those inculcated by the
Megillath Esther. The Maccabees had been inspired by the *Megillath Esther*, but as successful as they had been for a time,
their kingdom passed away. Herod the Idumean, and therefore
an Amalekite, took over under the protection of Rome, the
Amalek of that age. Already Judas the Galilean, the founder
of the Zealots, had paid the price. All were in some way paying
the price in the time of Jesus, enjoying the benefits conferred
by Rome, and fearing the retribution of the Zealots. Judas'
grandson (Eleazar the despot of Masada, as Josephus called him)
made his followers pay the price and then paid it himself, the
last brave but desperate bid for a freedom which, even when they
had it briefly at the beginning of the revolt, they lost in
fighting Jew against Jew. But Jesus was their king with Roman
approval, just as Esther had been made Ahasuerus' queen when

Haman was thwarted and Mordecai shared the government. But such a fate would never have done for Jesus. He did not belong to this world. He had said repeatedly that he must go to his Father. He was shown as their king. But they did not want him; the chief priests and the officers when they saw him cried out "Crucify him, crucify him", just as Esther and Mordecai had had done to Haman. But in pressing for his crucifixion, they were pressing for his enthronement which he had envisaged from the beginning (Jn. 3:14; 8:28; 12:32; 12:34). There was irony[222] in Esther; there is a deeper irony here. Pilate told them: "Take him yourselves, and crucify him: for I find no crime in him." The Jews could not let that pass (Jn. 19:7). The Jews answered him: "We have a law, and by that law he ought to die because he made himself the Son of God." This is the same as in Jn. 10:33 where the Jews answered him: "For a good work we stone you not, but for blasphemy, and because that you being a man, make yourself God." Jesus' answer to that had been (Jn. 10:35): "Do you say of him, whom the Father sanctified and sent into the world, you blaspheme because I said I am the Son of God?" When the believing Christian in Church heard this gospel read, he would say that the Jews had the matter the wrong way round. He was God and had made himself man. But the Jews were consistent. In Jn. 5:18 they had already sought to kill him because he called God his own Father, "making himself equal with God". Pilate was the more afraid when (Jn. 19:8) he heard this saying. He entered the palace again and there asked Jesus: "Where are you from?" Pilate became unsettled at Jesus' silence, and Pilate began to boast of his powers, how he had power to release him or to crucify him. Jesus pointed out that he (Pilate) would have no power or authority against him had it not been given him from above. This could refer to the emperor, but it was not that. It was

supernatural power, that of God. It was the same as when
Caiaphas prophesied, being high priest for that year, that
it was expedient for one man to die for the people, and the
result of his prophetic word, although he did not see it,
was that Jesus should die not only for that nation but that
he might also gather into one the children of God that were
scattered abroad. However, it is made clear to Pilate that
the one that had delivered Jesus into Pilate's hands had committed the greater sin than he. This does exonerate Pilate
somewhat and fixes the blame on Caiaphas and the Jews. Pilate
(v. 12) then sought to release Jesus, but the Jews retorted:
"If thou release this man you are not Caesar's friend." It
was a clever attack, for Pilate could not afford to be in the
position of having the Jews denounce him to Caesar. Pilate,
like the Jews, thought more of the glory which comes from men
than from God. Pilate had Jesus brought out and he himself
sat in the judgment seat. Time was getting on and preparation
of the Passover had to be accomplished, lambs slaughtered in
the Temple before sunset and the beginning of Passover. He
said again to the Jews: "Behold your King." The Jews cried
out: "Away with him, away with him, crucify him." When Pilate
said, "Shall I crucify your King?", the chief priests answered:
"We have no king but Caesar" (Jn. 19:15). This is a shocking
remark. In the benediction after the *Shema'* Yahweh is King;
so in saying this they were denying God, as the writer of the
Fourth Gospel believed they were doing by denying the kingship
of Jesus. They held on to their Temple and its services, and
they were afraid to upset Rome in any way. They had already
lost their God when they could say: "We have no king but Caesar."

Pilate could not be less in his devotion to Caesar than the
chief priests. He was as concerned to receive glory from men as
the Jews (Jn. 5:44), and he did not care for the glory that had

come from God. He did not really stop seriously to inquire
what is truth. He handed Jesus over to be crucified. Jesus
bore his cross himself to Golgotha where he was crucified with
two others (who they are is not stated in the Fourth Gospel).
Jesus' cross was in the middle. Pilate insisted on the title
"Jesus of Nazareth, the King of the Jews" being put on Jesus'
cross in Hebrew, Latin and Greek. The chief priests found this
offensive as it was near the city and they wanted Pilate to
change it and write that "He said I am King of the Jews".
Pilate said: "What I have written, I have written." Jesus
was enthroned on his cross as King of the Jews. The Zealots[223]
maintained that they had no King but God. Jesus is crucified
between two others, most likely Zealots, as the King of the
Jews. The irony according to the writer of the gospel is that,
despite appearance, it is true. They have raised up Yahweh on
His throne and glorified the Son of Man. Here as elsewhere the
writer of this gospel shows concern for what is said, i.e. what
is written and not who said it. Jesus' enemies unwittingly are
made to testify to him. Even what the chief priests wanted
Pilate to write that he said "I am King of the Jews" would
testify at least to his claim to be Yahweh, King of the Jews
(I AM = Yahweh). The Fourth Evangelist is akin to the rabbinic
literal exegesis of Rabbi Akiba except he applies it not only
to words of the Torah but also to the words of Jesus and even
to words about Jesus.

Jn. 19:23-24 tells how the soldiers, having crucified
Jesus, took his garments and tore or cut them into four parts,
one for each soldier. There was his coat which was seamless
and woven from the top throughout. They did not tear or cut
it into four, but cast lots for it, which the Fourth Evangelist
assures us was so that the scripture, unbeknown to them, might
be fulfilled. The scripture cited is Ps. 22:18: "They parted

my garments among them, and upon my vesture did they cast lots."
This verse in the Psalm is accurately quoted, but it would
appear that this verse has given rise to the giving of a piece
of each garment to each of the four soldiers, except in the case
of his seamless robe for which they cast lots. The question
is whether the story, which the writer of the Fourth Gospel
gives, is so entirely derived from the Psalm that the detail
about the seamless robe is brought in to explain the word
"vesture" as if it were something additional to "my garments".
Actually "my vesture" may be merely the same as "my garments",
and it occurs in Ps. 22:18 simply because of Hebrew poetic par-
allelism.[224] The Synoptics use Ps. 22 (note the Marcan account
[Mk. 15:24] which does *not* mention the robe). It may be brought
in gladly by the Fourth Evangelist to stress the high priestly
character of Christ which is apparent in Jn. 17. Mark 15 cites
from or alludes to Ps. 22 verses 1, 7, 18. Matthew 27 cites
or alludes to Ps. 22:1, 7, 8, 17, 18. Luke 23 cites from Ps.
22, only verse 18, but it alludes to Ps. 69:21. The Marcan
account of the crucifixion (in addition to Ps. 22) possibly
alludes to Ps. 109:25, 35:28 and 40:15. Matthew 27 (in addition to Ps. 22) possibly alludes to Ps. 109:25. Luke 23 (in
addition to Ps. 22) alludes to Ps. 69:21.

Actually the one citation (at least as an allusion) in
the Fourth Gospel's crucifixion narrative is common to all
four gospels. There is no doubt that Ps. 22 has played a very
large role in shaping the form of the crucifixion narrative in
the Synoptics and in the Fourth Gospel.

But (Ps. 22:1) the cry of dereliction from the cross occurs
only in Mk. 15:34 and Mt. 27:46. The Fourth Gospel has not just
followed the Petrine tradition in using Ps. 22 in connection
with the crucifixion narrative. He clearly draws attention to
it in a way the others who use it more do not. They alluded to

it and where they cited it (i.e. Ps. 22:1) they did not here, or in the case of Ps. 22:18, quote it as a scripture which had to be fulfilled. The Fourth Evangelist, because his Christ has all power given to him, cannot even say, like Esther in her time of trials (according to rabbinic tradition, cf. Midrash on Psalms [Ps. 22]): "*Eli, Eli*, My God, my God, why has thou forsaken me?" Furthermore, this gospel stresses the constant harmonious rapport, nay complete union, between Jesus/Yahweh and *El*/God the Father. But, since the Fourth Gospel does draw allusive contrasts between the work of the hero and heroine of the *Megillath Esther* (for the deliverance of the Jews of Shushan) and Jesus (for his redemptive work for mankind), it cannot afford to neglect Ps. 22. It should be pointed out that while the Midrash on Psalms (Ps. 22) does in general identify many of its verses with details in the story of Esther, especially before she went into Ahasuerus, yet there is a tradition there given that the *Ayeleth Shahar* of the title of that Psalm is not Esther but God. The Fourth Gospel writer could then use the Psalm as referring to Jesus as God while also making use of the known view that the Psalm alluded to Esther. The Midrash on Psalms on Ps. 22:18 is very specific about that verse. Esther's enemies, who hoped for her downfall as a result of coming to Ahasuerus unannounced, were already deciding which of her garments, etc. they should have. The mocking by the passers-by, the chief priests, and scribes, which is so prominent a feature in Mark,[225] and the darkness[226] from the sixth to the ninth hour are omitted. Instead there is Jesus' concern for his mother and her future welfare and his making arrangements for the disciple whom he loved to be a son to her (cf. Jn. 19:26-27). John 19:28 states that Jesus' knowing that all things are now finished said: "I thirst." But this was so that the scripture might be accomplished. The scripture in question is Ps. 69:21: "They

gave me also gall for my meat, and in my thirst they gave me
vinegar to drink." He who had said to the Samaritan woman,
"Give me to drink", and had offered her the living water, he
who had said to the Jews at Tabernacles in the Temple, "If
any man thirst let him come to me and drink", when he says to
the Jews "I thirst" is given vinegar. When he had received
the vinegar, he said (Jn. 19:30): "It is finished." He bowed
his head and gave up his spirit. The Nestorians say the Son
of God did not die on the cross, only the man Jesus as the
Spirit of God had left him. This is a dangerous distinction
and leads to adoptionism. The other end of the scale is shown
by the Acts of John where the Christ speaks with John on the
Mount of Olives while the Jews think they see Jesus being
crucified. The Fourth Gospel believes that Jesus Christ was
the Son of God and that he is divine, but that it was through
a human family (Jn. 6:42) he came into the world of men to
save them. This redemption was by God, and it was not easy
for God, who to achieve His aim had to accomplish it not from
outside the world of men, but in human society as a man. But
the Fourth Gospel, while believing in a genuine humanity of
Jesus Christ, confesses first and foremost his Godhead. The
Fourth Gospel does not make a distinction between perfect
humanity and the Godhead. "You are gods,[227] but shall die like
men" (Jn. 10:35). But if men confess Jesus as the Son of God
and that he and the Father are one, this is eternal life. The
medium is the message. By belief in Jesus they believe in God
the Father and can become sons of God. Merely saying they
love Jesus is not enough; they show it by loving one another.
The aim of the divine scheme of salvation is not "individual
salvation" or "individual sonship", but that men love Jesus
and thereby love God and love one another. The aim is oneness
of humanity and oneness not just of individuals but of humanity

with Jesus, just as he is one with God. This does not mean
being swallowed up in God. It means, it is true, that redeemed
humanity can be divine, because the divinity is truly human.
But as there is distinction within the Godhead--even the Jews
did admit that the *Middath Din*[228] (the Attribute of Mercy) belonged to *YHWH* the LORD, while the *Middath Rahamin* (the Attribute of Justice) belonged to *Elohim* God--though it is harmonious unity. So also humanity, one with Christ and one in their
loving service of one another, can keep their individuality
while bowing their wills in loving service of God and their
fellowman.

CHAPTER 13

The Canonicity of Esther
and that of the Fourth Gospel

Because it was the *Preparation* before the Sabbath which was also Passover, Pilate hastened the deaths of those crucified with Jesus. But as Jesus was already dead, they did not break his legs. This came to pass, says the Evangelist, that the scripture might be fulfilled: "A bone of him shall not be broken." This statement is based on Ex. 12:46, "neither shall you break a bone thereof" (the paschal lamb), and Num. 9:12, "nor break a bone thereof" (also the paschal lamb). The Fourth Gospel can and wants us to see Jesus as the paschal lamb because at the time he was on the cross the paschal lambs were being slain in the Temple. Luke (Lk. 23:45; cf. Mk. 15:38; Mt. 27:51) has the veil in the Temple rent, dividing the Holy of Holies from the *Hekhal* or nave of the Temple. But with a different and earlier date for Passover they could not equate the crucifixion with the sacrificing of the paschal lamb.

Jn. 19:34 told how one of the soldiers, finding Jesus already apparently dead, "with a spear pierced his side, and straightaway there came out blood and water". This incident is of great importance to the writer of the gospel. "And he (Jn. 19:35) that has seen has borne witness, and his witness is true." Here again it all depends what "has seen" means-- presumably not with the eyes of the flesh alone, which in this gospel are blind, and probably not even with them at all. By "blood and water" the writer of this gospel would want us to

refer to the blood[229] of the Eucharistic offering, and the
water of baptism, both essential to salvation and adoption to
sonship. The crucifixion is the glorification of Christ; it
is also the central point of the gospel. Just as he said:
"If I be lifted up, I will draw all men to me." The crucified
Christ draws together the various strands in the gospel. From
one point of view, i.e. the dogmatic, the gospel is catechetical instruction on the faith, instruction on the sacraments of
baptism and the Eucharist. From another point of view, i.e.
the apologetic, the gospel is the answer to Esther and the Jews.
This latter determines the literary form which parallels the
movement of events in the *Megillath Esther*. Literary form and
allusion are important for the writer of the gospel as they
convey the answer to the claims of the Jews. As already remarked, the *Megillath Esther* pattern has been superimposed on
an earlier gospel pattern derived from Mark and through him
from Peter. But the crucifixion was not central in Mark; the
Passover meal was. The crucifixion and the slaying of the
paschal lamb are identified in the Fourth Gospel; nevertheless,
the Last Supper has been retained not as a paschal meal but to
provide background for the teaching of the specifically Christian social ethic and to highlight the contrast of the betrayer
Judas and his master. Besides being the glorification of
Christ, the crucifixion is the discrediting of the chief priests,
the Jews *par excellence* who have no king but Caesar. The crucifixion is the illustration of Jesus' word that he who loves his
life loses it, but he who loses it brings forth much fruit. The
Esther pattern and the Exodus pattern of the death of the first-
born converge at the crucifixion. Both were examples of divine
irony. The redeemer of the Jews redeems by being crucified,
and Haman appears to go scot free. Instead of the slaying of
the Egyptians, the Hebrew redeemer, the first-born himself, is

slain. But how do the catechetical and the Esther patterns
(i.e. the dogmatic and the apologetic) converge? In looking
back over the gospel, the main teaching on baptism is to the
Samaritan woman and to Nicodemus. The setting for neither of
these events fits into the "dinner pattern", though the setting
for the Eucharistic instruction occurs in connection with the
second "dinner", i.e. the feeding of the five thousand. The
Temple feasts at Jerusalem are all occasions for manifesting
who he is. Besides beginning the persecution of Jesus, the
unnamed feast (Jn. 5:1) begins the testimony to the Jews as to
who he is. Their obtuseness and hostility serve to give opportunity and occasion for Jesus to give dogmatic instruction on
who he is. The dogmatic and the apologetic interests are combined with the feasts from Jn. 5:1 and Purim, i.e. the catechetical lecture and the Esther patterns. Just as Haman had
cast lots[230] as to when was the best time to act against the
Jews, the Jews toy for a similar period of a year to deal with
Jesus, but it was not yet his hour. I submit that this Evangelist deliberately stressed the water and the blood from the
side of Jesus to show that the sacramental element of the catechetical pattern is also related to the central pivot of this
gospel, the crucifixion of Jesus. Note how Jn. 19:35 is not
only an emphatic testimony to the essential truth of the blood
and water from the side of the crucified Jesus, but it stresses
why the writer of the gospel said it: "that ye also may believe".
What they are to believe is not just that water and blood came
out when the spear pierced his side, but that they may *believe*
in the same way as in Jn. 20:31: "And that believing you may
have life in his name." From the apparent emphasis in this
gospel on belief in who Jesus is, there is the danger that it
be thought to stress intellectual faith and also to be anti-
sacramental, especially as the Last Supper does not contain the

institution of the sacrament of his body and blood. It was
essential then for the Evangelist to show that the sacraments
are integrally related to the crucifixion and that the glorified Christ is the source of the sacraments. The phrase in
Jn. 19:35, "you also may believe", clearly links the sacraments to belief. Jn. 19:36 says: "For these things came to
pass that the scripture might be fulfilled, 'a bone of Him
shall not be broken'" (Ex. 12:46). This clearly identifies
the crucified Christ with the paschal lamb. He is the Lamb
of God as announced and so called by John the Baptist (Jn. 19:
37): "And again another scripture says: 'They shall look on
him whom they pierced'." This is from Zech. 12:10: "And I
will pour upon the house of David, and upon the inhabitants
of Jerusalem, the spirit of grace and of supplication; and
they shall look upon me" (or according to some Mss.) "him
whom they have pierced, and they shall mourn for him, as one
mourns for his only son, and shall be in bitterness for him,
as one that is in bitterness for his firstborn." This is an
important messianic[231] scriptural reference which the rabbis,
however, applied to the Messiah ben Joseph and not the Messiah
ben David. Joseph of Arimathaea (Jn. 19:38) figures in each
of the Synoptics as the one who asks Pilate for the body of
Jesus. Mt. 29:57 says that he was Jesus' disciple. The Fourth
Gospel significantly adds Jn. 19:38: "but secretly for fear
of the Jews". This phrase, which occurs elsewhere[232] in the
Fourth Gospel, is an allusion to Esther where after Haman's
overthrow "the fear of the Jews" is on the non-Jews. Mk. 15:
43 does not say he was a disciple, but "was looking for the
kingdom of God". Lk. 23:50, like Mk. 15:43, says that he was
a councilor (i.e. a member of the Sanhedrin). Neither Matthew
nor the Fourth Gospel say this. Lk. 23:51 says he had not con-
sented to their counsel. Lk. 23:51, like Mk. 15:43, says he

"was looking for the kingdom of God". It would appear that a good case could be made out for Joseph of Arimathaea and Nicodemus being one and the same person. But one could go further as the Acts of Pilate/Nicodemus did, and on the basis of Mt. 27:24, where Pilate said, "I am innocent of the blood of this righteous man", one could assert that Pilate is Nicodemus (whose name appears to be derived from $N^e k i \; Dam$). This is patently absurd. Yet in the rabbinic[233] sources there is a tortured etymology of Nakdimon's name which looks as if it were answering some other derivation. Possibly the fact that the Minim interpreted it as meaning "innocent of blood" was known to them. In addition to coming to Jesus by night, Nicodemus had spoken against a hasty condemnation of Jesus without hearing him (Jn. 7:50). But since the other gospels had Joseph of Arimathaea approach Pilate for the body of Jesus, the Fourth Gospel had to retain his services. From the rabbinic literature, it is plain there was a Nicodemus or Nakdaimon, though it is not at all clear, if we follow Thackeray's text, that Josephus knew of him. Josephus (B. J. II, 451) mentions a Gorion son of Nicomedes who was one of those sent by the Jews, who were besieging the Roman garrison under Metilius in Jerusalem, to give a pledge of security to Metilius. This war had broken out in Jerusalem in the summer of 66 A.D. As Thackeray (Loeb edition of Josephus)[234] notes on B. J. II, 451, the Latin has Gorion the son of Nicodemus instead of Gorion the son of Nicomedes. In B. J. II, 563 Joseph, son of Gorion, and Ananus the high priest (son of Annas) at the end of 66 A.D. were elected to the supreme control of the affairs in the city. They were moderates. Ananus was an ex-high priest, who had been appointed high priest by Agrippa II and deposed after three months on account of his part in the death of James, the brother of Jesus (cf. *Ant.* XX, 197ff.). If there is confusion

between "Ananus the high priest" (who is the son of Annas) and
Annas, it is also possible that Joseph (the son of Gorion) is
Joseph of Arimathaea. On the other hand, it may not be con-
fusion but a deliberate moving up of events nearer to the
period of the War. In rabbinic sources Nicodemus is called
Nakdimon b. Gurion (cf. Nicomedes son of Gorion above in
Josephus). It is quite possible to equate Joseph the son of
Gorion or Gorion the son of Joseph (B. J. IV, 159) with Gorion
the son of Nicomedes. It is quite likely that Joseph the son
of Gorion is identified with Joseph of Arimathaea, and Gorion,
the son of Nicomedes, or Nakdimon b. Gurion, give rise to
Nicodemus.[235] Both the Talmudic and the gospel form of the
name may be attempts to Hebraize a Greek name. The amount of
myrrh and aloes that Nicodemus brought for the burial of Jesus
testifies to his wealth. Jesus was crucified in a garden.
The cross is the tree of life, and Jesus is the fruit of the
tree of life which men are henceforth encouraged to eat. In
Gen. 3:22 the LORD God was worried, "lest he put forth his
hand and take also of the tree of life, and eat, and live for
ever". This was too dangerous, man having (Gen. 3:22) "become
as one of us (the *Elohim*) to know good and evil", and so the
LORD God sent him forth from the garden of Eden. But Jesus
came that men might have eternal life. The new tomb in which
Jesus was laid was also in the garden. Because of the preparation for the Sabbath, they laid him in the nearby new tomb.
It is almost as if Yahweh is resting on the Sabbath having
finished the new creation.

In Jn. 20 Mary Magdalene is first mentioned by name in
this gospel (Jn. 19:25), unless she be the same as Mary the
sister of Lazarus and Martha. In Jn. 20:11 and 16 she is
simply called Mary, and in v. 16 she is so called by Jesus.
It could be that while the Fourth Gospel could not depart from

the Synoptic tradition here that Mary Magdalene was at the
tomb of the risen Lord, the writer of this gospel indicates
her identity with Mary, the sister of Lazarus, who had anointed
his feet at the dinner party at Bethany. Early on the first
day of the week, while it was still dark, Mary Magdalene comes
to the tomb and sees the stone rolled away. She has come before dawn. The Syrian tradition (cf. Aphraates)[236] is that
Jesus arose on what we would call Saturday night, but it was
actually the eve of Sunday. But the Fourth Gospel has a day
of 12 hours (Jn. 11:9) separate from night. It is therefore
on Sunday morning that he rises before dawn. The Fourth Gospel
is careful to point out that he was buried before the Sabbath.
In Jn. 19:14, when Jesus is delivered to be crucified, we are
told: "Now it was the Preparation of the Passover; it was
about the sixth hour."[237]

That afternoon, in addition, the paschal lambs were
sacrificed at the Temple. They[238] were slaughtered, hung up,
and flayed (cf. M. Pes. 5, 8). Their blood was caught and
dashed on the altar.[239] The spear thrust in Jesus' side and
the shedding of his blood presented a significant parallel.
We do not know how long he was on the cross according to the
Fourth Gospel. Those present would want to go and sacrifice
their own lambs at the Temple. The "Jews' Preparation" in Jn.
19:42 could refer not only to the Preparation for Passover,
but also for the Sabbath. The latter is more likely (cf. Jn.
19:31): "Therefore, because it was the day of Preparation, so
that the bodies should not remain on the cross upon the Sabbath
...the Jews asked of Pilate that their legs might be broken",
i.e. to speed matters up. Because of the collocation of the
Preparation and Sabbath in this verse, and also the reference
to the "Jews' Preparation" in v. 42, it is probably being indicated to us that whatever elsewhere in this gospel, here we

must understand the Jewish mode of counting the day from evening to evening. It was therefore still light when he was buried, i.e. part of a day counts as a day. It was therefore on the third day that he rose. Though there is no mention of three days in this chapter (Jn. 20), yet Jesus had indicated in Jn. 2:19 that he would arise in 3 days. There is probably a parallel between Esther going in to see the king on the third day, but the gospel transcends it and fills it with new meaning when Jesus says to Mary (Jn. 20:17): "Touch me not, for I am not yet ascended to the Father; but go to my brethren and say to them, I ascend to my Father and your Father, and my God and your God." When on the evening of that day, the first day of the week, when the doors were shut where the disciples were, *"for fear of the Jews"* (Jn. 20:19), Jesus came and stood in their midst and said: "Peace be to you." He showed them his hands and his side. Then (v. 21) again he said, "Peace be to you", then added: "As the Father hath sent me, even so send I you." This is the commissioning of the apostles (cf. Jn. 17: 17). He asks God to sanctify them in the truth (v. 18): "As You did send me into the world, even so sent I them into the world." There he had been announcing his intention to God the Father. Now he sends them and breathing on them said: "Receive you the Holy Ghost: whosoever sins you forgive, they are forgiven them; whosoever sins you retain, they are retained." Jn. 7:39 mentions that the Spirit which they that believed on him were to receive was not yet given, because Jesus was not yet glorified. It is clear that when it was given he was glorified.

When Mary had spoken to Jesus he had said (Jn. 20:17): "Touch me not; for I am not yet ascended to the Father." But he emphasizes that he is ascending "to my Father and your Father, and my God and your God". Now when Thomas, who was

not with the others when Jesus came, said, when they told him
that they had seen the Lord (Jn. 20:25): "Unless I shall see
in his hands the print of the nails, and put my finger into
the print of the nails, and put my hand into his side, I will
not believe." Eight days later (Jn. 20:25) Jesus comes through
the closed doors and stands in the midst of the disciples with
whom Thomas was. After giving his Peace, he asks Thomas:
"Reach hither your hand, and put it into my side and be not
faithless, but believing." Thomas (Jn. 20:28) said: "My
LORD, and my God." Jesus' response was: "Because you have
seen me, you have believed; blessed are they that have not
seen and yet have believed." It is plain when Jesus met Mary
and would not let her touch him that he had not ascended to
God. If being ascended and glorified are the same, he had
ascended before he visited the disciples and breathed on them
the Holy Ghost (cf. Jn. 15:26) of whom Christ said: "I will
send to you from the Father, *even* the Spirit of truth, which
proceedeth from the Father." Presumably between Mary seeing
him in the garden and his coming to the disciples late that
very day, he had ascended, since he gave them the Holy Ghost.
But even if this is not allowed, he had ascended before Thomas,
eight days later, was told to put his hand into the wound in
his side. This means that in the Fourth Gospel the ascension
and the giving of the Spirit are on the resurrection day itself, or at least the giving of the Spirit takes place on that
day and the ascension within the first week thereafter. This
is quite different from Acts and even from Luke. The disciple
whom Jesus loved and Simon Peter, on being informed by Mary
Magdalene that the stone was taken away, ran to the tomb. Although outrun, the honour of first entering the tomb is given
to Peter. Jesus, unlike Lazarus, had come out *un*bound from
the grave and had disposed of the grave clothes in an orderly

fashion. Only after Simon Peter had gone in did the other
disciple do so, "and *he* saw and believed". It is most striking to be told in Jn. 20:9: "For as yet they knew not the
scripture, that he must rise again from the dead." The scripture concerned may be Ps. 16:10: "For Thou wilt not suffer
Thine holy one to see corruption." The gospel (Jn. 20:10)
says baldly: "So the disciples went away again into their
own home" (cf. Jn. 20:11). Mary, however, stood at the tomb
and wept. Then as she wept, she stooped and looked into the
tomb. She saw two angels in white, one at the head and one at
the feet, where the body of Jesus had lain. They give no information except to ask why she wept. It is rather pathetic
how she wants to hold on to a dead[240] Lord: "Because (Jn. 20:
13) they have taken away my Lord, and I know not where they
have laid him." She turned and beheld Jesus standing, and yet
she did not know him. Jesus asked why she wept, and whom she
sought. Mary asked him (the living Christ) where he had laid
him, so that she could take him (the dead Christ) away. This
is superb irony. She, however, recognized Jesus when he ad-
dressed her by name. It was she that told the disciples: "I
have seen the Lord."

Mary Magdalene and Thomas dominate this chapter in a way
that Simon Peter and the disciple whom Jesus loved do not.
They are all too much concerned with Christ as they knew him
in the flesh. To believe without having seen is more blessed
(the first to believe is the disciple whom Jesus loved [Jn.
20:8]), and the sum of belief is that Jesus is the Christ, the
Son of God, which John the Baptist had declared in the first
chapter. To believe this is to have life in his name, i.e.
life in and through him. But the positive response to Jesus
is fundamental. The medium is the message. It is not just
saying yes to the fact of Christ. He came because he is who

he is. It is not that we accept the fact of Christ and describe it how we will or ascribe to him what we will. While the Fourth Gospel does not claim finality for itself and would allow that we can be led constantly into new truth by his Spirit, yet the new truth is implicitly expected to be consistent with what the writer of the Fourth Gospel has told us of Christ. We cannot really separate the Christ of the Fourth Gospel from his words. His words are mainly about himself and his relation to God the Father, and our relation either as individuals or as humanity as a whole with him. The medium is the message, but the message is also the medium. God had to study the Torah[241] to keep up with the rabbis. The Synoptic Christ would have to study this gospel to find himself.

In Jn. 21 the third manifestation of Jesus to the disciples was at the sea of Tiberias. The first appearance was to Mary Magdalene, though she was not a disciple. Simon Peter, Thomas, Nathanael of Cana in Galilee, the sons of Zebedee, and two other disciples are by the sea. Following Simon Peter's lead, they went into the boat and fished all night and caught nothing. When day was breaking Jesus stood on the beach, but the disciples did not know that it was Jesus. Jesus still unrecognized asked them (Jn. 21:5): "Have you anything to eat?" When they answered "No" he said next: "Cast the net on the right side of the boat, and you shall find." They did, and "now they were not able to draw it for the multitude of the fishes". The disciple whom Jesus loved (Jn. 21:7) said to Peter: "It is the Lord." Compare how (Jn. 20:8) he also saw and believed earlier. Simon Peter did not wait for the boat to come to land. Dragging the net full of fishes he was pulled into the sea. When they came they saw a fire of coals and "fish laid on it and a loaf of bread". Jesus told them to bring the fish which they had caught. It was Simon Peter who drew the net with 153 great fishes to land; although there were so many, the net was not broken. The fish represent the Christians they will win from all races. Jerome[242] taught that there were 153 species of fish. Jesus told them to come and break their fast on the meal which he had prepared, a fish and a loaf. This reminds one of the ingredients of the repast offered to the 5,000. It had pointed to the Eucharist, and the Fourth Gospel there follows it up with the great sacramental teaching of Christ as the bread of life. Jesus provides the meal here too, even the fish and the loaf of bread, and he also provides the catch of fish which they bring to him. The gospel (Jn. 21:12) notes that none of the disciples ventured to ask who he was, knowing as they did that it was the Lord. Jesus (v. 13) is the host. He took the bread and gave it to them, and so also with the fish. We know he is the bread from the sacramental discourse in Jn. 6. Here we learn that he is the fish: *I. Ch. Th. U. S. IESOUS CHRISTOU THEOU UIUS SOTER* = Jesus Christ the Son of God the Saviour. This must be the origin of the anagram by which Christians afterwards identified themselves and confessed Christ. So when he gave the fish he clearly showed who he was.

In Jn. 21:15 after they had broken their fast, Jesus asked Simon Peter: "Simon, son of John, do you love me more than these?" The referent of "these" is perhaps the other disciples.

Jesus (Jn. 21:15) is appointing Peter to be the chief under-shepherd to him. When Simon Peter says: "Yes, Lord; thou knowest that I love thee", he says to him: "Feed my lambs." In the first half of this chapter Jesus is the great fisherman; now he is the great shepherd (cf. Jn. 10:11). Again he returns to the question: "Simon, son of John, dost thou love me?" When Peter reasserts his love for Christ, Jesus says to him: "Tend my sheep." A third time Jesus addresses the same question. Peter was now upset that Jesus asked a third time, "Dost thou

love me?" Jesus had made his point. Peter was reminded of
how he had boasted (Jn. 13:37): "I will lay down my life for
thee" before they had gone to the garden where Jesus delivered
himself up to his captors. In Jn. 18:27 Peter denied Christ
thrice before the cock crew, as Christ had said he would. So
Simon Peter (Jn. 21:17) now says: "LORD thou knowest all
things; thou knowest that I love thee." In Jn. 2:24, 25, when
at the first Passover in Jerusalem many believed on his name,
beholding his signs which he did, "but Jesus did not trust
himself unto them, for that he knew all men (v. 25) and because he needed not that anyone should bear witness concerning
man; for he himself knew what was in man". Jesus had forgiven
Simon Peter and said this third time: "Feed my sheep." The
Syriac version distinguishes between lambs, ewes, and rams,
i.e. the different age groups and sexes in the Church have
their different needs, and each and all must be given the
pastoral care appropriate to their needs. The reiteration of
"Feed my sheep" may merely be an attempt to drive the pastoral
charge home, and the Syriac with its different words for age
and gender of sheep may be a homiletic or midrashic development introduced by the Syriac translator for the benefit of
his co-religionists. In the graveyards of the Urmi (now Rezaiyeh) plain, the grave of a (warrior) priest, who had protected
his flock against the Kurds, etc., is marked by a tombstone in
the shape of a ram. Simon Peter's three-fold denial is ex-
punged, as it were, by the Lord's thrice repeated commission.
But now the Lord goes on, as it were, to take up Peter's boast
(Jn. 13:38): "I will lay down my life for thee." That was not
accepted before the arrest and crucifixion, but it will be when
he has carried out his commission (Jn. 21:18) in a solemn "verily, verily" pronouncement. When he was young he went where he
would, but when he will be old he will stretch forth his hands

and another shall gird him and carry him whither he did not
want to go. This is a graphic description of his arms being
stretched out, fixed to a cross, and the cross raised. Jn.
21:19 states that Jesus said this to signify by what manner
of death he should glorify God. When the Fourth Gospel was
written, Peter was probably dead thirty years.

The final command to Simon Peter is "Follow me". In
Jn. 13:37 Peter had asked: "Lord, why cannot I follow thee
even now." It was now as then: "but thou shalt follow afterwards" (Jn. 13:36).

Peter next turned round and seeing the disciple whom Jesus
loved following Jesus, Peter asked Jesus: "Lord what shall
this man do?" Jesus' reply was: "If I will that he tarry till
I come, what is that to thee? As for thee, follow me." Jn.
21:23 states that this saying went forth among the brethren
that that disciple should not die. This is an interesting
example of how a *logion* could be reshaped in transmission. The
writer of the Fourth Gospel underlines that Jesus did not say
he would not die, but only "If I will that he tarry till I come,
what is that to you?"

In Jn. 21:24 the writer of the Fourth Gospel apparently
identifies himself with the one of whom Simon Peter and Jesus
spoke. "This is the disciple who bears witness of these things
and who wrote these things." On the other hand, it could be
that it is those who refer to themselves as "we" who identify
the disciple under discussion by Simon Peter and Jesus as the
witness of these things.[243] "These things" need not be used
in a particularistic sense referring only to this final chapter
of the gospel but to the whole gospel. The claim that he wrote
"these things" would point to the writing of the whole gospel.
Thus the claim is made here that the disciple whom Jesus loved
bears witness to the contents of the gospel, and it is also

claimed that he wrote them all down. The last part of this verse (24) is an affirmation made by those who refer to themselves as "we" that his witness is true.

In Jn. 15:26 it is stated: "But when the Comforter is come, whom I will send unto you from the Father, even the Spirit of truth, who proceeds from the Father, He shall bear witness of me (v. 27) and you also bear witness, because you have been with me from the beginning." If we take this verse alongside Jn. 21:24, then it is the Spirit of truth which bears witness in and through the disciple in v. 24. He had already received the Holy Ghost (cf. Jn. 20:22). The others have received the Holy Spirit too and thereby are competent to bear witness.

Water is a symbol of the Spirit. In Jn. 7:38 Jesus said in the Temple at the Feast of Tabernacles: "He who believes on me, as the scripture has said, out of his belly shall flow rivers of living water. (v. 39) But this spake he of the Spirit." In rabbinic sources the water-pouring at Sukkoth is clearly associated with the giving of the Spirit. The Holy Spirit is primarily the Spirit of prophecy in rabbinic sources (cf. Targumic usage). Sifre 170 (to Dt. 18:18) says "I will put My words into his mouth" means "I put them into his mouth, but I do not speak with him face to face; know therefore that henceforth the Holy Spirit is put into the mouths of prophets". M. Song. R. 1.9 shows that "knowledge of God" is the Holy Spirit. According to Joel 2:28, 29, the Holy Spirit will be poured out upon all Israel in the messianic time.[244] M. Num. R. XV, 25 understands that all the people will be prophets. M. Song. R. 1.9 had held that whoever teaches the Torah in public partakes of the Holy Spirit. The Holy Spirit dwells only among a worthy generation and the frequency of His manifestations is proportionate to the worthiness of the people of that generation.

There was no manifestation of the Holy Spirit in the time of
the Second Temple (T. B. Yoma 21b), while there were many
during the time of Elijah (Tos. Sotah 12:5). The visible results of the activity of the Holy Spirit, according to the
rabbis, were the books of the Bible, all of which have been
composed under its inspiration. Traditional Judaism held the
view that every word of holy writ was inspired by the Spirit
of Holiness (i.e. God). This Spirit, in every case, was believed to have rested on a prophet; and consequently every
biblical book was said to have been written[245] by a prophet.
"Forty-eight prophets and seven prophetesses prophesied for
Israel. None of them took from or added anything to the Law,
except the reading of the roll of Esther" (T. B. Meg. 14a,
Baraitha). The rabbis were at pains to show that the biblical
books were written by prophets. A prophet under the influence
of the Holy Spirit knew both past and future. T. B. Baba Bathra 14b, the early and important *Baraitha* on the sequence and
authors of the biblical writings, assumes that not only the
Patriarchs and David and Solomon were prophets, but that the
author of every book of the Bible was a prophet. It finds him
either in the title or by deduction. Moses, Joshua, Samuel,
Ezra, and the Prophets wrote their own books. Moses wrote Job,
Joshua the last eight verses of the Torah (i.e. from Dt. 34:5),
"Moses, the servant of the Lord, died" to the end. Samuel
wrote Judges and Ruth. Jeremiah wrote the books of Kings as
well as his own book. David wrote the Psalms, and Solomon
wrote Proverbs, The Song of Songs, and Ecclesiastes (Seder
Olam XV). Ezra wrote Chronicles and Ezra-Nehemiah.[246] But
what about the Book of Esther? The Seder Olam held, on the
basis of Esth. 9:29, "Esther wrote", that Esther was a prophetess. "God" (M. Ex. R. XLVII, 7b) said to Moses: "Copy the
Torah, Prophets, and Hagiographa that you may have them in

writing; Hala<u>k</u>oth, Midrashim, Haggadoth, and Talmud, however,
are to be preserved only verbally." T. B. Meg. 14b seeks to
prove that Esther was a prophetess. This it does by pointing
out (Esth. 5:1) that it is written:

> 'Now it came to pass on the third day that
> Esther clothed herself in royalty.' Surely
> it should say 'royal apparel'? What this
> shows is that the Holy Spirit clothed her.
> It is written here, 'and she clothed',[247]
> and it is written in another place, 'Then
> the spirit clothed Amasai...' (I Chron.
> 12:19).

Actually T. B. Meg. 7a shows Esther commanding the wise men to
write an account of her for posterity. They refused till,
identifying Haman with Amalek, they found: "Write this for a
memorial in a book" (Ex. 17:14). Some of the wise men were in
favour of writing it on the basis of this injunction, others
were not since they held that the words "in a book" referred
not to the Book of Esther but to the account of Agag the Amalekite in I. Sam. 15.

> Rabbi Eliezer of Modi'im said however: 'Write
> this', namely what is written here (Ex. 17:8-
> 16 and Dt. 25:17-19), 'for a memorial', namely
> what is written in the prophets (I Sam. 15:2),
> 'in a book', namely, what is written in *The
> Megillah* (T. B. Meg. 7a).

This not only shows an example of rabbinic exegesis but how the
entry of the Book of Esther into the biblical canon was justified.

In T. B. Meg. 7a Rabbi Judah said in the name of Samuel:

> '[The Scroll] of Esther does not make the hands
> unclean.' Are we to infer from this that Samuel
> was of the opinion that Esther was not said (i.e.

composed) under the inspiration of the Holy
Spirit? How can this be, seeing that Samuel
had said that Esther was composed under the
inspiration of the Holy Spirit? It was composed to be recited (by heart) but not to be
written. The following objection was raised.
Rabbi Meir says that [the Scroll] of *Koheleth*
(Ecclesiastes) does not render the hands unclean, and that about the Song of Songs there
is a difference of opinion. R. Jose says that
the Song of Songs renders the hands unclean
and about *Koheleth* there is a difference of
opinion. R. Simeon says that *Koheleth* is one
of those matters in regard to which Beth
Shammai were more lenient and Beth Hillel more
stringent, but Ruth and the Song of Songs and
Esther [certainly] made the hands unclean!
Samuel concurred with R. Joshua. It has been
taught: R. Simeon b. Menasia said: '*Koheleth* does not render the hands unclean because it contains only the wisdom of Solomon'
[i.e. not of the Holy Spirit]. They said to
him: 'Was this then all that he composed?
Is it not stated elsewhere, "And he spoke
three thousand proverbs"' (I Kings 5:12).

The argument is that, since these were not written and
Ecclesiastes was, the conclusion may be drawn that the latter
was inspired, and it further says: "Add thou not to his word
words?"[248] Why this further quotation?

In case you might object that he composed very much and what it pleased him to
write he wrote and what it did not please
him he did not write. Therefore it says,
'Add thou not to his words' [which shows
that whatever he wrote down was inspired].
It has been taught: R. Eleazar said:
'Esther was composed under the inspiration
of the Holy Spirit, as it says: "And Haman
said in his heart"' (Esth. 6:6). [The argument is that the author could not know this
if he was not inspired.] R. Akiba says:
'Esther was composed under the inspiration

of the Holy Spirit, as it says, "And Esther
obtained favour in the eyes of all that looked
upon her"' (Esth. 2:15). [The argument is
that to know this was the case means the
writer was inspired.] R. Meir says: 'Esther
was composed under the inspiration of the
Holy Spirit, as it says: "And the thing became known to Mordecai"' (Esth. 2:22). [Who
revealed it to him, if not the Holy Spirit?]
R. Jose b. Durmaskith said: 'Esther was composed under the inspiration of the Holy Spirit
as it says: "But on the spoil they laid not
their hands"' (Esth. 9:10). [That this was
the case is again information from the Holy
Spirit who inspires the writer.] Said Samuel:
'Had I been there [when the Tannaim above
cited were discussing the matter], I would
have given a proof superior to all, namely
that it says: "They confirmed and took upon
them"' (Esth. 9:27). [This last means they
confirmed above (in heaven) what they took
upon themselves below.] Raba said: 'All
the proofs can be confuted except that of
Samuel which cannot be confuted.' [He then
proceeds to confute the proofs of Eleazar,
Akiba, Meir and R. Jose b. Durmaskith, one
by one.] R. Joseph said: 'It (that Esther
was written under the inspiration of the Holy
Spirit) can be proved from here: 'And these
days of Purim shall not fail from among the
Jews"' (Esth. 9:28). R. Nahman b. Isaac said:
'From here: "Nor the memorial of them perish
from their seed"' (Esth. 9:28 end) [because
the first half might refer only to that gener-
ation].

To return to Jn. 21:24. The fact that it is here stated
"and wrote these things" is a claim that this gospel is inspired
by the Holy Spirit and since it more than fulfills the require-
ments for entry into the canon of sacred scripture, it should
be admitted. Jn. 15:26 claimed that the Spirit, when sent,
shall bear witness. The disciples (Jn. 20:22) had already
received the Spirit. The disciple whom Jesus loved, inspired

by the Spirit, is bearing witness in this gospel. He is therefore prophesying about Christ, past and future, for the prophet
knew both past and future. But this gospel is not just proclaimed; it is *written* (just as the Jews claimed about the
Megillath Esther), and so with the inspiration by the Holy
Spirit of the disciple who wrote, it is not only fully canonical and on a level with the rest of the inspired scriptures
of the Jews but fulfills them and the Torah. The latter helped
Esther to become canonical because Haman was a descendant not
only of Agag but was also an Amalekite; and the curse put on
Amalekite and the injunction to wipe him and his seed out were
in the Torah. It is possible that the claims (Jn. 5:46): "for
he (Moses) wrote of me" and (Jn. 1:45): "We have found him of
whom Moses in the Law and the prophets did write" are mentioned
so as to relate this gospel, which contains Christ's words and
acts, to canonical scripture. It is just possible that the
very verse (Ex. 17:14) so important for the canonization of
Esther was in the mind of the writer of this gospel: "And the
Lord said unto Moses: 'Write this for a memorial in a book,
and rehearse it in the ears of Joshua[249] [LXX read Jesus] that
I will utterly blot out the remembrance of Amalek from under
heaven.'" It all depends whom Amalek is taken to be. In the
Fourth Gospel the real adversary of God is Satan. Even Judas
is not the real adversary, nor Annas and Caiaphas, but it is
Satan that seduces and uses them. We have seen parallels between the movement of this gospel and that of Esther; the
parallel to Haman is not Caiaphas or even Judas, but Satan,
who is the anti-Christ; the earthlings are but his tools. It
could be that the writer of the Fourth Gospel, besides giving
it the form it has as an answer to the *Megillath Esther* and
the ideals which the latter inculcated, has also hinted that
the same arguments being put forward for the canonicity of

Esther could apply to this written gospel. The writer had
shown that he knew what Jesus was thinking and what was happening in the mind of Judas. These were grounds for claiming his
being inspired by the Holy Spirit, just as much as Akiba and
the others had argued for Esther in T. B. Meg. 7a. Is this
why Raba confutes such arguments?

Jn. 21:25 states: "And there are also many other things
which Jesus did, and which, if every one of them should be
written, I suppose that even the world itself would not contain
the books that should be written." Ecclesiastes 12:11 speaks
of the words of the wise as goads (spears or thorns) and claims,
apparently, that all are derived from the one shepherd (cf. Jn.
10:14 and cf. also Jn. 21:15-17). The Midrashic interpretation
sees this as referring to the oral law and its relation to Moses.
The verse could be a justification for Ecclesiastes being in the
canon of scripture, whereas Eccles. 12:12 is closing the canon:
"And furthermore, my son, be admonished: of making many books
there is no end; and much study is a weariness of the flesh."
Ecclesiastes, as well as Esther, owed its inclusion in the canon
to Rabbi Akiba. It could be that the Fourth Gospel is alluding
in passing to Eccles. 12:12. It could also be warning anyone
who would add any more gospel accounts. It is the end of the
canon. In fact it is *the Gospel*.

What is the relation of this whole chapter (Jn. 21) to the
Esther pattern? After a day of killing (but taking no plunder,
for it was a *herem*) the Jews rested on the fourteenth of Adar
and made it a day of feasting and gladness. But the Jews of
Susa, having two days of killing, made the 15th their day of
feasting and gladness. It is possible that Jn. 20:19, which
tells of the disciples on the resurrection day in the evening
having assembled behind shut doors "for fear of the Jews", is
thinking of Esth. 9:2 and how "the fear of the Jews" fell upon

all the peoples of the Persian Empire after the crucifixion
of Haman, and the Jews through Esther having obtained the
right to do to their enemies what would have been done to
them. Then Jesus comes and gives them his peace. He com-
missions them as the Father had commissioned him. He gives
them the Holy Ghost and power to forgive sins, or to retain
sins. He is in control; he is Lord and they have his authority, a greater authority than Esther and Mordecai got from
Ahasuerus. It is not authority to slay their enemies. In
Jn. 21 the first half shows the extent of the mission. The
153 fish represent all mankind which they have to bring as a
Church to Christ the Son of God. He will meet his disciples'
needs by himself in the Eucharistic feast.

This is not a feast of excess like Purim, where it is
mandatory to drink till one cannot tell the difference between
Mordecai and Haman. Jesus' feast is a giving of himself and
strengthens us for further service.

The Jewish *haggadic Midrashim* spoke of the messianic
banquet in a new age at which Leviathan would be eaten. In
the cosmic struggle before or at creation, Leviathan the
great sea monster had been made captive. Part of the Holy
One's day when He was not studying Torah, or not making
marriages,[250] was taken up with playing with Leviathan, who
was kept to be eaten by the redeemed. The 153 fishes were
supposed to be all the varieties of fish in the sea. There
is no Leviathan among them. The meal by the lakeside (in Jn.
21) is a messianic meal and the writer of the Fourth Gospel
may deliberately be contrasting its simplicity and restraint
with haggadic fancies and excesses.

There had been a parallel between the incarnate Jesus
and Joseph, Jacob's son. Jacob is Man (*Ish Tam*); Jesus is
Son of Man, i.e. of Jacob after the flesh. In Esther, Morde-

cai is paralleled to Joseph in his advancement to almost royal
power. But Joseph's power, like Mordecai's power, is tawdry
and fleeting compared with even the power of the incarnate
Christ who had put aside his glory out of kindness towards
and consideration for men. Now that he has assumed it again,
there is still this divine restraint, true humility, and loving
kindness. One wonders if the first two Catholic Epistles of
John, in particular First John, do not bear the same relation
to the gospel as the letters of Mordecai mentioned in the Book
of Esther do to that book.

The second part of Jn. 21 tells us of the further service.
Christ is the one shepherd. In fairness to the Book of Esther,
the non-Jews who became proselytes seem to have shared in the
feasting. Purim is associated with giving to the poor and sending portions to one's friends. It is here in the context of the
parallel to the Jews' victory over their enemies that the victorious Christ is briefing his disciples. Devotion to Christ
is to be seen in devoted service to Christ's flock which is not
just the Jews, but as he said (Jn. 10:16): "Other sheep I have,
which are not of this fold: them also I must bring and they
shall hear my voice; and they shall become one flock, one shepherd." Peter, who had denied him, as the chief under-shepherd
is commissioned in particular to feed Christ's sheep and so
prove his love of Christ thus, before having the privilege of
glorifying God in a way similar to his Master's. There is no
promise of earthly power and authority such as Mordecai and
Esther enjoyed, nor any retribution exacted from their enemies.
Loving service and sacrifice is the reward here, and the goal
is bringing all mankind to God in Christ, not out of fear but
in love to him and all mankind. But Christ's three charges to
Peter could also be parallel contrasts to the letters sent out
by Mordecai and Esther with the king's authority to destroy the
Jews' enemies (Esth. 9:20ff., 26ff., 30ff.).

332

Esther 10:3 tells how Mordecai the Jew was next in rank
to King Ahasuerus. The Greek Esther adds:

> And Mordecai said: 'All this is God's doing.
> I remember the dream I had about these matters,
> nothing of which has failed to come true: the
> little spring that became a river, the light
> that shone, the sun, the flood of water.
> Esther is the river--she whom the king married
> and made queen. The two dragons are Haman and
> myself. The nations are those that banded to-
> gether to blot out the name of Jew. The single
> nation, mine, is Israel, those who cried out to
> God, and were saved. Yes, the Lord has saved
> his people; the Lord has delivered us from all
> these evils; God has worked such signs and
> great wonders as have never happened among the
> nations. Two destinies he appointed, one for
> his own people, one for the nations at large.
> And these two destinies were worked out at
> the hour and time and day laid down by God
> involving all the nations. In this way God
> has remembered his people and vindicated his
> heritage; and for them these days, the four-
> teenth and fifteenth of the month Adar, are
> to be days of assembly, of joy and gladness
> before God, through all generations and for
> ever among his people Israel.

The phrase "the two dragons" as applied to Haman and
Mordecai is interesting. There is the hint of a cosmic struggle
between evil and good. "The two destinies God has appointed,
one for the nations at large and another for His own people,
Israel" is contrary to the spirit of the Fourth Gospel, where
there will be one flock. It is every man who judges himself
by how he responds to God in Christ. The old division of Israel
and the nations does not apply. There is one flock but it is a
new flock.

It is worth noting the colophon to the Greek translation
of Esther. In the fourth year of the reign of Ptolemy and

Cleopatra, Dositheus, who affirmed that he was a priest and
Levite, and Ptolemy his son, brought the Epistle of Phrurai
(*Purim*)/foregoing letter (i.e. the Book of Esther) concerning
the Purim. They maintained it as being authentic, the translation having been made by Lysimachus the son of Ptolemy, a
member of the Jerusalem community. The date was 114 B.C.
This colophon refers to the translation of Esther, not the
additions which were not translations. The postscript obviously is commending not only the Book of Esther but inform-
ing them about Purim. The postscript with its testimony by
a member of the Jerusalem community that it is a genuine translation reminds one of Jn. 21:24: "And we know that his witness
is true." Even if this is appended to the Fourth Gospel as a
further parallel to the Book of Esther, the writer of the
Fourth Gospel went so much further in testifying to the Paraclete speaking through the disciple who wrote it. This served
two important purposes: it related the teaching on the Paraclete contained in the gospel to the Gospel itself; it showed
how this gospel could with perfect authority claim to know the
mind and thoughts and his communion with God, and by so doing
claim for itself canonicity as its rightful due. Prophecy had
ended with the last of the prophets. According to M. Aboth
1:1 the prophets were succeeded by the men of the great Synagogue, that nebulous body which was supposed to last from the
time of Ezra right down to Simon the Just. The story of Esther,
it is true, is set in the late Persian period, but, according
to the *Seder Olam Raba*, that whole period lasted only fifty
years. So Esther was regarded rather as belonging to the
period of the men of the great Synagogue, among whom some
prophets were supposed to survive. While this latter fact
did provide an escape clause to include Esther among the
prophets, it was not really pressed. It was the fact that

Esther was written and also that the writer knew what his characters sometimes thought which provided the grounds for including Esther. The case for the canonicity of Esther was indeed challenged long after Akiba--even among the Jews. But the Feast of Purim justified what Esther had written by making the reading of the Scroll (of Esther) an integral part of its celebration and that kept Esther within the canon. The Fourth Gospel never was within the Jewish canon of scripture, and during the second century A.D. its position in the Christian Church was challenged. But even though its position has long been acknowledged as the "Great Gospel" or the "Spiritual Gospel", it is both an enigma and a challenge.

If the mother of Jesus (Jn. 2:3) typifies the mother of the Church, i.e. the Synagogue, could it be that Jesus' mother, who stood by the cross, also there typifies the Synagogue? In the Johannine crucifixion narrative Jesus' one expressed concern on the cross is to make provision for her future welfare. He handed her over there to the disciple whom he loved, the disciple who claimed to write this gospel. To his mother, he said: "Woman, behold your son!" (Jn. 19:26). To the disciple, he said: "Behold your mother!" The Fourth Gospel has often been called "the most Greek of the gospels". It is not. Rather it is the most Hebraic and the most Jewish. It proclaims absolute monotheism and the universal love of God. This too was the vision of the Hebrew prophets. The disciple whom Jesus loved from that hour took his mother to his own home (Jn. 19:27). And if the mother is the Synagogue and the heart of the Synagogue liturgy is the *Shema'*, the Fourth Evangelist never forsook her, but sought to help her the better to understand the nature and extent of the love that the LORD/GOD offered her. In the gospel it is offered to all.

There is the haggadic midrash which tells how the LORD God offered the Torah to all men, but they refused. It was Israel's peculiar merit to have been unique in accepting it. The writer of the Fourth Gospel thinks of the LORD offering Himself, the Living God, to and for all men. He did not reject the Jews.

EPILOGUE

In the Fourth Gospel there is a tension and contrast
between light and darkness, God and Satan, Jesus and the Jews.
In fact the Jews are called in that gospel "sons of the devil".
In this gospel we see certain parallels alluding to the *Megillath Esther* and also contrast thereto. The Jews in the Fourth
Gospel are what Haman and his sons are in the *Megillath Esther*.
They are there a sort of collective Haman, though Judas Iscariot, Caiaphas, and Annas individually have a claim to that
name. But the Fourth Gospel would not have seen a mere malevo-
lent man as the real cause of opposition to Mordecai and the
Jews, just as it did not see Judas Iscariot as the real cause
of the betrayal of Jesus. It was the fact that Judas was under
the direct control of Satan. Not all the Jews were sons of
Satan and not only they; there were the good and the bad among
the non-Jews too. Most were blind and deaf. All men were
judged on how they reacted to a confrontation with Jesus and
his word. Actually as the gospel stands written for a Church
situation, they judged themselves on how they reacted to the
word (or words) about Jesus. There is in this gospel no advantage in being a Jew, but rather disadvantage, in that knowing
the Hebrew Bible they did not believe the word (preached) about
Jesus. I do not think we have, as in the *Manual of Discipline*,
the two camps--the sons of light and the sons of darkness.
Rather the whole world is in darkness. A little group of disciples had formed themselves round Jesus, and in the sixty
years before this gospel was written, they had developed into
a cluster of congregations. Nationality and citizenship in the

worldly or the Jewish sense meant nothing. Baptism and participation in the Eucharist were the sacraments necessary for entry and life in the new community. The choice of opting in or remaining out was an individual one, but how one responded to the word preached judged one. Once in the community how one treated one's fellow men judged the sincerety of one's belief. The Christian life is not static. One lives in the world, though not of it. One has to witness constantly for Christ and to resist Satan, in his various disguises. There is no doubt of the ultimate victory of light over darkness, of good over evil, but the battle still goes on. The difference that the incarnation made was that the Satan in man was met by God in man. It is part of the cosmic struggle. The victory of good over evil in the human plane was achieved and a society established perpetuating the fruits of the victory and offering the opportunity of each and every man or woman to enlist on God's side and participate in the victory that has been won and contribute to the universal extension of the divinely instituted new society. This society is not an end in itself but a step towards the union of each and all of its members and the whole body corporate, not only with each other, but with the Deity as adopted sons of God. The aim is the abolition of division, not by pretending it does not exist, but by the removal of evil in each and every one. The Fourth Gospel believes in the potential divinity of Man and the reality of the humanity of God. God and man are not basically antipathetic. If man was truly human, he would be divine. There is no doctrine of original sin in the Fourth Gospel. There is no doctrine of the fall. But there is a struggle between light and darkness, good and evil, the origin of which is not explained. But it is implied that the good (in a human sense) is the enemy of the best (in a divine sense). The struggle goes on as long as there is man and human society. Human society, in itself, is not evil but has to be continually remade and refined. If it is not, it becomes evil. Nationalism is not enough, not even that of Israel. Just as the individual like a seed must die for a seed to have more life and to give more life, so must existing human institutions. The Fourth Gospel did not see a future for the chosen people of the Hebrew Bible as a national religio-political entity. For its goal of unity to be achieved, God had to deal with the individual and with the world. It could be that the Church, as we know it now, stands in the way of the achievement of the union of man and God which comes with the beatific vision. The Pharisees' question to Jesus, who had given sight to the man born blind, was: "Are we also blind?" Jesus (Jn. 9:41) said unto them: "If you were blind, you would have no sin; but now you say, we see: your sin remains." Who are now the Pharisees? Is it the Churches?

NOTES

NOTES TO CHAPTER 1

1. See L. Finkelstein, *Akiba, Scholar, Saint and Martyr* (New York, 1936).

2. See L. Ginzberg, "Akiba ben Joseph," *Jewish Encyclopedia* (New York, 1916), I, 306.

3. That Aquila and Onkelos are one and the same (see P. E. Kahle, *The Cairo Geniza*, London, 1947, p. 118). This had already been stated by W. Bacher ("Targum", *JE*, XII, 58) on the basis of T. B. Meg. 3a and T. J. Meg. 71c, which in the giving of the same tradition on the authorship of the Targum to the Torah, have Onkelos and Aquila respectively. Bacher (*ibid.*, p. 59), while allowing that the final redaction was carried out in Babylonia, held: "The content of the Targums shows, moreover, that it was composed in Palestine in the second century; for both in its halakic and in its haggadic portions it may be traced in the great part to the school of Akiba and especially to the tannaim of that period." Louis Ginzberg ("Akiba", *JE*, I, 306) went further and stated "the so-called Targum Onkelos, which in matters of Halakah reflects Akiba's opinions completely".

4. T. B. Meg. 3a queries whether Onkelos did compose the Targum to the Torah, and gives a midrashic note by Rab on Neh. 8:8 that "with an interpretation" there meant Targum.

5. See Kahle, p. 123.

6. Probably the greater proportion of the community were regarded by the Pharisees as *Am ha-Arez* and therefore outside the community as the latter understood it. A Sadducean high priest could from this point of view be an *Am ha-Arez*. An *Am ha-Arez* could be someone who did not say the *Shema'* evening and morning so R. Eliezer (cf. T. B. Ber 74b); or in the plural *Amme ha-Arez* be those who called the sacred

Notes to p. 2

Ark the "chest" and the synagogue "the people's house" so
Ishmael b. Eleazar (T. B. Shab. 32a).

7. The *Minim*. Sometimes *Sadukim, Kuthim, Apikorsim*,
are used where the plain sense of Sadducees, Samaritans and
Epicureans is not applicable. So also with *Minim* sectaries,
heretics. These terms sometimes must be understood as referring to Jewish Christians. In T. B. Shab. 116a R. Tarfon
said: "The writings of the *Minim* deserve to be burned, even
though the holy name of God occurs therein, for paganism is
less dangerous than 'minuth'; the former fails to recognize
the truth of Judaism from want of knowledge, but the latter
denies what is fully known." Scrolls of the Law, *Tefillin*
and *Mezuzoth*, written by a *Min*, were burned (T. B. Gittin
45b; T. J. Shab. 14b; T. B. A. Z. 40b). An animal slaughtered
by a *Min* was forbidden (T. B. Hul, 13a).
Imma Shalom, the wife of R. Eliezer, was the sister
of Rabban Gamaliel II. Wishing to expose the venality of a
Min, who lived in the neighbourhood as a judge, and who prided
himself on his incorruptibility, she brought him secretly a
golden lamp and asked him to order her brother to divide the
inheritance with her. Their father, Rabban Simeon b. Gamaliel,
died at the destruction of the Temple. Rabban Gamaliel plead-
ed that, according to the Law of Moses, a daughter could not
inherit where there was a son. "Now that you are in captivity,"
replied the *Min*, "the Law of Moses is abolished and the Evangel is given which makes no distinction between sons and
daughters." The next day, before the case came on again,
Rabban Gamaliel had a Libyan ass secretly conveyed to him by
way of a bribe. The judge then said to the litigants: "The
Evangel, as having come last, is the foundation (the exponent
of the Law) and in it it is written: 'I have not come to
diminish the Law of Moses, nor to add thereto,'" etc. T. B.
Shab. 116a, b (Amsterdam edition). Tos. Shab 13 (14):5 refers
to the *Gillaion* and the books of the *Minim*. T. B. Shab. 116a
has the same phrase, reading *Zadukim* for *Minim* though this
latter is retained in the Munich MS. *Gillaion* meant a blank
parchment or margin of scrolls. R. Meir (T. B. Shab. 116a)
called the gospel falsehood (*'awen*) of blank paper (or of
revelation). R. Yohanan called it sin (*'awon*) of blank paper,
etc.
T. B. Hag. 5b tells us that when R. Joshua b. Hananiah
died it was said: "Who will now defend our cause against the
Minim?" (Rashi explains that the *Minim* referred to were the
disciples of Jesus [*Talmide Yeshu*] who do not believe in the
words of the wise.)
Justin Martyr, *Dial.*, 38, states: "And Trypho said:
'Sir, it were good for us if we obeyed our teachers, who laid

down a law that we should have no dealings with any of you, and that we should not have even any communication with you on these questions. For you utter many blasphemies, in that you seek to persuade us that this crucified man was with Moses and Aaron, and spoke to them in the pillar of the cloud; then that he became man, was crucified and ascended up to heaven, and comes again to earth, and ought to be worshipped.'" Inter-faith discussions were not encouraged by the establishment.

8. T. B. A. Z. 16b.

9. Called "The Scroll of the Law" (T. B. Hag. 5b).

10. R. Eliezer b. Hyrcanus was Akiba's Rabbi; but he was also a pupil of R. Joshua b. Hananiah. R. Nahum of Gimzo (T. B. Hag. 12a) and R. Tarphon (T. B. Ket. 84b) also instructed him.

11. Akiba's other principle was: "Words are amplifications." T. J. Shab. XIX, 17a, e.g. an infinitive before a finite verb (T. B. Sanh. 64b); the doubling of a word (T. B. Yeb. 71a); the repetition of a term by a synonym (T. J. Sot. VIII, 22b), see J. Z. Lauterbach, "Talmud Hermeneutics," *JE* XII, 31.

12. Cf. T. B. San. 45b, 46a.

13. G. F. Moore, *Judaism*, I, (Cambridge, 1927), p. 159.

14. J. Abelson, *The Immanence of God*, (London, 1912), p. 159.

15. Cf. p. 11 above.

16. T. B. B. M. 59b.

17. Actually the doctrine of God, e.g. His nature and attributes, was dependent on biblical exegesis.

18. See A. Marmorstein, *The Old Rabbinic Doctrine of God*, II: *Essays on Anthropomorphism*, (London, 1937), p. 29, etc.

19. E.g. where a noun was duplicated like *'ish, 'ish* or a verb *himmol yimmol* (Gen. 17:13) indicated to R. Akiba some new teaching. R. Ishmael and his school merely saw the Torah speaking the language of men, cf. Marmorstein, p. 119.

20. Cf. T. B. Hag. 14b.

344

21. Cf. also M. Song V:11, 4.

22. Cf. Ginzberg, "Akiba ben Joseph", *JE*, I, 308...
Akiba was an extremely strict and rational Jew. His doctrine
concerning the Messiah was the realistic and thoroughly Jewish
one, as his declaration that Bar Kocba was the Messiah shows.
He accordingly limited the Messianic Age to forty years, as
being within the scope of a man's life similar to the reigns
of David and Solomon against the usual conception of a mil-
lennium (Midr. Teh. XC 15). A distinction is, however, to
be made between the Messianic Age and the future world
(עולם הבא). To the future world all Israel will be admitted,
with the exception of the generation of the Wilderness and the
Ten Tribes (Sanh. XI 3, 110). But even this future world is
painted by Akiba in colours selected by his nationalist in-
clinations; for he makes the Messiah (whom according to Ezek.
XXXVII, 24, he identifies with David) the judge of all the
heathen world (Hag. 14a).

23. Justin (*Dial.*, 46) says to Trypho: "Let us consider
whether one may now observe all the Mosaic Institutions." And
he answered: "No, for we know that, as you said, it is not
possible either anywhere to sacrifice the lamb of the Passover,
or to offer the goats ordered for the Fast, or in short all
the other offerings." On being asked by Justin what he could
keep, Trypho replied: "To keep the Sabbath, to be circumcised, to observe months, and to be washed if you touch anything prohibited by Moses, or after sexual intercourse."

24. See M. Aboth. 3:16.

25. T. B. Ber. 33b.

26. Cf. Marmorstein, I, 105f., for the use of *Shamaim*
as a name of God.

NOTES TO CHAPTER 2

27. C.S.C.O. *Scriptores Syri*, 115-116, 1940.

28. *The Commentaries of Isho'dad of Merv*, ed. and trans.
by M. D. Gibson, I, 211 (trans.) and III, 102 (text), (Cambridge,
1911).

29. B. W. Bacon, *The Making of the New Testament*, (London, n.d.), p. 229f.

30. Justin (*Dial.*, 96) bitterly refers to Christians being cursed in Synagogues "and other nations effectively carry out the curse, putting to death those who simply confess themselves to be Christians, to all of whom we say 'You are our brethren'." See also *ibid.*, 133.

31. Irenaeus, *Haer.* 3, 3, 4b.

32. Irenaeus, 1, 11, 1.

33. See Marmorstein, I, 64, speaking of the *Lord of the World* in M. Ex. R. 31.1 says: "Owing to the unsatisfactory state of our texts we are unable to establish whether *Adon Olamim* was not the original, instead of *Adon ha'Olam*. It is quite impossible to assume that the Gnostic doctrine of the Jewish God as the Lord of this world, the Satan, the Demiurgos, the source of Evil, should not have influenced the theological speculations and the apologetical tendencies of the Rabbis."

34. See also Irenaeus, 1, 26, 1; esp. 3, 11, 1.

35. Justin (*Dial.*, 35) makes it plain that he regards such as "atheists, impious, unrighteous and sinful, and confessors of Jesus in name only".

36. A. Mingana, *Theodore on the Nicene Creed*, (Cambridge, 1932), ch. 5, p. 53; ch. 8, p. 84.

37. See Mingana, ch. 8, pp. 8, 9, n. 6.

38. See p. 20 above.

39. Irenaeus, 3, 3, 4.

40. Justin (*Dial.*, 35) condemns specifically Marcionites, Valentinians, Basilidians and Saturnilians.

41. Cf. T. B. Ta'anith, 19b-20a; T. B. Giṭṭin, 55b, 56b, 57a. According to T. B. Giṭṭin 56a he was one of the three wealthy men of Jerusalem during the siege. According to T. B. Ta'anith 19b, 20a he provides water for the use of pilgrims to Jerusalem. M. Shek. 5:1, in the list of Temple Officers, notes one in charge of provision of water.

42. Cf. T. B. Giṭ. 57a.

43. Jesus/or Joshua b. Gamla was a contemporary of Ananus, son of Ananus (i.e. Annas). Both were killed (cf. Jos. B. J. IV, 314-317) by the Idumean allies of the Zealots. Josephus (B. J. IV, 324) says that the capture of the city began with the death of Ananus. "With him (Ananus) was linked Jesus, who, though not comparable with Ananus, stood far above the rest" (Jos. B. J. IV, 322).

44. C. F. Burney, *The Aramaic Original of the Fourth Gospel*, (Oxford, 1922), p. 133.

45. Ex. 28:36; 39:30; Lev. 8:9.

46. The opening sentence of this prayer is a paraphrase of Isa. 45:7; however the reference to *YHWH* creating evil is removed and becomes "all things" in the prayer. After comparing the new day and renewal of creation, mention is made of His work on the Creation itself: "How manifold are Thy works, O *YHWH*. By Wisdom (*B^e Hakmah*) Thou made them all." This last is an important and significant phrase.

47. T. J. Meg. 1 70d.

48. It would explain the fact of the omission of Esther and Mordecai from Ben Sira's list of the heroes of Israel, if the Book of Esther had not been written when his list was compiled.

49. T. B. Meg. 15b interprets king *melek̲* (Esth. 6:12) as referring to the King of the World, i.e. God. Cf. also Pirke de Rabbi Eliezer ch. 50.

50. It is even suggested that Cain and Abel's sacrifice was on Hannukah, cf. M. Gen. R. 22.4.

51. Cf. the coins of John Hyrcanus (135-105 B.C.) with the legend *Yehohanan ha-Kohen ha-Godel we-Ḥeber or Rosh Ḥeber ha-Yehudim*; Ḥeber could be the senate: cf. also coins of Antigonus (40-37 B.C.) *Mattathiah ha-Kohen ha-Godel* sometimes followed by *we-Ḥeber ha-Yehudim*. Cf. "Numismatics", *JE*, IX, 354.

52. R. Hanina M. Pes. 1:6; Shek. 4:4; 6:1; Ed. 2:1, 2, 3; Ab. 3:2; Zeb. 9:3; 12:4; Men. 10:1; Neg. 1:4; Par. 3:1.

53. See Marmorstein, I, 215: "Jews, the children of Jacob, are the *true* Israel, but not the *New nation*, the offspring of Adam, Noah, Abraham, Isaac and Jacob, as the Church-Fathers taught."

54. Targum Pseudo-Jonathan, *ibid.*, says: "because thus it was to be done at the feast of Tabernacles".

55. See Justin's charge, *Dial.*, 112.

NOTES TO CHAPTER 3

56. See *The Fathers According to Rabbi Nathan*, trans. by J. Goldin, Yale Judaica Series, 10, (New Haven, 1955), p. 140f.

57. For a detailed account of these ten Descents one can refer to Pirke de Rabbi Eliezer, trans. by G. Friedlander, (London, 1916).

58. See Marmorstein, I, 150f.

59. *De Monachis* in *Patrologia Syriaca*, ed. R. Graffin, I, (Paris, 1894), p. 284.

60. *Ibid.*

61. Targum to Isaiah 17:11; 48:13; however cf. 56:5: "in the land where *My Shekinah dwells*".

62. L. Ginzberg, *The Legends of the Jews* (Philadelphia, 1947), p. 469 points out that the Prayer of Mordecai in the Greek Additions to Esther reads like an insertion in the first benediction of the *Amidah*. Certainly the Greek Esther 10:10, 11 resemble the early part of that benediction, whereas v. 15 resembles its close.

63. Y. Vainstein, *The Cycle of the Jewish Year*, 73 (Jerusalem, 1953), p. 25.

64. See M. Tam. 5:1.

65. I.e. in the standard form of the *Shemoneh Esreh*.

66. "The Original Form of the Anaphora of Addai and Mari," *JTS*, 30, 23-32.

67.   See the 3rd, 5th, 6th, 9th, and 15th benedictions of the *Shemoneh Esreh*.

68.   W. O. E. Oesterley and G. H. Box, *A Short Survey of the Literature of Rabbinical and Medieval Judaism*, (London, 1920), pp. 176-178.

69.   See A. J. MacLean, *The Ancient Church Orders*, (Cambridge, 1910), p. 38.

70.   See F. E. Brightman and C. E. Hammond, *Liturgies Eastern and Western*, I, p. 262.

71.   *Ibid.*, p. 516, VI, 30-32.

72.   See S. Singer, *Daily Prayer Book* (London, 1908), pp. 36-39.

73.   Ex. 20:2.

74.   See p. 78 above.

75.   See J. Abelson, *op. cit.*

76.   See p. 11 above.

77.   *The Book of Prayer and Order of Service According to the Custom of the Spanish and Portuguese Jews*, edited and revised by M. Gaster, I, *Daily and Occasional Prayers*, (London, 1936), p. 50.

78.   See p. 56 above.

NOTES TO CHAPTER 4

79.   *Das IV (Johannes) Evangelium und der Rabbinismus, Frankel's Monatschrift 37 Jahrgang*, p. 252 and 354.

80.   See p. 37 above.

81.   See p. 41 above.

82. 1 Macc. 7:48-49 speaks of the first Nicanor's day
as a great holiday and adds: "indeed they decided to celebrate it annually on the thirteenth Adar". II Macc. 15:36:
"And they all ordained with a unanimous vote never to let
that day go unobserved, but to mark with honour the thirteenth
day before the day of Mordecai" (i.e. Purim).

83. If Ahasuerus (Esth. 1:1) is Xerxes I, and Mordecai
is of the exiles taken with Jehoiachin (cf. Esth. 2:6) then
Mordecai was around 130 years old when the action in the Book
of Esther begins. His cousin Esther was a young septuagen-
arian (75, cf. T. B. Meg. 13a; M. Gen. R. 39:13). Abraham
had been 75 when he left his father's home. God had told him
that the deliverer of his descendants from Media would also
be seventy-five years old.

83a. According to Targum Sheni to Esther 3:14-15 it was
because Joseph's brethren had sold him into a foreign land
that their descendants were sold to a foreigner. However,
since Benjamin took no part in the selling of Joseph, his
descendants Mordecai and Esther became the Redeemers of
Israel. Aphraates, III, (*De Ieiunio*, ed. R. Graffin,
Patrologia Syriaca, Paris, 1894, p. 127) states that God
wrote that Amalek was to be destroyed by the sons of Rachel
and cites Joshua, Saul and Mordecai.

84. There is the question of the date of II Maccabees.
However relative to that of the Book of Esther is II Macc.
15:36, speaking of Nicanor's day as the day before the day
of Mordecai, presupposing the Book of Esther 9:21. But II
Maccabees could be as late as the first half of the first
century B.C. James Moffatt, allowing for the anti-Hasmonean
bias of the work, gave as a *terminus a quo* c. 106 B.C. Cf.
R. H. Charles, *The Apocrypha and Pseudepigrapha*, (Oxford,
1913), p. 129. If we accept the information of the postscript to the LXX Esther (11:1), it would appear that by
114 B.C. the observance of Purim (which might be called
Mordecai's Day, cf. LXX Esther 10:4, 13) was being canvassed
by an alleged Jerusalem priest before II Maccabees was
written.

85. R.V.   "The Lord hath sworn"
R.S.V. "A hand upon the banner of the Lord"
Jerusalem Bible "Lay hold of the banner of Yahweh"
Targum Onkelos: "With an oath has this been de-
clared from before the Fearful
One whose *Shekinah* is upon the
glorious throne; that war shall

be waged with the house of Amalek,
to destroy it from the generations
of the world."

Targum Pseudo-Jonathan: "Because the *Memra* of *Yeya*
has sworn by the throne of His
glory, that He by His *Memra* will
fight against those of the house
of Amalek and destroy them to three
generations: from the generation
of this world, from the generation
of the Messiah, and from the generation of the World to come."

Targum Jerushalmi: "The oath has come forth from beneath the throne of the Great One,
Lord of all the world, the first
king who shall sit upon the throne
of the kingdom of the children of
Israel, Saul the son of Kish, will
set the battle in array against
the house of Amalek and will slay
them; and those of them that remain Mordecai and Esther will destroy. *Yeya* has said by His *Memra*
that the memory of Amalek shall
perish for ever."

There are significant differences between Targum
Pseudo-Jonathan and Targum Jerushalmi. The latter regards
Mordecai and Esther as finishing off Amalek, they being as it
were the sole agents of Amalek's destruction. The former puts
the matter on a different plane. It is the *Memra* of *Yeya* that
will fight to destroy the house of Amalek and the fight will
be carried on in three ages: this age, the Messianic age and
the age to come. It could be significant that Mordecai and
Esther are not mentioned. At least Amalek's destruction was
not completed by them, but it could point to changing connotation being given to Amalek.

Shekinah in Targum Onkelos seems parallel to *Memra de
Yeya* in Targum Pseudo-Jonathan.

The Midrash on Psalms Ps. 9:10 on Ps. 9:7 states that
R. Levi taught in the name of R. Aha that the Name of God will
not be complete and the throne of the LORD will not be whole
until the remembrance of Amalek has perished. Interesting indeed is its Biblical *Asmakta* that in Ex. 17:16 *Yah* is written
instead of *YHWH* and *Kes* instead of *Kisse* (throne). The Massora
here may have known of such a haggadic midrash and have provided a proof for it.

86. *Makom*, see Marmorstein, I, 92.

87. M. Suk. 5:2, 3, 4.

88. M. Suk. 4:9, 10.

NOTES TO CHAPTER 5

89. Sunday being the First Day.

90. Targum to Eccles. 7:25 teaches that the Messiah will appear on a Sabbath.

91. Jacob's journey to Haran had been accompanied by five signs, among which was the vision at Bethel, and also the water rising upon the well for him at Haran. Cf. Targum Pseudo-Jonathan and Jerushalmi, on Gen. 28 begin.; the overflowing of the well is the 4th sign in the former and the 5th sign in the latter. One should recall this latter sign in connection with her statement that the well was deep and he had nothing to draw with (Jn. 4:11).

92. See *Code of Jewish Law. Kitzur Shulhan Aruh, A Compilation of Jewish Laws and Customs* by Rabbi Solomon Ganzfried, trans. by H. E. Goldin, rev. (New York, 1961).

93.. See Esth. 9:22, "sending portions one to another..."

94. See T. B. Meg. 7b. Rabbah and R. Zera at a Purim feast had kept this injunction. Rabbah arose and cut R. Zera's throat. Next day he prayed and revived him. When next year he asked R. Zera to the Purim feast with him, Zera declined saying: "A miracle does not occur on every occasion."

95. The Karaites observe the fast of Esther in Nisan on the three days before Passover, cf. L. Ginzberg, *ibid.*, VI, p. 473.

96. See also M. Song R. 30, 3.

97. This cuts across the Rabbinic view that God keeps the Sabbath.

NOTES TO CHAPTER 6

98.   See my article, "Identity and Date of Unnamed Feast of John 5:1," in *Near Eastern Studies in Honor of William Foxwell Albright*, ed. by Hans Goedicke, Baltimore, John Hopkins Press, 1971, p. 45.

99.   *Ibid.*, p. 49.

100.   Amalek in this world now, in the age of the Messiah, and in the world to come. The Rabbis were aware of the cosmic nature of the struggle with Amalek. "Never will the throne of God--the Lord of Truth, Justice and Love--be fully established until the seed of Amalek--the principle of hatred and wrong-doing--be destroyed forever." Cf. Pesik. R. 29b; Pesik R., ch. 12; cf. also Marmorstein, I, p. 174.

101.   Pirke de R. Eliezer, ch. 50; M. Esth. R. 3.17.

102.   Pirke de Rabbi Eliezer ch. 50 merely states that the king commanded people to bow down to him and show him reverence. It was Haman who made an image of an idol and had it embroidered on his clothes above his heart, so that whoever bowed to Haman bowed also to the idol. T. B. Sanh. 61b says it was the king who commanded divine honours to be paid to Haman.

103.   The enmity between Haman and Mordecai is in Targ. Esth. 3:6 traced back to Esau and Jacob. It is *Aphraates III Ieiunio* 13 who takes it back to Ham's jealousy of Shem. For the genealogy of Haman cf. Soferim 13:23; L. Ginzberg, *ibid.*, VI, p. 462 states: "With regard to Haman's descendants it is stated that some of them taught the Torah in Bene/Berak (comp. e.g. T. B. Sanh. 32b) and as the legend which makes him a descendant of proselytes might perhaps have been known to the Talmud (comp. Ginzberg, *Jewish Encyclopaedia*, I, 304) it is quite possible that Haman's descendant teaching at Bene Berak is none other than this great Tanna."

104.   Cf. Midrash on Psalms 22:19 where R. Samuel in the name of R. Hanina commenting on Ps. 22:4, "You who are enthroned on the praises of Israel", states that Esther pressed this point that if the Holy One did not hear her prayer there would be no praises of Israel to enthrone Him.

105.   E.g. I Macc. 13:42: "in the first year of Simon the great high priest and captain and leader of the Jews".

106.   The *Tamid* (evening) was offered early in the afternoon of Passover before the Passover lamb was sacrificed. If

the eve of Passover was also the eve of a Sabbath, the lamb
for the *Tamid* was slaughtered at a half after the sixth hour
and offered up at a half after the seventh hour. After this,
the Passover offering was slaughtered (M. Pes. 5:1). The
crucified Jesus in the Fourth Gospel fulfills, as it were,
both types.

107. Cf. the addition to the 16th benediction of the
Shemoneh Esreh said at Purim, "mentioned on p. 119." For the
full text, cf. S. Singer, *Daily Prayer Book*, pp. 51-52.

108. Cf. Mordecai's words to Esther, Esth. 4:13: "Do
not think you will escape in the king's house, more than all
the Jews."

109. Gen. 50:9-12. In both Targums he is a very military
messiah, with garments dipped in blood, and the mountains (in
Targ. Ps. Jon.) red with the blood of the slain, the rivers
(in Targ. Jer.) red with their blood. However, Targum Pseudo-
Jonathan adds: "He cannot look upon what is unclean, nor on
the shedding of the blood of the innocent: and his teeth
purer than milk cannot eat that which is stolen or torn: and
therefore his mountains are red with wine, his hills white
with corn, and with the cotes of lambs."
      Targum Jerushalmi shows us how to understand the
statements in Targum Pseudo-Jonathan about the Messiah. Because he is observant in the law as to matters of purity,
and will not eat *Terefah*, the very land is fertile.

110. See Justin Martyr in *Dial.*, 74, who finds the name
LORD (*Kurios*) in Ps. 96: "'Say among the nations, "The LORD
(reigns)"' refers to Christ. Trypho understands it as referring to the Father." In ch. 75 it is stated that the
name of God which was not revealed to Abraham or Jacob was
Jesus. It was in the power of this name that Joshua (Gk.
Iesous), whose name had previously been Hoshea, defeated
Amalek. It was after his name was changed to Joshua/Jesus
(Num. 13:16) that he received strength from His Spirit (i.e.
the Spirit of Jesus). The memorial of the injunction to destroy Amalek was to be laid up before Jesus (Joshua). But
this memorial of Amalek remained after the son of Nun (Joshua).
So it points to Jesus. Justin's *Dialogue with Trypho* is important as showing what claims Christians, not much more than
a generation after the Fourth Gospel was written, were making
in dialogue with Jews. The Epistle of Barnabas ch. 12 says
that the name Joshua was given the son of Nun "that all people
might hear the the Father would reveal all things concerning
His son Jesus 'to him'. Although the name is given on his

being sent to spy out the land, it is then that he is told:
"Take a book into your hands, and write what the LORD declares, that the Son of God will in the last days cut from
the roots all the house of Amalek."

111. In Esth. R. X.I on Esth. 6:1 "on that night the
king could not sleep" is interpreted as referring primarily
to God. Was there then a rabbinic precedent for interpreting
"King" in the Book of Esther as God? Rather we should note the
Midrash's interpretation of the action of the book as being on
two levels, viz. because Jews attended Ahasuerus' feast (Esth.
1:5) Satan accused them before God who decrees their doom. The
Torah wept as a widow before God, Elijah tried unsuccessfully
to get the Patriarchs to do something. However Moses "The
Faithful Shepherd" did respond and told Elijah to tell Mordecai (cf. Esth. R. 7.13). It is because the matter has already
been decreed by God that Haman can get the earthly king to
agree. Esth. R. 8.5 has Mordecai's dream as in the Greek
additions to Esther. While the two dragons in the Midrash
could be Mordecai and Haman, it is better to see them as referring to a cosmic struggle between God and Satan.

112. The present writer is aware of L. B. Paton's remark
(*The Book of Esther*, ICC, 2nd ed., Edinburgh, 1951, p. 101):
"Dislike of its (Esther's) revengeful spirit and doubts in
regard to its canonicity led the Fathers of the Eastern and
of the Western Church for the most part to ignore it." However Aphraates saw Esther as the figure of the Church (Aphraates, *De Persecutione* in *Patrologia Syriaca*, ed. R. Graffin,
I, Paris, 1894, p. 979f.). This is a very important section
as Mordecai like Joshua (cf. ftn. 110) is a figure of Christ:
Mordecai was persecuted, likewise Jesus was persecuted. Mordecai was persecuted by Haman the wicked, but Jesus was persecuted by the rebellious people. Mordecai by his prayer
delivered his people from the hands of Haman, but Jesus by
his prayer delivered his people from the hands of Satan.
Mordecai was delivered from the hands of his persecutors and
Jesus was freed from the hands of his persecutors. Because
Mordecai sat and wore sackcloth, he delivered Esther and his
people from the sword: and because Jesus put on a body and
humbled himself he delivered the Church and her sons from
death. Because of Mordecai Esther was pleasing to the king,
and went in and sat in Vashti's place, for the latter had
not carried out his (the king's) will. Through Jesus the
Church was pleasing to God and went in to the king instead
of the Synagogue which had not done His will. Mordecai ad-
vised Esther that she and her maidens should fast, so that
she and her people should be delivered from the hands of

Haman. But Jesus admonished his Church and her children so
that she and her sons should be delivered from the wrath (to
come). Mordecai accepted honour from Haman his persecutor,
but Jesus accepted great praise from his Father in exchange
for persecutions from the foolish people. Mordecai trod on
the neck of Haman his persecutor, and as for Jesus his enemies
were put under his feet. Before Mordecai Haman proclaimed:
"Thus let it be done to the man the king wishes to honour"
(Esth. 6:11). And as for Jesus, heralds went out from the
people (who were) the persecutors and said: "This is Jesus
the Son of God" (Mtt. 27:54). The blood of Mordecai was
required from Haman and his sons, the blood of Jesus his
persecutors received upon themselves and their sons.

The above is surely a very significant comparison
of Mordecai and Jesus. In this as in many other things
Aphraates may have preserved a picture of early Christian
apologetic specifically directed to Jews.

113. L. Ginzberg, *ibid.*, VI, 474 cites M. Esth. R. 5:11
end, as claiming that God would not permit the pious to
suffer more than three days and that accordingly Haman's
fall took place on 15th Nisan, three days after the decree
of annihilation was issued.

114. Cf. L. Ginzberg, *ibid.*, VI, 479 cites Targum Sheni
to Esther as saying that Haman took the same "lodging as
the son of Pandora", i.e. Jesus.

NOTES TO CHAPTER 7

115. Cf. Pirke de R. Eliezer, ch. 49. R. Eliezer said:
"...Every people who ate food in purity had its food provided
(according to the regulations of) purity; for it is said (Esth.
1:8): 'That they should do according to every man's pleasure.'"
M. Esth. R. 2:13 says on: "And the drinking was according to
the Law; none did compel." Esth. 1:8: "It varied according
to the Law (i.e. custom) of the various places...It was all
according to the custom of each people. For example for the
Samaritans who do not drink wine kept in leather bottles he
brought wine kept in jars."

Notes to pp. 164-170

116. "Fear of the Jews" *paḥad* could be a name for God,
cf. Gen. 31:42, 53 but *phobos* in the LXX Esth. 8:17, 9:2
and in Jn. 7:13; 19:38; 20:19, would mean dread inspired by
(the Jews).

117. But Jesus did not want to be the King Messiah such
as they wanted.

118. This reminds one of R. Meir's dictum (T. B. Meg. 7a)
that Esther was composed under the inspiration of the Holy
Spirit, as it says "and the thing became known to Mordecai"
(Esth. 2:22). The argument being "who revealed it to him,
if not the Holy Spirit?" "To be composed under the inspiration of the Holy Spirit" means is canonical.

119. "Holy One of God" is what the unclean spirit calls
Jesus (Mk. 1:24). Yahweh in Isaiah is frequently called the
Holy One of Israel, e.g. Isa. 43:14, "Yahweh, your Redeemer,
the Holy One of Israel", cf. also Isa. 48:17. Among the
Rabbis "The Holy One, Blessed be He" is the name of God in
the period of the Amoraim. Cf. Marmorstein, *ibid.*, I, p.
134.

120. There called water (cf. also Jn. 4:10, 11) just as
Jews thought of the Torah. "As water refreshes the body so
does the Torah refresh the soul" (M. Song R. 1.2). T. B.
Shab. 12a explains Isa. 3:1, "the whole stay of bread", as
referring to the Torah. As wine rejoices the heart in a
temporal sense, so the Torah rejoices the heart after a
spiritual manner, cf. M. Song R. 1:2.

121. T. B. A. Z. 5a.

122. *Adam*, Man, was one of God's names. Cf. Marmorstein,
I, p. 64, e.g. R. Judah b. Simon in Tanḥ. 1.24 sees *Adam* in
Eccl. 2:21 as one of God's names, basing this on Ezek. 1:26.
'Ish, *Man*, was also a name of God. Cf. Marmorstein, *ibid.*,
I, p. 65ff. who cites Nahum, the son of Simai who preached in
Tarsus on Ex. 12:3 ויקחו להם איש which R.V. renders "they
shall take to them every man..." He however took it as "Take
God to you". He meant that by performing the "duty of sacri-
ficing the paschal lamb the Israelite draws near to God"
(Tanh. IV, 30; Num. R. 9.1). This rendering of *'Ish* as God
here is typical of R. Akiba's literalism and anthropomorphism.

123. Actually in a sense the enmity of Haman against the
Jews is the continuation of the struggle between Haman's ancestor Esau and the Jews' ancestor Jacob. But the Early Church,

as typified by the Fourth Gospel, could not accept that the Jews were the descendants of Jacob.

124. Circumcision overrides the Sabbath was the opinion of R. Jose b. Halafta (M. Shab. 18:3). R. Jose b. Halafta is a contemporary of R. Meir and flourished in the middle of the 2nd century A.D. However in M. Shab. 19:1, R. Eliezer b. Hyrcanus would allow even wood to be cut on the Sabbath to make charcoal in order to forge the circumcision knife. R. Akiba laid down a general rule: any act of work that can be done on the eve of the Sabbath does not override the Sabbath. While in some ways restrictive (cf. M. Pes. 6:2; M. Men. 11:2, 3) this general rule of R. Akiba would allow circumcision on the Sabbath, if the eighth day which was *the* day for circumcision, fell on a Sabbath.

125. When Esther is taken into the king's harem, Esther did not declare who her people and kindred were, in this acting on the advice of Mordecai. In this we have a complete contrast between Esther and Christ. His critics thought they knew whence he was. In other words they testified to the fact that he had not concealed his origin. But the irony is though they could have known it, and thought they knew it, they did not know it.

126. Jn. 7:42 begins: "Has not the Scripture said..." What Scripture? Ps. 89:3, 4 might have been thought of for the Davidic ancestry, and Mic. 5:2 for Bethlehem.

127. A. Mingana, *Commentary of Theodore of Mopsuestia on the Nicene Creed*, Woodbrooke Studies, 5, (Cambridge, 1932), p. 75ff.

128. *Ibid.*, p. 88.

129. M. Shekalim 5:1 mentioned the functions of the members of that Temple Council. One member had to supply water for pilgrims. The story in T. B. Taan. 19b, 20a, which tells how Nakdimon on one occasion obtained this water, may point to Nicodemus exercising this function.

130. In Sifre 12a on Num. 6:25 Yahweh make His face to shine (lit. "give light") upon you is explained as meaning the light of the Torah. M. Deut. R. 7:3 states: "As oil gives light to the world, so too do the words of the Torah give light to the world." Cf. Jn. 1:17: "For the Law was given by Moses; grace and truth came by Jesus Christ."

131. Cf. Jer. 29:23, *'Anoki hu' yode'a (so Kethib) wa-'ed*, "I am He (who) knows and am witness" oracle of Yahweh. Eleazae ha-Kappar gives "witness" as one of the names of God (M. Aboth. 4:22).

132. Ex. 12:2 R.V.: "This month shall be to you the beginning of months." R. Akiba interpreted this in a literal sense. God showed Moses the New Moon (*Hodesh*--both new moon and month). R. Ishmael regarded this as not possible. It was Moses who showed the New Moon to the Israelites. Cf. Mek. 2b; cf. Marmorstein, II, p. 32, who adds: "This was one of three things which God showed to Moses with His finger. These are the New Moon, the making of the lamp, and the prohibition of unclean animals." On Ex. 20:18, "and all the people saw the thunderings" at the theophany at Sinai, R. Ishmael held that they saw the visible, and that they heard what could be heard. A. Marmorstein (*ibid.*) maintains R. Akiba favoured the more literal exposition when he says (Mek. 71a): "They see that which is heard, and hear that which is seen. Everything which came out of the mouth of the Power was immediately engraved on the tablets." This last is on the basis of Ps. 29:7.

133. Perhaps we might see its continuing influence on the Anaphora in "Fragment of an Anaphora of the Persian Rite," F. E. Brightman and C. E. Hammond, *Liturgies Eastern and Western*, I, (Oxford, 1896), pp. 513-515, III, IV, V, *passim*.

134. See *Ma'alah*, "Above", as a name of God, e.g. R. Hanina b. Hama: "A man does not hurt his finger below, unless it is decreed from Above" (T. B. Hul. 7b).

135. See Aphraates, *De Monachis* in *Patrologia Syriaca*, I, p. 275f.: "And when He was dwelling in the Height, He had no place to lay His head...And when He is God and Son of God, He took the likeness of a servant...And when He is the wakeful One who does not sleep, He was slumbering in the boat in the midst of the sea...And when He was Saviour (Lifegiver) of all mortals, He handed Himself over to the death of the cross."

136. Justin, *Dial.*, 94: "Just as God (who had forbidden the making of any image) commanded the sign of the brazen serpent, likewise though in the Law there is a curse on those who are crucified, yet no curse lies on the Christ of God, by whom all who have committed things worthy of a curse are saved."

137. See Jn. 3:14; 8:28. In Jn. 3:14, 15 Jesus in speaking to Nicodemus refers to Num. 21:9 as a type of his crucifixion and its lifegiving effects. Justin, *Dial.*, 91, 94, 114, sees the serpent of brass that Moses was commanded to raise, as a type of Christ's crucifixion. See also *The Epistle of Barnabas*, ch. 12. Both Barnabas (*ibid.*) and Justin (*Dial.*, 94, 112) made play of Moses' apparent transgression in making an image, and argue from this apparent inconsistency that this incident was a special sign pointing directly to the crucifixion, the slaying of the serpent Satan by Christ, and his healing those from Adam on that He had harmed.

138. See Pirke de Rabbi Eliezer, ch. 3 end. Wisdom, knowledge and understanding will be given to the King Messiah. This is stated on the basis of Isa. 11:2. This and the preceding verse are quoted by Trypho. Trypho's argument is that Justin had admitted that these verses referred to Christ, but that he maintained "Him to be pre-existent God incarnate by God's will..." Trypho wants to know how He can be shown to have been pre-existent God, who is filled with these powers of the Holy Ghost as if He lacked them. Justin's reply is to the point. These powers of the Spirit enumerated in the Scriptures came on Him "not because He stood in need of them, but because they would rest in Him, i.e. would find their accomplishment in Him: so that there would be no more prophets in your nation."...He imparts of His Spirit's power to those who believe in Him.

139. See also Mek. of Simon b. Yohai, p. 1f. Cf. Marmorstein, *ibid.*, II, p. 71, who ascribes such a doctrine to R. Akiba.

140. See Pirke de R. Eliezer ch. 39 beg. on the fourth descent of God viz. to Egypt based on Gen. 46:4, but cf. p. 47 above.

141. See Jn. 7:49 perhaps "This multitude who do not know the law are accursed." "Accursed" might mean put to the *herem*.

142. See Jerusalem under Simon bar Giora and John Gischala in Jos. B. J. V, 439-441.

143. See L. Ginzberg, *Legends of the Jews*, V, (Philadelphia, 1947).

144. In Dt. 18:18 (The LORD) states that He will put
His words into the mouth of the prophet like to Moses and
this prophet will speak to the people all that He commands
him. Whoever (cf. v. 19) will not hearken to the LORD God's
words which he speaks in His name, the LORD God will require
it of him. This is the other side of the coin. If the
prophet be *not* a false prophet, woe betide them if they reject him. God will exact retribution. But here in the
Fourth Gospel Jesus/Yahweh is judge just as he also is the
prophet.

NOTES TO CHAPTER 8

145. Marmorstein, I, p. 101, states that in the Haggadah
God is generally the owner of the flock, and Moses the
shepherd. God as the Shepherd, the older conception, occurs
however. He cites from the Midrash on Psalms Ps. 46:2 R.
Abba b. Kahana's comparison of God's deliverance of Israel
from Egypt, as a shepherd delivering the young from the
mother's womb. R. Hanina, the son of R. Aha, compared God
in Job's case to a shepherd who was inspecting his flock
when a wolf came and threatened it. The Shepherd (God) puts
a goat (Job) at the wolf's (Satan's) disposal (M. Gen. R.
57.3).

146. E.g. R. Akiba said: "One frog filled the land of
Egypt and brought about that terrible plague" (Tanḥ. ii,
Seder El., ch. vii; T. B. Sanh. 67b). True in Ps. 78:45
(46 Heb.) ẓepardea, "a frog", does occur as indeed the
singular is also found but with the definite article "the
frog" in Ex. 8:2 (though the plural occurs seven times in
Ex. 8:1-11).

147. Marcus Jastrow, *Dictionary of Talmud, Babli, Yerushalmi, Midrashic Literature and Targumim*, (New York, 1950).

148. One of the two benedictions before the morning *Shema'*.

149. The Targum Pseudo-Jonathan says of Melchizedek:
"And *Malka Zadika* who was Shem bar Noah, the King of Jerusalem, came forth to meet Abram and brought him bread and wine:

and in that time he ministered before *Eloha Ilaha*." The
Targum Jerushalmi says: "And Malki Zedek, king of Jerusalem,
who was Shem, who was the great priest of the Most High..."
In the Testament of Levi 8:11-15 it is said: "Levi thy seed
shall be divided into three offices, for a sign of the glory
of the Lord who is to come. And the first portion shall be
great, yea, greater than it shall now be. The second shall
be in the priesthood. And the third shall be called by a
new name, because a king shall arise in Judah and shall
establish a new priesthood, after the fashion of the Gentiles.
And his presence is beloved, as a prophet of the most High,
of the seed of Abraham our father." W. O. E. Oesterley, *The
Testament of the Twelve Patriarchs*, (London, 1917), p. xvl,
links this reference to king, priest and prophet all centered
in one person with Josephus' statement about John Hyrcanus
as possessor of the three greatest privileges, viz. "the
government of his nation, the dignity of the high priesthood,
and prophecy"; Oesterley then asserts (*ibid.*): "It is clear
that this is the ruler referred to in this passage, because
no other in all Jewish history combined these three offices
in himself." In regard to the "new name" spoken of in the
passage quoted, Charles points out that the Maccabaean high
priests "were the first Jewish priests to assume the title
'priests of the Most High God'. This title, anciently borne
by Melchizedek (Gen. 14:18) was revived by the new holders
of the high priesthood..." The title is found also in Jubilees 32:1; 32:16; Assumption of Moses 6:1; Jos. *Ant.* XVI
163, and Talmud T. B. R. H. 18b.

150. After the death of Simon the Just the pronouncing
of the Name, in the priestly Blessing in the Temple (T. B.
Yom. 49b), was stopped. Marmorstein, *ibid.*, I, pp. 24, 25,
thinks that it was the priests who, after the death of Simon
under Greek influence and Hellenistic teaching, held God has
no name, prohibited the pronunciation of the Tetragrammaton.
M. Tam. 7:2 says: "In the Temple they pronounced the Name as
it is written but in the provinces by a substituted word."
Marmorstein (*ibid.*) holds: "After a long struggle, the
teachers re-established the old usage of pronouncing the
Divine Name in the Temple." Taking into account the injunction in M. Ber. 9:5, "And it was ordained that a man should
salute his fellow with the use of the Name of God" (as in
Ruth 2:4; Judges 6:12), Marmorstein (*ibid.*) adds: "Moreover, even in common greetings they succeeded with their re-
form." This is too sweeping an assertion, but at least it
throws into relief the two attitudes. It is interesting that
M. Ber. 9:5 finds its Biblical support from the period of
Judges for greeting one's fellow with the Tetragrammaton.

M. Ber. 9:5 also cited Prov. 23:22 to stress that an ancient
custom (like using God's name in greeting) should not be
lightly set aside. Perhaps most significant of all is the
citation of Ps. 119:26 by M. Ber. 9:5: "And it is written,
it is time to work for *YHWH*: they have made void Your Law."
Perhaps we would be right in seeing the desire to use the Name
of God in greeting (as expressed in M. Ber. 9:5) as associated
both with Jewish Nationalism and devotion to the Torah. The
interpretation of Lev. 24:15f. varied according to time and
place.

151. Not even Jacob (Gen. 32:31) at Penuel, it was
Elohim he saw face to face.

152. The Divine Name *Elohim* according to the Rabbis shows
the *middath Din*, the attribute of judgment, whereas the Divine
Name *YHWH*, the *middath Rahamim*, the attribute of mercy. The
earliest example of this stated as a rule is Sifre, 27:
"Every place where *YHWH* is said this (means) the attribute
of mercy; every place where *Elohim* is said, this implies the
attribute of justice." In Midrash on Psalms, Ps. 56, 3 on
Ps. 56:11 this rule is ascribed to R. Nehorai whom A. Marmorstein, I, p. 47 identifies with R. Meir. However Philo Judaeus
had held just the opposite. *Theos = Elohim* the good, the God
of love and benevolence; *Kurios = Adonai* for *YHWH* and expresses
God's Lordship, as Ruler and Judge. Cf. Marmorstein, p. 43,
following *Dähne, Geschichtliche Darstellung der jud. alex.
Religions*: Philosophie, Halle, 1834, p. 231f. Mek. 37a cited
by Marmorstein, *ibid.*, I, p. 45, says: "God (*El*) the God
(*Elohim*) of my father, He treated me with the *middath rahamim*
the attribute *or* measure of mercy." Whence do we know that *El*
denotes the attribute of mercy? From Ps. 22:1, "My God (*Eli*),
My God (*Eli*), why have You forsaken me?"; Num. 12:13, "Hear
her, O God (*El*), I beseech You", and Ps. 118:27, "*YHWH* (is)
God (*El*) and He has given us light." It would appear that at
the time the Fourth Gospel was written *YHWH* represents the
attribute of judgment, and *Elohim* love and benevolence. This
being so, and if Jesus in the Fourth Gospel is LORD (= *YHWH*),
this is very important and would explain the claim made in Jn.
5:22: "Neither does the Father (cf. v. 18, i.e. *Theos*) judge
any man, but He has given all judgement to the Son." It has
often been observed that Jesus in the Fourth Gospel does not
do his healing miracles out of pity (as in the Synoptics). On
the other hand, *Theos* (= *El*) in the Fourth Gospel so loved
the world (Jn. 3:16) that He gave His only begotten Son, etc.
It is also surely very important that Ps. 22:1 is cited in
Mek. 37a as a proof that the attribute of mercy is intended
when the name *El* occurs. It is presumably possible that

because the Fourth Gospel identifies Jesus with Yahweh as Judge, that by the mid-second century the 2 *Middoth* ascribed to *YHWH* and *Elohim* respectively were reversed. In this connexion it may be significant that R. Akiba did not allow R. Ishmael's interpretation (Mek. 79a, T. B. Sanh. 66a, Soferim 4:5) of *Elohim* in Ex. 22:28 (Heb. 27) as judges and insisted on it being translated as God; cf. Marmorstein, *ibid.*, I, p. 14. This however may not be so much due to his being unwilling to associate the attribute of judgement with *Elohim* as because of his keen support of anthropomorphism. However R. Akiba's interpretation may be hinted at in Jn. 10: 34, 35. Justin, *Dial.*, ch. 124, interprets *Elohim* Ps. 82:6 as gods, but understanding it as pointing to what all men are potentially (as Adam was) "gods" and have power to become sons of the Highest (= *El Elyon*). But if they reject acknowledging Christ as God, they die like Adam.

153. W. O. E. Oesterley and T. H. Robinson, *Hebrew Religion: Its Origin and Development*, (London, 1933), p. 118f.

154. Cf. J. Morgenstern, *Some Significant Antecedents of Christianity*, (Leiden, 1966), p. 89, who states: "Many of the beliefs, traditions of cultic practices of this ancient Semitic, and specifically ancient Canaanite religion in the early, agricultural stages of the evolution were so deeply rooted that they lived on persistently in the folk religious belief and practice of a large segment of the rural population of Palestine down to the time of Jesus and even later."

155. Among the Rabbis mainly in liturgical compositions. However in the Tosefta Baba Ḳamma 7:2 both *Elyon* and *Koneh* (possessor) are used by Rabban Johanan ben Zakkai.

156. See above p. 46.

157. Certainly Yahweh is such not only in the O.T. but also in the rabbinic haggadah, cf. n. 191, p.

158. (a) Because of its plural form.
(b) Because in the Hebrew Bible it is so often defined by possessive pronominal suffixes, etc., till *Elohim* has almost as much as *Yahweh* a national connotation, e.g. *Yahweh Elohenu*.

159. Cf. Philo X, trans. by F. H. Colson and J. W. Earp, Loeb Classical Library, (London, 1962), p. 334.

160. Cf. Philo X, trans. by F. H. Colson, Loeb Classical Library, (London, 1962), p. 335.

161. Cf. Philo IV, trans. by F. H. Colson and G. H. Whitaker, Loeb Classical Library, (London, 1958), pp. 89-91.

162. Cf. "On the Creation", Philo I, trans. by F. H. Colson and G. H. Whitaker, Loeb Classical Library, (London, 1962), p. 55, § 69.

163. Cf. "Allegorical Interpretation", Philo I, trans. by F. H. Colson and G. H. Whitaker, Loeb Classical Library, (London, 1962), § 96, pp. 365, 367.

164. Cf. "The Confusion of Tongues", Philo IV, trans. by F. H. Colson and G. H. Whitaker, Loeb Classical Library, (London, 1958), pp. 89, 90.

165. Cf. n. 19 p. 19 above.

166. 1. El as the Father God. Cf. J. Morgenstein, p. 82.

167. Cf. also pp. 99-101 for fuller discussion.

168. Singer, *Daily Prayer Book*, (London, 1908), p. 52.

169. Cf. p. 221 above.

170. Cf. pp. 101-102 above.

171. Cf. pp. 200-201 above.

172. Midrash on Psalms, Ps. 82:1 understands it as "He is Judge among judges" and compares it with the similar use of *Elohim* in Ex. 22:8. It could have compared it with Mek. 97a. This is the view of R. Akiba who understood *Elohim* here as God, cf. n. 152 p. 211.

173. Cf. J. Morgenstern, pp. 94-95: "We have here no implication whatever of actual physical fatherhood and sonship in an earthly, human sense. Rather this relationship is altogether divine in character."

NOTES TO CHAPTER 9

174. Cf. pp. 114-115 above.

175. I.e. by the time this gospel was written.

176. On Amalek as rabbinic nickname for Rome, cf. my article "Amalek Saul and Paul the Apostle," *Abr Nahrain*, 13, (Leiden, 1972), p. 99.

177. In Esth. 3:8 it is "because of their laws that the Jews are to be put to death by Haman".

178. E.g. "the roaring lion" of Prov. 28:15 is Nebuchad-nezzar, "the ravenous bear" there mentioned is Ahasuerus, "the wicked ruler" is Haman, and "a poor people" is Israel.

179. I.e. to put out of the synagogue, "excommunicate", cf. Jn. 9:22.

180. Targum Sheni III to M. Esth. R. VII says Haman was an astrologer. He sought to fix the month for the execution of his fell plan. However like each day, the months were un-favourable to the Jews, except perhaps Adar, with the zodiacal sign of Pisces. Then he said: "Now I shall be able to swallow them as fish which swallow each other."

181. Cf. "Amalek" in Justin, *Dial.*, 131, cf. also n. 100 p. 135 above.

182. Cf. M. Sanh. 10:1. All Israelites have a share in the world to come; this is on the basis of Isa. 60:21. Then there are listed those who have no share in the world to come, viz. he that says that there is no resurrection of the dead prescribed in the Torah, and he that says that the Torah is not from Heaven (i.e. God), and an Epicurean. R. Akiba says: also he that reads the heretical books, or that utters a charm over a wound and says Ex. 15:26 (which ends: "for I am the LORD who heals you"). Abba Saul said: "Also he that pronounce the Name (*YHWH*) with its proper letters."

183. Mt. 19:19, esp. Mt. 22:39; Lk. 10:27.

184. B. J. II, 254-257.

185. B. J. II, 272-276.

Notes to pp. 243-252

186. B. J. II, 409f.

187. B. J. V, 440, 441.

NOTES TO CHAPTER 10

188. This looks as if it took place at Passover.

189. Cf. Aboth de R. Nathan IV.

190. Cf. p. 47f. above.

191. Cf. God's weeping in Rabbinic Haggadic Midrash. R. Eliezer b. Hyrcanus depicts God as sitting roaring like a lion in His pain over the destruction of the Temple, because He has lost His habitation (T. B. Ber. 3a). T. B. Hag. 5b says God is weeping because the pride or glory of the Kingdom of Heaven is crushed. Biblical basis for Yahweh's weeping could be found in Jer. 13:17. Marmorstein, *ibid.*, II, p. 70 states... the Rabbis do not mind speaking of God as being in trouble or pain, thinking of His as sharing His peoples' distress and exile. Esth. 6:1, "on that night the king could not sleep", is in M. Esth. R. X:1 referred to God whose throne was shaken, for He saw Israel in such distress. The question is asked how can God sleep in view of Ps. 121:4. Ah, but it can happen "when Israel is in distress, and the other nations are at ease"; that is why (Ps. 44:24) says: "Awake, why do You sleep My LORD (Adonai)?" Marmorstein's comment, *ibid.*, II, p. 70f. is very important: "The intimate connexion that is supposed to have existed between God and Israel and which lived in the minds of the Jewish teachers, induced them to preach the strange anthropopathic doctrine that God weeps or mourns." Marmorstein (*ibid.*) rightly connects this with the teaching of R. Joshua b. Hananiah (Mek. of R. Simon b. Yohai, p. 1f.) that because of God's boundless love and gracious protection towards His people Israel, His *Shekinah* went down with them to Egypt, crossed the sea with them, and brought them through the wilderness to His sanctuary. R. Akiba (cf. Mek. p. 17a) further developed this doctrine. The Exodus was not just the freeing of Hebrew slaves from bondage, but the release of God Himself. Scriptural basis for this is found in Ps. 91:15, 16. God was in servitude and bondage

during the whole time that His children were enslaved. As Marmorstein (*ibid.*) states: "This teaching was further extended by adding that not only in Egypt, but wherever His people were exiled and persecuted the *Shekinah*, the Divine Presence, or God Himself, is with them." This was an answer to the doubts of many a Jew after the Temple fell as to whether *YHWH* had deserted His people. It sought to emphasize "that God is and will remain" as Marmorstein, *ibid.*, II, p. 72 puts it "for ever in the community of Israel". Sifre Num. 84--the *Shekinah* suffers when Israel is distressed. There is little doubt that the writer of the Fourth Gospel was aware of such developments in Jewish apologetic and answering them by showing that his Jesus could satisfy all their needs and was with His own always in their joys and sorrows did they but know it.

192. M. Shek 6:3; M. Yom. 3:10; M. Sotah 1:5; M. Midd. 1:4; 2:3, 6; M. Neg. 14:8.

193. See *bosīma rāba* in Modern Assyrian of Rezaiyeh meaning literally "great perfume" but actually used for "very good", "very fine", or "splendid". *Bīsh, Bīsh* in the same dialect means bad, very bad; originally *bīsh* must have had the connotation of "evil smelling".

194. See T. B. Shab 104b; cf. also *Toledoth Jeshu*.

195. Judah Löw ben Bezaleel, d. 1609.

196. See n. 110 p. 148 and Justin's claim that Jesus was the Name of God revealed at the burning bush, and that the name of Jesus had a saving affect in Hebrew history.

197. Jn. 12:31 is Jesus' comment on the *Bath Kol* of Jn. 12:28. Targum Sheni to Esth. 3:7 states that when Haman cast lots to destroy the Jews, a *Bath Kol* was heard saying: "Fear not, congregation of Israel. If you turn with repentance to God the lot will fall on Haman instead of upon you." Haman is, as it were, the prince of this world.

198. Law could be oral law, and Haggadah at that.

199. In *Aphraates: De Paschate Patrologia Syriaca I*, ed. R. Graffin, (Paris, 1894), p. 527, the footwashing comes after the supper; it is there associated with the institution of Christian baptism. In Theodore of Mopsuestia, *Gospel of John, CSCO Scriptores Syri* III, 1940, p. 257, the footwashing is associated with a making ready to receive the baptism of the

Spirit. Isho'dad the Nestorian in Jn. 13:10 denies that the footwashing has anything to do with baptism. Cf. *The Commentaries of Isho'dad of Merv*, ed. and trans. by M. D. Gibson, I and II, (C.U.P., 1911), p. 261.

200. Cf. T. B. Ber. 64a: "Whoever is present at a banquet to which *Talmid Hakam* is invited enjoys, as it were, the effulgence of the *Shekinah*."

201. "He who contends against his Rabbi contends, as it were, against the *Shekinah*, for it is said (Num. 26:9): 'Who strove against the LORD and against Aaron...when they strove against the LORD.'" T. B. Sanh. 110a; Maimonides Hilkoth Talmud Torah. Sec. 5, halakah.

202. In Judaism even the allegorical school did not mind taking literally God's emotions, cf. Marmorstein, *ibid.*, II, pp. 68, 69.

NOTES TO CHAPTER 11

203. See p. 11 above.

204. See p. 254 above.

NOTES TO CHAPTER 12

205. Haman was the representative of Amalek, and the latter was the limb of Satan.

206. See p. 166 above.

207. Pilate as the representative of Roman power is as it were the epitome of Amalek, for Rome or Edom, as the Rabbis called her, was for them Amalek.

208. Josephus, *The Jewish War*, Books IV-VII, Loeb Classical Library, (London, 1961), p. 94n.

209. See Floyd V. Filson, *A New Testament History*, (London, 1965), p. 373.

210. Known to Polycrates of Ephesus, cf. n. 44 p. 32.

211. *Shinnui ha-Shem* T. B. R. H. 16b says: "Four things annul the decree that seals a person's fate: namely alms, prayer, change of name and change of deeds." Cf. *JE*, vol. 11, "*Shinnuy Ha-Shem*", p. 291, where the prayer effecting the change of name is given. In this prayer the following statement occurs: "We therefore...have changed the name of (mention here the former name) to the name of (mention the adopted name) who is now another person. The decree (i.e. of death from illness) shall not have any force with regard to him. Together with the change in name, so shall His (God's) decree be reversed from justice to mercy, from death to life, from illness to perfect health for (mention adopted name)."

212. E.g. in the Mishnah, only Ishmael, son of Fabi M. Parah Sotah 9:5, Jesus, son of Gamaliel M. Yeb. 6:4.

213. E.g. Eleazar, the brother of Judas Maccabaeus, B. J. I, 42A; Eleazar, son of Sameas, a Jewish hero. B. J. III, 229; Eleazar, captured at Machaerus, B. J. VII, 196-208, who was to be crucified, but was saved by the surrender of the garrison which resulted in the death of many of his people; Eleazar, father of Mary, B. J. VI, 201, the wealthy woman who had lost or given away everything, was starving and roasted her child, ate one half, and offered the other half to the horrified would-be food-stealers in the famine of the siege; Eleazar, nephew of Simon bar Gioras, B. J. VI, 227; Eleazar, son of Ananias, captain of the Temple, B. J. II, 409f., 424, 443ff., 450ff., who is credited by Josephus with starting the revolt in refusing priests the right to accept and offer sacrifices for non-Jews. Both Eleazar, nephew of Simon, and Eleazar, son of Ananias, minted coins. Eleazar, son of Ananias, had on his coins "The First Year of the Liberation of Jerusalem". Eleazar, nephew of Simon, was of a noble priestly family. His coins had "Eleazar the Priest" and on the other side "The First Year of the Redemption of Israel". Eleazar, son of Jairus, rebel defender of Masada, B. J. II, 447; VII, 253, 275, 297, his speeches to the besieged there counsel mutual destruction, VII, 320-388; 399. In the Medieval Hebrew Josiffan he is identified with Eleazar b. Ananias.

214. I.e. Segan or deputy high priest.

215. See Jer. 10:10 and "the sum or beginning of Yahweh's word is Truth" (Ps. 119:160). Ps. 15:2, Yahweh is the Speaker of Truth. God's seal is *'Emeth*, Truth. Cf. T. B. Shab 55a; Yoma 69b; Sanh. 64a. The (*'Emeth*) Truth here is explained by Notarikon as: א aleph God is the first; מ Mem besides Him there is no other; ת Tau He is the last, i.e. He has no successor.

216. See M. Ber. 2:2.

217. For *'Ani* as Name of God cf. what was said at the water-drawing at Sukkoth, T. B. Suk. 45a, 53a. The occurrence of "I am" pronouncements especially in the chapters in the Fourth Gospel apparently delivered at the period of Sukkoth, i.e. Tabernacles, is all the more appropriate.

218. Num. 15:37-41. This section specifically stresses the wearing of the *zizith* or fringes. R. Meir said: "Whosoever is particular in observing this commandment is to be regarded as if he had seen the countenance of the *Shekinah*" (T. J. Ber. 1:4). Cf. also R. Simon b. Yohai who holds the same view (T. B. Men. 43b). The very emphatic claim for this one commandment (which latter occurs only in the third section of the *Shema'*) may also point to a desire to popularize the recitation of this very section.

219. T. B. Shab. 119b.

220. Jn. 14:26; Jn. 15:26; Jn. 16:15.

221. See *ibid.*, §§ 300-309. This was one Jesus son of Ananias who at Tabernacles A.D. 62 stood in the Temple and pronounced doom on Jerusalem and the Temple. Even after the vicious scourging for seven years till he was killed in the siege he kept up his lament. Josephus, *ibid.*, 307 says: "His cries were loudest at the festivals."

222. See also p. 157 above.

223. The Pharisaic Rabbis though not so extreme, had scruples about writing the name of the ruler on the same page along with the name of God, cf. M. Yad. 4:8.

224. But cf. M. Ps. 22:18 where also "vesture" is regarded as additional to "garment".

225. See Mk. 15:29 and 31; Mt. 27:39 and 41; Lk. 23:35, 36.

226. Mk. 15:33; Mt. 27:45; Lk. 23:44.

227. Or is it a sort of modalism? At least is nominalism, cf. Abba b. Mamal (4th century A.D.). M. Ex. R. III:6, "God said to Moses, 'You want to know My name? I am called according to My deeds. When I judge the creatures I am called *Elohim*; when I fight the wicked I am *Zebaoth*; when I leave the sins of man in suspense I am *Shaddai*; and when I am compassionate I am *YHWH*."

228. Later to be reversed. Cf. Marmorstein, *ibid.*, I, p. 50. Commenting on Irenaeus, II, 35.3, he says: "This passage leaves no doubt that the two names (*Elohim* and *Adonai*) stood in the center of Gnostic speculations. It seemed natural that *kurios* should be interpreted as the God of the Jews, the God of rigid judgment, and *Elohim*, the general name of God, as the Highest God, the most perfect general name of God, the God of love and mercy. Consequently the teachers of the middle of the second century changed the order."

NOTES TO CHAPTER 13

229. See Isho'dad, *The Commentaries of Isho'dad of Merv*, ed. and trans. by M. D. Gibson, I and II, (C.U.P, 1911), p. 278.

230. See p. 157 above.

231. See T. B. Suk. 52a.

232. See Jn. 7:13; 20:19. For the verb, Jn. 9:22.

233. See T. B. Taan. 19b, 20a. Nakdimon had asked a non-Jew for the loan of twelve wells of water for the use of Temple pilgrims. He would repay in kind by a certain date, or pay a heavy forfeit in silver. The drought continued. Nakdimon entered the Temple and prayed: "Lord of the world, it is revealed and known to you that what I did I did not do for my own honour nor for the honour of my father's house, but for

Your honour, so that the pilgrims might have water." At once the sky filled with clouds and so much rain fell that not only were the twelve wells filled with water but there was much more besides. Nakdimon met the non-Jew and demanded payment for the extra water he had received. The latter replied: "I am aware that the Holy One, blessed be He, has disturbed the natural order of things on your account, but my claim against you for the money is still valid, for the sun has already set, and so the rain which fell belongs to me." Nakdimon re-entered the Temple and prayed: "Lord of the world, make it manifest that you have beloved ones in Your world." At once the clouds disappeared and the sun shone. Thereupon the non-Jew said to him: "Had not the sun broken through I should still have had a claim against you entitling me to get the forfeit in money from you as not having repaid in kind within the time limit."

This story is told to explain how he received the name Nakdimon because (in answer to his prayer) the sun shone out for him. Cf. also T. B. Gitt. 56a: *She nakdah lo hamah ba aburo*, for his sake, did the sun break through again (*Nakad*, to break through). Cf. Jastrow, *ibid.*, p. 931.

234. Josephus, Loeb Classical Library, (London, 1961).

235. It is quite possible that the writer of the Fourth Gospel had Josephus' *Jewish War* available. He also knew what Jewish tradition there was.

236. *De Paschate* in *Patrologia Syriaca*, ed. R. Graffin, I, p. 535.

237. The *Tamid* (daily whole-offering) of the evening was slaughtered at a half past the eighth hour and was offered up at half past the ninth hour. But if the eve of Passover fell on the eve of Sabbath, the *Tamid* was slaughtered at half past the sixth hour and offered at a half past the seventh hour. After this, the Passover offering was slaughtered (M. Pes. 5:1). The *Tamid* was the daily sin offering. When Jesus was crucified it would be approximately the same time that the daily evening lamb was slaughtered and sacrificed.

238. See M. Pes. 5, 9. The lamb was hung on one of the iron hooks fastened into walls and pillars, cf. M. Midd. 2:1. If such were not available there were thin, smooth staves which a man could put on his own and his fellow's shoulder and so hang and flay his offering.

239. M. Pes. 5:6. An Israelite slaughtered his own offering and the priest caught the blood....The priest nearest to the altar tossed the blood in one action against the base (of the altar).

240. See Mary the daughter of Eleazar in B. J. VI, 208, 211...and her dead child.

241. God keeps the commandments of the Torah, written and oral. T. B. Rosh ha-Shanah 17b depicts God in His Tallith prayer-shawl teaching Moses the order of the prayers.
    T. B. Sanh. 39a tells how God, after burying Moses, became defiled and purified Himself, not with water, but by fire. God kept the first Sabbath (Pirke de R. Eliezer, ch. XIX). God wears phylacteries (T. B. Ber. 7a). In the T. B. 'Abodah Zarah 3b Rab shows how God occupies Himself every day. He studies Torah; He judges the world; He feeds all living things from the smallest to the biggest; He plays with leviathan. In T. B. Ber. 8a the opinion was expressed by R. Hiyya bar Abba that since the destruction of the Temple there is only 4 cubits of the Halakah left to God. In Gen. R. LXIV 4 R. Berekiah gave the teaching of R. Judah b. Ezekiel that there is no day without a new teaching (on the Law) produced by God in His Beth ha-Midrash in Heaven. In T. B. Gittin 6b R. Abiathar and R. Jonathan gave different interpretations of Jud. 19:2 (the concubine of Gibeah). R. Abiathar met Elijah and enquired of him what God was doing then. Elijah told him that God was studying the subject of the concubine of Gibeah. On being asked what God said about it, Elijah reported: "He (God) says: 'My son Abiathar says so, and My son Jonathan says so.'" "What!" exclaimed the other, "Is there any doubt with Heaven (God)!" "No," said Elijah, "but both utter the words of the living God."
    Marmorstein, II, p. 65, says: "It is, of course, quite natural that scholars and students should exalt their occupation as divine and worthy of God Himself." The literal and anthropomorphic approach was not the only variety of Judaism, but since R. Akiba was both the exponent of the literal and the anthropomorphic we must give attention to this aspect of Judaism.

242. This unverified statement by Oppian is given by Jerome (Commentary on Ezekiel 47 in Migne's *Patrologia Latina*, XXV, 474) but it conflicts with Pliny's earlier estimate that only 74 species of fish were known (Natural History, IX, 43)

243. See the Hebrew Deuteronomy which is called *Debarim* after the initial words *Eleh Debarim* = "these things" or "words".

244. According to *Tanna debe Elijahu* on Joel 2:28, 29 the Holy Spirit will be poured equally upon Jews and pagans, both men and women, freemen and slaves.

245. The emphasis is on what is written. Cf. Pilate and what he wrote. R. Levi says: "Formerly, if a man did anything of importance, a prophet came and wrote it down" (M. Lev. R. 34:8).

246. Ezra is identified with Malachi T. B. Meg. 15a.

247. The [Holy Spirit] feminine as in early Syriac sources.

248. Prov. 30:6.

249. See Justin, *Dial.*, 131 for the application of Ex. 17:14 to Jesus.

250. In T. B. Sot. 2a a Jewish sage was asked: "What is God occupied with since the creation of the world?" The answer given was that He arranges marriages.

Aboth de R. Nathan IV, R. Akiba declared: "Blessed be God, the God of Israel, who has chosen the words of Torah and the words of the sages, for the words of the Torah and the words of the sages are established forever and to all eternity." For it is said (Eccles. 11:1): "Cast your bread upon the water, for you shall find it after many days."

A SELECTED BIBLIOGRAPHY

A. Primary

The Apocrypha and Pseudepigrapha of the Old Testament, ed. by
R. H. Charles. 2 vols., Oxford, Clarendon Press, 1913.

Apocryphal New Testament, tr. by M. R. James. Oxford, Clarendon Press, 1924.

The Babylonian Talmud, translated...under the editorship of
Rabbi Dr. I. Epstein. 35 vols., London, Soncino Press,
1948-1952.

Eusebius of Caesarea, *Demonstratio Evangelica*, tr. by W. J.
Ferrar. 2 vols., London, S.P.C.K., 1920.

Eusebius of Caesarea, *Preparatio Evangelica*, tr. by E. H.
Gifford. 2 vols., Oxford, Clarendon Press, 1903.

Flavius Josephus, *Jewish Antiquities*, Loeb Classical Library,
tr. by H. St. Thackeray and others. 7 vols., London,
Heineman, 1926-1965.

Flavius Josephus, *Jewish War*, Loeb Classical Library, tr.
by H. St. Thackeray and others. 2 vols., London,
Heineman, 1926-1965.

The Greek New Testament, ed. by Kurt Aland and others.
London, British and Foreign Bible Society, 1966.

Irenaeus of Lyons, *Adversus Haereses*, tr. by J. Keble. A
Library of Fathers of the Holy Catholic Church, vol.
42, Oxford, 1872.

The Jewish Encyclopedia, ed. by Isidore Singer. 12 vols.,
New York, Funk & Wagnalls, 1901-1906.

Justin Martyr, *Dialogue with Trypho*, tr. by A. L. Williams.
London, S.P.C.K., 1931.

Midrash on Psalms, tr. by W. G. Braude. New Haven, Yale
University Press, 1959.

Midrash Rabba Esther, tr. by M. Simon. London, Soncino
    Press, 1961.

Mikraoth Gedoloth. Warsaw, 1885.

The Minor Tractates of the Talmud, ed. by A. Cohen. 2 vols.,
    London, Soncino Press, 1965.

The Mishnah, tr. by Herbert Danby. London, Oxford University
    Press, 1933.

Philo of Alexandria. Loeb Classical Library, 10 vols.,
    London, Heineman, 1958-1963.

Pirke de Rabbi Eliezer, tr. by G. Friedlander. London, K.
    Paul, French and Trubner & Co., 1916.

Theodore of Mopsuestia, *Commentary on the Gospel of John*,
    new crit. ed. of the Syriac version with a Latin trans-
    lation by J. H. Vosté. CSCO, Louvain, 1940.

The Zohar, tr. by M. Simon and others. London, Sancino Press,
    1949.

B. <u>General</u>

Abelson, J., *The Immanence of God in Rabbinical Literature*.
    London, MacMillan, 1912.

Barrett, C. K., *The Gospel According to St. John*. London,
    S.P.C.K., 1960.

Bernard, T. D., *The Central Teaching of Jesus Christ*. London,
    MacMillan, 1892.

Borgen, Peder, *Bread from Heaven*. Leiden, Brill, 1965.

Bowman, John, *The Gospel of Mark: The New Christian Jewish
    Passover Haggadah*. Lieden, Brill, 1964.

Brighton, F. E., and Hammond, C. E., editors, *Liturgies
    Eastern and Western*, I. Oxford, Clarendon Press [1965].

Cassuto, U., *The Documentary Hypothesis*, tr. by I. Abraham. Jerusalem, Magnes Press, 1961.

Cohen, A., ed., *The Minor Tractates of the Talmud*. 2 vols., London, Soncino, 1965.

Dodd, C. H., *The Interpretation of the Fourth Gospel*. London, Cambridge University Press, 1960.

Drummond, J., *Philo Judaeus, the Jewish-Alexandrian Philosophy in its Development and Completion*. 2 vols., London, Williams and Norgate, 1888.

Filson, Floyd V., *A New Testament History*. London, S.C.M., 1968.

Finkelstein, L., *Akiba, Scholar, Saint and Martyr*. New York, Covier Friedes, 1936.

Friedmann, M., *Mechilta de-Rabbi Ismael*. Wien, 1870.

Friedmann, M., *Sifrê debê Rab*. Wien, 1864.

Gandz, Solomon and Klcin, Hyman, *The Code of Maimonides, The Book of Seasons*, tr. from the Hebrew. Yale Judaica Series, New Haven, Yale University Press, 1961.

Ganzfried, S., *Code of Jewish Law (Kitzur Shulhan Aruh)*, tr. by H. E. Goldin. New York, Hebrew Publishing Company, 1961.

Gärtner, B., *The Theology of the Gospel of Thomas*, tr. by E. J. Sharpe. London, Collins, 1961.

Gaster, Moses, *The Book of Prayer and Order of Service According to the Custom of the Spanish and Portuguese Jews*, edited and revised, vol. I: *Daily and Occasional Prayers*. London, Oxford University Press, 1936.

Ginzberg, L., *The Legends of the Jews*. 8 vols., Philadelphia, J.P.S.A., 1947.

Ginzberg, L., *On Jewish Law and Lore*. Philadelphia, J.P.S.A., 1962.

Gibson, M. D., ed. and tr., *The Commentaries of Isho'dad of Merv*. 2 vols., Cambridge, 1911.

Goldin, J., *The Fathers According to Rabbi Nathan*. New Haven, Yale University Press, 1955.

Graetz, H., *History of the Jews*, vol. II. Philadelphia, J.P.S.A., 1946.

Graffin, R., *Patrologia Syriaca*, vol. I. Paris, Firmin-Didot, 1894.

Hatch, E., and Redpath, H. A., *Concordance to the Septuagint*. Oxford, Clarendon Press, 1897.

Hoskyns, E. C., and Davey, F. N., *The Fourth Gospel*. 2 vols., London, Faher and Faher, 1939.

Kahle, P. E., *The Cairo Geniza*. London, Oxford University Press, 1947.

Lewittes, M., *The Code of Maimonides, The Book of Seasons*. New Haven, Yale University Press, 1961.

Marmorstein, A., *The Old Rabbinic Doctrine of God*; I, *The Names and Attributes of God*; II, *Essays on Anthropomorphism*. London, Oxford University Press, 1927-1937.

Mingana, A., *Commentary of Theodore of Mopsuestia on the Lord's Prayer and on the Sacraments of Baptism and the Eucharist*. Cambridge, Heffer, 1933.

Mingana, A., *Commentary of Theodore of Mopsuestia on the Nicene Creed*. Cambridge, Heffer, 1932.

Moore, George Fast, *Judaism*. 3 vols., Cambridge, Harvard University Press, 1927.

Morgenstern, J., *Some Significant Antecedents of Christianity*. Leiden, Brill, 1966.

Oesterley, W. O. E., and Box, G. H., *The Religion and Worship of the Synagogue*. London, Pitman & Sons, 1907.

Pope, M. H., *El in the Ugaritic Texts*. Leiden, Brill, 1958.

Sanday, W., *The Criticism of the Fourth Gospel*. London, Oxford University Press, 1905.

Singer, S., *A New Translation of "The Authorized Daily Prayer Book of the United Hebrew Congregation of the British Empire"*. London, Eyre & Spottisworde, 1908.

Sparks, H. F. D., *A Synopsis of the Gospels: The Synoptic Gospels with the Johannine Parallels*. London, A. & C. Black, 1964.

Strack, H. L., *B^{e}rakhoth, der Misna traktat* Lobsaguugen Leipzig, J. C. Hinrichs'sche Buchhandlung, 1915.

Streeter, B. H., *The Four Gospels: A Study of Origins*. Edinburgh, T. & T. Clark, 1936.

Van der Leeuw, G., *Religion in Essence and Manifestation*. London, Allen & Unwin, 1938.

Van Goudoever, J., *Biblical Calendars*. Leiden, Brill, 1959.

Vainstein, Y., *The Cycle of the Jewish Years*. Jerusalem, The World Zionist Organization, 1953.

Weiser, A., *The Psalms*. London, S.C.M., 1962.

Weiss, J., *Earliest Christianity: A History of the Period A.D. 30-150*, tr. by F. C. Grant. New York, Harpers, 1959.

Weiss, J. H., *Sifra Commentar 24 Leviticus*. Wien, 1862.

INDEX TO REFERENCES

I. *Old Testament*

GENESIS

1............205, 216
2:2,3,4.......205
2:7..........193
3:8..........45, 46, 47
3:22.........313
4:1,3,4,6,
  9,13,15,
  16,26.......191
5:29.........191
9:27.........48
11:5..........45, 47, 211
11:7..........46, 47
12:17.........126
14:18.........56, 64, 361
14:18-20......209
14:19.........209
14:22.........209
15:1,2,5,7....71
15:12.........125
17:1..........70, 212
17:8..........71
17:13.........343
17:22.........211
18:1,2,3,8,
  12,18.......187
18:21.........45, 46, 47
22:1-13.......202
22:7..........190
22:8..........190, 202
22:9..........64
22:14.........202
22:18.........190
23:27.........170
25:30.........188

31:42,53......356
32:31.........362
35:11.........211
36:11,12......188
44:4..........46
46:3..........208
46:4..........46, 47
49............72, 81
50:9-12.......353

EXODUS

1:22.........127
3:2ff........84
3:6..........69, 212,
  214
3:7-8........127
3:8..........45, 46,
        47, 69
3:12,13......69
3:14.........65, 69,
       84
3:15.........70, 73
3:16.........215
4:5..........85
4:11.........204
6:1ff........56
6:2..........84, 212,
       214
6:2ff........70, 212
6:3..........84, 212,
       214
6:23.........227

EXODUS (cont.)

7:1............85
8:1-11........360
12:1-20.......104
12:2..........358
12:3..........356
12:46.........306, 312
13:6..........124
15:2..........212
15:3..........211
15:11.........212
15:26.........365
17:8-16.......104, 120,
              325
17:14.........102, 142,
              325, 328
17:16.........49, 350
18:11.........104
19:18.........48
19:20.........45, 46, 48
20:1,2,3......83, 84
22:8..........364
22:28.........363
28:36.........346
30:11-16......104
33:3,9........51
33:20, 23.....50
34:5..........46
39:30.........346
40:35.........51

LEVITICUS

1:3...........201
1:5...........201, 202
1:6...........225
8:9...........346
16:7..........200, 201,
              220
17:6..........201, 202,
              225
19:2..........66
19:18.........80, 242,
              243
20:10.........175
24:15.........362
24:16.........233

NUMBERS

6:24..........61
6:25..........50
6:26..........61
7:1-89........104
9:12..........309
11:20.........50
11:25.........46, 48
12:5..........46
12:13.........362
13:16.........353
15:37-41......370
19:1-22.......104
35:30.........180

DEUTERONOMY

3:24..........50
4:2...........150
4:31..........211
4:35..........78
4:36..........84
5:39..........78
6:4...........72, 80,
              149, 241,
              242
6:4-9.........75
6:4ff.........80
6:5...........149, 241
6:15..........49
10:17.........56
11:18,20,
    33ff.......80
12:2..........56
12:32.........150
13:1ff........193
13:1-5........115, 151
13:3..........151, 153,
              169
13:5..........153
14:1..........217
14:23.........49
18:18.........115, 150,
              164, 174,
              194, 360
18:19.........360
18:20.........151

DEUTERONOMY (cont.)

18:20ff.......193
19:15.........180
21:6..........85
22:22,24......175
25:17-19......104, 105,
                325
28:58.........93
31:8..........52
32:3..........74
32:4..........211
32:6..........217
32:8..........212, 216
32:9..........212
32:18.........217
33:26.........52, 53
34:5..........324
42:11.........217

JOSHUA

22:22.........210

JUDGES

6:12..........361
19:2..........372

RUTH

2:4...........361

1 SAMUEL

15,15:2.......325
15:9..........105
28:13.........85

2 SAMUEL

2:3...........211

2 SAMUEL (cont.)

6:2...........76
22:10.........45

1 KINGS

5:12..........326

2 KINGS

17:23.........176
17:24.........114

1 CHRONICLES

12:19.........325

EZRA

1:3,7ff.,11...225
2:1,2.........225

NEHEMIAH

7:7...........225
8:8...........341
9:5,6.........93
9:7,15........206

ESTHER 1

1:1...........349
1:3...........156
1:4...........156, 164
1:5...........156, 161,
                163, 164
1:5ff.........162
1:7...........162, 163
1:8...........162, 355
1:10..........161
1:22..........156, 162

ESTHER 2

2:5...........108, 147
2:6...........349
2:8...........162
2:15..........327
2:17..........156
2:18..........137, 156,
             161, 163
2:22..........327, 356

ESTHER 3

3:1...........136, 166
3:2...........137, 231
3:3...........231
3:6...........137, 167,
             236, 281
3:7...........157, 167,
             245, 367
3:8...........236, 365
3:10..........157
3:13..........125, 127,
             128
3:14,15.......349

ESTHER 4

4:13..........353
4:14..........147, 148,
             155, 178,
             280
4:16..........118, 124,
             128, 129,
             154, 249
4:17..........124

ESTHER 5

5:1...........128, 325
5:2...........136
5:5,6,7.......156
5:8...........136, 156,
             157

ESTHER 5 (cont.)

5:12ff........136
5:14..........137

ESTHER 6

6:1...........137, 354,
             366
6:2...........137
6:6...........137, 326
6:7,8,9.......137
6:10..........138
6:11..........138, 355
6:12..........138, 346

ESTHER 7

7:1...........156
7:2...........156, 157
7:3...........136, 156
7:4...........136, 156,
             157
7:5...........156
7:6...........136, 275
7:10..........138, 157

ESTHER 8

8:1,2.........138
8:12..........158
8:15..........125, 138
8:16..........122, 123,
             124, 125,
             128
8:17..........138, 159,
             194
8:17 (LXX)....164, 356

ESTHER 9

9:1............155
9:2............194
9:2 (LXX).....164, 168,
             356
9:10..........327
9:13..........138
9:15..........108, 158
9:17,18.......158
9:20..........100
9:20-22.......148
9:20ff........332
9:21..........349
9:22..........123, 351
9:24..........167
9:26-29.......149
9:26ff........331
9:27..........100, 121,
             327
9:28..........327
9:29..........324
9:30ff........331
9:31..........128

ESTHER 10

10:3..........125, 158,
             332
10:4, 13
   (LXX).......349
10:5,10.......347

JOB

1:21..........93

PSALMS

2:7...........214
3:3...........64
7:17..........209
9:7...........350
15:2..........370

PSALMS (cont.)

16:10.........318
18:10.........45
22............148, 153,
             238, 279,
             304
22:1..........304, 305,
             362
22:2..........119, 123,
             126, 129,
             136
22:2-5........127
22:3..........118, 123
22:4..........127, 128
22:5..........125, 127,
             128
22:6..........126, 127,
             128
22:7..........128, 129,
             304
22:8..........128
22:11.........126
22:14,15......129
22:17,18......129, 304
23:1..........200, 201
23:2..........200
24:7,8,9,10...93
29:1,3........212
29:7..........358
33:6..........220
35:28.........304
37:37.........125
40:15.........304
41:9..........272
42:2..........211
44:24.........366
45:7..........85
47:2..........209
57:2..........209
57:3..........121
57:9..........126
68:20.........211
69:21.........304, 305
72:19.........93
78:45.........360
78:56.........209

PSALMS (cont.)

82:1.........228
82:6.........85, 226,
             227, 363
82:7.........227
84:2.........211
86:15........211
89:3.........357
89:4,29......266
91:15,16.....366
97:7.........85
109:25.......304
110:4........266
113:1........92
113:2........92, 120
113:4........92
118:27.......362
119:26.......362
119:160......370
121:4........366
146:10.......57, 98

PROVERBS

1:7.........216
8:22........216
23:22.......362
28:15.......365
30:6........374

ECCLESIASTES

1:26........356
2:21........356
11:1........374
12:11.......199

ISAIAH

1:2.........87
1:14,16,
  20........88
2:1.........220

ISAIAH (cont.)

3:1.........356
3:27........88
4:4.........88
5:16........64
5:25........18
6...........210
6:1,1ff.....268
6:3.........56, 57,
            67, 97,
            98
6:4.........52
6:8.........88
6:9.........86
6:10........86, 87,
            197,
            267
7:6.........88
7:14........26
9:2.........125
10:20.......88
11:4........88
12:2........88
15:45.......211
17:11.......347
21:17.......88
22:25.......88
25:8........88
25:9........87
26:2........96
26:3........87
26:4........88
26:13.......87
27:3........88
28:23.......88
30:33.......88
33:2........88
34:16.......88
36:7,15.....88
37:29,32....88
40:3........200, 263
40:4........88
40:10,11....200
41:8ff......91
41:11,13,14,
  16........88

ISAIAH (cont.)

42:1,5.........88
43:5..........88
43:7..........76
43:12.........91
43:14.........205
44:6..........205
44:24.........90
45:7..........346
45:12.........90
46:12.........88
48:11,12......90
48:13.........88, 347
48:14,15-17....91
48:16.........88
48:17.........356
49:3..........78
49:5,15.......88
51:2..........91
51:4,5,7......88
52:6..........88
53............267
53:1..........268
54:5,6........206, 207
54:7,8........207
54:13.........206
55:2,3........88
56:5..........347
56:6..........88, 203
56:7,8........203
58:14.........88
59:13,19......88
60:1..........125
60:9..........88
61:10.........88
62:2..........88
63:8,10,11,
   14.........88
63:16.........91
66:13,24......88

JEREMIAH

10:10.........370
13:17.........366

JEREMIAH (cont.)

23:6..........75
23:25.........53
29:23.........358
31:3..........34
31:32.........207

LAMENTATIONS

2:3...........81

EZEKIEL

1:1...........219
1:3...........219, 220
1:4,4-28......219
1:26..........210, 211,
            214, 218,
            219, 300
1:28..........210, 214
2:1...........219
3:12..........57, 97
9:4...........83
13:9..........191
16,16:44,46,
   60,62,63....176
23:23,49......191
28:24.........191
29:16.........191
37,37:19......202
37:24.........344
37:27.........202
37:28.........203, 264
38:2ff........46
38:23.........76, 93,
             95
44:2..........46
48:35.........77

DANIEL

3:12,19.......231
3:26..........209

DANIEL (cont.)

4:17,24,25,
  32,34......209
5:18,21......209
7:18,22,25,
  27.........209
9:4,11,36.....209

HOSEA

1:10.........211
2:16.........207
6:2..........154
11:9..........211

JOEL

2:28,29......323

JONAH

1:16.........65

JONAH (cont.)

2:11.........154
4:2..........211

MICAH

5:2..........357

ZECHARIAH

9:9..........260
12:10.........312
14.............174
14:4..........46
14:9..........72, 73
14:16.........99
14:17.........107

MALACHI

2:10,11......187
4:5,6........65

II. *New Testament*

MATTHEW

```
 1:18-23.......26
12:24..........150
15:33..........371
15:43..........312
19:19..........365
21:5...........260
21:9...........210
22:39..........365
26:6...........245
26:42..........263
26:62-75,75....291
27.............304
27:24..........313
27:39,41,45....371
27:46..........123, 304
27:51..........309
29:54..........355
29:57..........312
```

MARK

```
 1:11...........263
 1:24..........356
 3:22..........150
 5:7...........210
10:52..........246
11:10..........210
12:31..........80
13.............25
14:3...........245
14:7,8,10......259
14:36..........263
14:68,72.......291
15:24..........304
15:29,31.......371
15:34..........123, 304
15:38..........309
15:43..........312
```

LUKE

```
 1:31..........77
 1:32,35.......77, 210
 2:2...........253
 2:9...........26
 3:2...........284
 7:37,38.......258
10:27..........365
10:38..........245
10:40..........245, 258
10:41..........245
11:15,18.......150
22:42..........263
22:54-62.......291
22:61..........292
23.............304
23:35,36,44....371
23:45..........309
23:50,51.......312
```

JOHN 1

```
1.............68, 133,
              223, 241
1:1...........219
1:1ff.........216
1:1-3.........89
1:1-18........183
1:4ff.........220
1:11..........92, 270
1:14..........203, 297
1:16..........174
1:17..........71, 141,
              220, 357
1:18..........178, 191,
              210
1:19..........229
1:19-43,
  19ff........111
```

JOHN 1 (cont.)

1:23..........200
1:24..........179
1:29..........111, 133
1:30ff.......263
1:32..........169
1:33..........169, 263
1:34..........263
1:35..........111, 223,
               229
1:38..........271
1:40..........223
1:41..........170, 223,
               284
1:45..........170, 328
1:47..........217
1:48..........170
1:49..........218, 271
1:51..........170, 218,
               219, 220

JOHN 2

2............40, 133,
              161, 163,
              164, 169
2:1..........111, 161,
              169
2:2..........161
2:3..........113, 169,
              334
2:4..........113, 169
2:5..........113, 162,
              169
2:6,7,8,
  10........161
2:11.........115, 161
2:12.........111
2:13.........105
2:13-23......111
2:23.........105, 115,
              173
2:24,25......321
2:29,35,
  40........111

JOHN 3

3............32
3:2..........113, 115,
             151
3:5..........111
3:10.........211
3:12.........111
3:13.........111, 185,
             210
3:14.........111, 185,
             301, 359
3:15.........185, 206,
             359
3:16.........34, 111,
             362
3:18.........96, 228
3:22.........111
3:25.........229
3:27-36......111
3:27ff.......229
3:31.........183, 184
3:32.........184, 186,
             298
3:33.........298
3:34.........170
3:35.........203
3:36.........185, 269,
             298

JOHN 4

4............189
4:3,4........111
4:5..........116
4:6..........171
4:10.........356
4:11.........351, 356
4:12.........114, 218
4:18.........114
4:21.........144
4:22.........107
4:23.........296
4:25,26......115
4:35.........113
4:42.........115

JOHN 4 (cont.)

4:43..........106
4:46..........115

JOHN 5

5.............35, 36, 153,
              166, 168,
              169, 171,
              178, 186,
              192, 224,
              231, 234,
              240
5ff...........157, 173
5:1...........35, 40, 99,
              100, 105,
              134, 179,
              181, 311
5:7...........116
5:8...........151
5:9...........117, 168
5:10..........117, 131,
              168, 181
5:14..........176
5:15..........181
5:16..........166, 234
5:16-18.......167
5:17..........132, 179,
              205, 233
5:18..........39, 166,
              181, 182,
              188, 203,
              204, 205,
              210, 226,
              227, 233,
              293, 301
5:19..........186, 233
5:19ff........179
5:19-20.......269
5:22..........197, 362
5:23..........197
5:24..........240, 269
5:24-29.......241
5:25..........241, 242
5:28..........252
5:29-47.......39

JOHN 5 (cont.)

5:30a,b.......186
5:31..........177
5:32..........178, 263
5:33..........296
5:34..........178
5:35..........132
5:35-37.......149
5:36..........178, 179,
              228, 269
5:36b.........224
5:37..........149, 178,
              179, 182,
              210, 228
5:38..........178
5:39..........132, 141,
              146, 148
5:40..........148
5:41..........149
5:42..........149, 151
5:43..........96, 149,
              223, 224
5:44..........149, 168,
              269, 302
5:45-47.......36
5:46..........150, 328
5:47..........150

JOHN 6

6.............35, 36,
              40, 134,
              140, 164,
              165, 166,
              205, 319
6:4...........35, 116,
              134, 165,
              169
6:14..........105, 165,
              251
6:14-15.......164
6:15..........164, 251
6:18,19.......164
6:25..........271
6:26..........164
6:27..........165

JOHN 6 (cont.)

6:28.........165, 205
6:29,30......165
6:32,33,35....206
6:35b.........276
6:37.........226
6:38.........206
6:40.........269
6:41.........206
6:42.........169, 179,
              206, 306
6:45.........206
6:46.........178, 186
6:57.........228, 241
6:60.........165
6:62.........210, 267
6:63.........166, 276
6:64.........166
6:70.........167, 235
6:70-71......166
6:71.........166, 167

JOHN 7

7............166, 167,
              168, 169,
              175, 235,
              236
7:1..........166, 167,
              257
7:2..........105, 106
7:3..........171, 267
7:5..........171
7:8..........106, 167
7:10.........106, 168
7:11.........106, 258
7:12.........168
7:13.........158, 164,
              168, 356,
              371
7:14.........106
7:15.........185
7:16.........206
7:17.........106
7:19.........167, 168

JOHN 7 (cont.)

7:20.........168, 171,
              204, 235
7:21.........168
7:25.........167, 172,
              235
7:26,27......172, 195
7:28.........172, 183
7:29.........172, 228
7:30.........167, 235
7:31.........173, 186
7:32.........167, 173
7:33.........173, 174,
              179, 182,
              277
7:34.........173, 174,
              182
7:35.........182, 233,
              261, 277
7:36.........174
7:37.........174, 276
7:38.........276, 323
7:39.........174, 275,
              276, 316,
              323
7:41.........179
7:42.........172, 357
7:43.........166, 179,
              193
7:44.........167, 235
7:47,48......175
7:49.........175, 359
7:50.........313
7:53.........175

JOHN 8

8............186, 190,
              205
8:1-11.......175, 181
8:6..........177
8:12.........175, 177,
              269
8:12-20......180
8:13.........177, 182

JOHN 8 (cont.)

8:14..........179, 182,
                 195
8:15..........191
8:16..........179, 180,
                 186
8:17,18.......180
8:19..........182
8:20..........167
8:21..........174, 182
8:22..........182
8:23..........183, 184,
                 185, 194
8:24..........182, 183
8:25..........183
8:26..........184, 187
8:27..........184, 267
8:28..........185, 186,
                 301, 359
8:29..........185, 186,
                 190
8:30..........186
8:32..........296
8:34..........186
8:37..........167, 187,
                 235
8:38,39.......186
8:40..........167, 187,
                 235, 297
8:41..........187
8:42..........188, 228
8:43..........188
8:44..........188, 189,
                 191, 275
8:45,46.......235
8:48..........169, 182
8:49..........189
8:50,51.......190
8:52..........182
8:53,54,55....190
8:56..........92, 190
8:57..........182, 191
8:58..........92, 191,
                 204
8:59..........167, 191,
                 226, 229,
                 234, 245,
                 267

JOHN 9

9.............192, 200,
                 201, 205,
                 223, 224,
                 229
9:1-21........205
9:3...........193, 246
9:5,9,13......193
9:14..........32
9:16..........179, 193
9:17..........193
9:18,19.......194
9:22..........194, 201,
                 205, 268,
                 365, 371
9:24,26.......194
9:28,29.......195
9:31..........195, 196
9:32..........196
9:33,36.......197
9:38..........197, 234
9:39..........197
9:41..........339

JOHN 10

10............199, 200,
                 203, 229
                 230
10:1..........201
10:1-21.......205
10:3..........229
10:6..........199
10:7..........199, 200,
                 219
10:8..........199
10:9..........200, 202,
                 225
10:10.........201
10:11.........199, 200,
                 202, 224,
                 320
10:12,13......201
10:14.........200, 201,
                 329
10:15.........201, 202,
                 224

JOHN 10 (cont.)

10:16..........202, 226,
                331
10:17,18.......203
10:19..........179, 204,
                223, 235
10:20..........204
10:21..........204
10:22..........106, 221,
                226
10:22-39.......205
10:24..........223
10:25..........96, 223,
                224, 264
10:26,27.......224
10:28..........224, 226
10:30..........226, 227,
                241
10:31..........167, 226,
                234, 245
10:32..........228
10:33..........228, 301
10:34..........215, 363
10:35..........301, 306,
                363
10:36..........227, 228,
                233
10:37..........228
10:38..........228, 235
10:39..........167, 229
10:40,41,42....229

JOHN 11

11.............229, 240,
                245, 252
11:1...........238
11:2...........245
11:3...........251, 257
11:4...........193, 246,
                265
11:6...........257
11:7...........245, 257
11:9,10........245
11:11-14,
   15,16.......246

JOHN 11 (cont.)

11:17..........250
11:21..........240
11:23,24.......251
11:25,26.......251, 252
11:28..........251
11:33..........171, 251
11:35..........171, 252
11:36..........257
11:38..........171
11:40..........265
11:41,42,46....252
11:47..........232, 257,
                282, 300
11:47ff........157
11:48..........232, 237,
                260
11:49..........237
11:50..........232, 282
11:51..........232, 236
11:53..........237
11:54..........257
11:55..........105, 106,
                258
11:56,57.......258

JOHN 12

12.............233
12:1...........105, 166,
                258
12:2...........245, 258
12:3...........233, 259
12:6...........259
12:12..........106
12:12-15,
   13,16.......260
12:19..........260, 261
12:20..........106
12:20ff........261, 293
12:23..........261, 276
12:24..........261
12:26..........261
12:27..........262, 263,
                272
12:28..........263, 265

JOHN 12 (cont.)

12:29.........266
12:31.........233, 266
12:32.........185, 266,
                267, 293,
                301
12:33.........185, 293
12:34.........266, 301
12:36.........167, 267
12:37-43.......267
12:38.........268
12:40.........86, 268
12:41.........86, 92,
                197, 210,
                268
12:42,43.......268
12:44,44-50,
  45,46,47....269
12:47-49.......241
12:48.........241, 269
12:50.........293

JOHN 13

13.............270
13:1...........105, 270
                278
13:2...........236, 270
13:3,10,11,
  12,13.......271
13:14,16,17....272
13:19.........272, 278
13:20,21.......272
13:22.........275
13:23.........272
13:27.........273, 278
13:29.........106, 273
13:31.........275
13:32.........275
13:33.........277
13:34.........242
13:35.........243
13:36.........277
13:37.........246, 321,
                322
13:38.........278, 321

JOHN 14

14:6...........296
14:8,10,11....228
14:13.........96, 276
14:14.........96
14:14-17.......276
14:26.........96, 370

JOHN 15

15:8...........276
15:9...........35
15:12.........242, 243
15:13.........243, 257
15:16,21.......96
15:24.........228
15:26.........317, 323,
                327, 370
15:27.........323

JOHN 16

16:12.........270
16:13.........270, 280
16:15.........370
16:23,24.......96
16:28.........188

JOHN 17

17.............304
17:1-5.........276
17:2...........226
17:3...........226, 276
17:4,5.........276
17:6...........73, 96
17:12.........96, 281
17:14,15,16....183
17:17.........183, 193
17:18.........183, 228
17:19.........228
17:26.........73, 96

JOHN 18

18.............278
18:2...........278
18:3...........157, 282
18:4...........278
18:5...........276, 278
18:6...........235, 278
18:7...........281, 293
18:8,9.........281
18:11..........282
18:13..........232
18:14..........232, 282
18:15..........284, 285
18:16..........291
18:19ff........285
18:20..........184
18:22..........291, 292
18:27..........321
18:28..........105, 258,
               292
18:31,32,35....293
18:36..........154
18:37..........293
18:38..........298, 299
18:39..........105
18:40..........299

JOHN 19

19:3...........300
19:4...........299
19:6...........232, 299
19:7...........233, 301
19:8...........300, 301
19:12..........302
19:14..........106, 315
19:15..........302
19:20..........174
19:23,24.......303
19:25..........313
19:26,27.......305, 334
19:28..........171, 305
19:30..........306
19:31..........315
19:34..........309

JOHN 19 (cont.)

19:35..........309, 311,
               312
19:36,37.......312
19:38..........158, 164,
               312, 356
19:40..........252
19:42..........315

JOHN 20

20:7...........252
20:8,9,10......318
20:11..........313, 318
20:13..........318
20:16..........271, 313
20:17..........316
20:18..........277, 316
20:19..........158, 159,
               164, 168,
               174, 277,
               316, 329,
               356, 371
20:21..........316
20:22..........174, 323,
               327
20:23..........174
20:25..........317
20:28..........210, 215,
               317
20:29..........288
20:31..........96, 185,
               224, 226,
               241, 311

JOHN 21

21.............329, 330,
               331
21:5,7,8,
   12,13.......319
21:15..........320
21:15-17.......329
21:17,18.......321

JOHN 21 (cont.)

21:19.........322
21:20,21......284
21:23.........322
21:24.........285, 288,
              322, 323,
              327
21:25.........329

JOHN 22

22:18.........303

ACTS

3:2...........253
4:6...........286
5:37.........253

GALATIANS

3:8...........190

COLOSSIANS

2:9...........169

HEBREWS

7:1...........209

1 JOHN

4:20.........80, 243

III. *The Apocrypha and Pseudepigrapha of the Old Testament*

1 MACCABEES

4:36..........39
4:59..........100
7:48-49......349
7:49..........118
13:42..........352
13:51..........360

2 MACCABEES

1:9..........103
1:18..........39
10:8..........39, 100
15:36..........101, 118,
          349

JUBILEES

32:1,16........361

TESTAMENT OF LEVI

8:11-15......361

ASSUMPTION OF MOSES

6:1...........361

IV. *From the Targums*

ONKELOS

On Genesis

    1...............220
    3:8............47
    9:27...........48
    11:5...........47
    11:7...........47
    14:23..........49
    15:1ff.........92
    18:21..........47
    46:4...........47

On Exodus

    3:8............47
    17:16..........49
    19:18..........48
    19:20..........48
    20:1...........83
    33:9,10........51
    33:20..........50
    40:35..........51
    46:4...........47

On Numbers

    6:25...........50
    11:20..........50
    11:25..........48, 50

On Deuteronomy

    3:24...........50
    6:15...........49
    14:23..........49
    32:20..........55
    33:26..........52
    33:27..........216

On Esther

    2:13..........355
    3:6...........352
    10:1..........354, 366

On Ecclesiastes

    7:25..........351

On Isaiah

    1:2............87
    1:14,16,20....89
    3:27..........89
    4:4...........89
    5:25..........89
    6.............86, 87
    6:4...........52
    6:8...........89
    7:6...........89
    10:20.........89
    12:2..........89
    17:11.........347
    21:17.........89
    22:25.........89
    25:8..........89
    25:9..........87
    26:3..........87
    26:4..........89
    26:13.........87
    27:3..........88
    28:23.........89
    29:22.........91
    30:33.........89
    33:2..........88
    34:16.........89
    36:5,7........89
    37:29.........88
    37:32.........89
    40:4..........89

On Isaiah (cont.)

```
41:8ff.........91
41:10..........89
41:11..........88
41:13,14.......88, 89
41:16..........89
42:1...........89
43:2...........89
43:5...........88, 89
43:11,12.......91
44:24..........90, 216
45:12..........90, 216
46:12..........88
48:11-13.......90
48:13..........89, 90,
                   347
48:15..........91
48:16..........88, 89, 91
48:17..........91
49:5...........89
49:15..........88
51:1...........88
51:2...........91
51:4,5,7.......88
52:6...........88
53.............141
55:2...........88
55:3,6.........88
56:5...........347
58:14..........89
59:13,19.......89
60:9...........88
61:10..........89
62:2...........89
63:8...........88
63:10,11,14....89
63:16..........91
66:13..........88
66:24..........89
```

JONATHAN

On Genesis

```
1..............216
3:8...........47
11:5,7.........47
15.............92
18:21..........47
46:4...........47
49.............187
```

On Exodus

```
3:8...........48
17:16..........49
19:18..........47
19:20..........47, 48
33:9,10........51
33:23..........50
40:35..........51
```

On Numbers

```
6:25..........50
11:25..........48
```

On Deuteronomy

```
6:15..........49
31:8...........52
33:26..........52
```

JERUSALEM

On Genesis

1	216
3:8	47
18:21	47
28	170, 218
49	81, 141, 187

On Exodus

17:16	49
19:18	48

On Exodus (cont.)

33:3,5,8	51
33:23	50

On Numbers

11:25	48

On Deuteronomy

33:20	55

402

V. *Rabbinical Literature*

Bab. 'Aḅodah Zarah

3b............5, 373
5a............342
16b............343
40b............356

'Aḅoth

3:2............446
3:16............344
4:22............358

Tos. Baḅa' Ḳama'

7:2............363

Bab. Baḅa' M'ẓi'a'

59b............343
86a............5

M. Baḅa' Bathrah

3:1............207

Bab. Baḅa' Bathrah

15b............37, 76
75b............76

M. B'rakhoth

2:2............80, 243,
            370
9:5............361, 362

Bab. B'rakhoth

3a............366
8a............373
29a............61
33b............344
64a............368
74b............341

Jer. B'rakhoth

1:4............55, 376
4............62

M. 'Eyduyoth

2:1,2,3......346

Bab. Giṭin

6b............373
45b............242
55b............345
56a,b..........345, 372
57a............345

Bab. Ḥagigah

5b............342, 343,
            366
12a,b..........343
14a............20

Bab. Ḥulin

7b............342

<u>Tos</u>. <u>K'thuboth</u>

1:1...........207

<u>Bab</u>. <u>K'thuboth</u>

84b...........343

<u>Bab</u>. <u>Kidushin</u>

71a...........73, 74

<u>M</u>. <u>M'gilah</u>

1:1...........101
1:2...........101, 117,
            118
2:1...........163
3:4...........104
3:6...........100, 104

<u>Bab</u>. <u>M'gilah</u>

3a............341
4a............118
7a............121, 141,
            152, 365
7b............123, 325,
            329, 351
11a...........234
12b...........147
13a...........349
13b...........177, 236
15a,b.........129, 131,
            136, 346,
            374
16b...........341
29a...........192
31c...........341

<u>Jer</u>. <u>M'gilah</u>

1.............131
70d...........131
71c...........341

<u>Bab</u>. <u>M'nahoth</u>

29b...........6, 19,
            181
43b...........55, 370

<u>M</u>. <u>Midoth</u>

1:4...........367
2:1...........372
2:3,6........367

<u>M</u>. <u>N'ga'im</u>

14:8..........367

<u>M</u>. <u>Parah</u>

3:1...........346

<u>M</u>. <u>P'sahim</u>

1:6...........346
5:1...........353, 372
5:6...........373
5:8...........315
5:9...........372
6:2...........357

Bab. P'sahim

50a............72
56a............80, 81
68b............123

Bab. Rosh Hashana

16b............369
17b............373
18b............361

M. Sanhedrin

10:1..........365
11:3..........110, 344
39a............373
45b............343
46a............343
61b............352
64a............370
64b............343
66a............363
67b............360
111a..........368

M. Shabath

4:4...........346
6:1...........346
18:3..........357
19:1..........357

Tos. Shabath

2:7...........207
13(14):5......342

Bab. Shabath

12a............356
14b............342

Bab. Shabath (cont.)

30a............79
30b............242
31a............80
32a............342
55a............370
104b..........367
119b..........95, 370

Jer. Shabath

17a............343
19.............343

Bab. Sh'bu'oth

116a,b........342

M. Sh'kalim

4:4...........346
5:1...........345, 357
6:1...........346
6:3...........367

M. Sotah

1:5...........367

Bab. Sotah

2a............374
3b............55
37b............73
49a............95

Jer. Sotah

8.............343
22b............343

M. Sukah

4:9,10........351
5:2,3,4.......351

Tos. Sukah

2:7..........207

Bab. Sukah

45a...........370
53a...........370

M. Tamid

5:1...........68, 93,
              293, 347
7:2...........93, 361

Bab. Tamid

32b...........54

M. Yadayim

4:8..........371

Bab. Y'bamoth

71a...........343

M. Yoma'

3:10.........367

Bab. Yoma'

21b...........323
49b...........361
69b...........370

Z'bahim

99:3..........346
12:4..........340

Sof'rim

4:5..........363
14:5,6........119
17:4..........118
21:3..........130

- - - - - - - - - -

Mekhilta

79a...........363
97a...........364

Sifre on Numbers

12a...........357

Sifre on Deuteronomy

170...........323

Shulhan Aruh
  Orah Hayyim

470,18........130

Genesis Rabbah

4:5...........53
5:11..........83
22:4..........346
24:2..........170
39:13.........349
44:17.........127
57:3..........360
64:4..........373

Exodus Rabbah

31:1..........345

Numbers Rabbah

13:4..........40

Deuteronomy Rabbah

7:3...........357

Ecclesiastes Rabbah

12:11.........200

Esther Rabbah

3:17..........352
4:14..........155, 280
8:6...........148
9:1...........155

Song of Songs Rabbah

1:2...........356
1:9...........323
5:4,11........344
30:3..........351
82:1..........364

Psalms Rabbah

9:7,10........350
22............124, 135,
              147, 148,
              162, 193,
              233, 238
22:2,3........177
22:4..........127, 352
22:5..........125, 154
22:6..........126, 127,
              128, 136
22:10.........126
22:15.........125
22:16.........126, 127,
              128
22:18.........127, 371
22:19.........352
22:20,21,
   24,25......128
22:27.........129

Pesikta Rabbati

29b...........352

Tanhuma

2.............360
4:30..........356

Midrash Tehillim

90:15.........344

Midrash Mishle

9,61..........131
10,10.........95
14,14.........95

Pirke de R. Eliezer

3............359
14............46
25............46
27............64
31............64
34............46
39............46, 359
40............65
43............65
45............66
46............66
49............355

Pirke de R. Eliezer
  (cont.)

50............124, 130,
               139, 147,
               355
51............66

'Aboth de R. Nathan
  on Genesis

3:8 (30b,6)...47, 192

VI. *Others*

Josephus, *Antiquities*

IV, 159........313
XI, 199-289....103
XI, 295........38
XII, 325......39
XII, 407,409...118
XIII, 297,
      298......17
XVI, 163.......361
XX, 197ff......287, 313
XVII, 23.......255
XVIII, 34......286

Josephus,
  Bellum Judaicum

I, 429.........369
II, 118........253
II, 243........287
II, 254-257....365
II, 272-276....365
II, 409ff......253, 366,
          369
II, 411-416....253
II, 240........286
II, 414,415,
    416........254
II, 424........369
II, 433,441,
    445........255
II, 447........252
II, 451........313
II, 454........255
II, 563........313
II, 566........287
III, 229.......369
IV, 126-127....282
IV, 173,174
    180-184....283
IV, 304-309....300
IV, 314-317....346
IV, 314-318....282, 299

Bellum Judaicum (cont.)

IV, 319-322....284
IV, 322,324....346
IV, 366,367....284
IV-VII.........369
V, 439-441.....359
V, 440-441.....366
V, 506.........282
VI, 201........369
VI, 208,211....373
VI, 227........369
VII, 196-208...369
VII, 196-209...255
VII, 253.......252, 253,
           369
VII, 275,297...369
VII, 320-336,
    337-339...246
VII, 320-388...369
VII, 341-388...247, 248
VII, 399.......250
VII, 401.......249
VII, 403,404...250

Justin Martyr,
  Dialogue

35.............245
38.............342
46.............344
74.............353
75.............353
91.............359
94.............358, 359
96.............345
112............347, 359
114............359
124............363
131............365, 375
133............345

Philo, I
  On The Creation

69 (p.55)......219

Philo, I
  *Allegorical Interpre-
  tation*

96 (pp. 365,
    367).......364

Philo, IV
  *The Confusion of
  Tongues*

145-148 (pp.
    89-91).....216, 217
146 (pp. 89-
    91).......219, 220

Philo, IV
  Who is the Heir

231 (p. 399)...219

Irenaeus, *Adversus
  Haereses*

1, 11, 1.......345
1, 26, 1.......345
3, 3, 4b.......345
3, 11, 1.......345

Eusebius, *Preparatio
  Evangelica*

1, 10..........213